D1295935

A CLINICAL APPROACH TO MARITAL PROBLEMS
Evaluation and Management

A CLINICAL APPROACH TO MARITAL PROBLEMS
Evaluation and Management

By

BERNARD L. GREENE, M.D.

Clinical Associate Professor of Psychiatry
College of Medicine, University of Illinois at the Medical Center
Chicago, Illinois
Adjunct Clinical Professor of Pastoral Psychology
Garrett Theological Seminary, Northwestern University Campus
Evanston, Illinois
Founder
Marital Department, Forest Hospital
Des Plaines, Illinois

CHARLES C THOMAS • **PUBLISHER**
Springfield • *Illinois* • *U.S.A.*

Published and Distributed Throughout the World by
CHARLES C THOMAS • PUBLISHER
BANNERSTONE HOUSE
301–327 East Lawrence Avenue, Springfield, Illinois, U.S.A.
NATCHEZ PLANTATION HOUSE
735 North Atlantic Boulevard, Fort Lauderdale, Florida, U.S.A.

With THOMAS BOOKS *careful attention is given to all details of manufacturing and design. It is the Publisher's desire to present books that are satisfactory as to their physical qualities and artistic possibilities and appropriate for their particular use.* THOMAS BOOKS *will be true to those laws of quality that assure a good name and good will.*

Printed in the United States of America

BB-14

To my wife
LENORE
and to my daughters
NORMA GAIL *and* **MARSHA JUNE**

PREFACE

Kaplan* has succinctly defined therapy as "a psychological treatment whereby a trained therapist develops a planned relationship with a patient or client with the expressed purpose of relieving suffering, it will include therapy carried out by a variety of individuals with differing backgrounds and training." For the purposes of this book, there is no need to differentiate the special areas of competence of the various disciplines. For simplicity, practitioners of all disciplines will be referred to as "therapist" (whether it be psychotherapy, marital counseling, multiclient interviewing, psychoanalysis, or any other). In this book therapy does not imply any particular level of treatment.

Many marriages are being lived out in a mood of quiet desperation while therapists talk about the durable incompatibility of many unions. The professional knows that there are many situations that look good on the surface but present serious hidden difficulties.

With the many serious problems in marriage, it is necessary for professionals to go outside of their regular academic training if they want to become skilled in the field of marriage therapy. Most professionals feel that their formal training in marital therapy was inadequate. Additional training has to be obtained either through study in a doctoral program or through prolonged clinical training experience in a hospital or counseling center. Academia has not yet solved the problem of giving men training that is adequate to the marital problems in the modern community.

The concepts in this book grew out of my experiences and thoughts as an active clinician (psychiatrist and psychoanalyst), as a synthesizer of the creativity of others, and finally, as a

* Alex H. Kaplan: Social work therapy and psychiatric psychotherapy, *Arch Gen Psychiat,* 9:95, 1963.

teacher. For the past ten years I have limited my clinical practice exclusively to marital disharmony. Initially, the teaching phase was limited to psychiatric residents, then to psychiatrists, psychologists and social workers. The third phase included marriage counselors and workers in the educational field. The final phase was the inclusion of the clergy. Special seminars for the latter were given at the Forest Hospital (a private psychiatric hospital in Des Plaines, Illinois) and at the Garrett Theological Seminary in Evanston, Illinois.

A clear distinction exists between marital therapy and individual psychotherapy. In marital therapy "the marriage is the patient," which means that the work is done with both husband and wife and that what is explored is the *relationship* which exists between them. In individual psychotherapy the area that is explored is primarily the intrapsychic dynamics of the individual.

Throughout this book the emphasis will be on the understanding of the multiple elements influencing a marriage. The very important relationship between the therapist and the marriage partners can only be stated but has to be dealt with in face-to-face relationships between the teacher and the student.

Since childhood patterns of reactions influence our adult methods of adjustment, it may help the student to visualize a jukebox with many "records" of old modes of reaction which are stimulated by current situations. The fact that tastes in music may vary can be the beginning of areas of conflict. It is important to recognize that "records" of childhood can be inappropriate in adult life. The playing of old "records" can lead to serious problems—premarital, marital or postmarital.

One of the goals in marital therapy is to help each individual mature to the point at which he or she is responding to present experiences and relationships in terms of the real meanings and values and not in terms of symbolic meanings from childhood.

The comprehensive approach used in this book is one of breadth as well as depth. My experience in the fields of classical psychoanalysis and psychiatry guarantees a depth approach. The choice of a general system theory as a model of analysis of marital problems guarantees breadth. The therapist should find no difficulty in discovering where he and his concerns fit into this approach.

The data to be presented in this book will be based on 750 couples with marital disharmony who were personally managed by me. Five hundred couples were taken from my private practice and 250 couples were seen at the marital department of the Forest Hospital. The data presented is not applicable for quantification. The disguised clinical vignettes to be presented do not prove anything in and by themselves. The orientation was primarily therapeutic and pragmatic.

This book has been organized in the following manner: Chapter I deals with an eclectic "organismic" model based on "general system theory," applicable to the social institution of marriage. Chapters II to XIX present a method of evaluating marriage problems and discuss the importance of the biographical marital questionnaire. Chapter XX is devoted to the conjoint diagnostic and disposition session. Finally, Chapters XXI to XXVIII discuss the prevention and management of marital problems.

BERNARD L. GREENE

ACKNOWLEDGMENTS

I wish to thank my dear friends, the Reverend Carroll A. Wise and Dr. Samuel Liebman, for the help given me in preparing this manuscript and for the many corrections they have suggested and Dr. Alfred P. Solomon, who first suggested I do marital therapy.

B.L.G.

CONTENTS

Part Two

Management of Marital Problems

A CLINICAL APPROACH TO MARITAL PROBLEMS

Evaluation and Management

Part One

Evaluation of Marital Problems

I

INTRODUCTION

There is no royal road to marital accord.
——Regina Flesch[1]

All therapists should attempt to participate more effectively in the resolution of today's exploding crises in marriage. Confronted with treating large numbers of couples with marital problems,[2] psychiatrists have had to adapt new skills to new settings and to collaborate with members of other helping professions.[3] Statistically, marital problems present the most common cause of psychiatric complaints, and psychiatrists rank far below other therapists as a source of therapy by families.[4] It is necessary that psychiatrists and members of the other helping professions move closer together in sharing their respective knowledge in alleviating marital disharmony. This book is designed to help the therapist become more effective. Obviously, one cannot teach the complex skills required for the full spectrum of therapies of marital discord,[5] but one can make the therapist able to deal more effectively with those that match his abilities or able to recognize those that exceed his qualifications and require the adroit involvement of a more experienced marriage counselor.

ORGANISMIC CONCEPTUAL FRAMEWORK

My current "organismic" conceptual framework has evolved over the past thirty-five years from the medical model of psychiatry and psychoanalysis to the present eclectic one, influenced by the general system theory of von Bertalanffy.[6,7] No one model, whether based on considerations of intrapsychic dynamics, interpersonal relationships, sociocultural factors, or ideological preferences, can describe the transactions within a marriage. All behavior has meaning, and all spouses are motivated by internal activities. In addition to this *intrapersonal system,* every individual has meaningful relationships with others (*interpersonal system*) and lives in a sociocultural matrix (*environmental system*). All three systems (see Fig. 1) have open boundaries and contain components in constant transactions of varying intensities. Marital disharmony results from these three systems

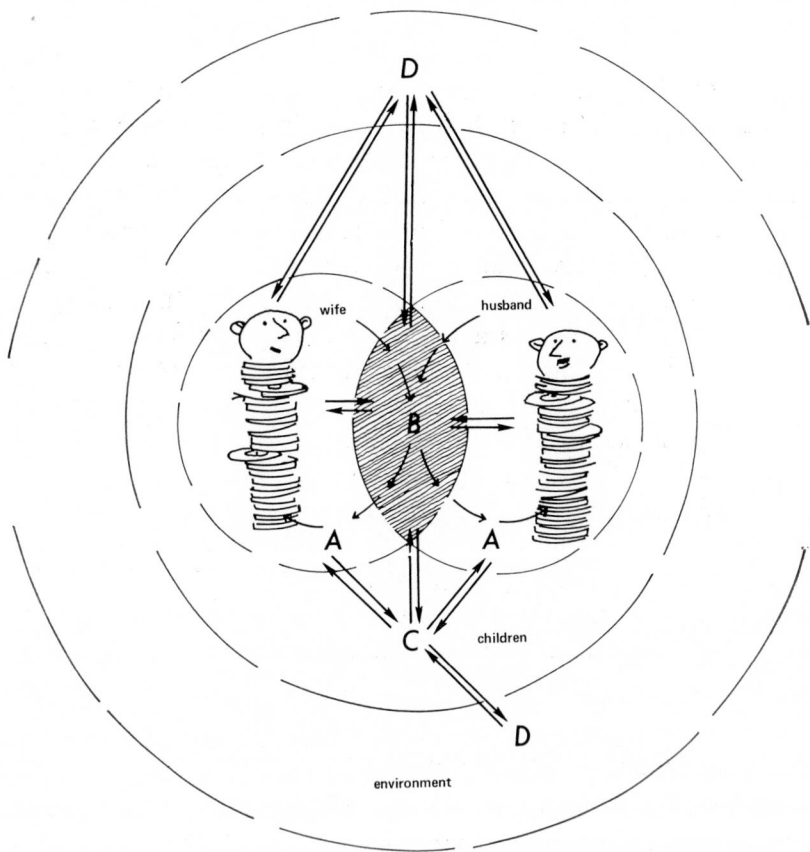

Figure 1. Marriage as an open system. *A,* Intrapersonal system; *B,* Interpersonal system (marital dyad); *C,* Interpersonal system (sibling subsystem) note *B+C*=family system; and *D,* Environmental system.

continually transacting with each other and creating permutations[8] which are dysfunctional.

In the past two decades, von Bertalanffy has introduced the term *general system theory* (GST) as a symbol for a key concept and thus initiated a trend toward unified "interdisciplinary" theory.[9,10] He defines a system as a complex of components in mutual interaction. He postulates complex open systems that have their own inherent lawfulness, such as feedback: "the result of a reaction is monitored back to the 'receptor' side so that the system is held stable or led toward a target or goal." In a recent paper,[11] von Bertalanffy states that to the system theorist, the totality of experience appears as a hierarchical order, the major levels of which are the inorganic, the living, and the symbolic world. He suggests abandoning the zoomorphic viewpoint, which tries to explain human behavior vis-à-vis animal behavior. He prefers the term *symbolic* to define those functions which separate human from animal behavior and form the sociocultural human superstructure. He notes that mankind does not consist of isolated individuals but is organized in a hierarchy of systems. Therefore, he suggests that the GST gives a theoretical framework for therapeutic measures such as family therapy. Since the marital dyad is a subsystem of the family, the GST is applicable to marital therapy.

Each system[12] consists of transacting elements within penetrable boundaries, thus insuring "openness." Each system has a temporal and spatial existence with structure derived from its past; its present is relatively stable, and its future has possible evolutionary potential. The constancy of the system is dependent upon a continuous exchange and flow of the transacting components. Each open system maintains its organization by goal-seeking activities characterized by "equifinality," indicating that the same final state can be reached from different initial conditions and in different ways. This is in contrast to equilibria in closed systems, which are determined by initial conditions. Each system may maintain itself by realignment of gradients, by partial sacrifice of structure or function or by decreasing its boundaries to permeability. Finally, each system is in active interplay with other systems in its environment which are significant for its viability. All systems are involved in encoding, processing, retrieving and transmitting information.[13]

I view the human being as a person with symbol-making abilities as well as a reacting organism utilizing thoughts, gestures, postures and total movement in relation to "significant others." Relationships can occur at random as a product of individual inclinations alone or can be affected by the values, ideas and sanctions of significant others. Thus, our focus is directed to the relationship between the parts of a wider system. There are no defenses or symptoms that are intrapersonal without involvement of others in a sociocultural matrix. It is not an uncommon clinical experience that the improvement of one family member sometimes results in the "illness" of another. Giovacchini,[14] among others,[15,16] gives some excellent examples of this rebound phenomenon. The following clinical example illustrates the interlocking of the three systems just described:

Mr. Abigail,[17] a blonde, well-dressed, dynamic married executive, in his mid-thirties, consulted me for *premarital counseling* (sic) (intrapersonal system). He related twelve years of marital dissatisfaction with an alcoholic wife (interpersonal system). He is dating a widow who fulfills his needs and is pressuring him to divorce his wife and marry her (interpersonal and environmental system). For the past eight months their relationship has been very rewarding. Unable to make a decision, he sought advice (interpersonal system).

His main concern was the fate of his two children (interpersonal system). Exploration of the total situation revealed that he had unconsciously encouraged his wife's dependent behavior, while she, also unconsciously, was gratifying his unfulfilled dependency needs (intra- and inter-personal systems). When Mrs. Abigail discovered that her husband had consulted me, she phoned for an appointment. With his permission, I agreed to see her for one session.

Mrs. Abigail appeared for her interview very anxious and frightened (intrapersonal, interpersonal and environmental systems). She described her husband as a very forceful, domineering man, highly successful in his business. She tried to meet his standards, but instead of praise, she received only further demands for perfection. Shortly after marriage she had given up and had begun to drink. As this progressed, she further infuriated her spouse. At the end of the interview I asked if she felt that her spouse's behavior had contributed to her mental condition and whether she might be better off without him. She replied: "Perhaps at the beginning of our marriage, yes, but now I am too dependent upon him."

Mr. Abigail was seen for the next three months, during which time I received a telephone call from his girlfriend, who was hysterical at his procrastination. She was advised to get counseling and be guided by her therapist's recommendations.

In the meantime, Mrs. Abigail had stopped drinking. Perhaps my question to her had confronted her with the possibility of divorce. Mr. Abigail reported that his relationship with his wife was better. She now was interested in going places with him. Although she had stopped drinking temporarily many times in the past, this time, she said, it would be permanent, since it was her idea and not coercion. At that time, Mr. Abigail began to develop moderately severe psychosomatic symptoms.

For a lengthy case history further illustrating the interlocking of the three systems see Hoffman and Long.[18]

THE TWO "JUKEBOXES" AND THE "SEESAW"

Behaviors of all kinds and all abstractions of communication reveal dilemmas, liabilities, assets and compromises of the person in *action*. The open-ended inclusive model of marital behavior based on the GST has led empirically to a simple pragmatic model, readily utilizable both for teaching and therapeutic purposes. The marriage institution is presented as consisting of two spouses (two jukeboxes with records—intrapersonal system), each unique in personality and seated at opposite ends of a seesaw[19] (interpersonal system). The transactions represented by the ongoing reciprocal swings of the seesaw may be pleasant or painful. Further, the playground on which the seesaw is found constitutes a complex social field of divergent environmental forces (environmental system) (see Fig. 2, courtesy of Reverend Bruce Mase).

The environmental forces include a number of subsystems which have varying effects upon each marriage. The family boundaries are not the same at all times or for all members, as the result of the life pattern of each individual and of each marriage. In our culture a newborn is considered a member of the family, but his membership is less clear when he marries and leaves. This kinship network plays an important role in marriage. As comparative studies of the various social classes of our society reveal different definitions regarding the composition of the nuclear family, sociocultural influences will be explored. Al-

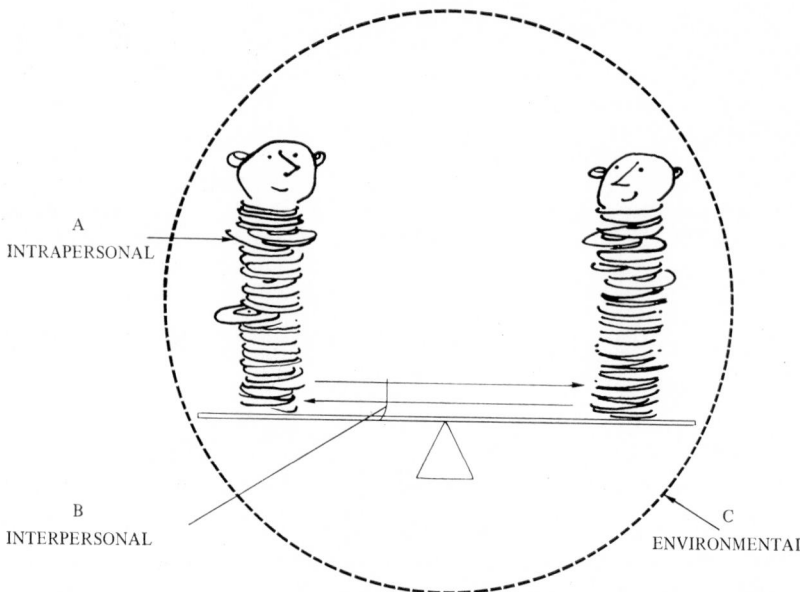

Figure 2. The suprasystem. *A*, Jukebox (intrapersonal system); *B*, Seesaw (interpersonal system); *C*, Sociocultural system of environmental forces (kinship networks, cultural values, and so on).

though each family's boundaries are spatially definable, these boundaries are permeable. Interchanges between the family and the subsystems, e.g. economic, occupational, religious, political, recreational, and so on, are constantly occurring. The complexity of our society with its progressive specialization forces the family to become structurally dependent on the multiple subsystems in its social matrix. In the management of marital problems, this structural dependence of the family makes it mandatory for the therapist to fully understand the interchanges between the nuclear family and its environment.

An individual may be compared to a jukebox containing a library of permanent stereophonic "records" (encoded informa-tion introjects stored in the brain of a neurophysiological nature whose structure awaits further scientific clarification, e.g. nucleic acids as repositories of information) capable of not only playing any past record but also capable of encoding (learn) new "records." A "record" can be considered to be a real phenomenon and not an abstraction and is the blend of the three main voices ("inner child," "parental" and "pia," i.e. perceptive-integrative-adaptive functions of the brain) reflecting the reality of either a past or present encoding. It is very common for a spouse to emphatically comment: "He sounds exactly like his mother and has the same mannerisms."

The voice of the *inner child* is present from birth and remains with the individual forever. The main attributes of the "inner child" include curiosity, creative play, creativity and sensuality. The voice of *pia* is nonemotional and is a data-processing mechanism with both an internal (intrapersonal system) and external (interpersonal and environmental systems) input. At birth the voices of the "pia" and of the "inner child" are indistinguishable.

With the development of object relationships and influenced by separation anxiety, the sound of the third important voice is heard. It is that of sociocultural values and attitudes that I refer to as the *parental,* after Berne.[20]

The jukebox contains an internal mechanism that plays the "records." The internal mechanism can be equated to the executive function of the brain.[21] The jukebox undergoes slow but progressive deterioration due to the inevitable aging process and to unavoidable trauma, e.g. illnesses or accidents. The deterioration is extremely variable, from imperceptible to gross changes, unique for each individual during his life cycle. This designation of the individual as a jukebox is mechanistic only for purposes of explanation.

The formation of character is the result of multiple systems of transactions in circularity (feedback loops), of which biology is only one factor, along with interpersonal and cultural determinants. The various possible determinants of the personality in action are explored in the presentation of the twenty-two items of the biographical marital questionnaire (hereinafter to be referred to as the BMQ and discussed in Chs. III to XIX, inclusive).

NOTES

1. Regina Flesch: Treatment goals and technique in marital discord, *Casework,* p. 388, 1949.
2. Clifford J. Sager, Ralph Gundlach, Malvina Kremer, Rosa Lenz, and Jack R. Royce (The married in treatment, *Arch Gen Psychiat, 19:*205, 1968) present their second phase of a study involving an intensive investigation of marital interaction—the effects of psychoanalysis on the marital state. They report data on 736 married patients and state, "Marital difficulties prompted about one half the patients in the sample to seek treatment."
3. Roy R. Grinker, Sr.: The sciences of psychiatry: fields, fences and riders. *Amer J Psychiat, 122:*367, 1965. I agree with Grinker, who notes: "Today the training, experience and discipline involved in the customary preparation for the role of therapist, based on the medical model, are assumed not to be important since nurses, social workers, psychologists, ministers, as well as psychiatrists, do some kind of psychotherapy. What one accomplishes and how one does it are more important than one's professional discipline."
4. Gerald Gurin, Joseph Veroff, and Sheila Feld: *Americans View Their Mental Health.* New York, Basic Books, 1960. Their statistics reveal that many couples with marital disharmony prefer to go to a non-psychiatric source of help. See also Jack R. Ewalt: *Action for Mental Health.* New York, Basic Books, 1961; and Elizabeth D. Ossario (Parish clergy and community health, *Psychiat Opinion, 3:*9, 1966), who finds in her research: "There is a great deal of variation in the amount of time any given minister spends in counseling. *Marital problems* [italics added] tended to make up the major portion of time any given minister spends counseling."
5. Bernard L. Greene (Ed.): *The Psychotherapies of Marital Disharmony.* New York, Free Press, Macmillan, 1965.
6. Ludwig von Bertalanffy: General system theory and psychiatry, in *American Handbook of Psychiatry.* (Silvano Arieti, Ed.). New York, Basic Books, 1966, Vol. III, pp. 705–721. See also von Bertalanffy: General system theory—a critical review, in *Modern Systems Research for the Behavioral Scientist* (Walter Buckley, Ed.). Chicago, Aldine, 1968, pp. 11–30. This book presents a practical and comprehensive understanding of system theory.
7. Ludwig von Bertalanffy: *Robots, Men and Minds.* New York, Braziller, 1967, and *General System Theory: Foundations, Development, Applications.* New York, Braziller, 1968. In their chapter, The Systems Concept, William J. Lederer and Don D. Jackson (*The Mirages of Marriage.* New York, Norton, 1968, pp. 87–97) succinctly present

system theory and state: "In this book, we are stressing the systems concept because *it is the most useful way of viewing marital interaction that has yet been developed* [italics added]." Also see Salvador Minuchin: The paraprofessional and the use of confrontation in the mental health field, *Amer J Orthopsychiat*, 39:728, 1969.

8. Harold A. Rashkis: Depression as a manifestation of the family as an open system, *Arch Gen Psychiat*, 19:57, 1968.

9. Edgar H. Auerswald prefers the term "ecological systems approach" (Interdisciplinary versus ecological approach, *Family Process*, 7:202, 1968). See also Andrew E. Curry: The family therapy situation as a system. *Family Process*, 5:131, 1966; Edward H. Knight: Psychotherapy-quo vadis?, *Psychiat Dig*, 29:8, 1968; and Harold D. Holder: Mental health and the search for new organizational strategies. *Arch Gen Psychiat, 20:*709, 1969.

10. Roy R. Grinker, Sr.: *Toward a Unified Theory of Human Behavior.* New York, Basic Books, 1965. A pioneer effort to unify general system theory in relation to human behavior. The new Second Edition (1967) includes a clear, concise summary of general system theory.

11. Ludwig von Bertalanffy: General System Theory and Psychiatry—An Overview. Paper presented at the American Psychiatric Association annual meeting, Detroit, Michigan May, 1967.

12. Von Bertalanfly: General system theory and psychiatry. In *American Handbook of Psychiatry* (Silvano Arieti Ed.). New York, Basic Books, 1966.

13. M. Ralph Kaufman, in a scholarly article on the medical or social model (Psychiatry—why "medical" or "social" model? *Arch Gen Psychiat, 17:*347, 1967), presents the thoughtful experience of an experienced teacher and clinician that deserves careful reading. Although his wording is different, his thinking, I believe, is consistent with the natural philosophic approach of von Bertalanffy.

14. Peter L. Giovacchini: Treatment of marital disharmonies: the classical approach, in *Psychotherapies of Marital Disharmony:* (Bernard L. Greene, Ed.). New York, Macmillan, 1965, pp. 39–82.

15. Ronald E. Fox (The effect of psychotherapy on the spouse, *Family Process,* 7:7, 1968) reviews some of the literature and attempts to assess the impact of the therapist and of treatment on the marriage.

16. Mildred Burgum: The father gets worse: a child guidance problem. *Amer J Orthopsychiat, 12:*474, 1942; Gordon Hamilton: *Psychotherapy in Child Guidance.* New York, Columbia Univ. Press, 1949, p. 282; Nathan W. Ackerman and Peter B. Neubauer: Failures in the psychotherapy of children. In *Failures in Psychiatric Treatment* (Paul H. Hoch, Ed.). New York, Grune & Stratton, 1948, pp. 86–88; John Bowlby: The study and reduction of group tensions in the family,

Hum Relations, 2:124, 1949; and, Ross Victor Speck, Clinical Director of the Eastern Psychiatric Hospital, Phladelphia, Penn. (communication to the author).

17. In order to preserve anonymity, I have altered certain details and henceforth use the names of hurricanes for clinical vignettes.

18. Lynn Hoffman and Lorence Long: A systems dilemma, *Family Process,* 8:211, 1969.

19. C. Eugene Waterman: Family Togetherness Without Closeness, Paper presented at the annual meeting of the American Orthopsychiatric Association, New York, March 17, 1965. A recent book by Ronald D. Laing, Herbert Phillipson, and A. Russell Lee (*Interpersonal Perception.* New York, Springer, 1966) deals with some of the components of the interpersonal system.

20. Eric Berne: Recent advances in transactional analysis, in *Current Psychiatric Therapies.* New York, Grune & Stratton, 1966, Vol. VI, pp. 114–124. See also Jean Piaget, who many scholars link with Freud with respect to his contributions to psychology, education and related disciplines (*The Origins of Intelligence in Children* (Margaret Cook, Trans.). New York, Int. Univs. Press, 1965, 3rd printing). Piaget's contributions illustrate the process of cognitive maturation to environmental reality.

21. Jarl E. Dyrud and Charles Donnelly (Executive functions of the ego, *Arch Gen Psychiat,* 20:257, 1969) prefer the term motility as their central concept rather than adaptation, ". . . for motility carries with it a precision not indicated by the term adaptation. Specifically, the concept of motility focuses more sharply on the ego's control and modification of movement as it operates in a field of consequences."

II

THE INITIAL INTERVIEWS

The techniques of marital therapy are undergoing profound changes toward spontaneous transactions occurring between patient* and therapist.

During the initial interview the patient sizes up the therapist[1,2] as an individual who is "impartial" and as a person capable of making some recommendations that will be helpful in the present crisis. He begins to develop conscious and unconscious attitudes toward the therapist.

The therapist gains diagnostic information, observes the kind of transactions going on and is in a position to do something.

It is my clinical experience that if you do not do something within the first ten minutes of the interview to alleviate anxiety and/or hostility (which is frequently a defense against severe apprehension), the patient may be lost because his anxiety level gets so high that a "working alliance"[3] cannot be established. Thus the initial interview is very important and the first ten minutes extremely so.

The request for help with a marital problem may be unilateral or bilateral. An early appointment is advisable, as marital crises respond best when dealt with at the height of tension. At one extreme are those who are adamant that they are not in need of help and that the problem is entirely due to their mate.

"Doctor, there is nothing wrong with me, and the only reason I agreed to come was that our minister strongly suggested I see you. We argue constantly. She blames me, but who can stand fifteen or thirty minutes of constant criticism without a retort and finally a heated argument. Why does she have to blow up over the smallest things and exaggerate its importance? Why does she have to build herself up into a screaming woman who can't be talked to? Why does she come back from visits with neighbors

* Hereinafter the individual coming for help will be designated patient.

and give me an exaggerated version of what made her mad? Why are the events which trigger these outbursts and tantrums so accumulative? She gets mad over small items—I dropped in for a beer at the tavern and started talking with the guys and before I knew it I was two hours late for dinner; she builds it into a huge argument. She then starts bringing up all the old fights and changing previous events to make more to fight over. I once told her mother off about a Christmas gift and she has never let me forget that one."

At the other end are those couples who are willing to do anything to alleviate the marital discord and who are eager for counsel.

Mr. Thora: "We want to save our marriage because we really like each other a lot. We have come to realize our individual problems, which do not affect our functioning in the world outside marriage in a detrimental way, seem to be causing a great deal of trouble. I'm self-centered. I procrastinate, I have to force myself to keep clean, and I can't change most habits as easily as I should—there is a terrible gap between my intellectual understanding of a problem and my visceral understanding of it. If you can help us . . . 'Thank You' is ridiculously inadequate."

Mrs. Thora: "Obviously we feel the marriage is worth saving or we would not be here. I feel it could be very good if our personal problems were straightened out. We have much to give each other and we had an awful lot of fun together. We have thought of each other as the other's best friend."

Very often a spouse will be uncooperative, either refusing to be interviewed, or coming under coercion. If a partner refuses to call for an appointment when requested by the patient, the therapist should take the initiative and telephone the individual, explaining that his information would be most valuable in dealing with the spouse's complaints. Infrequently (5%) will a partner refuse to be interviewed if the therapist employs tact.

Coercion may result from actual threat, "either we see a marriage counselor or we see a lawyer," or act, where one spouse has consulted a lawyer and started divorce proceedings. The hostility and/or anxiety is best dealt with by the technique used by experienced salesmen—"neutralization." The therapist responds to the overt or covert hostility by stating: "You are very angry at having been forced into coming here. No one likes to be coerced into doing anything. If you say you are not angry, you would be kidding yourself. However, I'm here to explore the situation with you, and it is your prerogative to continue or not." Usually this empathic statement "breaks the ice" and facilitates communication for a more cooperative atmosphere. Anger is a normal reaction to the invasion of one's privacy—the home is one's castle. Hostility can be a defense against the anxiety of a "family secret"[4] such as homosexuality or infidelity. Occasionally, anger may be due to past unfortunate experiences with therapy.

The stage is set for therapy on a transactional basis at the time of the first telephone call[5] or other request for an appointment. By holding the expectation that both partners participate in the initial evaluations, they usually do. At times one spouse may appear to be very cooperative, but it is soon observed that his cooperation is only lip service and that he is only going through the movements of therapy. This could be the game[6] of malingering, "Look How Hard I've Tried." Focusing on the marriage as a seesaw with a clearly stated rationale strongly influences the expectations and approach of the therapist as well as the expectations and behavior of the partners.

My concept of marriage is a *meaningful relationship* between husband and wife based on *mutual respect* which in turn is based on *self-respect.* I point out that it is the seesaw that is under observation and not the spouses seated at either end. They are advised that when their marriage stabilizes, it is their prerogative to revise the marriage contract to meet changing needs and circumstances if they so desire. Jackson's[7] definition of marriage as consisting of two facets, sexual and collaborative relationships, is stressed with the collaborative relationships to be more important and to consist of four characteristics: voluntary, permanent, exclusive (no other liaisons), and goal-oriented.

Marriage is considered a partnership. No problem can exist that does not affect each partner, and the solutions will come from both—"it takes two to tango." Thus an individual partner is released from sole responsibility.

The stage (clinical setting) is set for both spouses to view the transactions between them; both have a chance to experience what help might come from therapy without committing themselves beyond the initial evaluation. It is explained that the evaluation consists of one to three individual sessions (usually two), plus a final conjoint diagnostic and disposition session (CDD) where the transactions between the spouses can be observed firsthand. They are told that a statement will be made at the CDD session as to impressions and recommendations.

At this point I describe in simple language my frame of reference, drawing the seesaw, jukeboxes, and the base anchored in the sociocultural milieu (see Ch. I, Fig. 2). This conceptual frame is easily grasped by the couple. I stress learning theories with emphasis on encoding new "records" in one's jukebox. This diverting of responsibility away from the partners as individuals frees each to various degrees of some of the guilt they carry. This results in less need to be accusative or defensive, leading to a better understanding of how current responses have their roots in learned behavior of the past, i.e. one is playing "records" of the past no longer valid for current relationships.

If one spouse is unduly suspicious, I continue the evaluation conjointly from then on. This inclusion prevents the partner from being subjected to a barrage of questioning as to what was discussed in the sessions. Usually this type of complaint is common in what I have labeled the "DA syndrome" (district attorney syndrome, see Ch. X). Flexibility in approach is mandatory at all times.

The individual diagnostic phase permits each spouse to fully relate his presenting complaints. Being seen individually permits revealing family secrets (which in my experience are known by the partner either consciously or unconsciously[8]), and expression of feelings in their full flower without fear of retaliation from the partner. Conjoint interviews are indicated from the first session on when the therapist senses that individual sessions will call forth distortion by a patient. Continuing conjoint sessions should be permitted until a clear picture of the marital problem is obtained or until a working alliance is established with the suspicious mate, who can then accept individual interviews, if deemed necessary.

SILENCE

Perhaps at this point an understanding of silence on the part of one spouse would be helpful in its management.[9] Watzlawick[10] and associates, in their superb book on communication, postulate that it is impossible not to communicate in the presence of others. As they point out in one of their examples, the airplane passenger who closes his eyes is communicating that he does not wish to talk, and others "get the message" and leave him alone. In keeping with our conceptual frame of multicausality, the phenomena of silence can be viewed from at least three systems—intrapersonal, interpersonal and environmental. Symptoms, so-called ego defenses (such as projection, denial and rationalization), or even personality are not intrapersonal (intrapsychic) entities but the resultant of many influences interacting with significant others or environmental forces. For example, a child is not born with a phobia. It is a reaction to someone or something in its environment.

The intrapersonal system as pertaining to silence is the most obviously involved. The two most common causes, in my clinical experience, are related to pervasive anxiety about the new therapy or to the fear that the internal raging anger will become manifest and uncontrollable. Occasionally, silence can reflect intense introspection on the current crisis, it may be due to a depression, or it may be a manifestation of a schizoid personality with an unawareness and often inaccessibility of inner emotion. I have observed silence to be a psychotic flight from reality. Impaired intelligence or poor verbal facility may prevent one spouse from communicating his thoughts or feelings, as will an inadequate or poor self-image.

The most common reason for interpersonal impediments to communication is the presence of a family secret. This may be due to either the content of the secret or the relationship with the interviewer. The four most common types of secrets include extramarital affairs, homosexuality, incestuous experiences, or prejudices of racial or religious nature that cause one spouse to anticipate rejection by the therapist.

In the third system of environmental forces, silence may be a manifestation of an identification with silent parents, or it may be where outsiders (strangers) are viewed as potential hostile persons. Silence in the interview may complement the reaction of not completing the biographical marital questionnaire.

THE BIOGRAPHICAL MARITAL QUESTIONNAIRE (BMQ)

At the end of the first individual interview, the patient is given two BMQ's (see Appendix), one for each of the two partners, and told that the questionnaires hasten the evaluation if completed and mailed in before the next interview. It is suggested that each add as many sheets of information to the BMQ as they deem necessary. Data from the BMQ's have proved useful in obtaining background information on the spouses, sometimes being obtained more readily than it could have been in the initial individual diagnostic interviews. The BMQ, originally developed by Maholick[11] and his associates has undergone continuous modification,[12] with clinical usage and alteration in conceptual framework. Although all information is revealing as to structure, content and lacunae, questionnaires seldom bring one to the core of the phenomena.[13] Just as it is essential in the practice of medicine to have a wide knowledge of many areas of possible significance in an illness, the therapist should be exposed to a conceptual frame that permits a broad coverage of many potentially significant factors. In any couple only some of these factors may be of immediate concern. Unless the conceptual scheme is broad enough to encompass most of the factors that are likely to influence the marriage, critical conditions may be overlooked.

Procrastination in returning the BMQ, minimum statements or refusal to fill out the form are informative. A suspicious spouse may be very reluctant to put his thoughts or complaints in writing. Not infrequently, after rapport with the partner is established, by telling the patient that completing the form is important, since its contents can be read by the therapist during his leisure time or to refresh his memory later, an uncooperative spouse will complete the BMQ. Occasionally meagreness of data reflects limited schooling or intelligence, and the therapist can complete or complement the form. Psychotic preoccupation may prevent or distract the individual and reveal itself in both content and/or spareness of information. Procrastination may suggest an obsessive-compulsive personality or neurosis, since doubt is characteristic of these individuals, resulting in inability to commit themselves to definitive statements.

Refusal to fill out the BMQ may indicate hostility by a spouse to an outsider's invasion of his privacy. Rejection of the BMQ may indicate anger at the partner for involving another person in the solution of his marital strife, since one's narcissism is threatened by the suggestion that one cannot solve his own problems. Finally, refusal to fill out the BMQ may indicate lack of motivation in regard to maintaining the marriage and should alert the therapist to the possibility of the game "Look How Hard I've Tried."

The completed BMQ can also be valuable in the later interviews as points of departure for further exploration of unsettled areas in the marriage. The marital partner coming for help is deeply involved with himself and is often caught in a mass of undifferentiated feelings toward his spouse. Questions on the BMQ are designed to reveal feelings of the self and the partner about the affectional aspects of the marriage, feelings about kinship networks, division of responsibility in the home, and what each spouse views as the major areas of difficulty. It is important to be fully aware that statements, oral or written, cannot be taken at face value—people frequently say one thing and mean something else.[14] In the following chapters (III-XIX) each subheading of the BMQ will be explored, and reasons for ascertaining specific data and illustrative clinical vignettes will be presented.

NOTES

1. Alex H. Kaplan: Social work therapy and psychiatric psychotherapy, *Arch Gen Psychiat*, 9:95, 1963.
2. Daniel J. Levinson, John Merrifield, and Kenneth Berg: Becoming a

patient. Arch Gen Psychiat, 17:385, 1967; Arnold P. Goldstein (Maximizing the initial psychotherapeutic relationship, *Amer J Psychother,* 23:430, 1969) presents a scholarly article with excellent bibliography which describes his "approach to the goal of maximizing initial psychotherapeutic relationships, an approach relying singularly upon social-psychologic research for hypothesis development."

3. Ralph R. Greenson: *The Technique and Practice of Psychoanalysis.* New York, Int. Univs. Press, 1967, pp. 190–216. See also Myron G. Sandifer, Jr., Anthony Hordern, and Linda M. Green: The psychiatric interview: the impact of the first three minutes, *Amer J Psychiat, 126:*968, 1970.

4. Harold I. Eist and Adeline U. Mandel (Family treatment of ongoing incest behavior, *Family Process,* 7:216, 1968) end their article by noting: "Most often a secret is not revealed to avoid hypothesized negative consequences. Sometimes when it is revealed, it may be to invite negative consequences. Guilt expiation for instance would be one possible reason for revelation. Another would be to get the therapists to abandon him."

5. For an excellent presentation of the initial response for help over the telephone see Warren M. Brodey: *Changing the Family.* New York, Potter, 1968, pp.17–24. On pp. 39–56 he also clearly describes the role of the therapist in the initial session.

6. Eric Berne in his books *Transactional Analysis in Psychotherapy* and *Games People Play* (New York, Grove Press, 1961 and 1964) uses the term *game* to refer to sequences of behavior which are governed by rules and not to have any playful connotation.

7. Don D. Jackson: Family rules: the marital quid pro quo, *Arch Gen Psychiat, 12:*589, 1965. A different conception is by Kenneth R. Mitchell (*Menninger Quart, 23:*13, 1969) who describes three different kinds of marriage contracts, formal, informal, and secret. See also Henry V. Dicks: *Marital Tensions.* New York, Basic Books, 1967, p.7.

8. Robert Seidenberg (Fidelity and jealousy: socio-cultural considerations. *Med Aspects Hum Sexuality,* 3:8, 1969) notes: "First of all, the cuckold is very much like the cancer patient; he is the last to know, not because he is stupid, but because he often chooses to deny what he perceives." This is applicable to other types of "secrets."

9. Gerald H. Zuk (On the pathology of silencing strategies, *Family Process,* 4:32, 1965) describes silencing strategies as interpersonal processes. He illustrates a number of strategies observed in psychotherapy and attempts to assess some aspects of their structure and dynamics.

10. Paul Watzlawick, Janet Beavin, and Don D. Jackson: *Pragmatics of Human Communication.* New York, Norton, 1967.

11. Leonard T. Maholick and David S. Shapiro: Changing concepts of psychiatric evaluation, *Amer J Psychiat, 119*:233, 1962.
12. Bernard L. Greene: Training clergymen in marriage counseling, *Pastoral Counselor, 5*:42, 1967.
13. Michael Rutter and George W. Brown: The reliability and validity of measures of family life and relationships in families containing a psychiatric patient, *Soc Psychiat, 1*:38, 1966.
14. Susan R. Orden and Norman M. Bradburn (Dimensions of marriage happiness, *Amer J Sociol, 73*:715, 1968) note "There is also some evidence that people tend to give more socially desirable responses in personal interviews than they do in self-administered questionnaires (S. Sudman, A. Greeley, and L. Pinto, The effectiveness of self-administered questionnaires, *J Marketing Res, 12*:293, 1965)."

III

BIOGRAPHICAL MARITAL QUESTIONNAIRE

After date, name and address, the first item on the BMQ asks the age of the spouses (see Appendix). Two facts are sought in this question. The younger the individual, the easier it may be to change patterns of behavior. A marked differential in age arouses questions (for example, unresolved oedipal relationships or financial issues). There were relatively few young couples: only 6 percent in the PS (private series) and 8 percent in the MDS (marital department series) were twenty-five years or younger. Relatively few were elderly: only 4 percent in the PS and 2 percent in the MDS were fifty-six or older. In the largest group 39 percent (PS) and 41 percent (MDS) were between thirty-six and forty-five, 36 percent (PS) and 35 percent (MDS) were between twenty-six and thirty-five, 15 percent (PS) and 14 percent (MDS) were between forty-six and fifty-five (see Table I).

Vincent[1] has pointed out that most individuals normally experience sexual attractions toward a person in a different generation group at some time. He noted that a girl is indoctrinated to attract a man who is mature, sophisticated, financially secure and of the right social class. Such characteristics are much more likely to be associated with a man of forty than with a youth

TABLE I
AGE OF SPOUSES

	PS (1000)			MDS (500)		
Age	Male No.	Female No.	Total %	Male No.	Female No.	Total %
-25	9	48	6	11	32	8
26–35	148	210	36	78	95	35
36–45	220	171	39	107	98	41
46–55	95	59	15	45	23	14
56+	28	12	4	9	2	2

of twenty. Similarly, "a man in his early twenties is likely to find a greater degree of refinement, understanding, social finesse, and worldly wisdom in a woman his senior."

The therapist should be on the alert as to the possibility of something being amiss when a wife is twice as old as her husband:

Mrs. Anna opened the interview with the comment that she was twice as old as her husband. She wondered whether he married her for her money but then added that there had been bitter quarrels started by her husband accusing her of paying too much attention to her daughter (of a previous marriage), who was his peer. "We have had terrible arguments over minor things. In fact, last summer my daughter told us that if we could not act like grown-ups, she was not going to invite friends to visit. He doesn't want me to smoke because it's bad for my health. He is treating me like a father would treat his child."

She continued, "He was very upset today because I was not home when he returned from work earlier than usual. I can't go to bed when I want to anymore. I've been in the habit of watching the late TV shows to relax. He complains that I stay up too late and it's bad for my eyes. It is degrading me to argue about unimportant things. Until recently our marriage was a pleasure."

Mr. Anna, dressed in Ivy League style, was polite and cooperative in his first interview. His only complaint was the constant arguments: "Not frequent, but at times constant. I feel the actual substance of any of these is not important, but the fact that there are arguments is hurting our relationship, and my wife becomes upset. Most of the arguments seem to start when I make some request of her and then point out later that she ignored it. Beyond this, I have no complaint about our marriage, even though she is twice my age. I really believe our marriage can be successful and I want it to be."

It was apparent from the diagnostic phase with this couple that the important issue in the marriage was not a financial one.

Another age variable deals with the woman who marries a man twice her age. A variety of reasons are obtained for these unions—the most frequent, in my experience, relates to the woman's unresolved relationship with her father. The woman may be seeking for a father who left home early in her childhood and now may be trying to reestablish symbolically the father-daughter relationship with her husband. This may not necessarily lead to marital discord. I have observed a number of happy marriages with the wife continually referring to and calling her husband, "Daddy." On the other hand, this can lead to severe disharmony when the husband wants a wife and not a daughter. During the courtship, he thought her behavior was "cute." When he would come home from his office, he would be greeted at the door by his wife and three-year-old daughter; he would kiss them, sit down and have his wife on one knee and his daughter on the other and be distressed by the conflicted, competitive situation.

Another type of marital relationship, labeled "Pygmalion," is characterized by an attempt to mold the partner into an idealized concept of a spouse (see Ch. V). As you might expect, in the "Pygmalion" relationship one partner is much older than the other.

The second question on the BMQ (see Appendix) asks if this is the first marriage and its duration (see Table II).

A comparison of the two series (PS and MDS) reveals almost identical figures. Relatively few couples were married less than one year or more than twenty-five years, 6 percent in the PS versus 4 percent in the MDS. About 10 percent in each group were married twenty-one to twenty-five years, that is, one out of ten couples seen. In both series about equal numbers, one out of five, were married one to five, six to ten, eleven to fifteen, or sixteen to twenty years, respectively.

The third item in the BMQ (see Appendix) explores the religious practice of each spouse (see Table III).

Raising the issue of religion may reveal friction in the marriage because of differences in religious attitudes and values. This area is explored more fully under a separate heading (item 21 in the BMQ, see Appendix). Very often religious differences can

TABLE II
DURATION OF THE MARRIAGE

	PS		MDS	
Year	*No.*	%	*No.*	%
−1	31	6	10	4
1– 5	90	18	38	15
6–10	115	23	53	22
11–15	108	22	56	22
16–20	79	16	50	20
21–25	47	9	24	10
25+	30	6	19	7

TABLE III
RELIGION

	PS			MDS		
	Male *No.*	*Female* *No.*	*Total* *%*	*Male* *No.*	*Female* *No.*	*Total* *%*
Jewish	244	208	45	51	46	19
Non-Catholic	195	225	42	131	142	55
Catholic	61	67	13	68	62	26
Mixed marriages		72	15		50	20

cause marital conflicts, especially in attitudes about birth control or religious participation. As seen in Table III, there were definite differences in the ratios in the religions represented among the couples. In the two series this factor was due to the religion of the author and different locales of the couples. In the MDS the area includes many Catholic families. The number of mixed marriages was 15 percent in the PS in comparison to 20 percent in the MDS. A tragic example of mixed marriage was seen in the following couple:

Mr. Betty phoned for an appointment while in a state of great anxiety. When seen, he was very distraught and stated he had been married seven months, that his wife was six weeks pregnant, and that he was on the verge of leaving her: "She wanted the baby, I did not. We had arguments and she stopped taking birth control pills. All along she resented taking them because of her religious beliefs. I knew she had stopped the 'pill' but I thought she was in her safe period. Religion is the biggest thing, unseparable from our problem. My own identity is at stake. I'm reacting without being able to understand why I'm reacting. I keep emphasizing my Jewish identity to her, my wanting to go to Temple now on Friday nights and also wanting to take Hebrew classes on Monday nights. I was never religious before. Now I am reluctant to accompany her to Mass as I used to do before we were married. The day I called you I had packed my bags and was set to move out.

"It all began on our honeymoon. It was the High Holy Holidays. It was Yom Kippur and we were in Hawaii. I was looking for a Temple. I had never missed going before my marriage. I finally found an Orthodox Temple. We went together and I wore a yomulka and tallis. She looked at me and cried all during the service. We had been dating for two years and religion was our primary topic of discussion. I got married with great reservations. Thought if we didn't make a go of it, there would be an annulment. I had agreed to raise our children Catholic. I reasoned that if we were good parents, the children would be all right, that one religion was as good as another. I had frequently accompanied her to Mass. I really didn't think it made any difference. My family disowned me when I got engaged and her family too was very unhappy about our marriage. She is the most fascinating person I have ever known. I really love her but don't know what has come over me. This religious obsession with me now. She is bewildered and confused. I am too."

The fourth item on the BMQ asks the occupation[2] of both spouses (see Table IV).

Approximately 30 percent of the wives were employed or working in their own or their husbands' businesses. This is an important factor in contributing both to precipitation and resolution of marital discord. Both spouses contributing to the financial structure of the family changes both power and decision-making processes. Occasionally, the male may react to his wife's working as a rejection of her emotional or nurturance role, re-

TABLE IV
OCCUPATION

| | *PS* | | *MDS* | |
	Male	*Female*	*Male*	*Female*
Owner of or in family business	189	20	35	5
Executive	145	7	63	3
Professional	135	70	68	22
White-collar	31	53	53	45
Blue-collar	0	0	31	0

sulting in the common marital game of "Uproar" (see Ch. XX). The type of occupation at times gives clues as to the personality of the individual, e.g. an accountant might be more comfortable with mathematical figures than with the human figure and more apt to be of obsessive-compulsive character structure and be married to a wife whose main complaint is that he does not meet her emotional needs. On the other hand, a salesman would tend to be more gregarious, outgoing, and one might expect a major complaint to be neglect in the sexual area or infidelity.

The working wife has more opportunities to meet other men when she goes with the girls for a drink at a nearby bar after work.

A glance at Table IV shows 13 percent of the husbands in the MDS to be blue-collar workers. Because of the different class memberships, therapist and patient may fail to communicate. It is a difficult task for a middle-class professional to change the whole structure of a way of life, nor should he attempt to do so. He cannot preach sobriety when alcoholic intemperance is the accepted code. Saving for the future has little meaning for a blue-collar individual whose job status may change from day to day. The therapeutic role of the professional needs careful scrutiny with this type of person. The blue-collar spouse needs to be treated as an individual whose culture is often in conflict with that of the middle-class therapists. The blue-collar individual seeks to be understood in terms of his own needs and his own way of life.

McGuire,[3] two decades ago, estimated that about one fourth of all Americans move up from the class in which they were born. He pointed out that social climbing by lower-class individuals required learning the behavior patterns of the new group (e.g. saving for the future) and discarding the patterns of the old (e.g. swearing, dirty jokes). In my two series, PS and MDS, none of the wives classified themselves as blue-collar. Thus 13 percent of the men in the MDS had moved upward, resulting in marital disharmony in some marriages. It would seem that the conduct of therapy without recognition of the cultural context of both oneself and the couple is not good.

Therapy with both spouses rather than with the individual only quite definitely heightens the likelihood that problems of cultural values will be thrust into the therapist's awareness.

The fifth item in the BMQ (see Appendix) deals with the issue of education (see Table V) and also gives a clue as to the status of the individual in the social milieu.

The lower the level of education attained, the more active and directive the therapy should be. The individual with limited

TABLE V
LEVEL OF EDUCATION

	PS		MDS	
	Male *No.(%)*	*Female* *No.(%)*	*Male* *No.(%)*	*Female* *No.(%)*
Grammar school	11(2)	5(1)	5(2)	5(2)
High school	79(16)	171(34)	76(30)	129(52)
Some college	88(18)	150(30)	50(20)	64(25)
College graduate	168(33)	148(30)	75(30)	45(18)
Postgraduate degrees	154(31)	26(5)	44(18)	7(3)

education wants direct answers and guidance in contrast to the person with a middle- or upper-class orientation, who seeks psychological or intellectual answers for his problem. Recently the literature has shown the trend to include more and more people in therapy procedures, especially with the advent of prepaid health insurance. Our two series are not typical of the majority of couples seeking help with marital problems, since 36 percent in the PS and 21 percent in the MDS had several college degrees. College graduates made up about one third of the couples in the PS and one third of the men in the MDS: only 20 percent of the women in the MDS graduate from college.

The sixth item on the BMQ (see Appendix) and an extremely important one in the CDD session asks the number of children and their ages. Children can be a major source of marital discord, either in terms of scapegoating, alliances with one of the spouses, in terms of disciplining, and so on. These issues will be explored more fully under item 15 (see Appendix). Table VI compares the number of children in the two series. Both series had about the same distribution, with two children being the most frequent: 36 percent in the PS and 28 percent in the MDS. In both groups, 16 percent in the PS and 14 percent in the MDS, there were no children. Approximately one fourth of the couples in both series had three children. Thirteen percent (13%) in the PS and 22 percent in the MDS had four or more children.

The seventh item of the BMQ (see Appendix) asks the source of referral. There were eight sources as shown in Table VII.

Psychiatrists accounted for the majority of referrals in both series: 43 percent in the PS versus 35 percent in the MDS. This could indicate either a disinterest or failure in dealing with marital problems. The 32 percent referrals from the clergy[4] and social agencies in the MDS may be due to publicity resulting

TABLE VI
CHILDREN IN THE FAMILY

Children	PS	MDS
None	79	34
One	65	25
Two	180	69
Three	114	65
Four or more	62	57

TABLE VII
SOURCE OF REFERRAL

	PS	MDS
Psychiatrist	217	87
Physician	93	35
Social worker, social agency or counselor	65	51
Previous patients	38	5
Clergyman	33	29
Lawyer	21	11
Friend	21	27
Psychologist	12	5

from both the annual clergymen's institute and monthly Forest Hospital lectures for professionals. The source of referral at times is valuable in revealing previous help obtained. At times, after a certain period of progress with a couple, it may be wise to refer the couple back to the original referring agency or individual.

NOTES

1. Clark E. Vincent: Sexual interest in someone older or younger. *Med Aspects Hum Sexuality, 2:6, 1968.*
2. James A. Peterson: The executive and his family. *Med Aspects Hum Sexuality, 3:6, 1969.* This article portrays how the "successful executive is often a driven man, taxed by career responsibilities and bored with the traditional marital role." In addition, he suggests four possible reasons for infidelity: (1) to prove his masculinity, (2) as a release from vocational dissatisfaction, (3) the presence of an "office wife"— his secretary shares more things with him than does his wife, and (4) the opportunities for sexual adventures as a result of vocational travel mobility.
3. Carson McGuire: Social stratification and mobility patterns, *Amer Sociol Rev, 15:195, 1950.*
4. Richard F. Larson (Clerical and psychiatric conceptions of the clergyman's role in the therapeutic setting, *Social Prob, 11:419, 1964*) presents a study "concerned with conceptions of psychiatrists and members of the clergy regarding the role of the clergyman in the treatment process. . . . Particular emphasis was placed on the extent of the clergyman's . . . referral policies." Another article, Attitudes and opinions of clergymen about mental health and causes of mental illness. *Ment Hyg, 49:32, 1965,* he states that the referral rate by clergy to psychiatrists to be 3 percent. This figure is half of my percentage in the private series—7 percent.

IV

SPECIFIC COMPLAINTS

Marital complaints can be classified clinically into specific areas and within these areas into specific clusters. One must obtain quickly the complaints that the spouses have about each other.[1] Although complaints (content) are very important in creating marital disharmony, the relationship between the spouses is the crucial factor. Item 8 (see Appendix) asks each spouse to list his specific complaints about the marriage and then to describe them in detail. This item is the most important of the entire BMQ, and although at first structured, the partners are encouraged to verbalize their complaints freely and spontaneously. When the BMQ was first modified in 1962, the ten most common complaints about the marriage in 136 couples were listed in the following order of frequency:

1. Spouse does not fulfill emotional needs.
2. Constant arguments.
3. Sexual dissatisfaction.
4. Financial disagreements.
5. Infidelity.
6. In-law trouble.
7. Lack of communication.
8. Alcoholism.
9. Conflicts about the children.
10. Suspicious spouse.

The current (fifth) revision of the BMQ based on 750 couples shows that the most frequent complaint now to be lack of communication (see Table VIII).

As was to be expected, more than one complaint was the usual finding. The following clinical vignette is one where both

TABLE VIII
SPECIFIC MARITAL COMPLAINTS

	PS*			MDS†			Grand Total
	Male	Female	Total	Male	Female	Total	
Lack of communication	254	244	498	121	150	271	769
Constant arguments	246	230	476	125	132	257	733
Unfulfilled emotional needs	168	250	418	78	137	215	633
Sexual dissatisfaction	214	186	400	94	108	202	602
Financial disagreements	118	105	223	61	94	155	378
In-law trouble	84	79	163	35	59	94	257
Infidelity	70	86	156	46	29	75	230
Conflicts about children	59	94	153	15	20	35	188
Domineering spouse	55	70	125	7	10	17	142
Suspicious spouse	51	40	91	12	10	22	113
Alcoholism	15	50	65	10	21	31	96
Physical attack	8	35	43	2	23	25	68

* Includes 500 couples.
† Includes 250 couples.

spouses had circled all the complaints on the form, although their main complaint was continuous quarreling about their son:

Mr. and Mrs. Beulah are both professional people, married twenty-five years—first marriage for each. Mrs. Beulah is in the main attacking of, hostile to, and depreciative of her husband, while he makes only a half-hearted attempt to ward off her attacks on him. Only toward the end of the CDD session was there any display on her part of some support and concern for her husband.

In initiating the interview, Mrs. Beulah took the lead, saying that they were here primarily because of their son, who is an underachiever in high school. They were referred by the school counselor, who stated they need marital counseling for their son's sake.

Mr. Beulah stated that for a long time they both felt they could work it out between them. Though he feels it is deep-seated and their difficulties are increasing, he is now willing to accept counseling.

Mrs. Beulah indicated that she would go along, expressing reservations about the efficacy of treatment and fearful it will upset her. She suggested that her husband speak first.

He commented that she thinks he drinks too much (alcoholism). He has two martinis at noon with his associates and several highballs at dinner.

She interrupted to ask about the two screwballs (slip of the tongue), "I mean the two screwdrivers" he had this morning. He countered that he was upset this morning because of what happened last night.

She replied that she is tired of having the wool pulled over her eyes. He has been running around with a woman (her complaint No. 2) for a year, he never told her the truth (the third complaint is lack of communication) and she has had to check up on him. He denies seeing this woman: she is his secretary, and it is merely an employer-employee relationship (his complaint, she is a suspicious spouse).

She interrupts to add that the incident of last night had to do with her husband's leaving the house to go shopping and that he was gone unduly long. She checked about for him, and drove over to these friends of theirs and found him there with a drink in his hand. He states: "She blew her stack," created a scene and embarrassed him (his complaint of constant arguments). She replied: "I am short tempered."

At this point she became aggressive, angry, attacking, and demanded to know where her money goes (her next complaint is a financial one), is sure her husband spends it at bars, and she resents this use of her money.

He switches to claim that her accusations about his secretary were blown up beyond proportion and beyond the reality of what happened between them. She counterattacks and states that he used her money on this other woman. He comments that even prior to their sons difficulty in school, she would constantly haggle and accuse him of being interested in other woman. They would wrangle every morning, and the boy would go off to school in tears.

There followed accusations and counteraccusations that each was not doing enough for their son, he in terms of care, and she in not enough father and son companionship.

Mr. Beulah goes on to say he feels his wife is bored with him, does not tune in to his needs, and rejects his friends (his complaint: unfulfilled emotional needs). She retorts, she refuses to go bar hopping, which is what he and his friends like to do. So he goes off by himself or out with his secretary.

Mrs. Beulah again returns to the money issue and lays into her husband. She suggests that he has been rolled. He denies this, and she claims that he has dissipated their funds. He retorts that between them they earn twenty-five thousand dollars a year, and that there are no money problems.

He describes himself as composed, never losing his temper; he blocks off emotional outbursts, and claims that he cannt be provoked. She, however, claims that he is cutting in his remarks and in this manner gets in his licks.

She turns to ask her husband what his secretary has that she hasn't. She attacks him while he only defends and fends off. She considers that she is too old to learn and never had it anyhow, feels that the attraction between her husband and that woman had to do with sex. He replies that they have a good sexual relationship. She complains, however, that at night her husband falls asleep when she makes a sexual overture. He wants it only in the morning and at a time she feels unable to respond. He counters that it has to be when she is in the mood, the stars in the proper position, the time at night only and in a completely darkened room (thus, both complain of sexual dissatisfaction).

I raise the question of the way they are rearing their son, and whether this is an issue between them. Mrs. Beulah felt it had been more of an issue in the past because of his parents' interference (her next complaint is in-law trouble). She describes her husband as being more lenient towards their son on the advice of his parents. She feels her son is a headstrong, difficult to manage adolescent, and at times rebellious. She also feels, at times her husband wasn't available, which only made matters worse. He feels that if he would reprimand the boy, Mrs. Beulah would call him down, so he began avoiding taking any responsibility (both complain about child rearing). They both feel that their son is quite skilled in pitting one parent against the other. They consider him an intellectually sharp youngster, who baits his parents, pits them against each other, and is quite perceptive as to what goes on in the household. With this comment both became silent.

Communication may be pathological in its absence or in too frequent quarreling. The most common marital complaint was lack of communication.[2] In the PS both husbands and wives expressed the same percentage of lack of communication, approximately 50 percent, whereas in the MDS more women complained in the ratio of 60 to 48 percent. In this age of mass communication it is interesting that the number one complaint of conflicted couples is lack of communication.

There are many ways of communicating and relating in a marriage that are unique to the spouses and understood only by them. Currently there is no generally acceptable, complete theory of human communication. Jurgen Ruesch[3,4] was the first psychiatrist to write extensively on the pragmatic and theoretical exploration of communication. He states:[5]

The various communication theories have achieved their present positions of eminence because they have the characteristics of general system theories. Properties or functions described are no longer bound to a structure of a given magnitude, as is the case with the abstractions of the behavioral or social scientists, in as much as input, output, and central processes are characteristic of cell, organ, organism, group, society, or automaton.

In order to communicate and relate to each other, the marital couple must share a code or language. Further, Ruesch[6] points out that matters get more complicated when one considers actions as messages, since involuntary messages may cause as much reaction as intentional ones. Nonverbal communication includes gestures, facial expressions, posture, voice inflection, the pace and sequence of the words themselves, and so on.

The recent book by Watzlawick[7] and associates on pragmatic communication is a must reading for therapists. They present some attributes of communication that fundamentally influence interpersonal relationships. They discuss these attributes in the nature of tentative axioms. The first axiom was previously described in Chapter II where it was postulated that it is impossible not to communicate in the presence of others.

Another axiom differentiates between content and relationship. Frequently arguments are focused on content when the real source of conflict is the disturbed relationship between the couple.

> If a husband brings home flowers for his wife, the content will be the flowers but the relationship will determine the transaction between them. She may comment that it was very thoughtful of him to bring the flowers, give him a kiss and state that they will make a lovely center *piece* on the dinner table. Or, she may angrily state that if he is trying to buy *peace* for his rudeness at the breakfast table, he has another guess coming. On the other hand, she may coyly state that although the flowers will make a lovely center piece, does he have ideas in mind for later in the evening, another sort of "piece?"

Another axiom is that the relationship between individuals is influenced by the dynamic punctuation of the messages between the persons. A common example is in the marital game described by Eric Berne[8] "If It Weren't For Him" (see Ch. XX), where the husband complains that the reason he does not cut the grass is because his wife is always nagging him to do so, whereas the wife retorts that unless she nags him he never does anything around the house.

Still another axiom describes how individuals "communicate both digitally and analogically," with the content feature of communication transmitted as digital and the relationship aspect conveyed as analogical. The digital mode of communication is an arbitrary code of using a word to establish a relation between a name and thing. Analogical communication is nonverbal and includes facial expressions, gestures, body positions, voice modifications and similar phenomena.

The last axiom advanced is that all communicational transactions are either symmetrical or complementary. In the complementary relationship one spouse's behavior complements that of his partner's leading to dovetailing and closure, whereas in the symmetrical type the partners tend to mirror each other's behavior, resulting in escalation and the second most common marital game, "Uproar" (see Ch. XX).

Clinically these axioms have been found to be extremely useful in the management of marital problems. For example, the impossibility of not communicating makes all marriages interpersonal and communicative and helps explain a technical maneuver later to be presented as Transient Structured Distance (see Ch. XXI).

Although the previously described axioms have enhanced my understanding of pathological communication, the following factors in order of frequency were found to be present in our conflicted couples:

1. Narcissistic spouse—whose orientation is self-centered and not on the marriage.
2. Indifference—an actual negative approach toward the partner's feelings, needs, and wishes or even a lack of respect for him leading to a lack of concern.
3. Inability—an incapability to reinforce and support the partner; what Berne refers to as "stroking."
4. Inflexibility—a rigid set of attitudes and values which do not permit the individual to deviate from a fixed pattern or code.
5. Inexperience—a lack of experience in positive, meaningful relationships.
6. Crossed transactions—digital and analogic modes of communicating in which areas of verbal and nonverbal communications have little in common.
7. Avoidance maneuvers—where one partner avoids communication by withdrawing (however, since in a marriage one cannot not communicate, the partner still gets the message of rejection).
8. Distortion—messages are received, but not as sent.

The following extracts from clinical cases illustrate the above enumerated factors in couples complaining of lack of communication.

Narcissistic spouse (1), the most common complaint is illustrated below.

Mrs. Blanche bitterly stated: "He seems more of an observer to life than a participant and is wrapped up in his own private world to an extreme degree."

Mr. Blanche calmly commented: "She is impatient in discussing anything. She is highly emotional and can easily get upset. She insists on having things her way." (Symmetrical escalation in this couple.) "At the height of her temper she is very insulting. Her words are very sharp and hurting. She is more concerned about her career than her home and family." (Both spouses accuse the other of being self-centered.)

The CDD session highlighted their narcissistic orientation.

He was very polite, talked about their marital problems in an intellectual manner, and seemed embarrassed at seeking marriage therapy. She gave the impression of being a somewhat angy individual. She was however also very courteous, handled the conversation around their marital difficulties in an intellectual manner, gave the impression that there was little hope for change in the marriage but was willing to seek marital counseling because her husband wished this. Both spouses seemed reluctant to state their conflicts in any manner which might reflect discredit on the other. Both stated that their marriage seemed to have developed down to a more practical situation rather than a marriage, and both agreed that they went their own way and both were strong willed (lack of complementary closure). Both complained that there was little communication between them, that they do not or cannot talk things through, and that both accused each other of not comprehending their communications although both are college graduates. Their major difficulties and arguments seemed to evolve around finances, as they argue over what to buy, how to save, and what to do with their money. (The symmetrical escalation in this couple is a good example of a disturbance of communication due to confusion between content and relationship, based on the question of who was right regarding some minor content matter, each accusing the other of being self-centered.)

Indifference (2), the second most common complaint, with an actual negative approach toward partner's feelings, needs, and/or wishes, developed gradually in the majority of these conflicted couples. Just as recent sensory deprivation experiments have demonstrated the importance of varying levels of sensory input for the stability of the individual, similarly the stability of the marital relationship demands that spouses reinforce not only their own but their partner's self-definition, i.e. their self-image. As Watzlawick *et al.*[9] have succinctly stated: "On the relationship level people do not communicate about facts outside their relationship but offer each other definitions of that relationship and, by implication, of themselves." Indifference, which is a deadly form of rejection, implies the partner no longer exist. As one individual aptly stated: "I may as well be talking to the wall in most cases as to talk to her." The following vignette is illustrative of both the gradual and destroying development of indifference in a marriage and how different views of reality of the marriage (discrepant punctuation) led to severe marital disharmony:

Mrs. Bridget began the conjoint session by bitterly complaining about her husband: "When we first were married, Jim started going to school and I was away from home for the first time, pregnant, in a strange locale, and didn't know anyone. There was no time spent together because he always had to study. We didn't go out very often, and the only conversation I had to offer was neighborhood gossip, which he made plain he wasn't interested in. My rules around the home are never backed up by him and only when his own things are disturbed does he correct the children. The farther apart we grew in communication the farther apart we grew sexually, and gradually I wasn't anxious for his advances. Most of the time I was too tired physically and mentally and furious at his indifference of my feelings and needs. He'd demand sex relations regardless or start an argument. So to avoid trouble I'd submit to pacify him. Now I don't care at all. I've got to the point where I find that reading or painting or knitting satisfy the need I once had for companionship, and I don't miss him and the fights being with him bring."

Mr. Bridget replied: "I admit that when I was at school I was too wrapped up in myself and my studies. But now she avoids me, and seldom tells me of the children's problems as they develop. She must be left alone, shut-up in her bedroom, she reads for hours until midnight or later. No show of affection is normal among man and wife, she claims. When I try to communicate with her, she withdraws and then blames me for being indifferent."

Inability (3), the third factor in the complaint of lack of communication, occurred in two thirds of the couples. This inability to support and reinforce the partner is primarily the replaying of a past faulty parental model of identification. One spouse succinctly put it: "We are not in close communication with each other and never have been. It is a definite *lack* in both of us to give to each other. I feel we cannot nourish it now."

The following couple, whose courtship was smooth, noneventful, and nonpassionate, gave the following history:

Mr. Caroline started the interview by stating that probably their basic problem was total lack of communication and that their sex life was not satisfactory to his wife.

Mrs. Caroline interrupted, with controlled anger, and added: "What little sex we have (note the needle[10]) has been quite satisfactory and there is a financial problem and a basic religious difference. There has been a budgeting problem since the very start of marriage, as he will tend to stay in bed till late in the morning and is always late for work. We are different in makeup, I have a lot of get up and go, and he is just the opposite. When we were courting, I misinterpreted his inability to give of himself as the mark of a gentleman and respect for me as a woman."

Mr. Caroline comments that in his childhood there was little display of affection between his parents and very little communication: "Our family was like that painting of the New England farmer, his wife, and pitchfork. I would like to talk to her but it doesn't come easily. On the other hand, I've been raked over the coals for the last ten years and receive nothing but constant criticism from her. I have to do everything on schedule, and this irritates me no end. I do not want to eat as soon as I get home from work but would like to relax a little with a highball."

Mrs. Caroline at this point started to cry and stated she does not know why he hates her so. She is, she supposes, very critical, but she doesn't like to see him go to work unshaven, with holes in his shoes, and she supposes that instead of bringing him up to her normal standards, she has slipped down to his (another needle).

He retorts that the lack of sex is probably due to his anger, as they argue all day long and she expects to have sex that night.

Inflexibility (4), on the part of a spouse was a factor in 20 percent of the couples. Characteristic of this behavior was a personality that did not permit deviation from a fixed pattern or code.

Two spouses stated this type of behavior succinctly:

"We do not seem able to sit down like two human beings and reason something. A decision is made by him and that's that. He insists all I want is my own way. Sometimes I am wrong, but often my ideas are good for everyone and I do want my way because I believe it is a good one. He calls it petticoat government, or, wearing the pants!"

The following vignette is illustrative:

Mr. and Mrs. Catherine were referred by their respective divorce lawyers. Mrs. Catherine related the following: "Lack of communication has always been a problem between us. He's a schemer and I'm a dreamer. Our minds start working on opposite poles, and sometimes it takes forever for them to meet. I hurt his feelings by what I say, and he hurts mine by what he says, with or without any intention of doing so. Until recently I practically had to make an appointment with him to talk anything over.

It is difficult for him to talk anything over seriously with me and invariably it goes through an argument before a solution can be reached. The argument part for years produced a harangue in him and tears in me. Finally, a year ago, I realized I was not that bad and began to talk back. I was confident enough to be able to defend myself rationally. I was not able to do this before, because I know that most of the things my husband complains of in me have plenty of truth in them, and for this I have no defense and can only try to improve. I can tell him why, but that does not seem to help. But I had not known specifically what was wrong with him. It took years and years to get the vaguest glimmerings of what was really the matter with him. During the past year especially, I have been reading what psychology books for the laymen I could find. But mostly I have just thought and thought about it. I still can't understand what he says to me sometimes. Or if I can understand it, it doesn't make sense to me. He often tells me how stupid I am, and it must be because I can't see from his viewpoint. When I believe he is wrong and point this out and tell why, he can be expected to fly into a rage. So the pattern of his anger and my tears which lasted for fifteen years has now changed to his anger and my calmness. I get very upset, but I am outwardly calm, and he is angry and violent in word especially and in gesture sometimes. It's almost as if I have to lie to satisfy him, that is, in order to resolve an argument. Because if I persist in my own judgment, we never effect a meeting. Everything has to be *his* way about the management of finances, the rearing of children, the appearance of the home, and so on."

Inexperience (5), crossed transactions (6), avoidance maneuvers (7), and distortion (8) occurred in the remaining 20 percent of the factors involved in pathological communication patterns. An example of inexperience is the following:

He seems to lack a basic understanding of women and their variable moods. I'd like a more outward show of affection and conversation! He just doesn't have the experience. Marriage should be the beginning of life, not the end.

In crossed transactions frequently the problem is in content and relationship communication. Digital messages (content) are concise, but analogic communication (relationship) is antithetical, frequently resulting in incompatible interpretations. As one husband complained:

We are on different wavelengths. We have a constant communication problem and misinterpret each other. She takes everything I say literally. She says she can't tell when I am jesting and when I am serious. When I bring her a box of candy, I don't know whether she will react with pleasure, suspicion, or anger. Intellectually we communicate well, emotionally we do not. I write poetry which she judges by mechanical standards and fails to recognize the spiritual and emotional content to any significant degree. She does not appear to appreciate my expression of love, beauty or compassion.

In avoidance maneuvers, one spouse avoids communicating by withdrawing:

I don't communicate with her because I am always fearful of bringing about an argument in talking about most problems. My wife is quick tempered and usually takes things the wrong way. So I keep my distance.

Another spouse related:

Whenever we have an argument, there is one of two methods used—"cold war" sometimes lasting as long as ten days and I would always be the one to break the ice even though the disagreement was started by him: or he would lose his temper and hit me. So I avoid him as much as possible.

Still another woman bitterly complained:

He is noncommunicative. I can't talk to him. He won't admit I am right. I am right 98 percent of the time. He has taken all the fun out of life. He tolerates all my abuse and doesn't defend himself. I am talkative and he is closemouthed. He says he avoids talking to me in order to avoid arguments. I scream to get a rise out of him and can't get it.

Finally, in 5 percent of the complaints was the factor of distortion where spouses distort messages received:

She interprets things I say in her own way, which tends to distort and create tension and arguments.

The second most common marital complaint, constant arguments, is the other main group of pathological communication. Fifty-five percent of the couples in the PS and MDS complained of both lack of communication and constant arguments. The distribution of this complaint was about the same in both the PS and the MDS, and it was almost equally distributed between both sexes, being 48 percent in the PS and 51 percent in the MDS. This type of marital conflict will be more fully described in Chapter XX in the marital game of "Uproar."

An understanding of phenomenon of disagreement is contingent upon the phenomena of ambivalence that Freud[11] stressed in his writings. In every relationship from infancy on to marriage, one cannot have a close and loving interrelation without also having anger and disagreement.[12] It is impossible to live and avoid frustration with its corresponding affect of anger. Every therapist has to encounter the ambivalent reactions of his patients as well as his own ambivalent reactions to them.

NOTES

1. Peter A. Martin: *Selected Papers of Peter A. Martin*. Detroit (self-published) 1966, pp. 129–198.
2. Antonio J. Ferreira and William D. Winter (Information exchange and silence in normal and abnormal families, *Family Process*, 7:251, 1968) in an interesting research study have corroborated their hypothesis that "abnormal families do spend more time in *silence* [italics added] than normal families."
3. Jurgen Ruesch: *Therapeutic Communication*. New York, Norton, 1963.
4. Jurgen Ruesch and Gregory Bateson: *Communications: The Social Matrix of Psychiatry*. New York, Norton, 1951. For the past decade and until recently, Bateson has strongly influenced the Palo Alto group (Mental Research Institute) in California, for example, his "double-bind" concept.
5. Jurgen Ruesch: Social process, *Arch Gen Psychiat*, 15:577, 1967.
6. Jurgen Ruesch and Weldon Kees: *Nonverbal Communication*. Berkeley, U. of Calif Press, 1956.
7. Paul Watzlawick, Janet H. Beavin, and Don D. Jackson: *Pragmatics of Human Communication, A Study of Interactional Patterns, Pathologies, and Paradoxes*. New York, Norton, 1967. See also Don D. Jackson and Arthur M. Bodin: Paradoxical communication and the marital paradox, in *The Marriage Relationship* (Salo Rosenbaum and Ian Alger, Eds. New York, Basic Books, 1968, pp. 3–20; and, Ray L. Birdwhistell: Communicative signals and their clinical assessment, *Voices*, 1:37, 1965.
8. Eric Berne: *Games People Play*. New York, Grove Press, 1964.
9. Watzlawick, *et al., op. cit.*
10. When a couple is anchored in therapy, I frequently interrupt and state that this is a needle, an observation which usually causes the partner to retaliate. I then relate the story of the frozen porcupines huddling for warmth. As soon as the ice melts, they begin to prick each other again and draw apart and get cold again.
11. Freud broke many of the idols of traditional psychology when he introduced his psychodynamic theory of behavior. His seminal ideas require no emphasis here. Psychoanalysis postulates that behavior is primarily the outcome of a hypothesized interplay of intrapsychic vectors, considered to follow closely the thermodynamic laws of

energy in physics. The interdependence between man and his environmental matrix remained a neglected field of orthodox psychoanalytic study. Certain basic psychoanalytic concepts remain important for understanding human behavior: the unconscious, transference, ambivalence, conflict and repression.

12. J. Mervyn Dickinson: You should fight with your wife, *Together, 41,* 1967. See also Israel W. Charny's excellent article and bibliography, Marital love and hate (*Family Process,* 8:1, 1969), who writes: "In each marriage the choice is not between happiness and unhappiness, but between a respectful, cooperative state of nonviolent tension, where quite often we must experience anger though often we may also enjoy a more positive, empathizing love; or a state of increasingly violent, demoralizing, depersonalizing destruction of one or another." Also, James L. Hawkins: Associations between companionship, hostility, and marital satisfaction, *J Marriage Family, 30:*647, 1968.

V

UNFULFILLED EMOTIONAL NEEDS

When the BMQ was first developed, the most frequent marital complaint was unfulfilled emotional needs. Currently this complaint is third in frequency and occurred in 42 percent of the couples. Interestingly, the frequency is about the same in both the PS and MDS. However, as to be expected, women complained more frequently than men in the ratio of about three to two (see Table VIII Ch. IV). Perhaps the relatively smaller number of women in the PS could be due to more plentiful economic resources, e.g. to employ maids or to belong to country clubs. Hence, the needs of these women are met elsewhere. The frustration of emotional needs centered about the "inner child" of the spouse. The leading complaint could be defined as "no stroking" or "critical" behavior from the partner as described by Berne.[1] The other principal area of complaint was that he, i.e. his "inner child," was unloveable. At this time it might be advantageous to discuss "records" and their phenomenological manifestations (voices).

In Chapter I, I briefly presented the marriage institution as consisting of two spouses (jukeboxes), each unique in personality and seated at opposite ends of a seesaw (see Fig. 1). Each jukebox contains a library of permanent stereophonic "records." If all the records could be exposed on the seesaw, the current marital relationship could be understood from the present configuration of the "records." My patients and my students readily grasp the concept of a stereophonic "record" with a blending of various voices. These voices in each "record," vary in intensity so that at times one may hear a solo, duo, or trio, with all three voices being expressed at the same time. The "pia" and "inner child" voices are of biological origin and are undifferentiated until the onset of object relationships when the infant is about six months old. The complex subject of object relationships will be further elaborated upon in Chapter XIV. The "pia" voice is presented as nonemotional and purely data processing of both internal and external stimuli. The voice of the "inner child" remains about the same throughout life. "Parental" and "pia" voices are subject to both biological aging and environmental stresses. The "parental" voice expresses the sociocultural matrix and can consist of one voice or any combination of voices, from parental (solo or duo of both parents) to trios or quartets and so on, of siblings, from chamber groups of peers to an entire symphony of the various social institutions of society in general. At all times the "parental" voices express value orientations and/ or "stroking" attitudes. The attributes of the "parental" voices will be developed in Chapter XV.

Before describing the voice of the "inner child," which is the loudest whiner in the complaint of unfulfilled needs, I would like to discuss the "pia" voice in detail. It is important to keep in mind that the "pia" voice is present from birth and relates to nonemotional data processing of the brain. The three principal functions of the "pia" voice are _perceptive_, _integrative_, and _a_daptive. The perceptive function concerns itself with the input of internal and external stimuli. The former come from the various needs of the "inner child" and the internalized values and attitudes of the "parental" voices, which include parents and others in the external environment of the individual. The external stimuli perceived by the "pia" pertain to ever-changing forces in the sociocultural matrix. The integrative function of the "pia" consists of data scanning, data processing, and data storage in the form of memories. The adaptive function helps the individual see reality as it is to him.

A "record" is viewed as a pragmatic unit of communication.[2] All behavior is communication (verbal and nonverbal) and therefore influences and is influenced by others. Thus the "pia" voice be affected strongly by chronological and experiential forces. Panzetta,[3] describes the action model as grounded in "pragmatic activism" and based on ego-interpersonal-environmental involvement. The neo-Freudian concept of ego best describes the "pia" voice. The seesaw and its anchoring base best introduce the complementarity of forces which determine behavior due to the mutuality and interdependence of the individual and his environment. The environment consists of the "existent social order, structures and institutions of the locale involved."[4] All three determinants—intrapersonal, interpersonal and environmental—are converted into a common energy unit and stored in the brain in the form of a "record," capable of replay, consciously and unconsciously.

The "pia" voice is a combination of various theoretical formulations. In the past forty-seven years, since Freud[5] described the structure of the ego in 1923,[6] advances have been made in theory and therapy by psychoanalysts as well as others who utilize psychoanalytic concepts. Anna Freud's classic book[7] in 1936 and Hartmann's monograph[8] stimulated interest in ego functions. Erik Erikson's[9] concept of equilibrium of forces also is important in evaluating the role of the "pia" voice in the individual's total functioning, internally and externally. Freud's formulation of the ego concept varied over the years in relation to different aspects of the ego or its functioning. In his first phase of conceptualization, which ended around 1900 with the publication of *The Interpretation of Dreams*,[10] Freud conceived of the ego as an intrapsychic structure responsible for such functions as reality testing, perception, reasoning, memory, and so on. During the second phase, ending in 1923, his interest was directed to intensive study of instincts and their vicissitudes.[11] In the third and last phase, ending with his death in 1939, he again emphasized the organization and primacy of the ego's integrative functions. Ferenczi[12] likewise was concerned with functioning of the ego, as revealed by his studies on reality testing and adaptation. Anna Freud in 1936 focused on the defensive mechanisms of the ego against instinctual drives and external dangers. This pointed the way to the development of the theory of adaptation—the relationship of the person to his

environment. A year later, Hartmann's important monograph on
ego psychology and adaptation initiated modern psychoanalytic
theory.

An important result of Hartmann's stress on adaptation was
a further unfolding of the functions of the ego. He noted that
the infant is endowed with a number of inborn capacities for
development, which include perception, memory, motility, and
so on. These capacities have an inherent maturational unfolding, are autonomous and do not arise out of conflict. Thus the
formulation that the human being at birth has only a simple,
primary id is no longer tenable. It is now viewed as an undifferentiated id-ego mass. This undifferentiated mass, an abstract construct, can be viewed from the phenomenological
viewpoint of "pia" and "inner child" voices. Hartmann emphasized the function of adaptation of these autonomous, inborn
capacities in relation to the environmental forces, e.g. perception
helps the infant and child to adapt to his environment, both
human and nonhuman. He also postulated that individuals are
born with an inherent coordination with their environment,
which he called a "state of adaptedness," which is relatively con-
flict-free (e.g. the baby's cry) and that the environment provides
relatively stable human and cultural responses, the "average
expectable environment" (e.g. mother's or a maternal surrogate's
response). The state of adaptedness allows the growing child
to modify his responses to all the forces in his environment.
Another useful concept of Hartmann is that of "apparatuses of
secondary autonomy." In this, behavior that once was involved
in conflict and served essentially defensive ends may continue
as an adaptive pattern of behavior, removed from the original
instinctual gratification, and autonomous in the service of adaptation to the environment. According to Hartmann, the growing
child has two parallel lines of development. Implicit in these
two concepts of autonomy is the construct of the relative independence of the ego from the id. This independence is a
marked change from Freud's concept of the ego splitting off
from the id. Thus the "pia" voice is present at birth but does
not begin to manifest itself until about six months of age when

perception progresses to the point of establishing object relationships. The concepts of Erikson on adaptation supplement the postulate of Hartmann that each individual has an inborn capacity to adapt to an average expectable environment. Erikson has amplified this postulate with the concept of mutuality and "cogwheeling" between generations.

The "inner child" of the individual plays an important role in marriage. Its needs vary with the various phases of maturation. The earliest emotional needs correspond to the early symbiotic relationship between the infant and its mother. Thus closeness, warmth, tenderness, fondling and kissing are basic to the normal emotional maturation of a person. Creative play also arises early in development. The second year in life ushers in the wonderful world of curiosity. With progressive maturation of the individual, "libidinal" needs[13] begin to become important. Thus it is not surprising that sexual dissatisfaction is the fourth most common marital complaint and will be discussed in the next chapter (VI). Missildine[14] begins his excellent book with the following: "Somewhere, sometime, you were a child. This is one of the great obvious, seemingly meaningless and forgotten common denominators of adult life. In trying to be adults we mistakenly try to ignore our lives as children, discount our childhood and omit it in our considerations of ourselves and others. This is the basic cause of much adult distress and unhappiness." The ongoing voice of the "inner child" influences and often determines and dominates the individual's relationships, depending on the intensity of its tone in resonance or dissonance with the "parental" and "pia" voices. From infancy on we are dealing primarily with the feelings and behavior patterns of our "inner child." As Missildine notes: "We disown, ignore or dismiss them, 'overcome' them, scolding and belittling ourselves as 'childish' and for not being 'grown up.' Yet the very nature of emotional development makes it impossible to do this."[15] Much marital discord could be eliminated if couples had a deeper understanding of how to live in harmony with their "inner child." In Chapter XIX, where we ask the question about social and recreational activities, further information is given about the "inner child." An important pragmatic concept found to be useful clinically is Franz Alexander's[16] "surplus energy" postulate. He describes the individual as having a daily specified amount of energy that is primarily for utilitarian functions as eating, breathing, and so on. Any excess energy left over is discharged in either play or sex, depending on inclination, maturation, external circumstances, and others.

In reviewing the complaint of nonfulfillment of emotional needs, six principal categories were found in the following order of frequency:

1. Frustration of dependency needs.
2. Making the "inner child" feel inadequate.
3. Making the "inner child" feel unloveable.
4. Avoidance of household responsibilities—housekeeping for females and house maintenance for males.
5. Seeing partner as "another child in the household."
6. Differences in recreational needs.

Frequently the above categories were found in varying combinations. A typical example of the first category, frustration of dependency needs, follows:

"He is not happy about the things that make me happy such as the Christmas season, birthdays, some aspects of vacations, or when I am ill. If I had a physical problem, he would ignore me. I severely burned my hand several years ago, and he never asked how it was or if it was healing. I have been ill, and he has never offered to do anything around the house or even come upstairs to see how I was. He has gone to bed ill every time one of our children was born, and I've had to take care of the baby and him!"

The second category of unfulfilled emotional needs, a variation of the marital game described by Berne as "Yes But," consists of making the partner's "inner child" feel inadequate.

Mr. and Mrs. Charlotte were referred for marital therapy. His main complaint was that recently she had started to drink too much: "She doesn't get drunk, but I think that three highballs when we are out socially is too much. When she has a few drinks, she tells me off when we get home. We have been married fifteen years, and this has never happened bfore. I saw my father's deterioration from his drinking. He was a kind and soft man, a steady worker as a grocery clerk. Occasionally he would stop after work and have a few beers with friends at the local tavern. When he got home he would always catch hell from Mother. Mother was the strong person in the family, relatively good-natured, domineering, immaculate housekeeper and a good cook. She was always criticizing father in everything he did around the house."

Mrs. Charlotte was a petite, pleasant, cooperative, effacing woman in her mid-thirties, who had worked in the same office since her marriage as a private secretary: "We have never quarreled until recently when he told me I drink too much. I am not an alcoholic, but recently when I've had a few drinks I have told him off. We have no children because he wanted it that way. Everything has to be his way. He feels everything I do should be perfect. In the kitchen he will stand and count my steps and correct me if I'm not logical and precise. He can't stand doors left ajar. When I am in the kitchen, he watches the way I prepare the food, what pans or pots to use, what condiments to add, etc. . . . This makes me nervous. He is a good cook, in fact everything he does is good—painting, electrical work, you name it. At times he will come home with some clothes he bought for me that he saw in a women's shop on display. He has good taste, knows my size, but I would prefer to buy my own clothes. I don't say anything, but more and more I have begun to feel like a half-wit and stupid, yet I have a lot of responsibility at work and my boss thinks highly of me. He first praises then criticizes me."

This couple is a good example of the syndrome I call "Pygmalion," where the husband or wife tries to make the partner into the idealized image of a marital mate. Mr. Charlotte is a good example of an individual playing the "records" of his mother in his "parental" voice.

The third type of couple is one where the spouse makes his partner's "inner child" feel unloveable. Since one's self-esteem and self-respect is usually contingent upon what others feel about one, this type of relationship can be very damaging to a couple. The following vignette is illustrative:

Mr. and Mrs. Clara came at the request of their respective divorce lawyers. Mr. Clara, a contented bachelor at thirty, had been pressured into marriage by his wife, saying that after three years of steady dating, either he marry her or else. Both are intelligent, had many mutual interests and happy in their respective careers. Mr. Clara admitted that after marriage he began to withdraw emotionally from his wife when she became more and more possessive of him and that he felt with marriage she was showing her true self.

Mrs. Clara denied being possessive but complained that her husband was too wrapped up in his work and too exhausted when he got home to care about her needs and wants: "I've gotten to the feeling I really should leave him, yet I'm afraid to be alone. I hate to lose what I have, modest

though it be . . . . He is so exhausted when he comes home. He puts so
much into his job . . . . It dawned upon me, most of the time when he
wants sex he has to get half gassed. I must be a lousy love object that
he has to be intoxicated to make love. . . . I try to meet his needs but
I don't get any feedback. I don't sense any particular respect for me,
many times down right antagonism. He never apologizes when he is wrong.
That's all I want, not to be crapped on and ignored, to be treated like
you don't exist is the worse thing in the world. The other night I made
a special gourmet meal he likes, but not a word of praise or thanks. At
times I get the feeling I am repulsive to him."

The fourth most common complaint dealt with the avoidance
of household responsibilities; especially in a male, not to be
fed is not to be loved. Since many women equate, unconsciously,
home with self, avoidance of household maintenance by the
husband is equated with rejection of her as woman. The following abstracts are typical:

"I am furious at my wife. She is lazy and ungiving to me and the
children. I can't count on her for anything. I have the feeling that any
man who treated her decently and nicely could have been her husband.
No affection given and apparently none expected. I have to make my
own breakfast. She usually gets up about ten in the morning. It's a good
thing we have a cook or the children wouldn't be fed either. She wants
to be a 'free agent' with all the benefits of being wife but none or few
of the responsibilities."

In another couple it was the wife, an aggressive woman married
to a passive, effeminate man, who complained as follows:

"The masculine duties around here I used to do, such as cut, rake
and fertilize the grass, wash halls and paint, refinish the furniture, tile
the floors, refinish window sills, etc. . . . These are things he should
have done. They are not a woman's responsibility. Whenever I ask him
to do something, he always says, tomorrow. Yet tomorrow never comes
around, and I end up doing it."

The fifth type of complaint of nonfulfilled emotional needs
was that of seeing partner as "another child in the household."
Typical is the following:

"He does not fulfill my emotional needs in that I do not feel protected
by him at all, except financially. His instinctive response to anything I say
is, No! He is more of an observer to life than a participant and is wrapped
up in his own private world to an extreme degree. I feel like my husband's
mother, always pushing him to things. I am the boss of the family and
definitely do not want to be. If we go out for an evening, it is my sug-

gestion. I have to decide where to go and what to do. I consider myself having three children, my husband being the third child. I need someone to lean on, to look up to."

The last category of this type of emotional marital complaint relates to differences in recreational needs of the "inner child." This topic will be more fully described in Chapter XIX, where the nineteenth item on the BMQ gives valuable information on the creativity, curiosity and creative play of the "inner child." Typical of this complaint is the following:

"My husband and I share little in common, he likes Westerns and I like Puccini."

NOTES

1. Eric Berne: *Transactional Analysis in Psychotherapy*. New York, Grove Press, 1961.
2. Paul Watzlawick, Janet H. Beavin, and Don D. Jackson: *Pragmatics of Human Communication*. New York, Norton, 1967.
3. Anthony F. Panzetta: Causal and action models in social psychiatry, *Arch Gen Psychiat, 16:*290, 1967.
4. *Ibid.*
5. My experience indicates that most clergymen no longer view the concepts of Freud as antireligious but parallel the thinking of Father O'Brien (John A. O'Brien: What the clergy is doing, *Psychiat Opinion,* 3:15, 1966): " . . . clergy now distinguish between his remarkable insights into the workings of the human mind, particularly the subconscious, in which he achieved unusual competence, and his views on religion—a field in which he was an amateur (especially when compared with the scholarly analysis of religion by Max Weber in his book *The Sociology of Religion*. Boston, Beacon Press, 1964. Author's note). They accept whatever has proven helpful in psychiatry, and that comprises a great deal. Indeed, Freud himself has acknowledged that psychoanalysis is not hostile to religion. Writing to a lifelong friend, Reverend Oscar Pfister, Freud said: "In itself, psychoanalysis is neither religious nor non-religious, but an impartial tool which both priest and layman may use in the service of suffering. . . ."
6. Sigmund Freud: *The Ego and the Id*. London, Hogarth Press, 1927.
7. Anna Freud: *The Ego and the Mechanisms of Defense*. London, Hogarth Press, 1937.
8. Heinz Hartmann: *Ego Psychology and the Problem of Adaptation*. New York, Int. Univs. Press, 1958.

9. Erik Erikson: *Identity and The Life Cycle. Psychological Issues.* New York, Int. Univs. Press, 1959, Vol I

10. Sigmund Freud: *The Interpretation of Dreams.* New York, Basic Books, 1958.

11. Sigmund Freud: *"Instincts and Their Vicissitudes, Collected Papers.* London, Hogarth Press, 1948, Vol. IV pp. 60–83.

12. Sandor Ferenczi: *Further Contributions to The Theory and Technique of Psychoanalysis.* London, Hogarth Press, 1926.

13. The term libidinal, influenced by Freudian abstractions, will be used to describe a wide spectrum of feelings and behavior, ranging from warmth to sexual intimacy, depending on the biopsychosocial level of the individual. In this book sensual will be equated with libidinal.

14. W. Hugh Missildine: *Your Inner Child of the Past.* New York, Simon and Schuster, 1963.

15. *Ibid.*

16. Franz Alexander: Lectures at The Chicago Institute for Psychoanalysis, 1948.

VI

SEXUAL DISSATISFACTION

The fourth most frequent marital complaint was that of sexual dissatisfaction.[1] The frequency was the same in both series, except that the ratio was the exact opposite as regards gender. Eighty percent of the couples complained of sexual dissatisfaction: 214 males versus 186 females in the PS and 94 males versus 108 females in the MDS. Just as the two most common marital complaints were due to pathological communication, the next two most common complaints related to the "inner child" and dealt with unfulfilled emotional needs and sexual dissatisfaction. The ancient institution of marriage involves ever-changing relationships, and with each generation new kinds of sexual problems arise.[2] Mass communication, mobility of the population with approximately 20 percent of the families moving each year, the impact of the contraceptive "pill," recent studies on sexology (particularly the physiological studies of Masters and Johnson,[3] and the psychological studies of Mary J. Sherfey[4]) are only a few factors that have influenced sexual expectations and disappointments leading to marital conflicts.

The two series of conflicted couples were combined, since the ratio of sexual dissatisfaction was about the same. In the PS group I selected 250 of the 312 couples who were treated more intensively. In the 250 couples in the MDS group, the data available to me came from the individual initial sessions performed by someone else and a personal interview with each couple in a CDD session. The sexual complaints of the women fell into three main categories: displeasure with the sexual act, frequency of sex, and husband's performance in sexuality (see Table IX).

The sexual complaints of the men fell into the four main categories of frequency, displeasure in the sexual act, perfor-

TABLE IX
FEMALES COMPLAINING OF SEXUAL DISSATISFACTION

	No.	*Total*
No pleasure in the sexual act		
In general	176	
Perverse demand by partner	8	
		184
Frequency		
Too demanding	22	
Infrequent	87	
Nonexistent	20	
		129
Inadequate performance of partner		
Premature ejaculation	29	
Inhibited	13	
		42

mance of partner, and own inability to perform adequately (see Table X).

A surprising finding was that only in 175 couples, or in 35 percent, did both partners complain of their sexual relationship. Thus, although many marriages begin with feelings of pleasure in their sexual fulfillment, in at least one third of these, sexual dissatisfaction occurs for very complicated reasons in both spouses. On the other hand, there are many painful marriages—the so-called durable incompatible marriage,[5] with pleasurable sexual relationships.

GENERAL COMMENTS ON SEXOLOGY

The sexual drive is an instinctual one, closely intertwined with the individual's intrapersonal, interpersonal and environmental

TABLE X
MALES COMPLAINING OF SEXUAL DISSATISFACTION

	No.	*Total*
Frequency		
Infrequent	116	
Nonexistent	16	
		132
No pleasure in the act		
Wife frigid	98	
In general	20	
		118
Performance		
Wife inhibited	47	
Wife too agressive	17	
		64
Own inadequacy		15

systems. All three systems are interlocked but vary in importance with the chronological age of the individual. The sexual feelings (intrapersonal) and behavior of a person are a reaction to the parental attitudes (interpersonal) in which he was raised. These attitudes, in turn, were handed down by their parents and were largely molded by broad cultural viewpoints specific to their social class (environmental forces). As a result of the interlocking of these three systems, distortions and misconceptions[6] have often become part of what should be accepted as normal— "doing what comes natural."

A clarification of the phenomenological concept of the libidinal voice of the "inner child" is indicated at this point. The persistency of this libidinal voice has been shown in the elderly by the current studies of Masters and Johnson.[7] Sexual performance in the elderly is dependent upon cultural attitudes, availability and cooperation of the partner, and physical condition of the individual. On the other hand, the libidinal voice in an infant includes a wide spectrum of feelings and behavior. We must distinguish between gender and sex[8] as well as between genitality and sexuality. Gender differentiation in infancy merely indicates "male or female, without any necessary implications of sexual capacity until a later time, for it is only later that the male or female will have some knowledge and skill with regard to the genitals and their ultimate role in the sex act."[9] A penile erection in an infant, a very common observation as any mother will observe, is a manifestation of the libidinal voice of the "inner child"; however, it is certainly not a sexual response but simply a neurophysiological reflex act. The research of Money[10] and the Hampsons[11] and others on intersexuality and imprinting and the establishment of the gender role have emphasized that an individual's behavior as a male or female is strongly influenced by the cultural factors of how a male or female should behave rather than by an awareness of the sexual significance of one's gender. In fact, regardless of the anatomical state of the sexual organs, it is difficult to encode new libidinal "records" after the age of three. For example, if a mother dresses her male child as a girl, encourages his interest in dolls and clothes, stresses the importance of being passive and playing with girls, discourages all efforts of masculine behavior while praising his use of cosmetics and interest in aesthetic endeavors, this encoding in his "records" results in continuing effeminate behavior, which will be most resistant to behavioral change later, should he consciously so desire. The following clinical extract remains vividly in my mind, although it occurred in 1943, about twenty-seven years ago:

During W.W. II, an officer was referred to my neuropsychiatric service. He had been in combat for the past six months and decorated twice for bravery. He had been evacuated from his unit because of pneumonia. While convalescing, he began to complain of inability to hear. Otologic examination was negative, so he was sent for neuropsychiatric consultation which was also negative. A diagnosis of hysterical deafness was made. He was told that my examination was negative, and unless his hearing returned by the following day, I would do an intravenous sodium pentothal (truth serum) examination.

The next day he told me that he had been malingering and related the following history. An only child, his mother had been disappointed at his birth, since she wanted a girl. His father was a meek-mannered man, rarely home, since his work required considerable traveling. He had been dressed as a girl, wore curls, and discouraged from playing with boys until he entered kindergarten. The ensuing ridicule forced his mother to get his hair cut. However, he avoided playing with his male schoolmates because of their teasing and preferred the company either of girls or much younger boys. He would make up plays and always played the role of the girl, wearing dresses and makeup. His father, although displeased, said nothing and his mother thought it was "so cute."

In high school he was seduced by a male drama teacher and thus began his homosexual relationships. These continued intermittently until he graduated from college. While working as a teacher, he met his wife and told her about his deviant sexual behavior. A real relationship developed, and he detailed the long, laborious effort of three years in which he practiced talking in a deep masculine manner and walking in a noneffeminate way.

With his complete change in behavior he married, had several children and was making a good adjustment in all areas when he was drafted into the army. He had no difficulty adjusting, since his wife was living only one hundred miles away, and when he felt any homosexual tension, he would drive to his home and relieve his sexual tension with his wife. However, when he was sent overseas with his unit, he had noticed increasing homosexual tension, and being out in combat, he had no way to cope with this feeling. Afraid of acting out and disgracing his family, he had seized the opportunity of his recent illness to feign deafness to get back to his family.

This case material demonstrates how a mother imprinted a

female role in a male child, which, most remarkably, this man was able to change by creating new "records." As Salzman notes: "Only when the genital as a sexual organ is involved in an activity or influences behavior should it be part of a gender involvement . . . being dressed as a girl means being identified with privileges or denials regarding gender rather than sexual identity."[12] Thus learning and social experiences clearly influence sexual behavior.

Leon Salzman[13] delineates a dozen sexual myths that should be exposed and laid to rest. He writes:

> Man's psychology, and particularly his sexual functions, remain the last bastion of ignorance and therefore involve the greatest number of myths and superstitions. . . . In the monotheistic religions, sex became identified with sin, which severely influenced man's attitudes toward sex and encouraged ignorance and myth-making about the sex function. Both historically and theologically, the female has been considered inferior to the male as well as more sinful. She has therefore been especially burdened by a false, distorted, insistent, and damaging views of sex.

In marriage there are two people on the seesaw, and one cannot understand a sexual complaint without evaluating the sexual attitudes of both spouses and their interpersonal systems. Since both are seated at opposite ends of the seesaw, both are equally responsible for sexual incompatibility. The myth of male primacy is no longer tenable. On the seesaw what goes up must also come down. The wife, far from being passive in sexual intercourse, is an equally active participant, i.e. for maximum sexual pleasure each spouse must be passive and aggressive with equal cooperative participation.[14] Thus the myth of "female coital nonaggressiveness" has made both men and women "feel guilty, inferior, inadequate, or even 'homosexual' when their inclinations are somewhat different from prevailing prejudices concerning the role of each sex." The following couple illustrates how destroying the myth of female coital nonaggressiveness lead to the development of a satisfactory marriage after ten years of marital disharmony:

> Mr. and Mrs. Jacquette were referred for counseling. Both were attractive, intelligent individuals who had met in their senior year of college at a local church dance. Their courtship was smooth. After graduation they

married and left for a honeymoon. Both agreed that their wedding night was a complete disaster because of their sexual inexperience.

Mr. Jacquette added: "I was unable to complete the act of intercourse, and this initial experience resulted in a great lack of confidence which has never left me. Since then, I've hardly ever initiated sexual activity for fear that I would not be able to follow through in the completion of the act. My wife has always been very passive and has never initiated any sexual overture. For the past three years we have not attempted intercourse."

Mrs. Jacquette, with controlled anger replied that her family were early settlers in this area and respected as leaders in the community and church. At no time in her childhood had she seen any overt expression of affection between her parents. When she was about four years old, she and the boy next door were playing doctor and nurse and were peeking under each others clothes when they were discovered by her mother. She never forgot the look of disgust and worry on her mother's face and was told that a "Cynthia girl does not do that sort of thing!" Shortly after she began to menstruate. Her mother accidentally found her masturbating and again had the same look of disgust and worry and stated that a "Cynthia girl does not touch that area!" Since that time she has felt ashamed, guilty and embarrassed about any sexual feelings and thoughts.

Mr. Jacquette commented that he was convinced that their marital problems were due to the fact that "we've never gotten to the basic problems surrounding our marriage, I've never been able to express real feelings."

Mrs. Jacquette added that she, too, had been unable to express her feelings, sexually or otherwise, and was inwardly very angry at his behavior of the past year when he did not come home from work on Friday nights. He ostensibly "went to the movies" but "movies don't let out at two or three in the morning." She had never questioned him but suspected a return of his previous homosexual fantasies while not wanting to add to the existing complications. She knew he had therapy for this condition previously.

Since there were no family secrets in this marriage, they were treated with weekly conjoint sessions (see Ch. XXV).

Mrs. Jacquette is a good example of a woman raised with the standards of Puritan morality handed down from generations in her family, i.e. a woman is submissive, expected to be patient and long-suffering, to be passive and nonaggressive, and accept the particular program of her husband's sexual activity.

Mary Jane Sherfey[15] in 1966 destroyed the myth of male embryological equality. Her investigation was the "product of a fairly global approach to the study of man," requiring familiarity with twelve disciplines. She established that the female sex is primal. The early embryo is female! There is no bisexual phase of embryonic development. Genetic sex is established at conception, but the effect of the sex genes is not manifested until about the sixth week of fetal life. During this period all fetuses are morphologically female. If the genetic sex is male, the male hormones (androgens) suppress the growth of the ovaries and induce the male growth characteristics. Sherfey points out that female development is autonomous, whereas the male fetus must undergo differentiation necessary for masculine characteristics.

Masters and Johnson's[16] physiological studies, and Sherfey's among others, have been helpful in the understanding of the physiology of the female sexual apparatus, its role in sexual intercourse and the mechanism of orgasm. As a result, as Salzman points out, four sexual myths have been demolished: vaginal orgasm, ideal coital position, simultaneous orgasm, and superiority of the large penis. The orgastic response of men and women during sexual intercourse is physiologically similar. Masters'[17] data emphasize similarities rather than differences in the response of the female and male to sexual stimulation. Their research resolved the theoretical difference between clitoral and vaginal orgasm emphasized by Freud. Freud's notion of separate clitoral and vaginal orgasms, with the vaginal as the mature and desirable and the clitoral orgasm as evidence of immaturity, resulted in much marital dissatisfaction, especially in middle-class, educated women. Strong efforts and feelings of inadequacy on the part of women to achieve vaginal orgasms or of making the husbands feel inadequate as a lover if they do not have vaginal orgasms have produced much marital discord. Clitoral and vaginal orgasms are not separate. In fact, the female orgasm is normally initiated by clitoral stimulation and it consists of a series of spasmodic contractions of the vaginal muscles and surrounding perineal area. The female orgasm is a total body response with idiosyncratic variations in intensity and timing. A careful reading of Masters and Johnson's book is mandatory for the therapy of sexual complaints.

The removal of the myth of vaginal orgasm should encourage all types of foreplay through clitoral contact and massage. Sexual intercourse should be practiced

in whatever manner is conducive to the greatest mutual enjoyment, provided there is no physiological or psychological damage to either partner.
The manner of stimulating the penis or clitoris whether by means of finger,
mouth, or vaginal insertion, should not be viewed in terms of normality
or maturity . . . an enlightened attitude toward sex should avoid as-
signing priorities to particular methods of achieving sexual satisfaction.[18]

Salzman, in his continuing cogent comments, proceeds to destroy
other sexual myths which are responsible for much marital as
well as sexual complaints. Thus, recent studies emphasize the
child's curiosity and other adaptive interests instead of the myth
of the infant sex drive. Sensual and sexual are two different
entities. "Sex as such is rarely a human need until adolescence,
and it is misleading to apply the adult label 'sexual' to genital
play, penile or clitoral, prior to gonadal maturation." He next
points out that the myth of masturbation causing mental illness
is no longer valid nor is the "belief that interference with the
full expression of the sex instinct" a primary source of emotional
problems. The extraordinary capacity of libidinal activities to
fulfill many needs of an individual aside from procreation makes
the issue of sex important in therapy.

ADDITIONAL DATA

In contrasting the two tables on sexual dissatisfaction, it is
apparent that the most common complaint of the women was
displeasure with the sexual act, whereas the men complained
mainly about the infrequency of coition. The following clinical
extracts are typical:

Mr. Deborah: "I feel that the specific complaint is sexual and that the
tension on both our parts is the result of this condition. At least characteristically that is the sequence. We have never had a satisfactory
sexual relationship in our four years of marriage. At first it was primarily
dissatisfaction on her part. 'I hate sex' was one of her favorite expressions
following the act. This was probably caused by a failure on my part to
stimulate her sufficiently, but I also feel that she failed to give herself
over to full participation. It was always as if her mind was partially elsewhere. This dissatisfaction on her part affected my satisfaction, and consequently, our frequency decreased. This situation has been getting increasingly worse the four years of our marriage. The sex problem became
one where each felt an obligation; consequently it became a duty and

little else. Now it has reached the point where each expects no pleasure from the act."

Mrs. Deborah: "He is a quiet, undemonstrative man, who never gives me any indication of my worth. An unsatisfactory sexual life seems to be the overshadowing problem however. Beyond the first few months of our marriage he seemed to have minimal interest. From my reading I determined that he was to do specific things to interest me, but he never did. I was always anxious to continue trying, but I guess he didn't find it too satisfactory and would rather not bother. Very soon in our marriage the attitude toward sex became one of rehabilitating the act and not enjoying it on its own merit. It became rather laborious and consequently diminished in frequency to nothing."

In another couple where the only marital complaint was sexual dissatisfaction, both complained as follows:

Mrs. Diane: "Sex seemed all right until I discovered I was trying to do what he wanted me to do and found he really wasn't doing any of the things I asked him to do. First he doesn't take sufficient time to arouse me, then he leaves me freezing in the bed while he flounders in the bathroom looking for a rubber protective, and yet when he returns five minutes later he expects me to be warm and receptive. He truly found me disappointed and angry. Sometimes I've decided against letting this pathetic idiot arouse me again. I started out giving and I ended up hating the sexual act. I feel this is a failure on his part, possibly because of all the arguments over the years about sex, that prevents me from participating. I can't help but think that any normal man would give me these considerations if I asked. When I do he calls me crazy or stupid or demanding.
I call it equality!"

Mr. Diane: "My only complaint about our marriage is the infrequency of our sex. I feel it has been far below par, once a month or so. I have always found her frigid. Now I am told that I am a poor partner. Not preparing with precaution, towel or cloth, Vaseline® and the like. We would reach a sexual point and I would get up for the necessary articles and upon my return everything would be gone. Frustration from her and disgust for me. I was the bungler."

The most common sexual complaint among the women was displeasure with the sexual act. There were a variety of factors mentioned from frigidity to perversity in the partner:

"He has developed competence in the mechanics[19] of making love but still fails to be interested in me as a person to whom he is making love."

"I have the capacity for refusing sex or carrying through the sex act without absolutely no participation on my part. Mother told me she was that way too, a woman's duty."

"He has made me come to hate sex. He dresses in my raincoat, puts on my rain boots and makes me tie his hands behind him. Then I must assume the aggressive sexual role and seduce him. These demands make me feel depreciated in my feminine role."

The next most common sexual complaint in women related to frequency:[20] the great majority complained of infrequency, whereas there were equal complaints about too demanding husbands or nonexistent lovemaking.

"Ever since our marriage, my husband has desired sex very rarely. Once a month would be more than adequate on his part. When our son was born, we had no intercourse from the middle of my pregnancy till five months after the delivery. Our family doctor once gave him pills to stimulate desire on his part. My husband says there is nothing wrong with him physically; he has no desire."

"Ever since we have been married, he has made great sexual demands upon me. No matter whether I am tired, sick or even menstruating, he would like to have intercourse three or four times every night. When I refuse, he gets angry and beats me."

The third category of sexual complaints by women was regarding their partner's performance: twenty-nine women stated their husbands had premature ejaculations and thirteen stated their husbands were sexually inhibited. Typical is the following extract:

"Our sexual relationship is very poor. I have the feeling that my husband does not enjoy making love to me and tries to avoid any contact. He admits he feels like a little boy at making love and does not have any confidence in himself in this area and is afraid he will not be able to satisfy me; therefore, it is easier to avoid lovemaking. Yet his performance is good when he does make love. I myself am very inhibited, and find it difficult to show affection. This inhibition was broken down by my husband about six months after our marriage. Once I began to react sexually, he seemed to lose interest in sexual contact. After many months with very little lovemaking, I also lost interest in the sex act with my husband, but have not lost interest in sex. He acts so inhibited now."

A typical history of premature ejaculation is the following:

"We had premarital relations at his insistence. At one point I got pretty interested in sex. Once I got interested, he seemed to cool off. I think an awful lot was curiosity on my part. From the day we got back from our honeymoon, he would approach me sexually about every ten days to two weeks. I thought it was because we had premarital sex. When we did have relations, he would immediately have an orgasm and I was left unfulfilled. I went through an awful time. I talked to him about it. Last spring I got pretty adamant about it. I was really deflated. He just didn't approach me sexually, and when he did he came in a hurry."

Masters and Johnson[21] in their book gave an excellent description of both the anatomy and physiology of the male orgasm. The entire process varies in every individual and in the same person at different times and under different circumstances. We have no specific method of evaluating a man's potency. As Wershub,[22] an experienced urologist correctly states:

Successful coitus requires some degree of acculturation. Man's sexual behavior is largely determined by his social status and the sexual pattern of the particular segment of society of which he is a member. These factors may produce fear, confusion, and anxiety, and they are the underlying cause of more than 85 percent of the cases of sexual impotence. The younger and less experienced man is likely to ejaculate more rapidly than an older man or even a more sophisticated man of the same age. Complaints of rapid ejaculation are common during honeymoons, when the young man is nervous and overanxious.

Premature ejaculation usually involves all three systems of the individual. For example, the intrapersonal system may be most involved as with the husband who has premature ejaculation or even at times complete impotence with his wife, yet he can be completely potent with a prostitute.

The sexual complaints of the husbands fell in the four categories of frequency, pleasure, partner's performance, and their own sexual inadequacy. The main complaint in 55 percent of the men was that of infrequency. The reasons the husbands give vary from disinterest, fear of impregnating their spouse, religious objection, and so on. Typical case extracts include the following:

"My desires are either animalistic, immoral, childish, or perverted, depending on her mood at the time. Her favorite descriptive comment is 'Why must you make a production of it, can't we just do it?' She never makes advances toward me. It's always my part she says. She more or less thinks I am a sex maniac. I am getting to the point where I do not know if I am normal or not in craving so much sex, like sex about once or twice a week."

Another husband complains: "Our relations are infrequent because in the past I have refused to countenance the use of contraceptives, because I am a devout Catholic. My wife has complained that with the rhythm method she is only a part-time wife and therefore many times has refused me sexually. She has always been opposed to the Church's position on birth control. I am not happy with the Church's position on that matter either. However, I follow as a matter of faith. Accordingly, our marriage has been fairly stormy on this issue. My wife has lost the Church as a result. Because of this situation, I now received permission to practice birth control if my wife requests it, and if my wife will return to the Church. Her knowledge of this has only infuriated her, since all the responsibility rests upon her, and she frequently rejects me sexually."

The second most common complaint of the husbands was their lack of pleasure in having sexual intercourse with their wives. About 20 percent of the men complained that their wives were frigid sexually. In about 5 percent of the husbands, there was general displeasure in coitus, typical was the following comment:

"It's not pleasurable because I have the feeling that it's a duty she is performing. At times she will even have an orgasm, but most of the time she lays there inert. She never takes the lead in sexual matters and has never made a sexual overture to me in our ten years of marriage."

The game of "Frigid Woman" will be discussed in Chapter XX. The frequency of frigidity, as reported in the literature, varies from 15 percent to 90 percent, according to different observers.[23] I fully agree with the definition of Ruth Moulton,[24] who pragmatically defined frigidity,

. . . to refer to those women whose sexual response is so limited that there is evidence of repeated frustration or lack of any real satisfaction even with the use of flexible criteria. If the patient finds intercourse exciting, not merely pleasant, and reaches some climax with relaxation, I would not consider her frigid, even though I felt she could achieve greater sexual pleasure were she freer from conflict and anxiety.

In my data ninety-eight women, or one out of five, fell in the category of Moulton's definition of frigidity.

In spite of marked cultural changes, many women who function well in a number of complex roles still have more difficulty obtaining sexual pleasure than do a comparable group of men. Paradoxically, cultural permission for women to enjoy sex, in contrast to the old Puritan attitude that only women of ill-repute enjoyed sexual relationships, has produced new problems for women. Permission for sexual satisfaction has imposed a new pressure on women and on men. A woman feels inadequate if she fails to achieve orgasm. A man feels inadequate if he cannot satisfy his wife. This circularity frequently results in much marital discord.

Since all three systems (intrapersonal,[25] interpersonal and environmental) are involved in the causation of frigidity, it is unwise to look for the cause. In long-term therapy with couples in the PS, my clinical experience is in agreement with Moulton's: "Sometimes there are specific fears based on childhood traumata, but these only gather importance due to reinforcement from pervasive attitudes of significant people, operating insidiously and covertly over long periods of time."[26] The following specific sexual fears based on childhood trauma of rape, incest[27] or seductive behavior from an older person are shown in the following extracts:

"I was raised in a large family during the depression. To make ends meet Mother took in boarders. My parents quarreled frequently, mostly about Mother refusing to have sexual relations with Father. When I was approximately three years old, I saw one of the boarders rape my oldest sister. This frightened me a great deal and when I told Mother she cautioned me not to tell Father. She repeatedly warned me to beware of men but at times would ask me details of what happened."

Another woman states:

"My first recollection of my Father is brutality. When drunk he would beat me and try to have sex with me. To this day I am deathly afraid of sex. I never told Mother about Father's advances."

Cultural attitudes play a role in frigidity but in themselves rarely cause severe sexual inhibition unless enforced rigidly by parents who themselves are cold, nonresponsive, and unable to "stroke" their child. In fact, the parents frequently are unable to "stroke" the "inner child" of their partner as seen by the observation of the women in this series who described the parents of their marriage as good in only 16 percent (see Table XI).

The following extracts are illustrative of the cold, rejecting parents:

"My parents divorced when I was five years old. They tried to stay together because of my brother and me. My mother was only interested in her career, was cold and rejecting to me. She demanded perfection of me. I cannot ever remember her kissing me. I don't remember my father

TABLE XI
TYPE OF PARENTAL MARRIAGE IN FRIGID WOMEN

	PS	MDS
Good	20	13
Divorced	12	10
Poor	11	20
Separated	3	4
Death (while patient a child)	2	3

at all. He was always too busy to play with me. When I was a child Mother often warned me about getting a venereal disease off of toilet seats and against the evil intentions of men."

Or as another woman expressed it:

"My mother and dad were very good to each other, and have had a very happy marriage. They were also good to me but very un-understanding and expected too much from me. I never felt loved and trusted. They always thought I was going to get into some kind of trouble and expressed their doubts of my ability or anything I did. Our family was unaffectionate. When I wanted love the most, I never received it, so I rejected it any other time. I've always tried to do things to please them, but it was never enough. If only they could have given me some warmth and tenderness."

An important factor in frigidity in women is their relationship with their mothers (interpersonal system). Half of the mothers were described as cold, rejecting, and unable to "stroke" their daughters. Many of the mothers themselves had been unhappy with their lot as a woman, as seen through their daughter's eyes. In 10 percent the women expressed contempt for their mother's ineffectualness and submissiveness to a domineering father. Furious rage at the mother was marked in about 10 percent of the women. Table XII shows the role of the mother in both series.

The following extract is typical of many women with this complaint:

TABLE XII
ROLE OF MOTHER IN FRIGIDITY

	PS	MDS
Rejecting	24	25
Contempt for ineffectual, submissive mother	11	10
Mother unhappy in role as woman	9	10
Rage at mother	4	6

"Mother never encouraged anything fine. She discouraged any attempts on my part to better myself. I never could confide in her. Even when I started menstruating I could not approach her for advice. I asked my girlfriend. When she did find out I was menstruating she said: Now you have to be careful around men. It sounded so base and cruel. If anything bothered me, I couldn't tell her. First she would use it as a conversation piece, and secondly say: You had it coming to you. When I wanted the house clean, she would get angry at me and say: If I was any good, I would have been married a long time ago. I was twenty at that time."

"She felt unless one married by nineteen, it meant that no one wanted you. That I wanted it that way, she couldn't understand. She dressed like a slut, refused to do anything with her hair, refused to keep her nails clean. I was very angry at her. I always felt guilty about that. If she had an ounce of brains, she would have said: Save your money and get an education. Instead, we all had to go to work before finishing high school, even though my school adviser came to our home and pleaded with her. But to no avail, even though they could afford it. I was furiously angry at her. She was ignorant. She thought I was promiscuous, but I didn't permit that with boys. I was afraid of getting pregnant. We were always permitted to do anything we wanted. Why nothing happened sexually is beyond me. When I was young I did wish my parents would care. My girlfriends parents did care, made them be home at certain times and did not permit them in cars with fellows. Mother did not care if I was presentable going to school, but I did. I was always aware of how society acted. There wasn't any encouragement from her. Most galling was the way my father pushed her around."

In two thirds of the frigid women there was an inability to relate to their fathers in a constructive manner. Father was described as rejecting, disapproving, or disinterested. One father openly told his daughter that she was ugly and should resign herself to being a spinster. In those women in the private series, where intensive psychotherapy was instituted, many showed evidence of a deep, unrequited attachment to their fathers. Typical clinical extracts are the following:

I never could tune into my father. He was a domineering, dogmatic and selfish man. He always insisted on the choice cuts of meat for himself. Yet I respected him for his professional accomplishments. No matter how I tried to reach him, I was always unsuccessful. His attitude toward Mother and women in general was depreciatory. At no time did he ever attend a recital I was part of, yet he was an accomplished musician. He was proud of my grades but refused to go to school on parents' night."

Another frigid woman bitterly said:

"My father was very disappointed when I was born. He wanted a boy so badly. He refused to visit Mother in the hospital and for months didn't talk to her. I was a tomboy as a child and could hit a baseball farther and run faster than most boys in the neighborhood, but he would never come to watch me play. I wore jeans until I started high school, even though Mother bought me pretty dresses to go out in. Father was like a sphinx, like stone, silent and commanding."

In many of the women with frigidity their relationships and reactions to their husbands was important. In about 11 percent of the women, it was found that inability to have an orgasm was due to their husband's premature ejaculation. It is interesting to note that the frigid woman and the male with premature ejaculation frequently seek each other out.[28]

Another influence that these frigid women stressed was their partners' inability to fulfill their deep dependency needs to be taken care of ("stroking") that their own mothers had been unwilling or unable to give. This complaint was present in 25 percent of the women.

The third most common reason given for their lack of sexual responsiveness was their husbands' infidelity, expressed by about 8 percent of the women. Since infidelity is the seventh most common marital complaint, this topic will be dealt with in detail in Chapter IX.

Whereas about 8 percent complained that their husbands were too passive or inhibited, 6 percent of the women blamed their husbands' too aggressive, bombastic behavior as a cause of their frigidity. Table XIII records how these women viewed their husbands.

A conspicuous finding in 55 percent of these frigid women was the extreme fear of awareness or expression of their deep emotional feelings. This was, at times, manifested not by any

TABLE XIII

WIFE'S CONCEPT OF HUSBAND'S ROLE IN HER FRIGIDITY

	PS	MDS
Premature ejaculation	12	9
Frustration of dependency needs	8	10
Infidelity	7	9
Passive	6	9
Too aggressive	5	7
Pygmalion type	4	2
Homosexual	2	2

specific stated sexual anxiety but by an overall attitude of inability to react emotionally, as one husband aptly commented: "It is like kissing a mannequin!" In a number of women the need to withhold or control all emotions was part of their personality—frequently of an obsessive-compulsive character. Their verbalizations indicated that the need to control all emotion was due to the deep-seated fear that any strong emotion, sexual or aggressive, was potentially dangerous, leaving one vulnerable to retaliation or exploitation or even rejection. As Moulton[29] has pointed out, in some women the orgasm may be feared as a loss of self-image in which personality and/or body will disintegrate. "She may assume her psychic integrity rests on conscious control or she may feel her attractiveness completely depends on clothing, make-up and external appearance, and therefore cannot afford to let down her facade and forget herself long enough to enjoy herself." Grinstein[30] has beautifully described this type of "doll," whose narcissistic self-preoccupation allows her to look sexually feminine but prevents her from following through and remains sexually frigid. These women are dressed in the height of fashion, impeccably groomed, hair styled in the latest vogue and conspicuous by their excessive makeup.

Ninety-eight women with frigidity presented a variety of personality and psychiatric types ranging from the narcissistic "doll" to borderline psychotics (see Table XIV). The women were of all sizes and shapes, from petite to amazon.

Similarly, the husbands of these frigid women presented a wide range of character types and physical appearances, ranging from the polite, passive, inhibited, controlled male to the bombastic, aggressive individual. One woman described

TABLE XIV
CHARACTER TYPOLOGY OF FRIGID WOMEN

	PS	*MDS*
Narcissistic "doll"	15	14
Obsessive-compulsive	12	14
Depressive	7	8
Hysteric	6	5
Borderline psychotic	5	5
Paranoid	3	2
Adequate	0	2

her husband as a "bull in a china shop." He behaved that way in the conjoint diagnostic and disposition session. As expected, the major difference between the two groups of men was in their economic status: 75 percent of the men in the MDS earned considerably less than the men seen privately. In almost all other areas the two groups of men were similar.

In summary, the data, not quantifiable but indicating trends, points out that in spite of cultural permission now for women to enjoy sexual relationships, at least one in five fail to achieve pleasure in the act. Thus it is futile to look for the cause in any specific area. Sometimes there are specific fears based on childhood traumas which gather importance because of reinforcement from pervasive attitudes of significant others operating insidiously and covertly or overtly over long periods of time. Widespread cultural mores of a Victorian morality occasionally cause severe sexual inhibition, particularly when reflected by parents who themselves lack warmth. Occasionally, there are no specific fears about sexuality per se, but the lack of sexual responsiveness is only one aspect of a fear of loss of control of emotions in general, whether aggressive or sexual.

Frigidity may be representative of a personality problem rather than being a basic issue. A woman's reaction to her lack of sexual responsiveness varies considerably, from grave anxiety to indifference. Frigidity can result from intrapersonal factors of increased anger, decreased self-respect, or endogenous or reactive depressions. Many times interpersonal factors in relation to the partner are prominent, with either negative or positive feedback. All these variables defy neat structuring and necessitate exploration of all three systems of forces.

Judd Marmor[31] among others early raised doubts about Freud's theories about frigidity. The biological research of Sherfey and the physiological research of Johnson and Masters confirmed Marmor's postulate that the rich nerve supply in the clitorus would always be a source of sensual pleasure to the woman. Salzman's thoughtful article synthesized findings that exploded many sexual myths, beginning with penis envy as a bête noire of the female child. A distant or rejecting father, especially if mother was inadequate, depreciated or rejected her femininity, and would present a poor model for identification for a child. The maternal and paternal attitudes and values in the "parental" voices could produce a series of "records" in her jukebox which could raise doubt in this type of woman not only as to her sexual attractiveness and attributes but also in all areas pertaining to the feminine role. The so-called penis envy would not be anatomical but symbolic of the special forms of freedom men have in our society in spite of current "equality" between the sexes.

Finally, the psychosexual development of the female is more complex than that of the male. First she is dependent on her mother, then she relates to her father, and finally, she has to give up father to relate to another man. The male, however, is first dependent on his mother and then has to relate to another woman. Similarly, the female orgasm is more complex, as shown in the studies of Masters and Johnson,[32] since it involves the integration of sensations coming from two different foci, clitorial and vaginal. Moulton makes the following pertinent comment:

> Vaginal sensation is more diffuse, harder to describe, takes more maturity to absorb and withstand and, at its best, may allow a more complete response of the whole body than is usually available to men. Many women have arrived at a greater enjoyment of sexuality when they gave up comparing their responses to that of the men and allowed themselves a sensation more uniquely theirs. This development is hindered only by using the typical male sexual responses as a standard."

The third major category of sexual complaints by the men was related to the sexual performance of their partners' in terms of activity. Forty-seven men complained that their wives were too inhibited, whereas seventeen complained their wives were too aggressive. Typical of the latter complaint is the following:

> "When I am having sex with her, I feel her violent pelvic movements as though she is trying to rip my penis off. When I remonstrate with her about this, she ignores my complaint and persists in her behavior. I try to avoid sex with her."

A number of the inhibited wives turned out to be frigid women whose passive behavior, as interpreted by the man, was an expression of an overall personality problem. On the other hand, many of the inhibited wives were orgastic but very passive in their total behavior patterns, sexual as well as nonsexual. The following clinical extract was not unusual:

> Mr. and Mrs. Edna came for help because they felt they were not relating to each other as they wanted to. In addition to the complaints of unfulfilled emotional needs and lack of communication, both complained of sexual dissatisfaction.
>
> Mr. Edna quietly said: "My wife seems to be very passive about sexual relations, mainly because she does not reach a climax very often. The times she has experienced satisfaction have occurred when we have had something to drink that evening. She then would seem to overcome her passiveness that she normally exhibits about sex. Usually she just lays there as though her thoughts are elsewhere. While I do reach a physical climax each time we have relations, the knowledge that she does not fully participate physically lessens my enjoyment. Although I realize she is not aware of the reasons for her lack of response, I am irritated at times. However, should we find the underlying cause of this problem, I am sure our marriage would be happier."
>
> Mrs. Edna obviously quite embarrassed replied: "In the three years we have been married, I have only reached a climax about a dozen times; although this doesn't bother me, I know it's not normal. The lack of desire for sex doesn't seem to bother me, only in the way that I know this isn't fair to my husband. I might add also that it seems to take me a long time to get aroused and therefore after a while we'll just go ahead with the sex act. My father was a strict Lutheran minister and we children were not allowed to play cards, dance or smoke."

The fourth category of sexual complaint of the men was about their own inadequate sexual performance. The majority of these men complained primarily of premature ejaculation, some of impotence.[33] Inadequate male sexual performance was present in about 10 percent of the husbands. It is not surprising that only one third of the men openly stated their problem, since admission of sexual inadequacy is very painful. In about one third of the couples, both spouses talked about the complaint of premature ejaculation during the diagnostic phase. The following clinical extract of the Elizabeths is not uncommon during the CDD session:

> Mr. Elizabeth, well-mannered, polite, carefully dressed, quietly stated: "There's a lot of tension on the part of both of us."
>
> Mrs. Elizabeth, blonde, wearing black slacks and sweater, false eye lashes and heavy eye make-up, aggressively retorted: "We're tense because we don't get along. We've had trouble a long time. We've tried to talk

it out but that doesn't work. There is a lot of difference in our backgrounds, personalities, and goals."

Mr. Elizabeth: "Our main problem is a sexual one. We disagree on frequency. I don't have the desire as often as she does. When we do have intercourse, I have premature ejaculation, and she is left unsatisfied."

Mrs. Elizabeth: "I am insecure and can't take tension and now I go to pieces frequently and nag, scream, and cry a lot. He clams up when he is angry, whereas I shout."

Mr. Elizabeth: "There is no continuous or lasting problem except sex. We may fuss from time to time over other problems, but they are not recurring."

Mrs. Elizabeth: "Because of his lack of sexual interest, I don't trust him, I'm suspicious, feel he doesn't love me."

Mr. Elizabeth: "I'm in a highly competitive business with a demanding, nagging boss. . . ."

Mrs. Elizabeth (interrupting, and with heavy sarcasm): "Like me, dear!"

Mr. Elizabeth: "Between marital and work tensions, I am in a daze. I'm pooped all the time." (He proceeds to give an intellectualized approach to understanding of premature ejaculation. The whole sexual act produces anxiety in him, and her demands to try more often in hopes of increasing chances of successful intercourse put him under increased pressure, etc).

Mrs. Elizabeth bitterly comments: "I don't like being a housewife. I didn't go to college to learn to scrub floors and iron shirts, but if I try to take on too much, I get sick."

Just as in the evaluation of the data in frigidity in women, there are multiple factors in the occurrence of impaired sexuality in men with premature ejaculation. A remarkable finding was that at the time of consultation by the couple, no spouse was below the age of twenty-five years old. About one half of the men were between the ages of thirty to forty and about 25 percent were between forty and fifty. In the remaining 25 percent the men were either over fifty or younger than thirty. Outstanding was the finding that although the sexual problem began early in the marriage, only two couples had been married less than five years at the time of consultation. In fact, more than one half of the couples had been married between ten to twenty years. As a group, all the men, with few exceptions, were very successful in their occupations. Perhaps this could be a compensatory reaction to prove their masculinity in other areas. On the other hand, the high level of education achieved by most of these men could have also played an important factor in their economic success (four fifths of the men had some college education, the great majority having one or more degrees). In terms of ordinal position with regard to siblings, there were no correlations in my group of men. Premature ejaculation occurred twice as frequently in mixed marriages—religion—as in the total group. More than two thirds of the couples had two or more children external evidence of the man's virility.

An interesting finding was the manner in which these men with premature ejaculation viewed their marriages of their parents. In almost none of their parents' marriages had there been either a separation or divorce. In more than half of these men, they stated their parents had a good marriage. The composite manner in which the men in both series viewed their fathers was as follows: one-third saw them as very successful in their occupations, one-fourth viewed them as both domineering and aggressive, and about one-tenth saw them as rejecting or depreciating. The men pictured their mothers as follows: one-third as very good, one-third as seductive or possessive, and one-third as domineering or prudish. Another finding was that less than 1 percent stated their mothers to be rejecting. The following clinical extracts are illustrative of both the parents and their marriages:

"Mother was Victorian. She didn't like sex and made no bones about it. She came from a wealthy family and continually let Father know he was working for her family. Dad was a nice guy, but we didn't do much together. Mother insisted on washing me until I was fourteen years old when I insisted she stop. Although Father objected, it was I who had to make an issue of it."

Another man stated: "Father was never ambitious. He had no interest in me. Mother was totally narcissistic, pretentious, possessive, and viewed herself as a *femme fatale*."

Still another man commented: "My parents were devoted to each other. I had a strong father who resented me. He was domineering, successful business man. We never had any arguments around the house. When Father said to do something, it was done and no argument. Mother was a good person, warm and affectionate."

Or, as one man put it: "My parents were continually quarreling about everything from sex to finances. To mother sex was a dirty thing. She was very possessive of me. Mother and I got along well. We excluded my father. He thought my mother was stupid and I was taking after her. He and I argued a lot. Mother was very possessive and seductive to me."

The men with inadequate sexual performance presented a variety of personalities. In general, they tended to be well dressed and well groomed. Some were passive in manner, others tended to be aggressive and tried to dominate the interviews. Many of the couples dovetailed in that an aggressive male tended to have a passive wife and vice versa. About half the men complained that their wives were frigid. It was not uncommon to find the men in their courtships revealing nonpassionate behavior in their courting patterns. The usual history was the couple meeting in college, the courtship smooth, nonpassionate and of fairly long duration with the honeymoon pinpointing the problem of lack of sexual intimacy and inadequate sexual performance. Characteristic of the courtship and the honeymoon was talking and not action. Typical were the following:

Mr. Faye: "We met in college. We went together for five years. We were very close friends, no arguments, but we talked a lot about all sorts of things. Nothing serious until the last year we became engaged. All my friends, who were also her friends, warned me not to marry her because of her temper. Our honeymoon was very nice. But I have been criticized many times since it was over—that I wanted to do too much sightseeing to suit her and not enough lovemaking."

Mrs. Faye: "Our honeymoon was not a time spent in getting to know and love each other. Our sex was always poor. No foreplay, he was very quick in his emission and I felt cheated. I have never had an orgasm."

Mr. Frances: "We met in college. We went together for two years. It was a very casual relationship. We talked mostly and rarely petted. Our honeymoon was very poor. We were both very inexperienced."

Mrs. Frances: "Our courtship was very smooth and uneventful. We talked a lot, went to lectures, plays and concerts. We had no sex the first night. He said we should offer our first night to God. From the very beginning our sexual relationship has been very bad. He is very quick, to the point, that I can't move without his ejaculating. His opinion is that I am frigid. I don't think so, but I have no way of finding out with him."

Mr. Florence: "I met her on a blind date at school. We went together for six months. We talked and talked about everything for six months. I think I got married because I was looking for acceptance and was afraid I couldn't get a girl. On our honeymoon I felt trapped and I didn't think there was any way out. I don't think my wife was aware of my feelings."

Mrs. Florence: "On our honeymoon I felt my husband found me unattractive sexually. He did not like kissing me. I felt love and sex was an effort on his part. He thought I looked silly in sexy nightgowns. I found I couldn't enjoy sexual relations and felt he did not enjoy it."

The problem of premature ejaculation has multifaceted elements present in most of the men, involving all three systems: intrapersonal, interpersonal and environmental. The intrapersonal forces include both physiological and psychological factors. In many of the men, their inadequate sexual behavior started during adolesence. These men were usually outstanding in everything except sexuality. Characteristically they were successful outside their marriage. In some of the men there was great fear of their aggressive feelings, which manifested itself in avoidance of bodily physical sports. Frequently there was a history of an earlier confrontation either with a peer or sibling where murderous impulses had become subjective or almost carried out in reality. Since the act of sex requires both libidinal and aggressive feelings, inhibition in one area frequently results in impairment in the other. Occasionally, where there is great anger toward a seductive but frustrating mother, the "record" may be projected onto the wife (projective identification) and result in symbolic "urination" (instant ejaculation before vaginal entrance) instead of "fornication" (used in the sense of sexual intercourse instead of its legal definition).

The entire subject of the human sexual response is undergoing intensive reexamination. Although time consuming, it is necessary that the therapist attempt to keep up with the current literature.

NOTES

1. Henry V. Dicks: Symposium on sexual problems in marriage, *Proc Royal Society Med,* 52:867, 1959.
2. J. Richard Udry, in an erudite article containing an excellent bibliography (Sex and family life, *Med Aspects Hum Sexuality,* 2:66, 1968), presents sociological factors on the role which sex plays in marriage and family formation.
3. William H. Masters and Virginia E. Johnson: *Human Sexual Response,* Boston, Little, Brown, 1966. See also Paul H. Gebhard: Factors in marital orgasm, *Med Aspects Hum Sexuality,* 2:22, 1968.
4. Mary L. Sherfey: The evolution and nature of female sexuality in relation to psychoanalytic theory, *J Amer Psychoanal Assn, 14:*28, 1966.
5. John R. Cavanagh: The durable incompatible marriage, psychological characteristics of the mates, *Southern Med J,* 55:396, 1962. In their

book William J. Lederer and Don D. Jackson (*The Mirages of Marriage.* New York, Norton, 1968) on the marital relationship and its vicissitudes label this ongoing type of marriage "stable unsatisfactory." Henry V. Dicks (*Marital Tensions.* New York, Basic Books, 1967, p. 52) refers to this type of marriage as "cat and dog" type of interaction or sadomasochistic symbiosis.

6. Lionel S. Lewis and Dennis Brissett: Sex as work: a study of avocational counseling, *Med Aspects Hum Sexuality,* 2:14, 1968. This thoughtful study should be read by all therapists. The authors have studied fifteen sex manuals with wide circulation and concluded that "play, at least sexual play, has indeed been permeated with dimensions of a work ethic. The play of marital sex is presented by the counselors quite definitely as work. . . . Thus there seems to be two antagonistic forces operating in American society. On the one hand, there is an emphasis on work and, on the other hand, there is an emphasis on attaining maximum pleasure."

7. Masters and Johnson, *op. cit.;* and Jack Weinberg: Sexual expression in late life, *Amer J Psychiat,* 126:713, 1969.

8. Robert J. Stoller (*Sex and Gender: On The Development of Masculinity and Femininity.* New York, Science House, 1968) has written in interesting book on why men are men and women are women. Sex in this book refers to biological sex, and gender to the image that people have of themselves as male or female. The relationship between sex and gender is the focus of this book. The author presents a large body of clinical evidence to indicate that parental influences are decisive in molding gender identity, i.e. psychological sex is largely independent of biological sex.

9. Leon Salzman: Psychology of the female, *Arch Gen Psychiat,* 17:195, 1967. See also Judd Marmor: Changing Patterns of Femininity: Psychoanalytic Implications, in *The Marriage Relationship* (Salo Rosenbaum and Ian Alger, Eds.). New York, Basic Books, 1968, pp. 31–46.

10. John Money, J.G. Hampson and J.L. Hampson: Imprinting and the establishment of gender role, *Arch Neurol Psychiat,* 77:333, 1957. See also Richard Green and John Money: Stage-acting, role taking and effeminate impersonation during boyhood, *Arch Gen Psychiat,* 15:535, 1966, who found in some individuals no evidence that parents had steered their children into this role; a possible genetic role.

11. J.L. Hampson and J.G. Hampson: The Ontogenesis of Sexual Behavior in Man, in *Sex and Internal Secretions,* 3rd ed. (W.C. Young, Ed). Baltimore, Williams & Wilkins, 1961, Vol. II, pp. 1401–1432.

12. Salzman, *op. cit.*

13. Leon Salzman: Recently exploded sexual myths, *Med Aspects Hum Sexuality,* 1:6, 1967. See also Gert Heilbrunn: On sharing, *Amer J Psychotherapy,* 21:750, 1967.

14. Alfred Auerback (The battle of the sexes, *Med Aspects Hum Sexuality*, 1:6, 1967) quotes Havelock Ellis (*The Dance of Life*. Boston, Houghton Mifflin Co., 1929): "A man and woman dancing rhythmically together on a dance floor make an attractive sight. As they sway back and forth in rhythm with the music, their bodies blend together. While the man ostensibly leads and the woman follows, it actually is a *partnership* [italics added] with a high degree of communication through body contact. With a touch, a nod, or a word they change their dance step yet remain synchronized, moving in unison. The sexual act is a rhythmic coupling of male and female, the partners developing an awareness of each other's desires and bodily rhythms." Thus both husband and wife, particularly during the sexual act, are on a seesaw.

15. Sherfey, *op. cit.*

16. Masters and Johnson, *op. cit.*

17. William H. Masters: Clinical significance of the study of human sexual response, *Med Aspects Hum Sexuality*, 1:14, 1967 .

18. Salzman: *op. cit.*

19. In an interesting article in the *Saturday Review* (March 26, 1966, Antidotes for the New Puritanism), Rollo May expresses his views on sex and love in our culture and points out: "the new emphasis on technique in sex and love-making backfires . . . makes for a mechanistic attitude toward love-making, and goes along with alienation, feelings of loneliness, and depersonalization." I still vividly recall a patient's dream after she bitterly complained about the number of books her husband had brought home on sexual techniques: "My husband is at the airport. He gets into his airplane. Seats himself in the *cockpit*. Moves a number of dials and is disappointed when the plane does not take off. I look on with great disgust."

20. In the Kinsey studies (A.C. Kinsey, W.B. Pomeroy, and C.E. Martin: *Sexual Behavior in the Human Male*. Philadelphia, Saunders, 1948; and A.C. Kinsey, W.B. Pomeroy, C.E. Martin, and P.H. Gebbard: *Sexual Behavior in the Human Female*. Philadelphia, Saunders, 1953) the incidence of sexual intercourse is highest at the beginning of marriage. He and his associates found that males and females had intercourse 2.8 and 2.6 times a week, respectively, by the age of twenty. When they were about twice as old, sexual activity had decreased to a median of 1.5 times a week, and 0.6 times a week by age sixty. Roughly, in my clinical experience, sexual intercourse decreases once per week per decade, e.g. three times per week in the twenties, and so on. In the male, environmental demands and in the female, preoccupation with family matters play an important role. In an interesting article, David M. Reed (What is the normal for sexual relations in marriage, *Med Aspects Hum Sexuality*, 1:6, 1967) pinpoints:

"our concept of 'normal' marital sexuality must take account of the decline of the patriarchal family and the current 'sexual renaissance,' especially as it affects women." An interesting study by Robert R. Bell (Some emerging sexual expectation among women, *Med Aspects Hum Sexuality*, 1:65, 1967) shows that an increasing number of well-educated women have sexual needs greater than those of their partners. His figure of 25 percent among college-educated wives who complained of "too infrequent" sex parallels my finding of about 20 percent. Ralph R. Greenson (Sexual apathy in men, *Calif Med, 108:275*, 1968) notes that there has been a noticeable change in sexual behavior and responses in men and women since World War II. Women appear to be becoming sexually more assertive and demanding while men appear to have become more indifferent. Whereas thirty years ago "frigidity" was used exclusively in regard to women, today more men are found who display sexual coldness or disinterest—this he finds especially pronounced among men in their middle age. See also Eric Pfeiffer, Adriaan Verwoerdt, and Hsioh-Shan Wang: Sexual behavior in aged men and women, *Arch Gen Psychiat, 19:753*, 1968. Finally, the studies of Lee Rainwater (Some aspects of lower class sexual behavior, *Med Aspects Hum Sexuality, 11:15*, 1968) "Suggests that close examination of lower class sexual behavior tends to disprove certain widely-held stereotypes—themselves not unknown in social scientists' own attitudes." His study based on interviews with 409 individuals "chosen in such a way to represent the social class range of whites from upper-middle to lower-lower and Negroes at the upper-lower and lower-lower class levels" stated: "In short, thought we see some evidence to support the notion of a 'sexual renaissance' with respect to marital sexuality in the modern working class, we see no such evidence with respect to the less prosperous lower class." See also George Levinger: Sources of marital dissatisfaction among applicants for divorce, *Amer J Orthopsychiat, 36:803*, 1966, a study of 600 couples; Theodore N. Ferdinand: Sex behavior and the American class structure: a mosaic, *Med Aspects Hum Sexuality, 3:34*, 1969. See also Birgitta Linner: *Society and Sex in Sweden.* Sweden, Swedish Institute, 1965. See also Arnold A. Lazarus: Modes of treatment for sexual inadequacies, *Med Aspects Hum Sexuality, 3:53*, 1969, concerning sexual complaints in terms of frequency.

21. Masters and Johnson, *op. cit.*
22. Leonard P. Wershub: Premature ejaculation as a form of sexual impotence, *Med Aspects Hum Sexuality, 1:43*, 1967. Some of the dynamics of premature ejaculation are also found in retarded ejaculation. See Lionel Ovesey and Helen Meyers: Retarded ejaculation—psychodynamics and psychotherapy, *Amer J Psychotherapy, 22:185*, 1968.

23. Ruth Moulton: Multiple factors in frigidity, in *Sexuality of Women, Science and Psychoanalysis* (Jules H. Masserman Ed.) New York, London: Grune & Stratton, 1966, Vol. X pp 75–93. See also Salo Rosenbaum: The significance of the orgastic pretense, in *The Marriage Relationship*. New York, Basic Books, 1968, pp. 157–174.

24. Moulton, *op. cit.*

25. A recent study on some intrapersonal factors in sexual responsiveness in women was that of Seymour Fisher and Howard Osofsky: Sexual responsiveness in women, *Arch Gen Psychiat, 17:*214, 1967. They studied forty-two married women who were asked to rate themselves as to their own sexual responsiveness and by their own reports of actual and preferred frequencies of sex per week and the degree with which orgasm occurred. The most outstanding finding was the correlation of orgasm with the amount of oral fantasy and the enjoyment of eating. These investigators suggest that sexual responsiveness might be one aspect of a generalized capacity of obtain pleasure from persons or objects in the environmental matrix. See also Stanley R. Lesser and B. Ruth Easser: The marital life of the hysterical woman, *Med Aspects Hum Sexuality, 3:*27, 1969.

26. Moulton, *op. cit.*

27. Noel Lustig, John W. Dresser, Seth W. Spellman, and Thomas W. Murray: Incest: a family group survival pattern, *Arch Gen Psychiat, 14:*31, 1966. Also Harold I. Eist and Adeline U. Mandel (Family treatment of ongoing incest behavior, *Family Process, 7:*216, 1968) list a number of recent papers and monographs on the problem of incest behavior.

28. Bernard L. Greene and Alfred P. Solomon: Marital disharmony: concurrent psychoanalytic therapy of husband and wife by the same psychiatrist: the triangular transference transactions, *Amer J Psychotherapy, 17:*443, 1963.

29. Moulton, *op. cit.*

30. Alexander Grinstein: Profile of a doll—a female character type, *Psychoanaly Rev, 50:*162, 1963.

31. Judd Marmor: Some considerations concerning orgasm in the female, *Psychosom Med, 16:*240, 1954.

32. Masters and Johnson, *op. cit.*

33. J.M. Lewis: Impotence as a reflection of marital conflict, *Med Aspects Hum Sexuality, 3:*73, 1969.

VII

FINANCIAL DISAGREEMENTS

The fifth most common complaint among couples with marital discord was of financial disagreements and is representative of conflict in other areas of the marriage, for example, role[1] expectations and enactments. When dealing with sexual complaints, the voice of the "inner child" was most conspicuous in the "records" of the individual. In the complaint of financial disagreement, the "parental" voice, reflecting values and attitudes, was most prominent. While the money problems were voiced equally by the men in both series, the women of the MDS complained twice as frequently as those in the PS. This latter finding was not unexpected, since there was a marked financial disparity between the two groups. Money problems play a significant role in marital disharmony, regardless of the economic status of the couple. Table XV compares the two groups in terms of frequency of financial disagreement.

Changing socioeconomic forces have markedly influenced the role of money in marriage. These forces include the increasing mobility of families, with the uprooting of social networks;

TABLE XV
FINANCIAL COMPLAINTS

	PS			MDS		
	Male	*Female*	*Total*	*Male*	*Female*	*Total*
Poor management	116	80	196	94	58	152
Uncooperative	44	30	74	22	18	40
Incompetent	24	45	69	10	24	34
Does not confide	4	50	54	6	34	40
Selfish	24	28	52	16	20	36
Extravagant	28	20	48	16	22	38
Major purchases without mutuality	0	25	25	4	18	22
Poor provider	0	18	18	0	12	12
Parsimonious	0	14	14	0	24	24
Does not believe in saving, planning, et cetera.	4	5	9	24	16	40

technological advances, with more women entering the labor market and altering the respective roles of the spouses;[2] the exodus to the suburbs, with many families living beyond their means; and cultural differences between the spouses, manifesting itself in clashing attitudes about disbursement of monies, to name but a few. To provide objectivity on financial matters, an understanding is needed of the psychological and sociological aspects of money and their relationships to our economic establishment.

Money is a symbolic method utilized by civilized individuals or institutions to facilitate the movement of materials and services. In Western cultures money is the most common method to store assets, e.g. stocks or bank deposits. Recent changes in the economic processes of the world[3] have undermined the confidence in money per se, and some individuals and even some nations are accumulating gold bars, precious gems, precious objects of art, and so on. Ferenczi[4] (1914), on the ontogenesis of interest in money, alludes to the universality of money. By universality Ferenczi means that all individuals like to possess money. Fifty years later, Frances Feldman[5] (another must reading for marital therapists) again stresses the the universality of money:

> It has come to have value not only for what it will buy, but for itself—for it represents the power to buy or possess. Money simultaneously represents "dependence" and "independence": dependence to the extent that one can rely on it for obtaining the commodities one needs, and independence because its ownership implies competence and self-reliance. To many individuals, the possession of money connotes more than the realistic, practical use that rational man ascribes to it; it symbolizes not only economic, but social and emotional, security.

Feldman points out that social status, in many instances, is equated with the family's financial structure, "the higher the income, the higher the family's social status," and that this attitude is derived from equating income with production. "Therefore, the producer, with his material possessions that represent the fruit of his production, is a person of stature in our society. The earning and spending of money are symbols of success and have come to represent status aspirations." This is reflected in the strivings of many individuals to move into a higher social class.

Since World War II there has been a progressive increase in income received by families due to families containing two wage earners.[6] Not uncommonly the wife, in raising the standard of living in the family, has created a change in the previous pattern of spending and saving. Since 30 percent of the women[7] in the two groups (PS and MDS) worked part- or full-time, it was not surprising that the most common financial complaint was that of inadequate management of monies and poor budgeting. An important contributing factor to the financial problems of many couples has been the influence of mass media stressing the philosophy of "buy now, pay later." Thus, many couples incur relatively large debts early in the marriage. Compounding the financial problems has been the trend of moving to suburbia, with family changes in more children, increased housing costs, two cars in the garage, especially since the working wife needs her own transportation. An unexpected finding was the infrequent complaint of gambling from a marital partner. A recent article[8] by Bolen and Boyd reviews the pertinent literature on gambling.

Table XV presents data on financial complaints in terms of frequency. Inadequate management (including poor budgeting) was the most common complaint in both groups of couples and was twice as frequent in the MDS, where the couples had much less income. The clinical extract of the following couple pinpoints various factors contributing to the financial complaint of poor budgeting and inadequate management:

Conjoint session with Mr. and Mrs. Elsa. Mrs. Elsa looked wan and depressed. Mr. Elsa appeared resigned and defeated. Mrs. Elsa began the interview by stating that two checks bounced, and the bank had refused to reissue them. The session centered largely about money.

Mr. Elsa said he could state succinctly what the problem was. Their income did not meet their expenditures; consequently, they were having to rely upon subsidization from his wife's parents. When they began their marriage, they lived in the city in a three-room apartment, and with both working, there was no money problem. When Mrs. Elsa became pregnant and the unplanned baby was born, they decided to move to the suburbs since he was eligible for a GI mortgage as a veteran. With mortgage payments of approximately $125.00 per month, they felt that this could be readily handled within their income, and this sum of money met the standards of their lending agency. They also put up a garage, which made their total payment for the house and garage 170 dollars per month. At first he was reluctant to put this addition up, but the salesman and his wife talked him into it, besides it was only nine dollars a week extra. Living in the suburb created a hardship for his wife in terms of transportation. At first they shopped together in the evenings or on weekends, but later his wife became increasingly unhappy, since she was the only woman on the block without a car of her own. So they decided to buy a secondhand car. But instead, the car salesman convinced him to buy a new car for himself against his better judgement. Now they also had a fixed monthly expenditure for a new car. Their first car was a wedding gift from his in-laws. Things were not too bad financially until his wife talked him into a color TV set, again on installment payments. Consequently, they never had enough money. They were obliged to draw on his traveling expense account in order to meet household expenses and to draw upon his salary in order to meet his expenses at work. It was a vicious circle. He feels optimistic about his job, but his wife's last pregnancy required a major financial expenditure, since she needed an emergency cesarean section and additional nursing care.

Mrs. Elsa briefly aroused and flared at this, stated she did not ask to become pregnant, but that he wanted a boy! Could she help it that the umbilical cord was twisted around the baby's neck! She thought that the problem during her illness was also complicated, financially speaking, by him going out for dinner every night rather than cook for the girls and himself. He acknowledged that he had done this, and feels that he should have been more thrifty.

This couple got themselves in a financial bind, with frequent games of "Uproar" and "If it Weren't for Him" (see Ch. XX).

The second complaint of inadequate management of finances was uncooperativeness and is illustrated in the following vignette:

Mr. and Mrs. Emily state they are in the process of obtaining a divorce that will not become final until three months hence but they are still interested in seeing if they can salvage their marriage.

Mrs. Emily comments that although they are heavily in debt, her parents had suggested they get counseling and they would pay for the sessions. Their house is being foreclosed because of inability to maintain the mortgage payments.

Mr. Emily interrupts and states that he feels their problems are in the area of immaturity.

Mrs. Emily says she is resentful of his interest in expensive hobbies that they can ill afford: stereo-sets, ham radio, and, now pedigreed dogs.

Mr. Emily counterattacks by stating that she does not hesitate to ask for anything or suggesting anything even if she knows they are not financially able to.

She adds: she has spent too much money on clothes but he spends on his hobbies. They bought their house with a very small down payment borrowed from his boss. They were managing all right until both decided to put in complete air-conditioning in their home, also on time payments. Then they did another ill-advised thing: bought a new car and built a two-car garage, also on monthly payments. In short time they were unable to keep up with their creditors, even though his weekly take home pay is one hundred sixty dollars per week.

These two couples, and many like them seen in therapy (two thirds of the MDS and about one-third in the PS), view debt as a way of life. No longer is debt frowned upon as a disgrace. Only in small isolated areas are cash payments culturally acceptable. Buying a car on time and travel now and pay later are respectable and fashionable. Our mass media encourage individuals to mortgage the future in hedonistic joy today. Credit buying is influenced by three factors: age, education, and, sociocultural influences.

There was a sharp drop in installment buying in persons over forty years of age. Very few of the couples argued about credit buying when they were married over twenty-five years. In both the MDS and PS groups, those couples who had graduated from college were less likely to use extended credit—perhaps because their "parental" voices have different values and attitudes toward credit buying or perhaps, and most likely, their higher incomes gave them more available cash. Finally, sociocultural factors were important in attitudes toward credit buying. Children of first-generation immigrants used credit buying more frequently than the second-generation immigrants. The sociocultural factor was markedly seen in the fact that the complaint, "does not believe in saving," was ten times more frequent in the MDS than in the PS. This complaint is illustrated in the following extracts:

"We seem to have totally different standards of values. I feel bills should be paid first, as we did in our family. Then, if there is any money left, after putting some aside for future expenditures, such as house repair, vacations, or investments, you consider what you can have and plan to play. The surplus expendable money should be spent in such a manner as to bring greatest pleasure to the family as a whole. After all this, one considers one's personal indulgences. He is like his father, who lost all his money just before migrating to this country and lives for the day and does not worry about what will happen tomorrow."

Or in another couple:

"She doesn't believe in pension plans or savings accounts. Her father never had such a thing and never plans ahead. She lives only for today and never plans ahead. Before we married I don't believe she was ever able to save unless she had to pay cash for something. In fact, after we married, I found she owed money to different department stores. I am very poor at handling money myself, but she has tried to get me to draw money out of my pension plan."

And in another couple:

"We have different values. I believe we need to make some firm decisions on how we wish to live and what we wish to do with our income and then stick to it. He is always wanting to keep up with the Joneses and be like some of our neighbors who are very wealthy. He never invites his parents to our home because they speak with an accent (an excellent example where the child of first-generation immigrants uses credit plans to become acculturated and assimilated). I can't understand his attitude toward money. It's not like his parents', who do not owe money to anyone. Perhaps it's a reaction to his parents, who lived in the basement and rented the other part of their home until they paid off their mortgage. I think we should make some long range financial plans, discuss what our mutual and individuals desires are, reach a compromise, and try to keep within this framework. I met him when I was teaching school and he was the handsome maintenance man there. Besides, I had just turned thirty and thought I better get married before it was too late."

The third most common financial complaint, which occurred with the same frequency in both groups and with the same ratio between the sexes, was where one spouse regarded his partner as incompetent. The following comment succinctly states this in one sentence:

"She is a financial birdbrain, needs a leash in department stores and totally lacks fiscal foresight."

Or in another couple:

"In money matters, where to live, how to live, with whom to live, my husband allows no part of my opinions or desires to influence what is finally done. He gives in to me in superficial matters as long as it does not interfere with his desires and considers that giving in as being fair. And I majored in home economics in college."

In rebuttal, the husband defended his position: "She is a poor manager of funds, does not budget, criticizes my financial management, insists on nonrealistic living standards—a mansion instead of a home, expensive vacations, the latest type telephones, antique furniture, etc. . . . I would enjoy these things too, but I don't believe in living beyond my means."

The fourth financial complaint resulting in acrimonious arguments between the couple was the complaint of trust. This complaint was more frequent in the MDS and was voiced by the females (50 women versus 4 men in the PS, and 34 women versus 6 men in the MDS). One woman commented bitterly: "Until recently I didn't know we had two safety boxes in the bank, one in his name only. This made me mad!" A variation of the same complaint of lack of confiding is the following:

"My husband does not confide in me about money matters and never says no to any of my material wants, although he knows he cannot afford them. I have rarely purchased anything without asking him first and never made any major purchase without him being with me. Later I find out we shouldn't have made that particular purchase at the time.
I have no way of knowing what bills are paid and what bills are due, since he prefers to handle the money. Since his recent bankruptcy I find it very difficult to trust him in any financial matter."

The fifth complaint of a spouse being selfish, more frequent in the MDS, occurred in both groups in about the same ratio and was almost evenly divided between the sexes. Not uncommonly, this complaint was associated with the complaints of unfulfilled needs and sexual dissatisfaction. Typical of the complaint of selfishness is the following extract:

Mrs. Esther: "By keeping me on a tight allowance, I never have the freedom to buy something for myself. His clothes come first and his airplane next. The kids and I could wait until the very last minute.
Mr. Esther: "My wife has always felt that she should be made more self-sufficient financially. She resented the fact that the monies were doled out to her in the form of an allowance, and she was always without funds when her friends seemed to have all the money they needed all the time. This made her feel I did not trust her to handle money, and when she was given more money and responsibility to pay household expenses, the funds were never enough. I suppose she told you about my airplane, but a guy needs some recreation."

The financial complaint of extravagance was almost twice as frequent in the MDS than in the PS. Not infrequently the complaints of selfishness and extravagance were present at the same time. Typical of the complaint of extravagance is the following:

"I usually handled the money because my husband's lack of responsibility to pay bills. I could never agree or justify his purchases of automobiles, expensive cameras, special camera lenses, expensive stereo kits, to mention a few. All these items were not only more than we could afford, but he always lost interest in them after their purchase and traded them in for something better."

The seventh complaint of major purchases without mutuality was rarely verbalized by the men but confined primarily to the women with about the same frequency in both groups, about 7 percent. Since the majority of men in both groups were either in their own businesses or in executive positions involving major decision making, perhaps they made major purchases on their own without consulting their wives because this was a repetitive behavior pattern at work carried over into their homes.

The following extract is typical of the four men in the MDS who complained about their wives:

Mrs. Ethel: "I've always wanted to buy things it seemed to me, at the time, we needed, such as furniture, appliances, clothes, Christmas presents, dancing lessons for the kids, vacation trips and the fun things, but in my eyes completely worthwhile. While he wants these things too, he hates to delve into the savings account for them; if we do not have to do that, he worries about getting the money out of his monthly salary. He feels the weight of the children's college education to come. I really do not visualize it very well. I have always felt we were securely fixed, even though we do not save regularly. We have some stocks and savings. I know my husband can do well at his work, earn a good salary and I have always assumed he would do better as he got older. So I have never worried about the future. This undoubtedly makes him worry even more, making him feel alone in the responsibility. I wish I could help him more and I know I really don't understand economics. He is a smart mathematician and I am not. But I do not think he knows how much I appreciate his ability in this respect. I can manage the money he gives me, though occasionally I will run short because I made an error in subtraction or forgot to note a counter check. These things happen, although I try not to let them. He gets quite angry when this occurs, and we quarrel. He wants me to be a business partner, and yet he won't give me equal opportunity. I don't know what many of his plans are or what he has done in the past, and he doesn't tell me. Right now he has taken all our money and put it in a trust fund for the children's education. I don't know where it is. I am furious about this!"

Mr. Ethel: "I'm methodical, and my wife is a dreamer I am reluctant to disclose my income figure. She is careless regarding expenses and purchases. I believe in saving for the future, whereas she wants to spend everything now. Until recently she would make major purchases without consulting me, e.g. She bought a new washer and dryer without asking me. It was reduced and a good bargain and we would need a new one next year, she rationalizes. I was furious. We are unable to save out of my earnings for the childrens' education, so I've put our savings, which was mainly from inheritance, into a trust fund. She is a spender and I'm a saver. We just come from two different backgrounds. When my father came to this country, he had no money and did it all on his own. All our family had a college education."

The eighth complaint of the husband being a poor provider was about the same in both series. Not one male voiced this complaint in the 750 couples, since, as expected in our culture, the husband is suppose to provide the money. The following extract is not uncommon:

"We spend too much on baby-sitters and entertainment. We have never owned a home and probably never will. We have never had enough money for household help for me, even at times when I was very ill or after childbirth. We are always pressed to pay ordinary living expenses but always loaded if it is a matter of entertainment or having a good time or a luxury item. He could make more money if he tried harder. He is a lousy provider. We always live as though there is no tomorrow. We seldom have any savings. Never a reasonable budget. My husband considers his salary to be "mad money." The man will never live on a budget and still thinks he will find a pot of gold at the end of the rainbow. At this point he is swamped with bills, and we live from pay day to pay day. He has the ability to make more money but won't put out the effort."

The ninth complaint that the husband was parsimonious was verbalized only by the women in both groups. No male could admit that his wife is miserly and maintain his self-respect. This complaint was four times as frequent in the MDS as in the PS. The following extract is illustrative:

Mrs. Eva: "Financially, he was always a good provider, and we have never gone without things we needed. We have many arguments about money because he feels that I am extravagant, and I feel he is parisimonious, and he regards me as incompetent. Somewhere between is the truth. I do care for nice clothes for all of us, about setting a nice table, and having an attractive home. I consider my husband to be a big-time spender in public but a real tightwad at home."

Mr. Eva: "Until five years ago we lived within my income until we bought a home in the suburbs. My motive was to find a place where she could put down roots and find satisfactions. My income soon could barely cover all expenses because of her excessive demands. Our house had to be as nice as our neighbors', but their husbands earn much more than I do. We are continually falling behind on bills, creating an atmosphere for arguments. She calls me a miser, but I tell her I am being realistic. Sure I spend money when we entertain, but these are business clients."

In summary, all ten financial complaints usually occurred in combinations and involved all three systems: intrapersonal, interpersonal and environmental. Frequently the content varied, but the basic problem was in the relationship between the spouses.

NOTES

1. For our purposes we think of social roles as the functioning of an individual in society. At a lecture (October 1962, University of Chicago) John P. Spiegel defined social role as a goal-directed pattern of behavior, adapted by cultural values, for the position or function of an individual in a social situation *always* involving another role partner. An excellent description of role appears in an article by William F. Knoff: Role: a concept linking society and personality, *Amer J Psychiat, 117*:1010, 1961. The assignment of roles in marriage role complementarity, and the success or failure in carrying out roles are intertwined in the intrapersonal system of each spouse. The most frequent marital complaint is dissatisfaction with the behavior, roles assumed and assigned, of the other partner. See also James L. Hawkins and Kathryn Johnsen: Perception of Behavioral Conformity, Imputation of Consensus, and Marital Satisfaction, *Document #6*, 6–10–68, JLH, Draft #5.
2. Roland G. Tharp: Psychological patterning in marriage, *Psychol Bull, 60*:1, 1963. This is an excellent article in which theory and research are reviewed and integrated with sociological data on mate selection and marital happiness, including an extensive bibliography.
3. Max F. Millikan: Problems of underdevelopment: an economist's view, *Amer J Psychiat, 122*:1387, 1966.
4. Sandor Ferenczi: *Sex in Psychoanalysis: Contributions to Psychoanalysis.* Boston, Badger, Gorham Press, 1916, pp. 319–331.
5. Frances Lomas Feldman: *The Family in a Money World.* New York, Family Service Association of America, 1957. See also Max Gunther: How we feel about our money, reprinted from the *Saturday Evening Post*, Dec. 30, 1967, in *Reflections, 4*:36, 1968. Finally, highly recommended is a book by James A. Knight: *For the Love of Money,*

Philadelphia, Lippincott, 1968. Dr. Knight, a minister and psychiatrist, has had ample opportunities to view human behavior with respect to money. He states that the book:". . . . was stimulated by my psychiatric interest in the meaning of man's behavior toward money." This book contains an excellent bibliography.

6. Charles Winick: The beige epoch: depolarization of sex roles in America, *Med Aspects Hum Sexuality*, 3:69, 1969, notes that over 2,300,000 women earn more than their husbands.

7. Susan R. Orden and Norman M. Bradburn (Working wives and marriage happiness, *Amer J Sociol*, 74:392, 1969) find in their research that "A woman's freedom to choose among alternative life styles is an important predicator of happiness in marriage. Both partners are lower in marriage happiness if the wife participates in the labor market out of economic necessity. . . . This finding holds across educational levels, stages in the life cycle, and part-time and full-time employment." Their figures show 35 percent among married women who have an eighth-grade education or less to 45 percent for college-educated women work. Further, 29 percent of the wives of college-educated men work.

8. Darrel W. Bolen and William H. Boyd: Gambling and the gambler, *Arch Gen Psychiat*, 18:617, 1968. They define the compulsive gambler, the phenomena of gambling and discuss the different forms of gambling. In addition they present sociolegal, cultural, anthropological, personal-interpersonal characteristics of the gambler and gambling.

VIII

THE IN-LAW PROBLEM

Couples are frequently involved intensely with their kin. This relationship with family can either be helpful to the functioning of the marriage or be a source of strain and conflict. Thus in-law problems, the sixth most common marital complaint, were mentioned by about 17 percent of the patients. In the PS this complaint was equally distributed between the spouses, whereas in the MDS the women complained about twice as frequently as their partners. Although a kin conflict involves all three systems, the environmental system plays the most important role. The finding that twice as many women in the MDS complained of in-law interference was found to be related to the fact that the majority of these women were first immigrant children and from the lower middle class. On the other hand, most of the women in the PS were either from upper-middle or upper-class origin. Current sociological studies indicate that whereas parent-child ties and responsibilities to the family of childhood are stressed over those of others in lower-class families, in middle and upper classes priorities are given to the marriage.

The importance of the kinship group in marital problems is highlighted in an excellent book by Leichter and associates.[1] They stress that a knowledge of patterns of transaction with kin in general is necessary to understand the way in which marital conflicts are related to the structuring of kinship roles. Thus they present specific kin statuses and categories of kin in terms of laterality, generation, and sex with whom the individuals are in most contact. For example, a couple has more contact with their parents than with their siblings, and the most frequent relationship is with the wife's mother, followed by the husband's mother. This may explain the frequency of mother-in-law jokes. The breaking of ties with the family of childhood and the formation of new ties between the couple through marriage is frequently a transitional point of stress or crisis and is one of the important tasks in the courtship phase of the couple (see Ch. XIII). My observations (although limited mainly to middle and upper classes but including other social classes—using Hollinghead's[2] criteria for classification) confirm that the nuclear family is part of a larger "family field" and must structure its ties to the two families of orientation. Talcott Parsons[3] has described the structurally isolated nuclear family with its discontinuity and relative independence from adjacent adult generations, yet with the bilaterality of this system with both the husband's and wife's families potentially of equal importance in controlling property, giving support and advice. Thus each newly married couple must work out its own balance of ties, both dependent and independent, from the two families of childhood.

In a recent article[4] I described a nuclear dynamic model of the family (see Fig. 10). In constructing this model, some of the concepts of Eric Berne[5] have been most helpful, not only in structuring a discussion on the role of in-laws on the nuclear family, but also in the discussion of the multiple forces influencing a marriage. The external environmental factors influencing the outcome of a marriage would be outside the external boundary and consist mainly of sociocultural forces, the in-laws being one of those forces. The internal environmental forces would be those within the external boundary. Although all "good" marriages have conflicts, they are usually self-limited and kept within the nuclear family. In couples in conflict, about one out of five, there is difficulty in solving problems of how to relate to two sets of parents and of establishing family boundaries. One concept of GST, that of the permeability of systems (see Fig. 1), allows marital conflicts to spread to the original families, permitting the extended kin to be drawn into or play into the conflicts. This involvement may interfere with the resolution of the underlying areas of friction between the couple and may, in fact, lead to fixed conflicts. Thus, instead of unity of the couple resulting in collaboration, one or both spouses may become competitors in what they give or receive from their kin. The resultant feedback transactions between the individual and their kin may produce marital discord. Two main areas in the BMQ reveal information about relationships with the extended family: (1) the complaint of in-law interference, and (2), additional information about the childhood family.

Although the pioneer psychoanalysts, Abraham and Ferenczi, were well aware of the impact of extended families upon their patients, it remained for Ackerman[6] to fully emphasize the emotional impact of in-laws in family discord and to include them in the therapeutic setting. In 1962 Norman W. Bell[7] described four aspects of how extended kin relate either consciously or unconsciously with their married children. He distinguished these four aspects as an analytic device and found, as I did, that they were intertwined. He describes the different extended family relationships as follows:

1. Countervailing forces.
2. Stimulators of conflict.
3. Screens for projections of conflicts.
4. Competing objects of support and indulgence.[8]

The following data refers only to the couples in the PS where time permitted exploration of their relationships with their in-laws.

One hundred sixty-three spouses complained of in-law interference. In seventy-six couples the complaint was from both spouses. In terms of frequency, following Bell's categorization, the most common complaint was the use of in-laws as screens for the projection of conflicts. The original family need not be an active element in the marital disharmony of the couple. Instead, the extended family is used as a screen onto which a spouse can project feelings currently related to the partner or even be displacement of feelings toward parents or other objects of the past (projective identification, i.e. a past "record" is projected onto a current object and reacted to as in the past). Occasionally, even where the marital disharmony represents the projection of anger away from the original object, the substitute object (in-law or other relatives) may in reality be responsible for some of the hostility present. In some couples there was a splitting of past and current ambivalent feelings, with a spouse directing her negative sentiments towards the in-laws and the positive feelings towards extended kin. In thirty couples the extended families were used as a screen for the projection of conflicts. Typical were the two following case extracts:

Mr. and Mrs. Felice came for help at his insistence. He was dressed in typical Ivy League style and associated primarily with his relatives in their family-owned business. Mrs. Felice was an attractive, well-dressed, well-groomed woman, who originally had been her husband's secretary.

Mr. Felice began the interview by stating: "We have an occasional violent argument about my family. My wife comes from a very poor family. She always felt my family was rich and not too happy about our marriage. My wife is envious of the money my mother gives my sister for vacations. Yet, on our anniversay, mother gave us a five-hundred-dollar check as a gift. My father-in-law is a mailman and lives in a very modest neighborhood. My wife feels that although she comes from a very poor background, she has fine parents, better than mine. Her mother is a very dominating person. When her parents get to quarreling about their respective families, her mother will get furious, which angers him enough to strike her. Most of our difficulties are around my sister and my mother. I feel, by and large, it is my wife's fault. Her older sister was the favorite in her family. She accuses my mother of being dishonest and has made snide remarks about my sister's morals. My wife accuses me of being too close to my family, but I feel the conflict is deeper than this and is between my wife and me."

Mrs. Felice: "I am not particularly interested in coming for marriage counseling, since I don't feel we have any real problems in our marriage. I don't know what his problem is except he can't stand a dirty house. All our serious arguments are usually regarding some part of his family. I have never been accepted in his family because I was socially below them. His mother and father won't let him go. My parents were happy to get me married off. I dislike his mother because she is two-faced and domineering. I can't stand his sister because she thinks she is better than I. Besides, she puts on airs with me, just like my sister did."

In another couple:

Mr. Fidelia: "She keeps harping about my mother, a person my wife compares herself with, not me. This is just a reason for her to release pent up feelings. My mother happens to be her favorite target. Her mother, who is slovenly, a lousy housekeeper, and a bickering wife, can do no wrong and is perfect. Although by mother is her prime target, there are others."

Mrs. Fidelia: "He appeased and pacified his mother all our married life and expects me to do the same. His parents were the first people invited to our apartment after the honeymoon. He scrubbed and polished the floor until it shone, to prove to his mother I was a good housewife. His mother for many years has caused much dissention between both her sons and tried to cause trouble between the daughters-in-law. She has a very strong influence on my husband. My mother was that way with me until our first child was born."

In twenty-two couples, the extended families played a role in the marital discord by acting as stimulators of conflict. The in-laws were active elements in causing conflict because of their own unhappiness, which induced problems within the marriages of their children. The following couple is typical:

Mrs. Flora: "Our troubles began before we were married. My mother-in-law, who was unhappy in her marriage, took advantage of our youth and my desperate appeal for acceptance. After our marriage, she divorced her husband. I think she made trouble because she wasn't loved and didn't want to see others happy. She is referred to by my husband as a "lonely widow" and as such has spent much too much time with us and in our home. She is a nasty, bossy, imposing person, and although she has caused much unhappiness for us, my husband refuses to cut down the frequency of her visits or stand up for me in any way when his mother is involved in a given situation, although I may be right and she, wrong. My husband did tell me on many occasions not to discuss difficult subjects with her and to keep things impersonal. This is difficult for me to do. I usually wind up feeling sorry for her, and this gets me into trouble. I always felt unloved and unneeded as a child, and when my husband didn't take my side, I felt he thought the same things as long as he let her say them."

Mr. Flora: "We have enjoyed a nice relationship. However, during the entire time of our marriage, we had constant problems with our respective parents, primarily my wife with my mother, and her father and me. Both of these individuals were forceful and ruled their respective homes. My wife tried to be close to my mother but could not accept the resultant oppression of doing what was asked of her. I repeatedly suggested to my wife that she refrain from such attempts of closeness as she was attempting an abnormal thing. I suppose that was why my father divorced my mother. I feel sorry for my mother, she means well and is very lonely. When a couple of months ago my wife asked my mother to leave our home over a silly argument, our marriage itself became a horror. My mother is very unhappy, and I suspect she is trying to live vicariously through us."

Additional conflicts could be stimulated consciously or unconsciously by the extended family focusing on the weak spots in the nuclear family. Not uncommonly, the triggering incident for the marital discord is a gift from the parents. Ten couples fell in this category:

She: "My mother-in-law still treats her son as a baby. She spoils him. When saying good bye to us in private or public, she always asks: 'John do you need any money?'. She always has a roll of money on her. If he took it, which he usually did, she would say: 'Now that's all, no more!' She buys love from everyone. His dependence on her money has hindered his own development, interfered with his holding down a job, and caused many arguments."

The third type of situation, where the extended families played a role in the marital discord of eighteen couples, occurred where in-laws were used as countervailing forces. The partners may seek support from their kinship networks to support their crumbling marriage. It is not uncommon for one spouse to seek help from his parents and verbally attack his in-laws either alone or in cooperation with his kin. The feedback from this type of maneuvering is for his partner to counterattack, drawing upon her family for reserves and retaliating upon his parents. The circularity of this kind of behavior can lead to various forms of disruption of the family. The following case extracts are typical of some of the marriages where the extended families act as countervailing forces:

She: "To describe my mother-in-law would take a year. She is a vicious, conniving woman. My husband is the only one of her children who has stayed in Chicago. The others have all purposely moved away. My husband feels we are obligated to visit them every Friday night and yet is most hostile to his mother. She and I have had a few horrible battles where he is hesitant to stand up for me. He is constantly comparing his parents' wealth and mostly his mother's education and culture to my parents. He has stated he owes more to his parents because they sent him through college, whereas my parents only sent me to business college. We have had many arguments about our parents. My husband is very rude and crude to my mother, whom he only sees once a year, but he states she is crude, uneducated, and fails to see that my mother really liked him originally. My parents are pretty bitter about all this. The last time the two families were together at our wedding anniversary, my parents and his parents really said some nasty things to each other."

Another extract shows how the parents are drawn into the marital conflict:

"A whole chapter could be written about my dear mother-in-law. She has taken and taken from me. She is a most critical person, and yet in my home she never criticizes me. He runs to his family with all our problems. He has never accepted my family, though at first my mother sent us things. My folks are angry at his parents and won't even talk to them. Part of this is my fault for telling them about his mother."

And another illustrative example:

Mr. Georgiana: "In-laws are a constant source of irritation between us. I find nothing to say to them, since I can't speak on their level. They constantly invite us places, and I feel guilty in saying I do not want to go, even though I really do not want to go with them. I feel my wife has come from a very repressive atmosphere. In our family we are open and I can discuss anything with my parents. Her relationship with her family is a duty. My mother-in-law is a very immature idiot. I don't respect my father-in-law, and he knows it. When I pick on her mother, my wife comes to her defense. It just burns me up."

Mrs. Georgiana: "He has certain gripes about my family, hostilities toward my family. When we go out with them, he could be more friendly. It affects our relationship. Maybe I could ignore it when he says my mother is stupid and idiotic. Occasionally his parents and mine get into big arguments about us. His parents are so dogmatic and keep mixing in our affairs."

The fourth manner in which family networks play a role in marital disharmony is when they act as competing objects of support and indulgence. This aspect of interference by in-laws was observed in eighteen couples. The two main resources being contended for are material and affectional, either alone or in combination. The flow can be from the nuclear family to the in-laws or vice versa. An example in which the discord between the couple was due to a funneling of material goods and money to the extended family and which brought partners to their respective divorce lawyers follows:

Mr. Geraldine: "My point of view regarding my interest and motives with respect to my mother offers us an arena for discord. My wife resents my mother. This has gone on since we married. I admit my mother can, without so meaning, be somewhat difficult. She is possessive, I think; however, my wife is too critical. She resents that I give mother a fixed amount of money each week, although we can readily afford it. Also my brothers-in-law are on my payroll. They are dependable, so I pay them twice as much as they are worth. But I can afford it. She is not deprived of a single thing she wants. Yet my wife is a very giving person to everyone but my relatives. In the last two years she has not invited a single relative of mine to our home. I was raised in a household where relatives were always dropping in spontaneously. Not with my wife! They need a formal invitation. This infuriates me."

Mrs. Geraldine: "My mother-in-law and I do not agree on our respective places in the marriage between her son and myself. She tied her son to her apron strings and believes he should always stay tied. She resented me from the day we wed and considered me as 'that woman who came between us.' My husband has been brainwashed over the years by his mother. He can't even discuss our problems with me but runs to his family. Furthermore, I resent strongly his giving his mother money each week when she has ample funds of her own. Besides, his relatives are leaches on him."

In the following example, the flow of the resource was from the extended family to the nuclear and served the function of allowing the husband to rationalize his own shortcomings by externalizing them:

Mrs. Gertrude: "His folks have been supporting us for the past year. His parents are both independently wealthy. They firmly believe that everyone takes care of themselves separately. My family believes the opposite. My father is also well-to-do but not extremely wealthy. My father-in-law said to my father that if he would give us twenty thousand dollars, he would give a similar sum for a down payment on a house. My father doesn't believe in that. It has been a source of continuous arguments for me to ask my father for handouts. His mother indulges him in everything. If she didn't, he would take a good job and settle down. He has been a playboy long enough. I thought that after we married everything would change. But his mother won't let go of her *boy*—and he is thirty-five years old. She acts toward him like a girl friend instead of a mother. 'How do you like my new hairdo?' It's sickening. Love must be blind because I didn't notice this before our marriage. My husband is constantly criticizing my family—the money angle. He doesn't feel he should support me; he feels that the woman is supposed to pay her own way."

Mr. Gertrude: "I was brought up differently. My parents both received allowances from their parents when they were married. One reason they were opposed to our marriage was that her parents were not of the same social status. Her father is wealthy, but made it on his own. I feel resentful. I was led to believe by her that she had her own independent income. Then it turned out she didn't have enough income of her own. Her family makes no effort to help her. My parents think this is awful. The last time her parents and mine met there was a big argument over finances."

The other source of competition between the spouses resulting in marital friction relates to affection and/or attention directed toward an in-law. The most frequent complaint from a husband was the amount of time his wife spent on the telephone talking to her mother:

"My wife is abnormally close to her mother. She has to telephone her twice a day. Her nightly call to her mother infuriates me. I feel she is influenced by her, and this causes friction. When I come home from work I would like to have a cocktail before dinner and talk to her. Instead, she is on the phone with her mother. My wife feels my parents are horrible people who do not warrant the respect or concern that I might give them. She feels that they are awful people who deserve to be shot and, naturally, I resent this attitude."

Or in another example:

"My mother-in-law considers my family, husband and children as much hers as they are mine. She takes over the house when she is in it, and much more. When she visits, I have the feeling that it is not my home or creation. My husband just sits there and does nothing about it. He is an only child. She is my problem. Never lets go of him and monopolizes all his time as though I don't exist. For the first six years of our marriage, we had to spend every weekend with his parents. He has always resented any time I spent with my folks, who live out of town. I don't have a mother-in-law, I have a competitor."

In summary, the extended family can play an important role in promoting marital conflict in the nuclear family.[9] The most common process involves projection, where the in-laws are used as screens for the projection of conflicts. Other roles extended families play in producing marital discord in order of frequency are stimulators of conflict, countervailing forces, and competing objects of support and indulgence.

Kinship networks can contribute in a number of positive ways to the constructive functioning of a marriage. Marital disharmony related to the discharge of obligations toward one's family of childhood can frequently be stabilized by family rituals. At other times, conscious or unconscious scapegoating of the in-laws enables the marriage to continue, since destructive feelings between the spouses is directed away from the nuclear family.

NOTES

1. Hope Jensen Leichter and William E. Mitchell (with the collaboration of Candace Rogers and Judith Lieb): *Kinship and Casework.* New York, Russell Sage Found., 1967. Also very informative to a therapist is an article by Marvin B. Sussman (Adaptive, directive and integrative behavior of today's family, *Family Process,* 7:239, 1968) in which he concludes, "A reappraisal of the modern urban family shows that

the kin-related network assumes multiple postures, both dependent and independent, in interaction with other social institutions. As a voluntary system, the family competes for members with other social realms, also offering emotional, educational, economic and other supports. Based upon reciprocity with exchanges, often of an unequal nature, occurring through bargaining, the kin network acquires committments by providing rewards perceived as superior to those offered by alternative social structures. Once preferred, the kinship system rapidly instills tradition-laden obligations in its members."

2. August B. Hollingshead and Frederick C. Redlich: *Social Class and Mental Illness.* New York, Wiley, 1958.

3. Talcott Parsons: The Kinship System of Contemporary United States, in *Essays in Sociological Theory.* Glencoe, Free Press, 1954.

4. Bernard L. Greene: The Family in Therapy, in *American Family in Crisis.* Des Plaines, Forest Hospital Foundation Publications, 1965, pp. 35–46.

5. Eric Berne: *The Structure and Dynamics of Organizations and Groups.* Philadelphia, Lippincott, 1963.

6. Nathan W. Ackerman: Emotional Impact of the In-laws and Relatives, in *Emotional Forces in the Family* (Samuel Liebman, Ed.), Philadelphia, Lippincott, 1959.

7. Norman W. Bell: Extended family relationships of disturbed and well families, *Family Process,* 1:175, 1962.

8. *Ibid.*

9. Leichter, *et al., op. cit.,* describe three themes, which were repetitive in conflicts with husband's parents but infrequent with the wife's kin. These three themes were those of rejection-neglect, interference, and comparative loyalty. Rejection and neglect are two sides of the same coin. Rejection refers to exclusion from gatherings, criticism, and so on, whereas neglect refers to failure to fulfill obligations (social and/or material). The parents of the husband may feel rejected when obligations to wife's parents receive precedence over them, e.g.: "My husband's parents invited us to their Thanksgiving dinner, even though they knew my parents had previously invited us. We went to my parent's house! But not before a big argument between us, even though last year we went to his parent's dinner."

The second theme of interference referred to participation in the affairs of the couple by the relatives of the husband. The final theme was that of comparative loyalty of the husband to his wife and to his extended family, i.e. the wife feels the husband is more loyal to his relatives. An example of this situation was the following: "John and I had a bitter argument over the fact that one of his sisters complained about me. It was a distortion of what really happened. Instead of talking to me about it, he just believed her and got mad at me."

The three themes of rejection, interference and loyalty have various repercussions in the nuclear family. The husband's extended family may accuse his wife of trying to alienate him from them or even of showing preferences for her parents or relatives over his. On the other hand, the wife may suspect her in-laws of trying to take "advantage of his loyalty to them. She must insist that he support her if they criticize her, and reject their attempts to weaken her position as wife by intruding. . . . The wife is particularly likely to resent their hold on him, because in effect it reaffirms his status as a child in his parent's house instead of a man in her house. Since her prestige depends on his, she is doubly anxious to assert his independence, especially his independence of his mother, who often continues to treat him as a little boy." The authors point out another important fact involved in conflict with the husband's kin, namely, the wife's more frequent contact with his relatives, since she is expected, in our culture, to handle all social arrangements.

IX
INFIDELITY

The seventh most common marital complaint was that of infidelity. My statistics, which are conservative,[1-3] reveal that about one out of six spouses complained of his partner's unfaithfulness on the BMQ. The incidence of infidelity was about the same in both groups, 156 in the PS (500 couples) versus 75 in the MDS (250 couples) (see Table VIII). This figure is not accurate, since in the private series, where an important factor is the intensive character of the therapy, an additional one third of both men and women stated that they were or had been unfaithful to their partner, but that their spouse was consciously unaware of the situation. I emphasize unaware because of my clinical experience that there are very few family secrets and the partner is either consciously or unconsciously aware of his spouse's behavior. An interesting observation was finding more men in the MDS complaining of their wives being unfaithful than did the women, in the ratio of about five to three (see Table VIII). Surprising was the frequency in which a spouse's infidelity was forgiven and only caused marital discord when the partner persisted in being unfaithful. The distraught wife or tormented husband then initiated therapy in an effort to have the therapist stop the spouse's infidelity. However, in the majority of the couples a marital crisis ensued when the infidelity became known. Many men with premature ejaculation (one-half in the PS group) sought therapy because of guilt, feeling strongly that their poor sexual performance was responsible for their partner's unfaithfulness. An important pitfall to avoid is accepting the complaint of unfaithfulness at its face value. In a number of couples, one spouse was deeply disturbed emotionally, usually of a paranoid reaction.[4] Not infrequently the unjustly accused spouse may react with severe violence toward the partner. Only rarely have I encountered deliberate misrepresentation by a spouse, but this possibility should always be kept in mind.

In Chapter VI an adult's sexual activity was presented as epitomizing his personality. Infidelity will be described within the GST, utilizing the data from the PS group. For purposes of presentation, the forces present in infidelity will be detailed in terms of the three systems (intrapersonal, interpersonal and environmental).

The environmental system with its sociocultural forces plays an increasing role in contributing to marital unfaithfulness.[5] The emancipation of women, with an increasing number of working wives, provides opportunity and temptation. Vincent[6] has pointed out "occupational propinquity as a factor" in extramarital liaisons. He writes: "Eyebrows would quickly rise if a husband were to have coffee or lunch with the wife of his neighbor several times a week, but in a work situation equally close male-female relationships can develop during coffee breaks, lunch periods, and shared 'business projects' without raising any eyebrows." In a number of instances of infidelity, the relationship of a nonsexual nature between the "idealized boss" and his secretary began at the annual Christmas party, where the atmosphere and the available alcoholic beverages disrupted the usual boss-secretary arrangement (see the Lavinas, Ch. XXII).

Another sociocultural factor in infidelity is the current importance on looking sexy as stressed in magazines, books, plays and other mass media, with its covert incitement and encouragement for freer sexual behavior. This change in morality condones promiscuity. An increasing number of spouses no longer consider infidelity as a deviation from the norm. Willis[7] concludes: "Unfortunately, in our acceptance of the average state as normal and therefore desirable, the idealized conception of stability and fidelity for monogamous pairs sounds not only 'square' and unrealistic, but also may come to seem a kind of deviation in itself." Thus in some areas spouse swapping is not uncommon. In a number of spouses, both male and female, there was a tolerance of the infidelity as long as it was carried out in a discrete manner. Another sociocultural factor is the marked mobility of the population. This mobility removes the marital partners from the critical observations of their kinship networks. In addition to nuclear family mobility, there is the individual mobility of spouses, especially in upper-middle and upper classes, either for leisure or necessitated by occupational roles which afford opportunities and temptations for unfaithfulness:

Mr. Grace, a very successful business executive whose work entailed frequent out-of-town travel, married fifteen years, opened his initial interview with the following: "I have no specific complaints about my wife. I have just lost the feeling I once had for her and through no fault of hers of which I am aware. She has been a good, loving, loyal wife. She has had most of the responsibility of raising our children and they are a credit to her. I admire and respect her, but I no longer feel the love I once had for her. My work involves considerable travel. Then I met Alice, a colleague at a branch office. Our relationship was strictly professional for the past five years. We have a strict company policy about socializing. Then a year ago her husband suddenly died of a coronary heart attack. About six months ago I accidentally met her in a cocktail lounge at the hotel in which I was staying. I had always liked and respected her. She seemed lonely and told me how difficult it was to go home at night to an empty apartment. Gradually I established a close relationship with her. Now I feel like my wife is my sister. I would like to change in the way I now feel toward my wife."

Mrs. Grace tearfully stated: "I just don't understand what has happened. I accepted his traveling, since I knew it was important for his advancement. Until recently, we have had a wonderful marriage. Then he began to get preoccupied and I sensed a change in our sexual relationships. It was more of a duty than a pleasure as previously. Finally I asked him if he was ill or unhappy at work. He had always been truthful. He can't lie without betraying himself. Finally he told me about this other woman. I was terribly hurt. I hope you can help us."

Among other sociocultural forces has been the role of the contraceptive pill and other improvements in contraception. Contraception has removed one real deterrent to infidelity in many women—the fear of pregnancy.

In evaluating the forces operating in the intrapersonal and interpersonal systems of the spouses involved in infidelity, I found it expedient to categorize them in degree of awareness.[8] Thus motivating forces were found to be either conscious or unconscious, and present in different combinations. The conscious forces present in terms of frequency were as follows:

1. Sexual frustration.
2. Curiosity.
3. Revenge.
4. Ennui.
5. Recognition seeking.

The unconscious forces operating in infidelity could be classified in terms of frequency as follows:

1. Seeking "stroking" of the "inner child."
2. Rage at partner or parent.
3. Proof of masculinity.
4. Expression of immature personality.
5. Partner acting out "unconscious homosexual defense" of spouse.
6. Severe personality disturbance.
7. Denial of unconscious homosexuality.
8. Figurative penis envy.

Sexual frustration was the most common conscious factor, being present in about 70 percent of the spouses in the ratio of two males to one female. The following case extract is illustrative:

In a young couple married ten years, the husband's major and only complaint is his wife's sexual unresponsiveness to him. He wants intercourse nightly—wife says, sometimes two or three times a night. When she does not respond to his request, pleading fatigue, lack of interest, illness, and so on, he strikes her. This has gone on throughout their marriage.

The precipitating event for seeking counsel was another violent episode, following which the wife threatened to leave. Recently, because she feared getting pregnant again and was giving this as an excuse to avoid sex, the husband had a vasectomy (see Chap. XVIII) done to become sterile and improve their sex life. This only increased his sexual demands, and now when she refused him, he became violent. Throughout the CDD session, he kept pressing for answers regarding his wife's behavior as to whether it was normal for her to have energy for a social party at night but not for sex, or for her to have refused him sex during their engagement, necessitating his getting relief from prostitutes. During his following individual sessions, he again reiterated his complaints and admitted frequent extramarital affairs to relieve his sexual tension.

This man highlights a situation where marriage furnishes an easily available sexual partner, and what matters is not who relieves the sexual tension and anxiety but merely that it it be relieved.

Curiosity was the next common factor, being present in a little over 50 percent of the spouses in the ratio of three males to two females:

Mrs. Griselda began the initial conjoint session by complaining bitterly about her husband being unfaithful twice in the past six months. A dyed blonde, well groomed, heavy makeup, twice married, and wearing seductive clothes, she was at loss to understand his behavior, since their sexual relationships both before and during their marriage had always been satisfactory. Once they were engaged, she had suggested they be true to each other. He readily agreed, and she trusted him for the past ten years. If it hadn't been for a mysterious phone caller disclosing that her husband was sleeping with his receptionist, she would never had known. "I followed him to a motel with her. She was only nineteen years old, half his age. I threw him out, bag and baggage, but the next day I went and brought him home. He promised that he wouldn't do that again. But last weekend it happened again with another young girl. This time I got a phone call from her boyfriend, who was furious at her."

Mr. Griselda, with some embarrassment, defended his philandering by stating it was only one of those things and really meant nothing seriously. He loved his wife but had been curious. In their individual sessions, both had talked differently. Mr. Griselda had always had occasional affairs, even during their engagement. "I have always been very curious about women. I don't believe the saying, 'if you turn them upside down they are all the same.' I love my wife but my curiosity always gets the upper hand."

As Bellville[9] has written:

At times infidelity results from a dishonest marital contract. Perhaps more often men behave in such a way as to imply fidelity before marriage as well as swearing to it in the ceremony. After marriage they continue to have coitus with other women much the same as they did before. They feel this their privilege as long as their wives don't know about it.

In the above clinical extract, Mr. Griselda falsely entered into the marital contract, consciously knowing he did not intend to abide contractually to the aspect of exclusiveness. On the other hand, English[10] suggests:

First, I'd say they haven't been able to conclude as a result of the limited intimacy obtained with one man known as their "husband" that they know enough about what a woman, her body, and her abilities in love-making could mean to a man. . . . Naturally they have *curiosity* [italics added] about such an intimate and much "advertised" relationship as the sexual relationship and they want to know more about themselves and their possible emotional reactions with a man and for a man by way of this highly emotional intimate and personal relationship.

In about 40 percent of the spouses, revenge was the third most common factor in seeking extramarital affairs, and was equally distributed between the sexes:

Mrs. Hannah: "My husband is still seeing his secretary. Part of it is my fault. I have never had an orgasm with him. The first two years I was very much in love with him and enjoyed sex, even though I was frigid. Then I began to resent having to read the sex manuals he brought home and to be so specific about sexual foreplay. It took all the fun and spontaneity away. He has never excited me. He's tender and gentle and sweet and considerate. But no fire! It is obvious to me that I have aggravated the situation. He is a virile man. A year ago, the husband of my best friend said he would like to go to bed with me. I was flattered and intrigued at the time. I said something flip at the time. Every time we were together he would say something, squeeze my arm, and hold me tight when we were dancing. As the year progressed I became more intrigued with the idea, but my feelings were for my husband. Then we were out with this couple at a New Year's Eve party and something happened to me emotionally when he kissed me at midnight. I suddenly did not have any sexual feelings for my husband when we got home. He made an overture and I told him to leave me alone. I tried to be very kind and understanding. I rejected him. He was upset. A month later my husband flipped his lid and went to bed with some secretary in his office. I feel like I am living in the middle of hysterics when he told me he loved her. He certainly had reason to have an affair. I had been refusing him sex (frustration as a factor). I was mad! I was furious! I kept picturing this woman in his office. I decided not to do anything rash. This was a month ago. He wanted a divorce to marry this girl. He says she is a *woman* and makes him feel like a man. Finally, I woke up one day, was furious and seeking revenge. I said to myself, I've got to find out if I'm capable of orgasm and went to bed with my friend after saying no to him for one year. I haven't felt that womanly in ten years. I had guilt feelings about his wife. They are very happily married. I was relaxed, uninhibited, and enjoyed it. I not only enjoyed myself thoroughly, but to add dressing to the salad, I was also enjoying getting even with my husband. I have so many mixed feelings about it now. I'm old-fashioned, you make your bed and lie in it. Besides my husband is a nice guy, and I would like to salvage our marriage. Besides I am now orgastic with my husband. He thinks it is a reaction to his affair and that the other girl was a challenge to me. I know I am a woman now."

This woman illustrates how unconscious, conscious and accidental (situational) forces changed her sexual responsiveness.

The unconscious psychodynamics were revealed in her individual sessions.

Ennui (monotonous, bored, humdrum, tedious and "square" were some of the adjectives used by spouses to describe their current sexual relationships with their partners) was the fourth most common factor found and was equally distributed between the sexes. The following vignettes are typical:

"My husband is very systematic and proper in his personality. Our conversations center around immediate family incidents and our mutual friends in our social club. Other than that it is usually a business type of conversation on what things have to be done around the house, including budgeting, repairs, and entertainments. He constantly wants to set up programs for getting things done and have different couples over. This annoys me. But what really makes me mad is when he comes home at night from work, the whole family must line up and report what they have done that day. Like at his board of directors meetings. Gradually I lost more and more interest in my family life and thus became negligent about duties around the house. I was getting so bored of the humdrum existence at home, so I went back to teaching. My work was stimulating, and I felt in the swing of things. It all began when I began to stop for a drink at a nearby cocktail lounge. The conversation was stimulating, the people congenial, the atmosphere exciting, and one thing led to another."

And in another couple, the man stated:

"I fell in love with a young girl. Each day was the same monotonous routine. Getting up at seven in the morning and making the 7:45 commuter train to the office. Talking to the same customers day in and day out. Lunch at the same restaurant with the same fellows. The usual martini and usual jokes. Then I noticed this new office girl. At first I didn't think she would be interested in someone twenty years her senior, but she was. We fell in love, but the thought of leaving my wife and family never crossed my mind. My wife found out from her girl friend, who told her: "If you weren't my best friend I wouldn't tell you. But I saw your husband coming out of a motel with a young girl." I decided to leave this girl. This gal had just gotten a divorce herself. I was prepared to accept for a while my wife's torment and disgust. But that went on for six months and that was too much. She made me feel like an utter monster, and now I cannot bear her insecurity, emotional instability and her unhappiness. I feel ashamed and guilty as hell for having been the cause of it all. But she cannot forgive and forget. We need help!"

This last man illustrates what Reed[11] so aptly states: "Our problem is not the 'seven-year itch' of folklore and drama.

Rather, it is the seventeen-year restlessness that occurs in the second decade of marriage that is so problematic." Unfortunately, too many spouses stop working at their marriage as soon as the honeymoon is over.

The fifth most common conscious factor producing infidelity and occurring in about one fifth of the spouses with equal frequency was that of seeking recognition. The following extract was common:

> "I am unable to talk or discuss things with him. I seem to be on the defensive all the time. What might start out to be a simple discussion ends in an argument if I don't agree with his theory, and this seems to be all the time. I've felt lonely and neglected. He thought having the children here should be enough. He would come home when he felt like it; other peoples' problems came before mine. He belittled me in front of the children and made me feel insecure. I've felt a maid or housekeeper could do the job I was doing. I tried to do things to please him, like making special gourmet dinners; sometimes he would notice me, sometimes not. I needed to have someone listen to my silly quirks and ideas, but he would have no patience with me. Then I met Henry at a political meeting. I suddenly felt wanted, loved, important, and needed. He commented on my hairdo, my clothes, the cute way I talked and walked. I felt like someone again."

In explaining the dynamics of infidelity to spouses, I have found it expedient and pragmatic to utilize the jukebox concept. Thus the jukebox can be warped, the mechanism jammed and the same "record" can keep playing, or the wrong "record" can be played. In one fifth of the spouses, the internal mechanism of the jukebox was jammed. This was due to situational crises and/or to old "records" being played that were once appropriate in childhood or later, but which were currently inappropriate. The psychosocial manifestations of this jamming of the internal mechanism of the jukebox were revealed in the following severe psychiatric disturbances:

1. Hypomanic phase of a manic-depressive psychosis.
2. Paranoid state[12] or paranoid psychosis in which the complaint of infidelity is delusional.
3. Depressive reaction where the infidelity wards off an overt manifestation of depression.[13]
4. Chronic alcoholism.

The most common condition observed in my clinical material was the hypomanic behavior, characterized by pressure of speech, flight of ideas and increased motor activity—one reaction of this activity being infidelity. The following vignette is typical:

The Harriets were referred by the psychiatrist who has been and still is treating the father of Mr. Harriet for a manic-depressive condition of many years' duration. The couple had been happily married for three years, when the wife, going through a suit she was preparing for the cleaners, found a receipt for a motel room used by her husband. She angrily confronted him with the receipt; a bitter argument ensued during which he admitted being unfaithful, and he left home. After being separated for a month, he returned home with the understanding they would seek marriage counseling.

Mrs. Harriet, sad, attractive and smartly dressed, said: "I want to make every effort I can to help this marriage. I love him. I respect his ability and admire his talent. I respect him as a man, husband and a father. I just don't know why this happened. We are very compatible sexually and I look forward to sex with him. At times he gets very moody and doesn't talk, like his father. At other times he is a dynamo, and the least thing sets him off. The infidelity was a net result of our lack of communication, not the direct cause. The affair caused me great pain and much insecurity. When he came home and told me the affair was over I believed him. But I do know she stops in to see him at work. When it happens and I happen to know of it, the hurt and anxiety comes back to me. Why can't he totally ignore her? I know she works in the same building, and they will bump into each other. But why does she still come to see him and call him. He says it's to talk about her problems of work and boyfriends. Is he her psychologist?"

Mr. Harriett came in for his first session, casually, but smartly dressed. He was very personable and exuded a lot of warmth and charm: "Our problem is a lack of communication. We don't understand each other. A lack in me to give to her and vice versa, no excitement in the marriage. Everything stopped a year ago. I don't know whether I personally entered into the marriage with the right attitude. With my moods I should have stayed single. I was in love with her. I overlooked a lot of things about her. A lack of enthusiasm on her part to appreciate something as simple as walking down the street. I react to people. They give me ideas. I feel like I need that with a woman. I supposed Andy mentioned it. I was fooling around with another woman. It was good for me. My motor seemed to be racing. This girl didn't mean a thing to me. But since I've returned home, she keeps bothering me."

Further interviews revealed mood swings starting in high school, with ups and downs. In his freshman year in college, he was depressed for a month, could not study, was disinterested in the goings on in the fraternity house and kept to his room. He suddenly snapped out of it, was his old self for a year and then became very active in all sorts of extracurricular activities and had a series of love affairs.

This couple is characteristic of a marriage where one spouse has severe mood swings, which tax the equilibrium of his partner. His infidelity was only a symptom of his underlying emotional instability.

In several couples, the extramarital affair of one spouse was a restitutive attempt to ward off a depression. In a number of chronic alcoholics, the attempts at infidelity were made to overcome strong feelings of insecurity and lowered self-esteem due to either premature ejaculation or impotence with their wives. In about 10 percent of the complaint of infidelity, the partner was unjustly accused. Not infrequently the innocent spouse would react violently to the unjust accusation, not realizing his partner was ill with a paranoid condition. The following vignette was not uncommon:

Mr. and Mrs. Helen were referred for therapy by a psychiatric social worker who felt their problem was too difficult for her to counsel. Mr. Helen had recently become quite violent toward his wife, who, after twenty happy married years, began to accuse him of infidelity with a neighbor's wife. The arguments between the Helens had become so violent that the neighbors had called the police. Mr. and Mrs. Helen came together for their initial appointment.

Mrs. Helen was an attractive, well-dressed woman, in her late forties, quite tense and tearful during the interview. She was extremely well groomed, showing few signs of her age, in fact, she appeared at least ten years younger than her stated age.

Mr. Helen was tall, well built, a typical executive in dress and appearance with heavy black framed glasses, who looked about his stated age of sixty. He was pleasant and cooperative, but obviously tense, even though maintaining excellent control over his demeanor. He readily admitted losing his temper and was genuinely remorseful over this. He said he resented his wife's accusations and questioning. There is no validity to her charges.

Both expressed a sincere desire to maintain the marriage.

Mrs. Helen was next seen alone. She tearfully repeated her accusations. "If Herbert would only tell me the details of his affair, instead of becoming violent and flying off the handle. Why won't he admit his indiscretion and tell me how it all happened. Then I could forgive him. I know this is destroying our marriage. But even when I don't want to question him, something inside of me prevents me from keeping my mouth shut." (The repetitive playing of a record.")

When Mr. Helen came for his next appointment, he was quite business-like in his approach. "I hate to be accused ,of adultery when I haven't done anything. And I've heard it about two hundred times. It's absolutely nonsense. We belong to the same country club as our next door neighbors, and were a foursome on the golf course. Mabel hit a ball into the rough and I helped her look for it. That night my wife accused me of having sex with Mabel while I was looking for her ball. It's absolutely crazy. Since then its been almost nightly questioning about the details. I blew my cool last week and I struck her."

Mr. Helen, baffled by his wife's accusations, not only reacted violently but in retaliation had withdrawn from her sexually. His withdrawal only reinforced his wife's fears that her husband was getting sex elsewhere. And a vicious circle started of accusation—withdrawal, withdrawal—accusation.

This cycle was abruptly terminated when Mr. Helen, informed of his wife's illness, understood his need to be patient while his wife was undergoing intensive therapy. He was advised that his wife could not help herself when the mechanism jammed in her jukebox and she played the wrong "record."

In the second group of individuals with marital unfaithfulness due to unconscious forces, the jukebox itself was warped, resulting in repetitive antisocial or dyssocial behavior. Thus in about 50 percent of the spouses involved in infidelity in the ratio of three males to one female, the extramarital affairs were an expression of an immature personality. In personality (or character) disorders, behavior is "abnormal" primarily as judged by the value systems of others. Since the individual is unaware of this (a warped jukebox does not know it is damaged), he does not experience anxiety or guilt.

I use the term *warped* to indicate my poor prognosis in the treatment of these persons. The history of one such spouse is well described in the words of his wife, who came for advice in regard to her husband's drinking and philandering:

"Our courtship was both happy and sad. We met in the army where I was a nurse and he drove an ambulance. I was happy when he was sober and with me, and unhappy when he was chasing around with other women. Jack would get mean when he had been drinking. He would swear and get into trouble with whoever happened to be around. After-ward he would become repentant and beg my forgiveness with tears in his eyes, promising it would not happen again, and that all he needed was my love to help him straighten out. . . .My parents objected to his courting me, but I convinced them that he was the man I wanted to marry, that once we married, he would settle down. In spite of my pleas to drink moderately, Jack got drunk at the wedding reception and started fighting with some of the guests. . . . His best man drove us home and helped him upstairs to the new apartment that I had rented and furnished with my savings warding off blows as best he could in the process. He promptly fell asleep on the bed. I sat on a chair all night, frightened and crying but to proud to go home and face my parents' We told you so. He had good and bad days and could be in turn sweet and loving or coarse and brutal. Eventually he got several jobs but none lasted more than a few months because he would pick fights with his superiors. . . . I kept working, which was the only paycheck we could depend on. He never willingly shouldered any responsibility and began to drink and gamble more, and stay out more. . . . My friends told me he was chasing around with other women and that I should leave him. He came home only to change clothes and eat a quick snack."

The men and women in this category had behavior patterns that were inappropriate to their educational backgrounds and to the values and behavior of their parents or authorities. They were usually indifferent to the impact of their behavior on others.

In the third group of unconscious forces operating in persons with infidelity, the jukebox was adequate, the internal mechanism operational, but past inappropriate "records" were played too frequently in the present. In terms of decreasing frequency, the following "records" were played:

1. Unconsciously seeking "stroking"[14] of the "inner child."
2. Unconscious rage for a parent projected onto partner (projective identification).
3. Unconscious proof of masculinity.
4. Partner acting out unconscious homosexual defense of mate.
5. Denial of unconscious homosexual defense.
6. Figurative penis envy.

The following clinical vignettes will be illustrative of the above six categegories:

Unconsciously seeking "stroking" of the "inner child":

Mr. and Mrs. Henrietta; married for seven years, extremely sensitive and intelligent, sought help for their marriage. Mrs. Henrietta had impulsively confessed to her husband that she had been unfaithful. "I start all the fights. He just listens. Its the first time I have done anything independent. I have been messing around with someone for two months. I should not have told him. I always knew that if I told him, I would have to stop. He didn't want to know the details, but I wanted to tell him. I betrayed the other man. I really like him even though he is twice my age. After I told my husband, I packed a bag and started to leave the apartment but stopped when he began to cry. This is the first affair. The seven-year itch, when you wonder if you are still attractive. The complaints I have about our marriage are so general and difficult to label or call by certain phrases or words. I'm not sure sexual dissatisfaction is the right word in our case, though it seems more likely that the problem involves a basic inhibitedness that we have with each other physically, which ends in dissatisfaction. This then involves a lack of communication also. We both find it difficult to communicate sexual needs to each other. Early in our marriage we performed sex very often, probably because we knew this was something married people were expected to do. Sex is also very mechanical with us and always has been, except on a very few occasions. It is like pushing certain buttons and getting certain responses. He always asks me for sex or suggests it. I am completely incapable of letting him know in any way at all when I want it. I don't say or do a thing and then sometimes wake him up in the middle of the night to argue about our life in general and still can't tell him that what I really want is sex. Actually, I have awakened him for sex a few times and have either been rejected or he has told me the next day he was asleep through the whole thing! I am horribly oversensitive to things people say, and I will remember one rejecting comment for years. I do have orgasms though during intercourse. With the man that I have been having an affair with, sex is exciting but I have never experienced an orgasm with my lover."

Mrs. Henrietta described a very unhappy childhood with both parents rejecting her. "My father advocates 'building a shell around yourself so no one can hurt you.' He smokes long cigars and talks gruffly, but obviously he didn't do too well with his shell. Mother was also a very cold, rejecting person. Father was always communing with nature and mother was never home."

A variety of forces were operative in this couple, and only a few were pointed out in this extract: the rejection of the wife by her parents and the ensuing rage later projected onto the husband (projective identification). In addition, there was current anger from the cold, aloof husband that reinforced her anger. Perhaps her inability to have an orgasm with her lover, a father figure, could be related to incestuous anxiety.

Unconscious proof of masculinity, a common motivating factor in infidelity, is beautifully illustrated in the first dream of a man who was in a compulsive bind with his receptionist and unable to stop seeing her:

"I was surf board riding in the nude. I looked down and surprised to see that my testicles were the size of coconuts."

This man was unable to stop his affair until psychologically his testicles returned to normal size and only after more than one year of psychoanalysis.

The two factors relating to the unconscious role of the homosexual defense in infidelity (one partner acting out the unconscious homosexual defense of his mate) needs to be differentiated from the rather common phenomena of homosexual play in preadolescent boys and girls.[15] Is use the term *unconscious homosexual defense* as a normal, maturational process in the psychosocial development of every individual. It is a reaction to the libidinal voice of the "inner child" of the person and varies from warmth and tenderness to sexuality. I view the unconscious homosexual defense as a reaction to the retaliatory anxiety resulting from the competitive hostility of the child toward his adult rival of the same sex.[16] For example, the little boy wants all of his mother's affection and attention. To get all the affection (rob the giant who owns the goose that lays the golden egg), he is placed in a competitive position where his opponent looms large and awesome. From the child's view his father looks likes a giant. It matters not how one labels the anxiety: castration anxiety of Freud, existential anxiety of existentialism, and so on, the little boy, because of his retaliatory anxiety, has to deny his hostile, competitive feelings by saying to Father: "I don't want to eliminate you (so I can have all of Mother's affections and attention), I really love you." As soon as he reacts in this manner to someone of the same sex, he has established a homosexual defense—a secondary type of love for Father. Under normal circumstances, all boys have genuine positive feelings for Father from infancy on that are primary and noncompetitive. The little boy usually handles his unconscious homosexual defense by repression. It remains unconscious and can surface later in life when it is expressed in derogatory words, e.g. fairies or fags. In some children, the anxiety presents itself in aesthetic, effeminate and passive behavior. Or the anxiety can be reacted to with outbursts of rage. In a number of adolescents and men that I have treated in the past, their anxiety was so great that they became overt homosexuals. As if to say to Father: "Look Dad, I'm not interested in Mother, I'm only interested in men." Another group of men handle their homosexual defense by overt Don Juan heterosexuality. They go from one affair to another, pre-or extra-maritally. In a number of situations involving infidelity, one spouse was acting out the homosexual defense of his partner. By projecting the homosexual defense onto his mate, the mate became the vehicle for the release of the anxiety. This was dramatically illustrated in one couple where the wife developed considerable guilt about her extramarital sexual acts with other men. Her guilt about her cuckoldry changed to rage when she found out she was being used by her husband (unconsciously) to neutralize his homosexual anxiety. In one situation the husband insisted his best friend stay with his wife and children while he was in Europe on a business trip.

A factor playing a conscious and/or unconscious role in women with infidelity was their competitiveness with men, who were permitted special cultural prerogatives as to sexual expression. The issue was not sensuality but envy.

In comparing the groups PS and MDS, some interesting statistics were observed. Our total sample of 231 is too small to draw any firm conclusions about infidelity and can only indicate trends. In both groups, the women infrequently engage in extramarital affairs before thirty. Perhaps they are too busy with motherhood and housekeeping. On the other hand, there is a marked decrease in infidelity in women after forty-five years of age. The men in the MDS who are of a lower social class start earlier, from the age of twenty-five on. The men in the MDS between thirty to thirty-nine are unfaithful twice as often as the men of the PS of the same age. On the other hand, the men over forty-five in the PS are about three times more unfaithful than those of similar age in the MDS. An interesting finding was that infidelity per se does not disrupt many marriages, perhaps because of the furtiveness of the unfaithfulness or its conscious or unconscious acceptance by the partner. The majority of the marriages were of more than ten years in duration before there was a complaint by one spouse about infidelity. A sharp drop in this complaint occurs after the marriage is twenty years in duration. In both groups the ordinal position of the spouses revealed the oldest male to be most unfaithful. In both groups the higher the level of education, the greater the frequency in infidelity. In both groups the presence of two or more children in the family was no deterent to infidelity.

SUMMARY

The exclusive one-to-one relationship in our Western culture is not frequently realized, since it demands that the partner contain his frustration when his sexual needs are not met regardless of the cause. The marital contract of exclusiveness is both individually and culturally determined: each individual has an "inner child" whose libidinal voice varies in regard to its need from "stroking" to sexuality; secondly, marriage is frequently necessary for the socialization of children. The couple are "in love" when they announce their "engagement." But, the ability to "make love" requires experience and the prerequisite meaningful symbiotic child-mother relationships. These early experiences with mutual warmth, tenderness and intimacy come to full fruition in the permanent relationship of marriage. Reciprocal activation of meaningful "records," where the libidinal voice of the "inner child" is prominent, results in mutual pleasure and mutual trust. The harmonious balancing of the two jukeboxes on the seesaw of living is contingent upon individual integrity and maturity.[17] In almost every marriage internal and external environmental stimuli or situations may occur which will interfere with the harmonic playing of "records" focused on current reality and may deplete the energies of one or both spouses with resultant frustration of the "inner child." For example, a number of husbands in our two series (PS and MDS) became unfaithful during the pregnancy or birth of the first child. Real trouble arises when there is lack of understanding and incorrect data processing between husband and wife. This may result in infidelity if the relationship (interpersonal system) between the spouses rests on a shaky homeostasis, and the "inner child" (intrapersonal system) may look elsewhere for another "inner child" (interpersonal and environment systems) who is more understanding and giving. The conscious or unconscious feedback to the partner of this behavior may result in revengeful retaliation later, infidelity being one manifestation. Extramarital affairs are usually part of a broader problem troubling a majority of couples coming for help with marital disharmony. In a number of instances the infidelity was purely an extension of premarital patterns. Finally, in evaluating a complaint of adultery, both conscious and unconscious factors must be considered in addition to a delusional complaint in paranoid spouses.

NOTES

1. The studies of Kinsey and his associates (A.C. Kinsey, W.B. Pomeroy, and C.E. Martin: *Sexual Behavior in the Human Male,* and A.C. Kinsey, W.B. Pomeroy, C.E. Martin, and P.H. Gebhard: *Sexual Behavior in the Human Female.* Philadelphia, Saunders, 1948 and 1953, respectively) suggest that one half of all married men and more than one-quarter of all married women have committed adultery during the course of their married life.
2. Clark E. Vincent: The physician as counselor in postmarital and extramarital pregnancies, *Med Aspects Hum Sexuality,* 1:34, 1967.
3. Sandor S. Feldman: The attraction of the "The Other Woman," *J Hill Hosp.* 13:3, 1964; and, John F. Cuber: The mistress in American society, *Med Aspects Hum Sexuality,* 3:81, 1969.
4. Robert L. DuPont, Jr. and Henry Grunebaum (Willing victims: the husbands of paranoid women, *Amer J Psychiat, 115*:151, 1968) describe a marital syndrome associated with the diagnosis of paranoid state in married women. The husbands were passive, socially isolated, and unable to directly express angry or sexual feelings. The authors divided the wife's diagnosis into three groups, defining each group.
5. An interesting research study by Robert G. Ruder (Husband-Wife dyads versus married strangers, *Family Process* 7:233, 1968) may may also be of help in understanding the frequent statement made

by a spouse, "Why can't my spouse be as nice to me as he (she) is with a stranger," and also infidelity, as stated in his concluding paragraph: "Here then (spouses treat strangers more gently and more nicely than their spouses) is the possibility of one built-in source of instability in marriage, if it is really true that people are about as responsive to strangers as spouses, and strangers are nicer to them. People would be expected to have a more pleasant time with someone other than their own husband or wife, and to do so for reasons which have *nothing to do with the particular personnel involved* [italics added]." See also Julian Roebuck and S. Lee Spray (The cocktail lounge: A study of heterosexual relations in a public organization, *Reflections* 2:10, 1967) who describe the cocktail lounge facilitating casual sexual affairs between high-status married men and young, unattached women "conducted in a context of respectability." Further, their study indicated that the activities of the cocktail lounge "does not lead to a disruption of family ties." A follow-up study, two years later, showed that none of the married men to have been divorced.

6. Vincent, *op. cit.*
7. Stanley E. Willis, II: Sexual promiscuity as a symptom of personal and cultural anxiety, *Med Aspects Hum Sexuality*, 1:16, 1967; Alexander Wolf: the problem of infidelity, in *The Marriage Relationship* (Salo Rosenbaum and Ian Alger, Eds.), New York, Basic Books, 1968, pp. 175–196; and, Gerhard Neubeck, Carol Bellville, Arthur Johnson, and Titus P. Bellville: Roundtable: the significance of extramarital sex relations, *Med Aspects Hum Sexuality*, 3:33, 1969.
8. David R. Mace (Problems of Marital Infidelity in Counseling, in *Marital and Sexual Problems*, Richard H. Klemer, Ed., New York, Free Press of Glencoe, 1961) distinguishes five different types of unfaithful husbands: libertine, bored, curious, disturbed, and sexually frustrated. See also Joshua S. Golden: What is sexual promiscuity, *Med Aspects Hum Sexuality*, 2:47, 1968; Alfred Auerback: Satyriasis and nymphomania, *Med Aspects Hum Sexuality*, 2:39, 1968; and, Judd Marmor: Sex for nonsexual reasons, *Med Aspects Hum Sexuality*, 3:8, 1969.
9. Titus P. Bellville: A psychiatrist looks at infidelity, *Med Aspects Hum Sexuality*, 1:65, 1967.
10. O. Spurgeon English: Conversation with a married woman, *Voices*, 2:65, 1966.
11. David M. Reed: What is the normal for sexual relations in marriage, *Med Aspects Hum Sexuality*, 1:6, 1967. See also Miguel Prados: Marital problems of the middle aged group, *Canad Psychiat Ass J*, 7:97, 1962 writes: "As far as the spouses sexual relationship is concerned, sexual intimacy either does not exist anymore, or is scanty and unsatisfactory. . . . Even in cases which there are no objective

reasons—and this is the most frequent case—there exists in both spouses a mutual mistrust and suspicion regarding the other's loyalty. In extreme cases it might reach the intensity of a pathological jealousy, this being much more common amongst the wives than in the husbands."

12. DuPont and Grunebaum, *op. cit.*
13. Aaron T. Beck: Sexuality and depression, *Med Aspects Hum Sexuality*, 2:44, 1968.
14. Marc H. Hollender, Lester Luborsky, and Thomas J. Scaramella (Body contact and sexual excitement, *Arch Gen Psychiat*, 20:188, 1969) suggest another type of "stroking" that could lead to infidelity when they write: "Many women may fulfill their needs or desires for body contact by using sex to entice their husbands, but some turn to other men . . . for some women the need to be held or cuddled is a major determinant of promiscuity."
15. Carlfred B. Broderick: Preadolescent sexual behavior, *Med Aspects Hum Sexuality* 2:20, 1968.
16. Richard A. Gardner (Sexual fantasies in childhood, *Med Aspects Hum Sexuality*, 3:121, 1969) expresses my opinions on the phenomena which Freud referred to as the oedipus complex: "I do not believe that oedipal *problems* arise in the healthy family where the child receives genuine affection, tenderness, and respect from both parents. There are, however, occasional manifestations of what might be called oedipal *interest*. The child may speak on occasion of marrying the the parent of the opposite sex and getting rid of his rival. . . .But I do not believe that psychologically healthy children in this period have the desire for genital-sexual experiences with the parent, nor do I believe that their sexually tinged comments are associated with sexual-genital urges. What the healthy child may on occasion want is a little more affection and attention, undiluted by the rival."
17. Leon J. Saul (*Fidelity and Infidelity*. Philadelphia, Lippincott, 1967) offers an excellent guide to the basic elements that are necessary to assure what he calls a "harmonious marriage." See also Hyman Spotnitz and Lucy Freeman: *The Wandering Husband*. Englewood Cliffs, Prentice-Hall, 1964.

X

MISCELLANEOUS MARITAL COMPLAINTS

Beginning with the eighth complaint, conflicts about children, which occurred in 13 percent of the spouses with marital discord, there was a sharp drop in the frequency of marital complaints as follows: domineering spouse (9%), suspicious spouse (8%), alcoholism (6%), and physical attack (5%).

The conflict about children was not an unexpected finding, since the change in the marital setting from an exclusive duo (one-to-one relationship between the spouses) to a trio introduced additional elements into the marital system with the creation of the family system. The change from a duo to a trio or other combinations of family structure require new orchestrations, new differences in space and time among the members of the family, and dissonant and resonant voices, e.g. a crying, colicky baby for the first six months can tax the coping ability of one or both spouses. Whereas before the arrival of the first born, only two jukeboxes had to play in harmony, the addition of a new jukebox (child) may introduce conflict as to respective roles of each partner. The new jukebox can lead to friction between the parents, e.g. regarding child-rearing practices, competitive hostilities, and emotional deprivation.

All three systems (intrapersonal, interpersonal and environmental) are involved in the marital complaint concerning children. For example, in the environmental forces the two main influences are the interference of the kinship networks and financial rearrangements—two incomes produce more money and material advantages. The following clinical extracts are illustrative:

Mr. and Mrs. Winifred: well dressed, intelligent and both college graduates, were referred for counseling because of frequent arguments about their three children. Mrs. Winifred stated that their marriage was fine until she became pregnant after two years of marriage. They had both worked and had ample funds and time for each other. "When I told Jim I was pregnant, he wanted me to get an abortion, saying we had time for children when we were thirty. He wanted me to have the baby secretly and give it away for adoption when I tried to get an abortion and failed. I wanted that baby! He blamed my stupidity for getting pregnant. Our next child, also not planned, was less of a problem as Jim had resigned himself to his responsibilities at that point. I love my children and Jim never really wanted to do anything with and for them. This has led to frequent quarrels. When he would come home in the evening, I would find myself resenting them too, because of what he seemed to feel. My talking to a lawyer suddenly made him realize how important they are to his life."

Mr. Winifred: "My marriage has been one frustration after another. Never in the marriage has either one of us really been willing to give of ourselves. Throughout our marriage Mabel's lack of self-discipline has bothered me a great deal. She wanted children but she doesn't keep the house clean or even neat. She often watchs TV, often late into the night, and then is unable to get up and make breakfast for the children, let alone for me. Another point of great annoyance was her inability to discipline the children. Because of poor training in this area, the children were often out of control and then she would unmercifully scream at them. I was primarily interested in disciplining them to the point of rigid obedience so that I could control them easily so that they would not bother me. I was very harsh in my disciplining of them and she would get furious at me, and we would really argue. I can now see how all this influenced our oldest. He is a very sensitive child and at times appears withdrawn and emotionally deprived. I blame myself for much of this because when he was small I resented his presence and blamed him for my own frustrations in having to give up some of the things I was planning to get, especially a boat. At the time of his birth I did not want to be a parent and have always felt burdened by the children."

In another couple, the bitter quarreling about the children propelled them into marital therapy:

Mr. and Mrs. Wilhelmena were referred by her lawyer whom she had consulted about a divorce: "I'm unable to take any more of these bitter and silly quarrels about how to raise the children, his inconsistency regarding their discipline, his anger and pouting about how to raise them religiously and, to add salt to the wound, the influence of my mother-in-law. She considers my family, my husband and children as much hers as they are mine. She is not malicious about this, but when she visits, and this is too often, she takes over my house and much more. I have the feeling that it is not my home or creation. When I discuss these things with my husband, he explodes."

Mr. Wilhelmena, a quiet mannered, well-dressed, well-controlled professional man, stated he wanted to save the marriage, although their last quarrel about the children was just too much. When she threw the casserole of creamed lobster at me, I yelled back and should have clobbered her, but instead I cleaned up the mess. My wife was Catholic and I was Jewish when we married. We were married in a Roman Catholic Church, and I went along with that. When our first child was born, Nancy had him baptized without consulting me. This fried me, but I didn't say anything. Our children have been the primary force keeping our marriage together. I don't know what she has against my mother, who is always available as a baby sitter and who would do anything for them. I have always loved my children as individuals, and have had great pride in them since infancy. As children, I have been somewhat less attached to them. I was not prepared for their arrival. The timing of their conceptions was largely a matter of their mother's choice. She started haranguing me about having a baby during our honeymoon. I resisted on the basis that we were not financially ready and had plenty of time to start a family. She had no religious objection to using contraceptive measures. I wanted to put aside money for a house, furniture, travel and getting to know each other in the context of the marriage setting. After we spent most of our savings on furniture and moved into a rented house, her requests for a baby became more frequent. After a year of repeated requests for a baby, all her college friends had babies but us, and since our sexual relations had decreased to once or twice a week, I agreed partly on the basis of having the prospect of increasing the frequency and partly because it made me feel badly to continue refusing her. She has never let me forget that she had to wait a year to get pregnant, at the old age of twenty-two. At no time did I have or express the desire to have the baby. This has always infuriated Nancy. The three other children happened accidently on purpose, as a result of improper contraceptive measures on her part (note how he is playing the game of projection: "If It Weren't For Her"). Although I held the financial purse strings, she held the sexual purse strings, and during the pregnancies I could have sex whenever I wanted to. Her response was that she was sorry I did not want to have the children, but that *she did* and would not go along with waiting. As a result, I have been less than an ideal father as the children came along. I felt that they were forced on me, and I felt some initial resentment in each case. Nancy was interested in having babies but not in taking care of them, according to my standards. With each child I end up bathing them at night, feeding them, playing with them and setting limits in their behavior. This has led to innumerable quarrels."

The next marital complaint, the "Pygmalion syndrome" is characterized by one spouse acting in a domineering, depreciating and controlling manner toward his partner. This complaint occurred in about 9 percent of the spouses. The partner in this type of marital relationship reacted in any of a number of ways, e.g. alcoholism, "romancing" the charge account cards or a "sitdown strike." Not infrequently the attempt to mold the future spouse into a preconceived ideal partner occurs during the court-ship and frequently results in progressive disharmony after marriage. The following clinical vignette is typical:

Mr. and Mrs. Vivian were married for fifteen years and were childless. Mr. Vivian complained: "We are raising hell with each others nerves. I recently blew up when she had too much to drink at a dinner party."

Mr. Vivian was a tall, well-built man with a goatee, who always spoke slowly and deliberately. It seemed as though he habitually chose his words carefully and frequently paused for short periods while searching for the precise word he wanted to express his thoughts. His manner was pleasant and he seemed to be searching for answers to what may be causing the problems.

Casually he expressed the belief that he might be in error in his actions toward his wife. He spontaneously excluded sex or extramarital interests as being elements of their problem and prefered to label the discontent as related to apparent resentment, which he traced to having seen his wife drunk on several occasions. "I have been accused of being a perfectionist. In my own mind, no! But everything has to be just right. I have to be immaculately dressed and like my wife the same way. A straight line has to be straight. When I was a kid, I was taught to cook. I enjoy cooking. A sore spot has been because she has no desire to cook or keep house. I sit in the kitchen and watch my wife cook and add condiments and I enjoy it. She resents it if I make comments. But right is right."

Mrs. Vivian was a tall, slender woman with an intense businesslike demeanor. She spoke with concern of the difficulties which had arisen between her and her husband over the past two years. Her chief complaint was that he tended to criticize her household operations like an efficiency expert. He feels everything I do should be perfect. In the kitchen he will stand and count my steps and correct me if I'm not logical and precise. He can't stand doors left ajar. Jim has certain people he thinks are just right and thinks I should be like them, like his sister who has no children and has nothing to do but run a house. When I am in the kitchen, he watches the way I prepare food, whether I gently prepare the lettuce for salad, how I add the condiments, until I could go crazy. His constant telling me what to do has made me more nervous recently. I drink too much—at times in the past year or so. When I do, I can tell Jim things that normally I couldn't, because at that time he won't say anything but listen. He thinks I am an alcoholic. I drink too much at times but not consistently. I've always held responsible jobs. I used to play golf. I like sports, but Jim is always criticizing my game. He does everything to perfection. You name it, and he can do it with precision, and well!"

This couple illustrates the reaction of a spouse to her Pygmalion-acting husband who could only express her resentment while under the influence of liquor. Her therapy also revealed the use of alcohol to contain her hostility and neutralize her anxiety.

Another example was in a couple who had come for premarital counseling, refused to accept therapy and later returned for marital counseling. The complaints again presented were similar to those originally stated, except the content was different though the relationship had remained the same. The husband this time was the angry spouse instead of the angry suitor:

"I don't know why Tim is so angry at me and wanting to call off the wedding. All my suggestions have been for his benefit. Early in our courtship he would visit me twice a week but on other nights if I chanced to call after supper I would find that he had already gone to bed at 7 o'clock. He seemed perennially tired. In fact, I gave him a copy of *How Never to Be Tired.* He resents my correcting his table manners, which are very poor. I told him to chew with his mouth closed, to handle his silver in an acceptable manner, and not to place his napkin under his chin but on his lap. I learned also that he was averse to baths and toothbrushing, and since he perspires profusely, I suggested it was quite important that he bathe daily. I encouraged him to start college in the evenings. He went back to school with much protest. When he got his first grades, I pointed out he could have done better. That really made him mad."

And so they were married and lived unhappily until they returned for further help with their marriage. This time the criticisms focused primarily about his relationship to the children, his attitude about his household chores, e.g. the grass was not green enough, the hedges unevenly shaped, and so on.

A surprising finding in the seventy-eight spouses complaining of a critical partner was that the frequency was about four times more common among the couples in the PS. Although the content of the complaints in all of them varied, the discordant relationship was the same and usually was present in varying degrees during the courtship.

The tenth most common marital complaint involved an unjust accusation of infidelity by a suspicious spouse and occurred in about 8 percent of the spouses. One common form, the "district attorney (DA) syndrome," and which we have previously reported[1,2] is described in the following vignette:

Mr. Virginia angrily stated: "For the past year our relationship has been somewhat rocky. My work requires considerable travel. Before, during, and after each trip Jane makes constant references to infidelity, potential infidelity, how my time is spent, how the money is spent and on whom, whether the time and money was necessary, what time I leave to make my calls, what time I return and why, where I eat and with whom. I am facing a problem which to me is utterly fantastic and one I never had to face before. It is destroying what by all odds should be a very happy relationship. Now it seems I must spend most of my time proving that I have done nothing wrong when I am not with her."

Mrs. Virginia, with a resigned attitude: "I would like to have an understanding with John that our love is strong enough not to waver and that we won't ever be unfaithful to each other. The first year of our courtship was very smooth. He was fun to talk with, we liked doing the same things and got along well. But in the past year, since he began traveling, he is not confiding in me about past or present family affairs or about his business trips—where he went for dinner, his time schedules, who he saw while out of town or in town, no communication. Questions concerning my suspicions of other women seem to set him off violently. Often he strikes at me viciously, then says he is sorry. I have found lipstick on his shirts and handkerchiefs and blonde hair on his jacket. He claims they are mine. He gets angry when I question him and refuses to discuss it."

This couple is very typical of many married couples coming for help with the same type of marital complaint. Usually they have been fighting for years about suspected infidelity. Often a spouse will state that the repeated questioning is driving him insane, and that the partner is like a "district attorney." This type of complaint is related to the condition of pathological jealousy.

The eleventh marital complaint of alcoholism occurred in about 6 percent of the spouses. Alcoholism is classified psychiatrically as a personality disorder, but in the context of marriage it is best visualized as a role in the game which Eric Berne[3] labels "Alcoholic." He describes it in its full flower as a five-handed game. The central role is that of Alcoholic, who is "it," while the chief supporting role is that of the Persecutor, typically played by a member of the opposite sex. The Rescuer is often the family doctor, a clergyman or a good friend; the Patsy is often played by the alcoholic's mother, who gives him money and sympathizes with him; and the Agitator is the good guy who offers a drink without even being asked for one. In marriage the partner may play at least three supporting roles. At midnight the partner may be the Patsy, undressing the spouse and getting him into bed. On the next day, the partner can be both the Persecutor, berating the spouse for vile behavior, and the Rescuer, pleading with the spouse to stop drinking.

Various studies on alcoholism have noted the different meanings which can be attached to alcoholic patterns of drinking.[4] In our society different values and attitudes are attached to alcoholism, depending on social classes, religion or ethnical grouping. Lovald and Neuwirth[5] present the "notion that drinking constitutes role behavior. That is, the drinking of alcoholic beverages is learned like any other social role. Thus it includes more or less definite role expectations and entails the application of prescriptive and proscriptive sanctions to the role player who does not meet these expectations." They analyzed the research on alcoholism, focusing on two issues, the meaning of drinking in different social situations, and "the drinking role and the drinker's self-concept in situations where others define him as an alcoholic or problem drinker."

The evaluation of the complaint of alcoholism necessitates study of all three systems: intrapersonal, interpersonal and environmental. Intrapersonally, alcohol has both a physiological and psychological effect. Physiologically, alcohol acts as a depressant upon the central nervous system, affecting the more highly developed portions of the brain first—the neocortex. With increasing consumption of alcohol and the raising of the level of alcohol in the blood stream, those parts of the brain involved with sensation, movement and balance are involved. As Ewing[6] aptly puts it: "Alcohol has been used as a *social lubricant* [italics added], tranquilizer, and an anti-anxiety chemical for thousands of years." The "parental" voices of the records are mediated in those rostral parts of the brain which appear most sensitive to alcohol. Thus depending on the idiosyncratic reaction of the individual to alcohol and the level of alcohol in the circulating blood, there can be decreased self-awareness, less self-criticism with increased self-esteem, resulting in improved interpersonal transactions. The interplay of the interpersonal and environmental systems is carefully explored in the article by Lovald and Nuewirth.[7] They point out drinking as role behavior and some consequences in relation to "social control and self-concept." The self-concept is a psychological manifestation of the intrapersonal system of the individual. The "exposed drinker" of the skid row stereotype and the lower-class drinking styles are more visible than the "shielded drinker" of the middle and upper classes. Further, where one drinks, i.e. taverns versus private clubs or cocktail lounges[8] vis-à-vis home, and why one drinks, e.g. if the drinking is seen as self-controlled for the purpose of winning the esteem of others, can involve both interpersonal and environmental systems. Recent studies on alcoholism, e.g. treatment of the nonalcoholic spouse, can alter one's attitude in a positive direction in treating alcoholics, as the following clinical extract shows:

Mrs. Viola was referred for marital counseling because of her husband's excessive drinking. She had consulted her lawyer and had obtained separate maintenance. It was at this point that her husband had promised to stop drinking and would do anything for a reconciliation.[9] Mrs. Viola was very depressed during the first interview and cried frequently as she gave her tale of woe: "I am married to a devil, capable of anything under the sun. I am nuts to have stayed married to him this long. When he goes on a binge, he just takes off and leaves us without food or money. Then he returns, all remorse, begs my forgiveness, promises never to drink again, and I believe him." Although Mr. Viola had agreed to see me, I suggested that Mrs. Viola, alone, have treatment with me. She was seen sixty-four times, each session lasting forty-five minutes, over a period of ten months. Five years later, during which time her husband remained sober, I received a letter stating her husband was stable, sober, sweet and considerate.

The last complaint, twelfth in frequency, although there were other complaints in lesser amounts, was that of actual physical attack by a partner. This complaint occurred in about 5 percent of the spouses and was equally distributed in both the PS and MDS and with about the same frequency between the sexes.[10] As expected, only ten men complained of being attacked by their spouses in contrast to fifty-eight women who complained of physical abuse (see Table VIII). A variety of psychodynamic and interpersonal patterns were present in the spouses complaining of physical abuse. Surprisingly, there was no correlation between educational level of the partner and this complaint, e.g., one man, a college graduate and president of his corporation, repeatedly struck his wife during bitter quarreling about the disciplining of their teen-age son. A noninfrequent cause of physical attack on a spouse was the result of a suspicious spouse provoking her partner by incessant questioning about alleged infidelity as seen occasionally in the "district attorney syndrome."

Often alcoholism of one spouse produced both bitter quarreling and assault, either from the spouse under the influence of excessive drinking or against the inebriated partner. Rarely, a spouse may react violently due to excessive irritability, as seen in the following extract:

Mr. Victoria: "I am always in a hurry. I'm impatient with her. So I nag her to have things ready when I want them. All my life I've been on edge. I snap at people. My heavy work schedule is the biggest cause of our problems. I'm so tense at night she has to rub my back before I can go to sleep. I get about four hours of sleep at night, I am tired all the time. When we argue about my working so hard and long hours, I get angry and strike her. Then I feel badly. I work full time and after work I have my own contracting business. I want to get ahead, eventually be able to give up my job and be my own boss. I am doing this only for the children and her."

Mrs. Victoria: "He doesn't seem to respect my beliefs and views. I think the arguments bother me more than the beatings. He is in business with his uncle at night and holds down a full-time job as supervisor during the daytime. When I complain that we can get along nicely on his salary, he accuses me of not wanting him to be independent. When I complain he is never at home, that the children do not have a father, and I, no husband, he gets mad. One word leads to another and many times he strikes me and then is full of remorse the next hour."

A frequent cause of a violent argument ending in a physical assault results when the husband reacts with panic to the request of his partner for a divorce. In some of these situations the wife has the unconscious meaning of an alter phallus and the threat of divorce is unconsciously equated to castration.[11]

In this chapter, five specific types of marital complaints were presented: conflicts about children, domineering spouses, suspicious spouses, excessive drinking, and physical assault. Although there were other complaints occasionally verbalized, all the complaints described in Chapters IV and X, inclusive, regardless of frequency, were examples of *content*, the real issue that needed exploring was that of *relationship*.

NOTES

1. Bernard L. Greene and Noel Lustig: Contraindications to marriage, *Med Aspects Hum Sexuality*, 2:4, 1968.

2. Philip Polatin: Jealousy: *Med Aspects Hum Sexuality*, 2:6, 1968.

3. Eric Berne: *Games People Play*. New York, Grove Press, 1964. See

also Claude M. Steiner (The alcoholic game, *Transactional Analysis Bull*, 7:6, 1968), who elaborates upon Berne's game of "Alcoholic" by categorizing three subtypes: Drunk and Proud, Lush, and Wino.

4. D.W. Pittman and C.R. Snyder (Eds.): *Society, Culture, and Drinking Patterns*. New York, Wiley, 1962.

5. Keith Lovald and Gertrud Neuwirth: Exposed and shielded drinking, *Arch Gen Psychiat, 19*:95, 1968.

6. John A. Ewing: Alcohol, sex, and marriage, *Med Aspects Hum Sexuality, 2*:43, 1968. In this excellent article he also gives a "good working definition (of the alcoholic) as someone whose uncontrolled excessive drinking is harmful to himself, his marriage, his family, or his work. He is unable to do anything about the problem, and in many instances he is not able to recognize it."

7. Lovald and Neuwirth, *op. cit.*

8. Julian Roebuck and S. Lee Spray: The cocktail lounge: A study of heterosexual relations in a public organization, *Reflections, 2*:10, 1967.

9. Martin H. Stein: The unconscious meaning of the marital bond, in *Neurotic Interaction in Marriage*, (Victor W. Eisenstein, Ed.), New York, Basic Books, 1956, pp. 65–80. Also Shirley Gehrke and Martin Kirschenbaum (Survival patterns in family conjoint therapy, *Family Process, 6*:67, 1967) discuss the survival myth that I have also found to be a factor in some individuals who react to the request for divorce with panic.

10. John E. Mayer (People's imagery, *Family Process, 6*:27, 1967) states in a footnote: "In her recent study of blue collar marriages, Mirra Komarovsky notes that violent quarrels, at times accompanied by beatings, are mentioned by 17% of the high school men and by 27% of the less educated" (*Blue-Collar Marriage*, New York, Random House, 1962, p. 195). Our figure, although relatively high, is perhaps an understatement. See the research study of Kaspar D. Naegele: Some problems in the study of hostility and aggression in middle-class American families, in *A Modern Introduction to the Family* (Norman W. Bell and Ezra F. Vogel, Eds.). New York, The Free Press, 1960, p. 427. He suggests that while mothers will tell of extreme annoyance, and "blow up" at their children, "it is, however, very difficult to get these mothers to admit the same behavior vis-à-vis their husbands." See also George Levinger: Marital Satisfaction and Complaint. Paper presented at 1965 Annual Meeting of American Orthopsychiatric Association, New York. And in Notes and Comments, *Amer J Psychotherapy, 21*:837, 1967, he quotes the FBI Uniform Crime Reports, which estimates 10,920 murders committed in the United States in 1966: "Killings within the family made up 29% of all murders in 1966: over one-half of these involved spouse killing spouse (mostly men killing women)."

11. Stein, *op. cit.*

XI

WHY ARE YOU *NOW* SEEKING HELP?

The question "Why are you *now* seeking help?" is a recent addition to the BMQ. It pinpoints the reason the couple is consulting the therapist. Furthermore, it helps the couple to crystallize their thinking in their request for help. For the therapist it focuses in on the "here and now" as to the precipitating crisis.

Table XVI lists the nine most common reasons in item 9 of the BMQ in order of decreasing frequency.[1] In 35 percent or about one third of the couples, divorce proceedings had started, one spouse had actually threatened divorce "either we see a psychiatrist or a lawyer," or the partners were actually separated. In about 15 percent of the couples, the reason was about equally divided in an acute crisis involving a child,[2] a suicidal threat, or an acute alcoholic situation. In 10 percent of the couples, the discovery of adultery on the part of a partner led to a crisis in the marriage. In about 40 percent of the couples, the request for help was to improve the marriage. Many of these marriages could be classified as "durable incompatible."

TABLE XVI
REASONS FOR SEEKING THERAPY

	Percentage
Possibility of divorce	25
Improvement of marriage	24
Constant quarreling	14
Infidelity	10
Separated—attempting reconciliation	7
Acute crisis involving a child	6
Alcoholism	5
Suicidal threat	5
Suspicious spouse causing partner to threaten separation	3
Others	1

Although it is twenty-five years since Erich Lindemann's[3] classic article on acute grief introduced crisis concepts, it has been only in the last decade that crises studies have received prominence in the literature of the behavioral sciences. As Table XVI clearly demonstrates, at least 50 percent of the couples were in an acute crisis. A crisis results from a combination of factors: maturational, and situational, threatening external events. As Lucille Austin[4] cogently writes:

Rooted squarely in psychoanalytic personality theory, crisis theory uses psychoanalytic insights in combination with selected social science concepts to extend and enrich the concept of the person-situation configuration as the unit of attention in psychosocial treatment. . . . *These formulations describe the dynamics for change that are mobilized under stress and that are more accessible to intervention at the point the client comes for help than they are likely to be at a later point* [italics added].

Gerald Caplan[5] writes: "The crises of life, precipitated by temporarily insoluble problems, are way stations at each of which there is the opportunity for learning new problem-solving skills."

Building on Freud's theories of psychosexual development, Erikson[6] developed a theory of psychosocial development based on the gradual unfolding of the personality through phase-specific crises precipitated by both environmental and societal pressures and the person's readiness and capacity to deal with these pressures. Otto Pollak[7] extended the theories of Freud, Erikson, Hartmann[8] and others and presented a framework of value in dealing especially with the family. Neo-Freudians, especially Sandor Rado among others, have differentiated between the adaptive process of *coping* with a crisis and *defensive* Freudian *mechanisms* as crystallized by Anna Freud[9] in her classic monograph.

The psychic activities of the adaptive process has been defined as coping behavior and consist of all the strategies utilized by a person to deal with a current threat to his psychosocial stability. Thus coping is a universal and more inclusive name than defense and not associated with the negative implications of the term defense. The important differentiation between coping and defense is that there are adaptive phenomena which serve no defensive purpose. On the other hand, the psychoanalytic usage of the term defense generally connotes two functions: (1) restraining and containing the instinctual drives of the id, and (2) serving adaptation to the environment. Freud would certainly have been interested in and perhaps incorporated into his writings recent information from ethology,[10] e.g. imprinting, which pointed out the interrelationships between learning and instinct.

The adaptive process of coping behavior is a reaction to a crisis and consists of intrapersonal defensive responses, which protect the person from disruptive levels of anxiety, as objectively evaluated from the degree of comfort shown by the individual and defensive responses directed either toward the interpersonal or environmental systems and judged for effectiveness in social terms. The relationship between the intrapersonal defensive aspects of coping and the total coping process is a very intimate mixture. Thus if the relationship is a constructive one, the individual can freely focus on the current crisis. On the other hand, if the intrapersonal defensive responses are inadequate, the individual will be overwhelmed with anxiety. Another destructive relationship occurs when the adaptive coping defenses become so distracting to the individual that he is unable to concentrate effectively on his external problem. Thus coping maneuvers can be scaled on a continuum with an indeterminate range of defensive strength in the center which permits optimum coping, whereas deviations at either end of this continuum would have unfavorable effects on coping behavior. Finally, I have found Reuben Hill's[11] truncated form of a roller coaster very useful in explaining the adjustment to a crisis. Thus each crisis results in disintegration with the usual phases of recovery and reintegration. I have modified his profile to include three levels of reorganization: regression, fixation, or progression. The use of the angle of recovery has been very useful clinically when patients complain of impatience (see Fig. 3). The concept of crisis resolution as formulated by Gerald Caplan[12] and presented by Lydia Rapoport[13] involves "correct cognitive perception" of the problem, "management of affect" through awareness of feelings and their discharge, and develop-

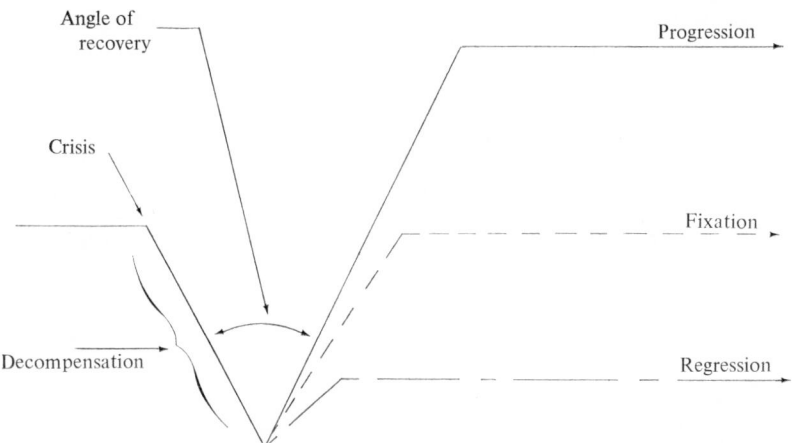

Figure 3. Adjustment to a crisis (after Ruben Hill).

ment of patterns of seeking and using help" that is action oriented.

Erikson's[14] theory of psychosocial development describes the relationship of the individual to the interpersonal and environmental systems and the functions of the ego in the intrapersonal system with respect to the individual's adaptive processes. He examines so-called growth crises through phase-specific stages in the individual's development of interpersonal relationships. Erikson, influenced by his psychoanalytic background, correlates the psychosocial crises of various ages with the particular psychosexual problems of the stages of instinctual development. He states that each individual solves the problem of adaptation in his own unique way. For example, in infancy the psychosexual adaptive problems center on the oral zone and the incorporative function; its resolution confronts the infant with the dilemma of trust versus mistrust in relation to the mother. The problem of trust versus mistrust, in Erikson's theory of psychosocial development, represents a universal adaptive crisis. According to Erikson, each individual develops through an unique innate maturational design. He has extended the study of the adaptive processes beyond the early and adolescent stages of development to encompass the entire human life cycle.

While psychoanalysis clarifies the limits of the individual's adaptive potential at different phases of psychosexual development, the theories of adaptation help to comprehend the impact of the interpersonal and environmental systems on the developing psyche. The concepts developed by Hartmann[15] and his collaborators and Erikson supplement each other. Hartmann *et al.* hypothecated the role of the *autonomous functions of the ego* in the determination of personality and neurosis. Hartmann suggested that the individual has an innate capacity to adapt to an "average expectable environment," and Erikson executed with detail this idea with his concepts of mutuality and "cogwheeling" between generations. His concept of cogwheeling is a variant of Therese Benedek's[16] thesis of symbiosis—a sense of mutuality that develops between the mother and child. (The subject of object relationships will be further discussed in Ch. XIV under the subject of remarriage). The mother and child each exercise adaptive functions in relation to one another, specific to the needs of each at his phase-specific crisis in his respective life cycle. Thus the generations are cogwheeled together because of their mutual needs. The concept of autonomous ego functions elaborated by Hartmann and his co-workers is related to Erikson's thesis of particular modes of functioning. He describes how a characteristic function of a specific body zone becomes separated from that zone and then functions autonomously. For example, the process of incorporation is originally oral, but the infant gradually, as a result of interpersonal and environmental influences, soon "takes in" in other symbolic manners. This change in the function in incorporation and response to multiple external influences results in variations in cultural patterns and resultant diversity in marital patterns.

The marriage therapist, if possible, should keep abreast of the studies from others in the helping professions.[17] Maturational crises are experienced by all individuals as part of the life cycle and are characterized by expectable behavioral, cognitive and affectional reactions. For example, the normal hostile, competitive reactions of the child to the parent of the same sex, the complex biopsychosocial reactions at puberty, the "stormy decade of adolescence," the "getting married phase," and so on, all represent maturational crises that must be mastered before the individual can proceed for further development. On the other hand, the differentiation between maturational and situational crises at times is difficult. Thus the mourning process following death, desertion or divorce represent situational crises, and puberty constitutes a maturational crisis; but the birth of the first child has both maturational and situational elements. The combined impact of a situational crisis superimposed on a maturational crisis can often result in a major crisis, for example, where the birth of the first child was the beginning of alcoholism in the father. A not uncommon finding in women following the delivery of their first child is the so-called "baby blues." I have found the studies of Rhona Rapoport[18] on the "critical transition points in the *normal, expectable* development of the family life cycle" of great value.

Finally, in understanding the maturational and situational crises in marriage, the observations of Otto Pollak[19] are extremely valuable in dealing with marital disharmony. He uses sociological and psychoanalytic concepts to characterize various forms of marital relationships and suggests "types of dysfunction between the marriage partners and their possible causation in terms of secondary gains in the realm of psychodynamics and of unresolved problems created by social change." His characterization gives equal attention to the perceptual principle of figure (intrapersonal system) and his background (interpersonal and environmental systems). Thus he is fully aware of the psychodynamics of intrapsychic conflict, unconscious motivation and ambivalence as well as interpersonal and environmental influences of transactional patterns, group processes and social roles involved in social change. As an outstanding sociologist, he correctly conceives of the family as a social organization that goes through four phases of development in its life cycle, with differences in "life tasks" (crises) at each phase. The first phase reflects the effort of the newlyweds to form a new family system distinct from their background families;[20] the second phase is that of child bearing and child rearing, the third is where the children leave home—this is referred to in the literature as the "empty nest" syndrome,[21] and, the last phase is again a dyadic one, and finally one spouse is the survivor. Pollak suggests that at every phase there exist different dimensions of complementary need that serve current satisfaction and preparation for the future. He classifies the dimensions of need complementarity in four areas:

1. Interpersonal reorientation.
2. Sexual sphere.
3. Economic sphere.
4. Ego strengthening.[22]

The dimensions of need complementarity vary in importance as the family passes from one developmental phase to another. Each phase is separated from another by a "crisis of transition." This systematization follows Gerald Caplan's conception of the strategic meaning of crisis for development.[23] Pollak next discusses how the interaction patterns can be violated in various ways, resulting in the production of crises, which result in marital discord. A careful reading of his essay[24] will be most rewarding for every therapist.

NOTES

1. David A. Hamburg and John E. Adams in an outstanding article on coping behavior in crisis situations list seventeen examples of common stressful experiences that have been emphasized in recent research and clinical discussions (A perspective on coping behavior, *Arch Gen Psychiat, 17*:277, 1967). Further, Herbert C. Schulberg and Alan Sheldon in surveying the literature on crisis have been "struck by the arbitrary, varying, and even elusive qualities currently associated with the term crisis. . . ." They raise many challenging questions about the characteristics of crisis (The probability of crisis and strategies for preventive intervention, *Arch Gen Psychiat, 18*:533, 1968). On the other hand, Arden A. Flint, Jr. (Crisis in marriage— reification or reality?, *Amer J Orthopsychiat, 38*:560, 1968) in a philosophical existential article questions whether there are marital crises as categories. He uses the vaudevillian two-man horse costume to describe the marital relationship.

Crises are realities not categories, although frequently the marital disharmony centers around content when it is the relationship between the spouses that need the therapeutic focus. Crises are realities when the therapist is confronted with a serious marital problem that involves the interplay of three systems, with their numerous subsystems, all transacting with each other in cyclical feedback. Also see Carl A. Whitaker and Milton H. Miller: A reevaluation of "Psychiatric Help" when divorce impends, *Amer J Psychiat, 126*:611, 1969.

2. Daniel R. Miller and Jack C. Westman (Family teamwork and psychotherapy, *Family Process, 5*:49, 1966) describe their studies with children with underachievement producing an acute marital crisis.
3. Erich Lindemann: Symptomatology and management of acute grief, *Amer J Psychiat, 101*:141, 1944. It should be noted that Anton T. Boisen anticipated crises studies almost a decade before Lindemann's classic paper when he wrote: "He succeeds in affecting a synthesis between the *crisis experience* [italics added] and his subsequent life which enables him to grow in the direction of inner unification and social adaptation on a basis conceived as universal." (*The Exploration of the Inner World*. Chicago, Willett, Clark & Co., 1936, p. ix).
4. Lucille N. Austin: Foreword, in *Crisis Intervention: Selected Readings* (Howard J. Parad, Ed.). New York, Family Service Association of America (44 East 23rd St., 10010), 1965. This book is another must reading for all therapists. For a six-month follow-up of 150 family crisis therapy cases, see Donald G. Langsley, Kalman Flomenhaft, and Pavel Machotka: Follow-up evaluation of family crisis therapy, *Amer J Orthopsychiat, 39*:753, 1969.
5. Gerald Caplan: *An Approach to Community Mental Health*. New York, Grune & Stratton, 1961.
6. Erik H. Erikson: Identity and the life cycle. *Psychol Issues, 1*:1, 1959.
7. Otto Pollak: Sociological and Psychoanalytic Concepts in Family Diagnosis, in *The Psychotherapies of Marital Disharmony* (B.L. Greene, Ed.). New York, MacMillan, 1965, pp. 15–26.
8. Heinz Hartmann: *Ego Psychology and the Problem of Adaptation*. New York, Int. Univs. Press, 1958.
9. Anna Freud: *The Ego and the Mechanisms of Defence*. New York, Int. Univs. Press, 1946.
10. Leonard S. Zegans: An appraisal of ethological contributions to psychiatric theory and research, *Amer J Psychiat, 124*:729, 1967. The author believes that ethology may make its most important contribution to the study of man by facilitating the accurate and rich description of how people communicate motivational and affective messages to one another in a natural rather than an experimental setting. The article contains an excellent number of references.
11. Reuben Hill: Generic Features of Families Under Stress. In *Crisis*

Intervention: Selected Readings (Howard J. Parad, Ed.) New York Family Service Association of America, 1965, pp. 32–52.

12. Gerald Caplan: Patterns of parental response to the crisis of premature birth. *Psychiatry, 23:*365, 1960.

13. Lydia Rapoport: The state of crisis: Some Theoretical Considerations. In *Crisis Intervention: Selected Readings* (Howard J. Parad, Ed.) New York, Family Service Association of America, 1965, pp. 22–31.

14. Erikson, *op. cit.*

15. Heinz Hartmann and Ernst Kris: The genetic approach in psychoanalysis. *Psychoanal Study Child, 1:*11, 1945. This was the opening article in the first volume of an annual book under Anglo-American cooperation that was to become a must reading for all professionals interested in the study of the child. See also Heinz Hartmann, Ernst Kris, and Rudolph M. Lowenstein: Comments on the formation of psychic structure, *Psychoanal Study Child, 2:*11, 1946.

16. Therese Benedek: The psychosomatic implications of the primary unit: mother-child. *Amer J Orthopsychiat, 19:*642, 1949.

17. Donald G. Langsley, Frank S. Pittman III, Paval Machotka, and Kalman Flomenhaft (Family crisis therapy--results and implications, *Family Process, 7:*145–158, 1968) have attempted a classification of crises: "(1) The "bolt from the blue" crisis, (2) The caretaker crisis, (3) The developmental crisis, (4) The exacerbation crisis." For example, "The 'bolt from the blue' views the unexpected external hazard as the important contribution; given a strong enough external shock, any family or person will capitulate." The authors are not satisfied with this classification. See also Judd Marmor: The crisis of middle age, *Psychiat Dig, 29:*17, 1968.

18. Rhona Rapoport: Normal crises, family structure, and mental health. *Family Process, 2:*68, 1963.

19. Otto Pollak: A family diagnosis model. Proceedings of the conference on family diagnosis. *Social Serv Rev, 34:*19, 1960.

20. Harold L. Raush, Wells Goodrich, and John D. Campbell in an interesting article (Adaptation to the first years of marriage, *Psychiatry, 26:*368, 1963) present a viewpoint of evaluating initial marital adaptation within an open structure to illustrate modes of communication: "such as developing modes for resolving conflicts and making decisions, become particularly salient in cultures which foster an open marital structure. In contrast to a closed marital structure, in which coping involves an adaptation to what *is* and the primary conflicts and resolutions are *intrapersonal,* the open marital structure requires working out what *is* to *be* and the primary conflicts and esolutions are *interpersonal* processes required for defining the development of the dyadic system." Another pragmatic use of crisis intervention has been found in the treatment of psychosocial crises in the

emergency service at the Massachusetts General Hospital in Boston. Frankel and associates have found that: "A flexible and multidisciplinary approach to these problems is considered to be the most effective means of handling them and of applying principles of crisis intervention." See Fred H. Frankel, Morris E. Chafetz, and Howard T. Blane: Treatment of psycho-social crises in the emergency service of a general hospital. *JAMA, 195*:626, 1966; and Paul Glasser in (Family equilibrium during psychotherapy, *Family Process, 2*:245, 1963) has provided an excellent bibliography on family crisis studies, marital adjustment studies, family development theory, role theory, and social psychiatry.

21. Alvin I. Goldfarb: Marital problems of older persons, in *The Marriage Relationship* (Salo Rosenbaum and Ian Alger, Eds.). New York, Basic Books, 1968, p. 109. He writes: "The departure of children 'from the nest' may improve good marriages. On the other hand, it may accentuate the defects of bad marriages as the common interest in child rearing is lost, or a scapegoat escapes and the husband and wife are thrown back upon each other for emotional gratification, companionship, diversion, and purposeful activity." See also Eva Y. Deykin, Shirley Jacobson, Gerald Klerman, and Najda Solomon: The empty nest: psychosocial aspects of conflict between depressed women and their grown children, *Amer J Psychiat, 122*:1422, 1966; and Roy D. Waldman: Neurosis and the social structure, *Amer J Orthopsychiat, 38*:92, 1968.

22. Otto Pollak: *Social Serv Rev, 34*:19, 1960.

23. Gerald Caplan, *op. cit.*

24. Otto Pollak: In *The Psychotherapies of Marital Disharmony* (B. L. Greene, Ed.). New York, Macmillan, 1965, p. 15–26.

XII

PREVIOUS HELP RECEIVED AND QUESTION OF SUICIDE

The tenth item on the BMQ (see Appendix) deals with the subject of previous help received by the couple. Frequently information is obtained as to therapy in regard to a personal, emotional problem, either antedating the marriage, during the current marriage, or following a previous marriage. Information from the question of previous help received has been valuable in four areas:

1. Motivation—Whether the couple was aware of conflict in their marriage, and when they first sought help for their problem.
2. Type of help received—This gives a clue as to whether the couple want directive or explorative techniques.
3. Who gave the previous help—If the CDD reveals that the marital problem is a symptom of a disturbed personality, then referral back to the previous therapist is possible if an earlier good relationship existed.
4. Another dimension of information about the spouses from a previous therapist. (It is important to obtain a written permission from the couple before contacting the therapist involved.)

Table XVII presents the data on previous help received by the couples of both series.

In one half of the couples in the PS, no help had been sought previously, in contrast to one sixth in the MDS. Women sought help with their marriage more often than their husbands. An interesting finding was the failure of previous help to reequilibrate the marriage.

TABLE XVII
PREVIOUS HELP RECEIVED FOR THE MARRIAGE*

	PS	MDS
None	248	42
Psychiatrist	138	72
Clergyman	40	68
Physician	36	33
Social worker	24	37
Psychologist	20	22
Counselor	14	29
Lawyer	10	3

* Note: some couples sought therapy from several sources.

The eleventh item on the BMQ concerning suicide, the most recent addition to the questionnaire, is of extreme importance for therapists. Both spouses are queried, since the denial mechanism is extremely prominent in attempted suicide. This attempt has such a dramatic impact on the entire family[1] that everyone wants to forget its occurrence. Very often the nonsuicidal spouse does not relate this attempt by his partner, either of conscious or nonconscious wishes that "his partner would drop dead" or because of guilt about this hostility. A history of attempted suicide, or as occasionally happens in answering this question that the patient has been thinking of suicide, should immediately alert the therapist to the need of sharing this responsibility. Thus should another attempt be made, prompt emergency measures can be instituted, since about four out of five people who commit suicide have previously attempted or threatened suicide. Therefore, I direct the question, "Have *you* or *your* spouse ever attempted suicide?" to both spouses. This item was incorporated in the questionnaire at the marital department after a woman was hospitalized following a serious suicidal attempt. The couple had been receiving counseling from a therapist in training. Ironically, neither spouse had related the wife's serious suicidal attempt five years previously, although both were college graduates and quite verbal. The suicidal attempt followed a day of bitter quarreling between the couple, during which time the wife had consumed a fifth of Bourbon, the husband had taken away his wife's sewing machine, and she retaliated by smashing his newly completed boat model.

Many suicides occur when the individual is under the influence of alcohol.[2] A review of the clinical material in this couple revealed the underlying depression in the woman that an experienced therapist would have been alerted to. The highlights in this woman's clinical material follows as it pertains to her underlying depression:

"I would like to point out that my husband has completely destroyed my self-confidence. This has had a tremendous depressing effect on me. My morale is at a very low ebb. He criticizes my hat-making, until it brings tears to my eyes, while neighbors beg me to make hats for them regardless of price. He ridicules my hats, while guests rave about them. He continually insults me in front of his friends and mine. I have reached the point where I realize that the two of us cannot be together except alone. . . . I am so completely undermined and bewildered. . . . I feel so alone. . . . I am so confused and very sad. . . ."

The above was interspersed with other material and thus buried in a maze of complaints, both marital and hypochondriacal. However, in fifteen conjoint sessions, at no time was the subject of a previous, serious suicidal attempt by the wife mentioned.

The two most important factors for the therapist to keep in mind in the prevention of suicide is a high suspicion index and his availability to the patient at all times—day and night.[3] If the therapist cannot be available because of circumstances beyond his control, he should impress upon the partner the seriousness of the situation and the importance of close surveillance. Unfortunately, there are many times when hospitalization is either refused by the individual or when there are no valid legal reasons for commitment or when a calculated risk is necessary—hospitalization could crystallize a chronic psychiatric illness. Since marital discord and other interpersonal disputes are frequent precipitants of suicidal attempts, and since 60 percent of the therapist's practice revolves around marital disharmony, suicide must be at all times a concern of the therapist. Incidentally, depression is the most common psychiatric diagnosis made.[4]

Since suicide is an end point of depression, I shall present some concepts about depressive states. We know little more currently than Shakespeare[5] did about depression at the turn of the seventeenth century, when he opened his play, *The Merchant of Venice,* with Antonio speaking as follows:

> "In sooth I know not why I am so sad.
> It wearies me; you say it wearies you;
> But how I caught it, found it, or came by it,
> What stuff 'tis made of, whereof it is born,
> I am to learn."

Although we do not know what causes cyclothymic reactions or how to adequately classify the various types of depression, I have previously conceptualized cyclothymic reactions[6] along a continuum that may be divided into three categories:

1. *Cyclothymic tendencies, mild* mood swings that pass reasonably rapidly and consist of sadness, depression, or feeling blue and that are present in everyone.
2. A *cyclothymic personality* is characterized by *moderate* highs and lows in mood. This type of an individual frequently relates, if questioned, a past history of several depressive episodes of increasing frequency, intensity and duration. Especially in premarital counseling with this type of person, caution is indicated in advising marriage.
3. *Cyclothymic psychosis* (manic-depressive psychosis) is characterized by *severe* mood swings, with or without hospitalization for threatened or attempted suicide.

Often the severe cyclothymic personality develops manic-depressive psychosis and frequently has a turbulent marital history. In the cyclothymic psychosis, recurrent episodes of either manic or hypomanic spiraling, or severe depressive reactions with or without suicidal attempts, are devastating to the other spouse and extremely disturbing to children. The following clinical vignette shows the progression from a cyclothymic personality to a cyclothymic psychosis:

A twenty-five year old man, handsome and well built, was seen in an emergency consultation. He was in a severe (but not psychotic) anxious depression and extremely worried about his impending wedding. He was going to complete his last graduate course requirement in two weeks and to be married the next day. His history revealed two depressive episodes. One occurred in his senior year in high school and lasted a week; the other occurred just before he graduated college. This one was deeper than the first and lasted almost three weeks.

This man had been well until the previous two weeks when he became restless and irritable. He awoke each morning at four, had trouble concentrating, felt worthless, and was concerned about his approaching marriage. The courtship had been smooth, uneventful, and happy. His fiancee was attractive, intelligent, and a college graduate. She was happily looking forward to their marriage.

The depression began to lift when I suggested he postpone his marriage while he received intensive psychotherapy. Treatment was continued under another therapist, who advised the patient not to marry. However, two years later he did marry. He was hospitalized after a suicidal attempt when his first child was six months old.

Having observed and treated cyclothymic personalities and cyclothymic psychotics over the past thirty-three years, I fully believe now that the condition primarily involves the intrapersonal system of the individual and is due essentially to underlying biochemical changes.[7] I agree with Grinker, Sr.,[8] who pinpoints time as the essential therapeutic element in these disorders. He writes: "Ego depletion, lack of self-esteem, regressed behavior and felt-hopelessness, and the concomitant exposure of severe intrapsychic conflicts require time for restitution. That time is the essential element in all so-called specific psychotherapeutic, milieu, and somatotherapeutic remedies for depression seems possible."

The psychodynamic conceptualizations of depression were influenced by Freud's[9] seminal paper on "Mourning and Melancholia." He was well aware of the difficulty of unifying the various depressive syndromes into one psychodynamic formulation: "Even in descriptive psychiatry the definition of melancholia is uncertain; it takes on various clinical forms (some of them suggesting somatic rather than psychogenic affections) that do not seem definitely to warrant reduction to a *unity* [italics added]." This paper crystallized melancholia as a form of self-reproach, resulting from anger against a loved object whose internalized mental representation (introject) has temporarily become part of the patient's own ego. Grinker, Sr.[10] suggests that the various psychodynamic formulations on depression are "not representative of causes except as *stressors* long before the onset and that later they are augmented as the *results* of the depressive process."

In my experience, although all three systems of the individual are involved in varying degrees, I find it useful to view a depressed individual as either reacting from primarily intrapersonal forces (the so-called endogenous or autonomous type) or as reacting to a specific environmental precipitant (the so-called reactive depression).[11] Time is the important factor in reversing the depression, and this usually occurs spontaneously. Frequently, I have observed that a brief hospitalization with only several electroconvulsive treatments hastens the remissive process. On the other hand, when the person is reacting to a specific environmental precipitant, like the request for a divorce—in the couple to be presented next—psychotherapy is the indicated approach. The following vignette is typical of the reactive depressive reaction:

Mrs. Vera is a small, thin, bespectacled brunette, who was referred by her minister for both marital counseling and treatment of her depression. Initially she maintained a firm control over both her feelings and her verbalizations, as evidenced by a seeming pursing of her lips and a precise, clipped manner of speech. As the sessions progress, she seemed to be able to relax her controls and express deep feelings of both depression and a longing for resolution of her marital difficulties. Aside from a prolonged period of inadequate sexual adjustment and seeming inability to communicate her feelings with her husband, Mrs. Vera bemoaned her husband's abrupt announcement that he wanted a divorce. Married six years, and one child, she complained about their sexual adjustment. Although her husband complained that she is frigid, she stated that she wasn't, that their premarital sexual adjustment was very enjoyable. She was orgastic, but everything changed on their honeymoon. "He no longer was romantic, no foreplay, and acted as a brute. I tried to tell him, but he didn't say anything or answer. I resented him more and more, and our sex relations deteriorated to twice a year. In addition, I resented his traveling and his being home only on weekends. But when he asked for a divorce I went to pieces. I couldn't stop crying. Being home alone all week, all I think is what I've done to him and our child. (*Cries.*) I was so lonely. I don't want a divorce. I am so remorseful about what I have done." At this point Mrs. Vera cried uncontrollably, and stated that the only solution was to kill herself and her child. She was given considerable reassurance, told that there was hope, since her husband was cooperating in the therapy, and told to call me at any time, day or night, if she felt the need to.

Mr. Vera was a well-dressed, executive type, Ivy League type of individual with a pleasant and cooperative manner. He spoke freely about the events which had led him to seek help with his marital situation but showed some confusion about the direction he is going. On the other hand, even with the complaints he had about his wife's frigidity, he seemed genuinely concerned about hurting her and their daughter by a possible divorce. On the other hand, he deeply questioned whether there could be any satisfactory resolution within the marriage, since he had no feelings of love but just "admiration" for his wife. Besides, the other woman met all his needs, both emotional and sexual. However, he agreed to enter into therapy, particularly when it was pointed out to him that his wife could kill not only herself but their child.

This couple illustrates a reactive depression on the part of the spouse to the request for divorce, with the depression resulting from a turning in of hostility. Unable to attack her husband, she wants to destroy the introjected mental representation of her partner, but in doing this she would have destroyed herself.

This chapter dealt with the subject of previous help received by the couple and pointed out how this item was valuable in the four areas of motivation, type of help received, possibility of referral and possibility of another dimension of information about the couple from a previous therapist. The second topic discussed suicide, previous attempt or current rumination. The etiology and classification of depression still remains an enigma. Two main categories of depression were described.

NOTES

1. Peter R. Whitis: The legacy of a child's suicide. *Family Process*, 7:159, 1968.

2. F.A. Whitlock and K. Schapira: Attempted suicide in Newcastle-upon-Tyne, *Brit J Psychiat, 113*:423, 1967. In this article, the authors point out that in their experience with 274 patients admitted after making a suicidal attempt, nearly one third of the patients had ingested alcohol before the attempt.

3. The Suicide Prevention Center in Los Angeles under the direction of Edwin S. Shneidman, Norman L. Faberow and Robert E. Litman has been in the forefront in furthering basic understanding about the phenomenon of suicide. Two of their psychiatric social workers, Sam M. Heilig and David J. Klugman (The Social Worker in a Suicide Prevention Center, in *Crisis Intervention: Selected Readings*, Howard J. Parad, Ed., New York, Family Service Association of America, 1965) have written about their role at the Center, which can be most useful in helping a therapist cope with a patient considering suicide. Also a recent review of the literature by F.A. Whitlock and J.E. Edwards

(Pregnancy and attempted suicide, *Compr Psychiat,* 9:1, 1968) shows that contrary to popular belief, both suicide and attempted suicide can occur in pregnant women. In their study they found 6.2 percent of women pregnant who had attempted suicide in a group of 483 women admitted to public hospitals in Brisbane. See also Paul W. Pretzel: Training ministers in suicide prevention. *Pastoral Counselor,* 5:34, 1967. A new journal, *Bulletin of Suicidology,* edited by Edwin S. Shneidman and David D. Swenson, whose purpose is to facilitate information on suicide and to provide abstracts of the recent literature on suicide and suicide prevention can be obtained by writing to the National Clearinghouse for Mental Health Information, National Institute of Mental Health, Chevy Chase, Md. 20203.

4. Morris Fishbein (Studies of suicide, *Med World News,* 9:96, 1968) states that "according to Dr. Erwin Stengel, professor emeritus of psychiatry at the University of Sheffield in England, about one out of ten of the 200,000 suicide attempts in the U.S. each year is fatal. While most of the people who have attempted suicide and failed go on to lead fairly normal lives, those who have tried once are likely to try again. Hence the need for psychiatric and social attention. Dr. Stengel is convinced that suicides are rarely planned, but rather represent a gamble in which intrapsychic and interpersonal factors are important."

5. William Shakespeare: "The Merchant of Venice," in *The Complete Works of William Shakespeare* (William Aldis Wright, Ed.). Philadelphia, Blakiston, 1936, pp. 447–476.

6. Bernard L. Greene and Noel Lustig: Contraindications to marriage, *Med Aspects Hum Sexuality,* 2:4, 1968.

7. Saul H. Rosenthal and Jon E. Gudeman (The Endogenous depressive pattern, *Arch Gen Psychiat, 16:241,* 1967) suggest that the term *autonomous depression,* after Gillispie, offers a better description of the pattern used so commonly to describe "endogenous depression." They point out that whereas "endogenous implies that the cause of the illness is known to be an internal mechanism, autonomous merely describes the course and lack of environmental reactivity." Their studies investigated clinical reaction patterns in depression and their relationship to premorbid personality traits and historical data. Clinical ratings were done on one hundred depressed female patients and subjected to correlational techniques and factor analysis. Their results show a "first factor made up of symptoms and signs which correspond to the classical concept of the endogenous depressive pattern. This factor correlates significantly with absent precipitant, a history of prior manic and depressive episodes, obsessive and depressive personality traits, and a lack of emotional reactivity."

8. Roy R. Grinker, Sr.: Reception of communications by patients in depressive states, *Arch Gen Psychiat, 10:576,* 1964. Also see Sidney S.

Furst and Mortimor Ostow: The psychodynamics of suicide, *Bull NY Acad Med, 41:*190, 1965; A. J. Malerstein: Depression as pivotal affect. *Amer J Psychotherapy, 22:*202, 1968; and Jan Fawcett, Melitta Leff, and William E. Bunney: Suicide. *Arch Gen Psychiat, 21:*129, 1969.

9. Sigmund Freud: Mourning and Melancholia, in *Collected Papers Vol IV,* London: Hogarth Press, 1948, pp 152–172. Other psychoanalysts. especially Abraham, Melanie Klein, Jacobson and Bibring have extended Freud's conceptual approach to include constitutional factors of fixation of the libido on the oral level, infantile struggle between love and hate, insufficient separation between object-representation and self-representation and focus on ego psychology, and so on.

10. Grinker, Sr., *op. cit.*

11. Earl Cohen, Jerome A. Motto, and Richard H. Seiden (An instrument for evaluating suicide potential: a preliminary study, *Amer J Psychiat, 122:*886, 1966) are attempting to develop a clinical instrument made up largely of demographic variables to test its validity in prognosticating subsequent suicidal behavior. The factors studied were of two clusters: (1) in the predicted direction and (2) not in the predicted direction. For example, alcoholism, drug addiction, delinquency and recent loss were all found to be in the predicted direction. They conclude: "The factors related to suicide are multiple and complex; they involve an intense interplay of social, cultural, economic, physiologic and intrapsychic phenomena which have thus far defied therapeutic intervention."

12. My experience parallels that of Mathew Ross: Suicide among college students, *Amer J Psychiat, 126:*220, 1969, who comments: ". . . often leading questions about suicidal thoughts are necessary, for direct questioning will often reveal otherwise concealed suicidal intentions. There is no evidence that such questions asked in a proper way have any aggravating effect upon the patient. The reverse is usually true. . . ."

XIII

GETTING MARRIED PHASE

Love is not blind, it is deaf.

The marriage cycle consists of two main phases, the getting married phase and the married phase proper. In Chapter XI, I presented the marriage phase proper as delineated by Otto Pollak and divided by him into four dimensions of need complementarity. The twelfth item in the BMQ inquiring into the getting married phase has three subheadings:

a. How did you meet your spouse?
b. Describe your courtship.
c. Discuss your honeymoon.

MATE SELECTION

Marriage is the fusion of two individuals who are unique in their own existence and have met, not through the strategy of intelligence, not through the magic of romance, but through sheer chance.[1] Table XVIII, shows how 750 couples met.

A glance at Table XVIII reveals that about 40 percent of the couples were introduced by either a friend or relative. This observation indicates the trend of mate selection by homogamy,

TABLE XVIII
HOW SPOUSES MET

	PS	*MDS*
Through friend or relative	225	100
At school	111	55
At work	85	33
Pickup	37	30
Neighborhood	30	15
Church	12	15

that is, "likes marry likes." Since marriage is fundamental in almost all societies, every social class has definitions of who may marry, for example, certain individuals are unequivocally prohibited as marriage partners due to incest taboo. In their book on marriage, Winch and McGinnis[2] have selected articles by Hollingshead,[3] Glick and Landau,[4] Koller,[5] and Ktsanes and Ktsanes[6] to illustrate that cultural and psychic determinants in mate selection are homogamous[7] with respect to race, age and class position. They state: "In a highly significant number of cases the person one marries is very similar culturally to one's self." Glick and Landau comment in their article: "Age is one of several important factors that tend to limit the choice of a marriage partner. There is a tendency in American society for men to marry a wife a few years younger than they are." Twenty years later La Barre[8] notes the declining ages of first marriages: "Today one out of every four eighteen-year-old girls is married, as are one out of every eight, seventeen-year-old girls and one out of approximately every sixteen, sixteen-year-old girls."

Koller[9] in his article on mate selection has verified the pioneer work by Bossard[10] on residential propinquity and also included occupational propinquity in choosing a marital partner. He finds in his studies that "there appears to be a stronger than fifty-fifty chance that a young boy or girl will marry someone living very close to his residence." My figures (see Table XVIII) show that approximately 50 percent of the couples in both series, PS and MDS, selected their partner because of residential or occupational propinquity: school, work, neighborhood or church. In 5 percent in the PS and 12 percent in the MDS was the mate selection purely accidental, i.e. due to a "pick up."

Ktsanes and Ktsanes[11] illustrate the theory of complementary needs first set forth by Winch[12-14] in 1952. They view mate selection as operating on the theory of complementary needs rather than on psychological similarity.

Tharp[15] believes:

Mates are selected from a field of eligibles. This field is determined by homogamy as to race, ethnic origin, social class, age, religion, and by residential propinquity. Exploration of this field is a function of unknown psychological viables. Cultural homogamys provide for a measure of similarity between mates with respect to social value, and personality characteristics. Mate-selection (courtship) roles manifest needs and expectations which differ in content and organization from marriage roles.

My clinical experience indicates that all three systems (intrapersonal, interpersonal and environmental) contribute to the selection of a mate and that GST provides a better framework to understand mate selection.

Having selected a potential mate, the next step in the marriage cycle is the courtship. The challenge of courtship entails a progression of transitional stages from aloneness to intimacy. Each transitional point creates a crisis, either for maturation, fixation, or regression. If the crisis is handled adequately, the individual matures. If the stress engendered by the crisis is not coped with advantageously, old psychological conflicts may be reactivated or new conflicts may arise with behavioral reactions. The courtship period ends with the *rite de passage* of the wedding, and throughout the courtship the couple fluctuates between separation and joining. Rubinstein[16] presents the distortion and dilemma in marital choice (and applicable to courtship) based on the dynamics of projective identification (see Ch. XX) where the engaged couple are not relating to each other as real persons but through each other in terms of their internalized mental representations of objects ("records"). Thus there are numerous transitional points during the courtship that have elements attached to them that are novel for the engaged couple. This is especially valid in our society where *rites de passage* are limited and where anticipatory socialization for the roles in marriage tends to be minimal.[17] As Frank Cox[18] points out, "There is a great deal of difference between individual dating patterns and the norms. In addition, these patterns evolve and change with time. . . ." The changing cultural pattern of going steady in high school, college, and even in grade school is a recent innovation. As Cox states: "This tendency to 'go steady' combined with a slowly declining average age at marriage tends to limit drastically the number of meaningful heterosexual relations available to the young person." The pattern "to go steady" is a symptom of the generalized insecurity in our culture. Going steady reduces the necessity to compete, assures dates for social events and avoids the risk of rejection. A grave disadvantage of going steady is the limited experience with the opposite sex, impaired judgement concerning a future spouse, and a limiting of the chances for wider testing of personalities and possible meanings of love. Ehrmann's[19] book on premarital dating behavior is helpful in understanding the impact of going steady in college students.

As used in this book, the item "describe your courtship" includes both the courting and engagement phases. Although the great majority of couples meet by sheer accident, marriage partners choose each other for highly specific conscious and unconscious reasons. This selection represents the summation of normal and appropriate goals, as well as various neurotic and symbolic needs which must be met either intrapsychically or interpersonally. The continuation of the courtship is dependent on the development of object relationships. Each individual brings into a relationship his own unique personality. Sklarew[20] has recently reported a stimulating pilot study on courtship. The issues he raises include "consolidation of sexual identity; commitment (to a relationship, occupational goals, and values); conformity-rebellion; lessening ties to parents; intimacy-isolation; empathy, and the handling of doubting in a heterosexual relationship." Table XIX presents some general data on courtship observed in the couples in the PS.

The tasks that confront engaged persons involve all three systems (see fig. 1). Different individuals accomplish the tasks at different times; some only begin to deal with them during the period of engagement, whereas others have accomplished many of them by time they get engaged. In ordering observations on courtship, the outline suggested by Otto Pollak of the four dimensions of need complementarity has been followed (see Ch. XI). Another key organizing concept is that of *fit*, suggested by Rhona Rapoport.[21] Her two papers are valuable in understanding the phenomena confronted by the couple in the getting married phase of marriage cycle. A good fit may be

TABLE XIX
GENERAL DATA IN COURTSHIP IN PRIVATE SERIES

	No.
Duration of courtship	
Less than 6 months	108
Less than 1 year	122
1 to 2 years	169
2 to 3 years	29
3 years and up	72
Areas of conflict	
First appeared in courtship and persisted after marriage	249 (50%)
Premarital pregnancy	51 (10%)

	Male	Female
Nonconflictual courtship		
Yes	201	302
No	299	198
Premarital sex	184	92

arrived at in various ways. The couple need not be identical in the way they do things or in their personality configurations. An engaged couple may have a similar orientation to some aspect of life and the result may be conflict or unhappy competition in the relationship. On the other hand, dissonant orientations do not necessarily indicate a poor fit. Frequently they complement one another. Rapoport points out that the essential point is the effect of their "fitting together" actions.

TRANSACTIONS IN COURTSHIP

Interpersonal Reorientation

Of prime importance is providing a new and age-appropriate anchor of intimate association in place of parental anchor. Disengagement involves separation from all relationships, both kinship and social, that interfere with commitment to the marital relationship. At this point it is important to differentiate between kinship bonds and the concept of role. The concept of role deals with the expectations, obligations and rights of the person in a particular status and encompasses more than the concept of bond. Furthermore, each role includes reciprocal positions related to it, e.g. father-son, father-daughter relationships, and so on. On the other hand, the concept of bond implies a hierarchy of ties of obligations and feelings between those in set reciprocal status that pattern the organization of a kinship network, i.e. the bond between son and mother is stronger than the bond between siblings. Thus disengagement on the part of the engaged couple from their respective kin is not an easy task. As Leichter[22] *et al.* point out:

The right of kin to give and thereby to initiate exchange processes adds to the hold of kinship. Ritual and economic, psychological and social mesh in exchanges among kin; cultural norms define expectations of reciprocity as legitimate. The sequential processes or reciprocity and the resulting imbalances increases the binding quality of kinship ties, making them difficult to change.

Thus the disengagement from respective kinship networks is not an easy task for many individuals. Some deal with this issue before engagement, whereas others deal with it primarily during the engagement period.

The following clinical extract illustrates where the wife was unable to disengage herself from her family:

Mr. and Mrs. Veronica, married only three months, had been quarreling constantly about their relationships with their parents. Mrs. Veronica stated bitterly that there were absolutely no mutual interests and compatibility between them. She states that he seems to be of the opinion that because he gave in for the eleven months of courtship to her relationship to her family that he now expects her to give in for the rest of the marriage. She adds that he complains that she wants everything her way, but quickly states that the simple fact is that he never does anything so she has to take over and do it herself.

Mr. Veronica adds that a lot she says is true, but actually what he is doing is trying to avoid arguments. Whenever he disagrees with her, she claims he is calling her stupid and challenging her womanhood. The problems in the marriage started when they got engaged because he was too agreeable and that after marriage he was not as prone to say yes all the time as he was before. During the engagement they were with his wife's parents a great deal. He didn't think this was right, as he felt that occasionally they should visit his parents. But his wife insisted, and he made no issue about it, although he felt it was not right.

Mrs. Veronica interrupted to state that he never objected, and besides her father insisted they come.

Mr. Veronica complained the problem was her mother. She must talk to her mother every night for a few hours, that every other afternoon the two of them spend the afternoon together either shopping, dining out, seeing a play, and so on. That doesn't bother him, since he is at work, but her coming over every other night to visit is too much. He feels his mother-in-law undermines him by buying his wife many things that he should be buying. He gets into trouble when he agrees with his mother-in-law and also get into trouble when he disagrees with her. Either way he loses. But what really gripes him is the close relationship she has with her mother. He thought when he married, his wife would change. "Two is a marriage, but three is a crowd. I can't see why she has to call her mother about everything that happens between us."

Disengagement involves separation from any type relationship that interferes with marriage. These close relationships may be with sibling, parent, friend, relative, or others. Important to evaluate is how the individuals accommodated their premarital gratifications to their courtship. Some persons feel that getting married does not necessitate relinquishing premarital gratifications. For example, it may be extremely difficult for a woman to give up the thrill of romantic premarital behavior: Mrs. Valeria, the belle of the campus with repeated romances until trapped by impregnation, never forgave her husband for this happening.

Sexual Sphere

This includes transactions proceeding toward harmony in biological completion. The task of developing a mutually satisfactory sexual adjustment for the courtship period is contingent on each individual's norms about sexuality behavior for an engaged couple. While 36 percent of the men admitted premarital sexual intercourse with their fiancees, only 18 percent of the women admitted premarital sex during the engagement. As Halleck[23] has stated in his discussion of sexual problems of college students:

One of the least accurate and most destructive impressions of sexuality in America has been promulgated by newspapers, periodicals, and television. These media have convinced most Americans that we are in the midst of a major sexual revolution. The phrase implies that premarital sexual intercourse and sexual promiscuity have become more commonplace than they were in past decades. The facts are different. Whatever revolution exists is primarily one of *attitude* [italics added]."

Beverly Mead *et al.*[24] in a panel discussion present divergent opinions on the psychological effects of premarital intercourse. The repercussions of premarital sexuality vary from severe to none, depending on the degree the three systems (intra-personal, interpersonal and environmental) are involved. Important variables in each individual to premarital sex include sex, age, personality makeup, environmental circumstances, values, and other factors such as premarital pregnancy.

My observations in premarital pregnancy, which occurred in 10 percent of the couples in the PS, parallels that of La Barre,[25] Vincent,[26] and others. A successful marriage can start with premarital pregnancy. On the other hand, premarital pregnancy creates a crisis of considerable magnitude.[27] The following couple is illustrative:

Mr. and Mrs. Jacqueline were referred for therapy because of the husband's compulsive ruminating that his wife would become unfaithful. He stated that for the past two years she seemed disinterested in sex with him, and he was suspecting another man.

Mrs. Jacqueline began her first session as follows: "I guess I always wanted and tried to have a perfect marriage, but after the first two years I began to have doubts about whether or not I married the right person. I knew I cared and respected Bob very much. But since we had to get married, as I was pregnant, I never felt I had chosen Bob. I began to wonder if I really loved him. Slowly, I guess, I became unsure of making love, that is, I didn't feel excited anymore. I didn't enjoy going to bed, in fact, at times I disliked it, but tried not to let Bob feel this. . . . I tried to keep it inside, but I became more and more confused. I knew I cared very much in every other way for Bob, but when it came to sex, most of the time it didn't excite me or arouse any feeling in me whatsoever. Before this, I had orgasm all the time. I began to fantasy about other men. I was a freshman in college when I got pregnant and married. I really enjoyed school, all the social activities and resented it when I got pregnant. I didn't want to get married, but my father insisted when he found out. I've always resented that I was unable to finish college."

Mr. Jacqueline: "Sexual dissatisfaction is probably the best topic to describe our trouble, although I don't believe it's dissatisfaction but rather a lack of one or both to work for satisfaction. My wife is very attractive and excites me easily. The problem is that in the last two years of our marriage, I have failed to help her reach a climax. For the first two years she was very satisfied, then this lonely, unsatisfied feeling developed, and now she has built this thing up to something like she has and I don't understand what has happened."

In their first conjoint session, Mrs. Jacqueline related being very angry at her father for forcing her to get married, and at her husband who told her he had planned to get her pregnant because he was afraid she was going to marry someone else.

Mr. Jacqueline interrupted to comment that they were in love and that he was angry at her when she didn't want to marry him.

In the fourth conjoint session, Mrs. Jacqueline related the following dream: "We are at a party. We were switching partners. It was okay with me. But I got upset when Bob went over and asked a girl to dance before I was asked. He held her close while they danced. I was angry and said, You always do more than you are supposed to!"

The associations revealed that her impregnation occurred when she accepted his invitation to meet him at his friend's apartment to discuss their relationship.

When asked why she had gone to the apartment, she replied smilingly: I didn't expect anything to happen. The remaining conjoint sessions dealt with their respective guilt and anger.

This couple demonstrates the unconscious collusion between the mates. Her material revealed her feeling of being trapped into marriage, yet she willingly met him at his friend's apartment.

Financial Sphere

This includes transactions dealing with division of labor between earner and homemaker and clarification as to the wife working to enable mate to complete education (academic or vocational), both working toward a down payment on a house, boat, and so on. The role expectations of the two individuals can be categorized under two main activities, to provide for the material things in living and to provide nurturance-succorance, whether it be woman's or man's work. Whatever the work situation, either male or female, regardless of which individual assumes primarily the instrumental role, there has to be a realistic conception of the economic problems. The task accepted must not only be intrapersonal in terms of the individual's capacity to contribute to the economic needs of the marriage, but also each must work out an arrangement ego-syntonic to their own self-images. Usually the male is expected to take on the instrumental role, and the female the nurturant-affectional role. However, with the progressively decreasing age of persons entering into marriage, more and more middle-class girls continue to work while their husbands are completing their studies.

Ego-Strengthening Sphere

This involves transactions in which each engaged person helps the other to learn future spouse roles. Ideally, each one of the engaged couple accords to the other the freedom to express individuality and help in the maintenance of their self-esteem and self-image. In addition, both are involved in establishing a couple identity, learning how to communicate and support each other in the planning for the wedding, honeymoon (if possible), and the early phase of marriage. Mutuality instead of narcissistic adaptive defenses become important.

The phase of getting married affords the therapist the opportunity for prevention of future marital discord. In 50 percent of the couples observed, areas of conflict that first appeared in the courtship persisted after marriage. The following couple is an example of the mirroring of courtship and marital conflictual patterns:

Mrs. Urania describing her courtship: "We courted each other for about a year and one-half. Mostly we continued seeing each other because I had nobody on the scene. We spent most weekends visiting an out-of-town best friend of mine. During this time we did not sleep together, and our relationship might be described as comfortable. Ted drank heavily and his conduct, when drunk, was boorish. We decided to get married when this girl friend married. I was tired of being a bachelor girl and felt it was time to progress to marriage and settle down. Ted did not excite or arouse me, but I felt this was a sign of mature judgment in selecting a marriage partner. I was aware that Ted had a drinking problem but felt once we had a home of our own and children, and he was no longer living with his eccentric mother who pampered him, he would relax and become moderate in his drinking. I was wrong. He continued to drink, and his mother was very much in the picture. I was pretty certain he was not in love with me, and I know I was not in love with him, but kept it pretty much out of my mind. Our sexual relationship has never been satisfactory since our honeymoon, but I should have known that as he was not the passionate kind from our courtship. But he was handsome, well educated, and I knew he would always be a good provider. I thought we could learn to love each other." (In answering the question of specific complaints about marriage in the BMQ, she had circled all except infidelity and stated: "All of the above, in varying degrees, have been causes for the disintegration of our marriage (sic?), which I believe, was ill-founded to begin with. Neither of us had the right to marry the other.")

Mr. Urania: "We went together steady for about a year and a half. For the most part, it was smooth, but there was one very stormy event when I struck her. This resulted in an estrangement of approximately three months. Our relationship was renewed on my wife's initiative. I wanted to marry my wife because I admired her and was convinced that the marriage would work to the benefit of both parties. I was unable to achieve satisfactory sexual intercourse during our premarital attempts."

And so they married, had children, and a marriage no different than their courtship. This couple is a good illustration of a poor courtship where the three main tasks confronting each partner in the engagement were not dealt with: preparation for their respective roles as husband and wife, disengagement from premarital relationships, and lack of accommodation to the other's needs.

HONEYMOON

The final stage of the getting-married phase is the honeymoon, which usually involves a psychosocial crisis.[28] The honeymoon has been arbitrarily included as part of the getting-married phase. In 71 percent of the couples in the PS, some type of honeymoon occurred. Table XX gives some of the data obtained.

The principal transactions during the honeymoon relate to the spheres of interpersonal reorientation, ego strengthening and sexuality. In one third of the couples, areas of conflict that appeared on the honeymoon continued in the marriage, e.g. games of mutual escalation.

TABLE XX
THE HONEYMOON IN THE PRIVATE SERIES

			Couples
None			149
Honeymoon			355
Areas of conflict			
First appeared on the honeymoon and persisted during the marriage.			172
Games of "Uproar"			53
Sexual relationship	*Male*	*Female*	
Satisfactory	280	245	
Unsatisfactory	75	112	
Total experience			
Unsatisfactory	26	55	
Satisfactory for both			285
Unsatisfactory for both			74

The honeymoon usually provides the couple with the real challenge of intimacy, especially if there has been no previous premarital sexual intercourse. Thus not only the challenge of sexuality but the shift from aloneness to intimacy comes to the forefront.

A frequent cause of argument on the honeymoon revolves around the topic of residence. Residence is an area dealing with interpersonal reorientation. Not uncommonly, one spouse had assumed that this issue was not important enough to have warranted discussion during the courtship. Residence is patterned and related to social values and expectations and is a basic concept of kinship networks. Marriage inevitably involves a dislocation for one or both partners, and frequently there is great emotional investment cathected to where one lives in relation to relatives. The following couple illustrates the importance of residence.

Mr. and Mrs. Ulrica were born in San Diego and lived there most of their lives. A job change caused them to move to Chicago. Mrs. Ulrica feels this is the crux of their problem. She says she is very unhappy here and wants to go back home, but her husband wants to stay in Chicago. Two years ago, his firm wished to send him here to manage the local distributing office. He wanted to accept the offer, which involved a promotion and a substantial increase in salary. He reluctantly turned it down when she bitterly opposed moving. Recently he was offered the same opportunity and accepted it over her protests. He is the only person who has benefited from the move. Most important, Mrs. Ulrica misses her family and friends. Furthermore, when they were on their honeymoon, they had argued about where to live, and she had told him specifically that she did not intend to leave San Diego and her parents regardless of circumstances, and he had promised to stay put.

Mr. Ulrica retorts, he had expected her to change after they married. . . .

This woman typifies a childish overdependence on her parents. In other couples, the dependence of one spouse disrupted the honeymoon by the frequent daily telephone communications with the parents.

The honeymoon period was a traumatic time for many of the couples. A glance at Table XX shows that the total honeymoon experience was twice as unsatisfactory for the women as for the men. In 15 percent of the couples, the total honeymoon experience was unsatisfactory for both spouses. On the other hand, 57 percent of the couples were satisfied with their honeymoon as a total experience. When asked specifically about their feelings in regard to sexuality on their honeymoon, about one fifth of the women were dissatisfied. The following clinical extracts show reactions of the dissatisfied couples to their honeymoon:

He: "It was not successful as far as being intimate. My wife's vagina was not large enough for me to enter. She didn't disrobe or attempt any relation the first night. She had absolutely no knowledge of what intercourse was about."

She: "I was disappointed. I thought he was sophisticated and knew his way around. He was the most popular man on campus and a star athlete. We never did consummate[29] the marriage on our honeymoon. And he blamed me for being ignorant."

It it not uncommon to hear the complaint by a spouse of too much traveling (travel serves many purposes: anxiety about performance, useful as an avoidance maneuver, avoidance of intimacy, and so on). The following example was typical:

He: "Wild. My fault. I was ignorant. We traveled 6,000 miles in two weeks. I had to be a big shot and visit all the spots I had been to when in the armed service."

She: "We drove and drove and drove. He visited all his former army buddies and their wives. I was disappointed. He was very inconsiderate."

The following extracts are illustrative of sexual complaints that started on the honeymoon and continued throughout the marriage:

He: "Our honeymoon was fine in all areas."

She: "Our troubles started on our honeymoon. Not only did he forget to take contraceptives, but sexually he was much too fast and has been ever since (note the discrepancy in how each spouse viewed their honeymoon)."

He: "Unsatisfactory. It started on our honeymoon. I found out she was unable to have an .orgasm. She complained constantly that I paid attention to everyone but her. This stunned me."

She: "Our honeymoon was most unsatisfactory in all areas. When I couldn't have an orgasm, he reacted and made a big deal of it. We had to see several psychiatrists, and this on our honeymoon. Besides he was paying attention to his friends more than to me."

He: "Very enjoyable. Her behavior was that of complete enjoyment. There was a blow-up over sex. Very short argument. We had had adequate sexual relations during our engagement."

She: "It went pretty well. He was deeply hurt over something I said when I didn't reach a climax in intercourse. I always had before with him. This probably began our sex problems. Since that night, he has had premature ejaculations."

The other complaints verbalized by one or both spouses about their honeymoons included:

He: "We went to Canada on a canoe trip, my wife wanted to go to Florida. The trip ended in an argument in which I struck her. This was the start of a long list of my faults which my wife has listed and never forgets."

She: "Our first argument started on our honeymoon. He, in a rage, hit me, not hard, but it was the beginning of many such incidents. Our sexual adjustment was normal."

He: "Our honeymoon was wonderful. Toward the end, we had a few bitter discussions about my mother and her father."

She: "We were both extremely naive. We were very young and had many obstacles to overcome. He was very considerate and willing to please me in any way possible. We did have several battles over our parents. He resented my calling my mother every day."

He: "I do not have a great love for running all over to see everything. That was taken as disinterest on my part. After you've seen one museum, you've seen them all. I have been told I deliberately ruined our honeymoon."

She: "The longest ten days of my life. He was more interested in sleeping, not sex, than seeing or doing."

He: "The honeymoon was fine, although there were some rough periods. She was doing unnecessary criticizing about my table manners. At one time during the honeymoon she said she wasn't sure she loved me. That hurt very much, and I still recall that vividly. I had raised the issue when she seemed mopey. Sexually everything was fine, also during our engagement."

She: "On our honeymoon I criticized his manners. His table manners were terrible, especially for a college graduate. Sexually everything was fine. On our honeymoon I was still thinking of the other man."

SUMMARY

The marriage cycle consists of two main phases, the getting married phase and the married phase proper. The getting married phase consists of three subphases: choice of mate, the courtship and the honeymoon. The honeymoon has been arbitrarily included with the getting married phase, although it begins the marriage cycle. Following Otto Pollak, each phase was dealt with in terms of the four dimensions of need complementarity.

The trend of mate selection is by homogamy, with psychological and cultural factors playing an important role. In our couples approximately 50 percent selected their partner because of residential or occupational propinquity. Further, having selected a mate, there is a progression of transitional stages from aloneness to intimacy. Each transitional point creates a crisis. The tasks confronting the engaged couple are threefold: disengagement, role assignment, and compromise as to mutuality of conflictual areas, e.g. sexual and kinship. In 50 percent of the couples, areas of conflict that first appeared in the courtship and honeymoon persisted during the marriage.

NOTES

1. Robert O. Blood, Jr.: *Marriage*. New York, The Free Press of Glencoe, 1962, p. 38.
2. Robert F. Winch and Robert McGinnis: *Selected Studies in Marriage and the Family*. New York, Henry Holt, 1954, pp. 398–435. See also Lilly Ottenheimer: Psychodynamics of the choice of mate, in *The Marriage Relationship* (Salo Rosenbaum and Ian Alger, Eds.). New York, Basic Books, 1968, pp. 59–69. She states "that the choice of a mate is not accidental or random but is deeply influenced by unconscious factors" derived from the oedipal and preoedipal phases of development.
3. August B. Hollingshead: Cultural factors in the selection of marriage mates, *Amer Sociol Rev, 15:*619, 1950.
4. Paul C. Glick and Emanuel Landau: Age as a factor in marriage, *Amer Sociol Rev, 15:*517, 1950. See also J. Joel Moss: Teen-age marriage: Cross-national trends and sociological factors in the decision of when to marry, *J Marriage Family, 27:*230, 1965; Lee G. Burchinal: Trends and prospects for young marriages in the United States, *J Marriage Family, 27:*243, 1965.
5. Marvin R. Koller: Residential and occupational propinquity, *Amer Sociol Rev, 13:*613, 1948.
6. Thomas Ktsanes and Virginia Ktsanes: The theory of complementary

needs in mate-selection, in *Selected Studies Marriage and the Family* (Robert F. Winch and Robert McGinnis, Eds.): New York, Henry Holt, 1954, p. 435.

7. Two studies by Golden and his associates (Jules Golden, Nathan Mandel, Bernard C. Glueck, Jr., and Zetta Feder: A summary description of fifty "normal" white males, *Amer J Psychiat, 119*:48, 1962, and *Arch Gen Psychiat, 9*:614, 1963) of fifty "normal" white males and the thirty-eight available wives of the forty men who were married at the time of their investigation are consistent with Hollingshead's thesis of homogamy. Their sample consisted of fifty of the seventy-three subjects of a population of 2000 boys, who twelve years earlier as ninth-grade pupils had obtained a perfectly normal MMPI (Minnesota Multiphasic Personality Inventory) test. The subjects (age 26–27) as a group were found to be unusually well-adjusted socially and psychologically, although their lives seemed mundane and dull, similar to the findings of Roy Grinker, Sr., studies on "homoclites." Golden *et al.* found that these essentially healthy individuals select healthy spouses. Further, "in keeping with the reported dominance of the male or mutuality of leadership in 84 percent of these couples, the stereotype of the ascendancy of the American wife and 'Momism' is not applicable to this sample." Thirty-six of the wives would probably be considered emotionally healthy in their intrapersonal, interpersonal and environmental adaptations. There had been no separation or divorces of the forty men. As with the men, Golden *et al.* found the overaall impression of these women as one of remarkable homogeneity and high uniformity. Thirty-five had a conventional religious ceremony. Twenty-one were religiously devout, fifteen of conventional belief, and two of qualified belief. The women gave their religions as follows, twenty-two Protestant, fourteen Catholic and two Jewish. Twenty-seven had no religious difference or conflict over religion. In six, there was a difference in religion but without conflict. In only five was the difference in religion a basis for mild contention.

8. Maurine La Barre: Pregnancy experiences among married adolescents, *Amer J Orthopsychiat, 38*:47, 1968.

9. Koller, *op. cit.*

10. James H.S. Bossard: *Marriage and Family.* Philadelphia, Univ. Penn Press, 1940, pp. 79–92.

11. Ktsanes and Ktsanes, *op. cit.*

12. Robert F. Winch: *The Modern Family.* New York, Henry Holt, 1952, pp. 209–13.

13. Robert F. Winch: *The Modern Family,* 2nd ed. New York, Henry Holt, 1963.

14. Winch and McGinnis, *op. cit.*

15. Roland G. Tharp: Psychological patterning in marriage, *Psychol Bull*, 60:1, 1963.
16. David Rubinstein: Distortion and dilemma in marital choice, *Voices*, 2:60, 1966.
17. James G. Frazer: *The New Golden Bough*. New York, Criterion Books, 1959.
18. Frank D. Cox: The honeymoon is over, *Voices*, 2:85, 1966. This is an excellent article about the early years of marriage.
19. Winston Ehrmann: *Premarital Dating Behavior*. New York, Henry Holt, 1959. An informative book in which is studied the premarital sexual activities in dating as reported by one thousand male and female college students in questionnaires and by one hundred of these students in personal interviews. The students' vivid unstructured comments provide interesting insights into the personalities and problems of youth.
20. Bruce H. Sklarew: Courtship—The Origin of the Family. Paper presented at the annual meeting of the American Psychiatric Association, May 7, 1964, Los Angeles, California.
21. Rhona Rapoport: The family and psychiatric treatment, *Psychiatry*, 23:53, 1960, and, Normal crises, family structure and mental health, *Family Process*, 2:68, 1963.
22. Hope J. Leichter and William E. Mitchell (with collaboration of Candace Rogers and Judith Lieb): *Kinship and Casework*. New York, Russell Sage Foundation, 1967.
23. Seymour L. Halleck: Sexual problems of college students, *Med Aspects Hum Sexuality*, 2:14, 1968. See also John H. Gagnon and William Simon: Prospects for change in American sexual patterns, *Med Aspects Hum Sexuality*, 4:100, 1970.
24. Beverly T. Mead, M.D.; William L. Peltz, M.D.; Mervyn S. Sanders, M.D.; Rev. Perry Lefevre; Father John L. Thomas, S.J.; and Rabbi Jeshaia Schnitzer: What are the psychological effects of premarital intercourse? *Med Aspects Hum Sexuality*, 2:22, 1968. In a round-table—How does premarital sex affect marriage?—Eugene B. Linton, David R. Mace, John M. Pixley, and Rev. David Burr (in *Med Aspects Hum Sexuality*, 2:14, 1968), Dr. Mace stated: "The percentage of premarital virgins who . . . turned to extramarital sex relations was 13 percent. The figure for non-virgins was 29 percent—more than double." See also Thomas P. Lowry: First coitus, *Med Aspects Hum Sexuality*, 3:91 , 1969.
25. La Barre, *op. cit.*
26. Every therapist should read the informative article by Clark E. Vincent: The physician as counselor in non-marital and premarital pregnancies, *Med Aspects Hum Sexuality*, 1:28, 1967. His observations and advice to physicians are applicable to the clergy. See also Esther

O. Fisher: *Help For Today's Troubled Marriages*. New York, Hawthorn Books, 1968, p. 199; and Nenabelle G. Dame, George H. Finck, Ruth G. Mayos, Beatrice S. Reiner, and Brady O. Smith: Conflict in marriage following premarital pregnancy, *Amer J Orthopsychiat*, *33:*468, 1966.

27. Toby B. Bieber and Irving Bieber: Resistance to marriage, in *The Marriage Relationship* (Salo Rosenbaum and Ian Alger, Eds.). New York, Basic Books, 1968, pp. 47–58.

28. Rhona Rapoport and Robert N. Rapoport: New light on the honeymoon, *Hum Relations*, *17:*33, 1964.

29. L.J. Friedman: *Virgin Wives: A Study of Unconsummated Marriages*. London, Tavistock Publications, 1962.

XIV
PREVIOUS MARRIAGES

The thirteenth item on the BMQ raises the issue of previous marriages (see Appendix). Information about a former marriage may provide insight into his marital object choices as well as his object relationships.[1,2] Knowledge of previous marriages is also helpful in evaluating the current conflicts of the conflicted couple. However, the family myths, the paucity of scientific studies, and the many variables make generalizations mandatory. The three main variables include the following:

1. The many contradictions in the literature about the outcome of a remarriage.
2. The unreliability of retrospective data.[3]
3. The heterogeneous composition of the remarried population—the three marital types (single, divorced, and widowed) intermarry, and each party is unique as to marital background (once divorced, twice divorced, and so on).

Table XXI shows the marital patterns in the 750 couples. Thus, 21 percent in the PS had been previously maried vis-à-vis 15 percent in the MDS.

TABLE XXI
MARITAL PATTERNS

	PS		MDS	
Marriage	*Male*	*Female*	*Male*	*Female*
First	391	397	216	210
Second	88	75	24	32
Third	8	17	8	4
Fourth	5	0	0	2
Widow		11		2
Widower	8		2	

The greater frequency of remarriage in the PS could be partially due to economic and cultural factors. The spouses in the PS were in a much higher economic bracket and could afford the luxury of sequential marriages. Cultural factors in the MDS contributed toward maintenance of the marriage, e.g. there were twice as many Catholics in the MDS. Sixteen percent (16%) of the spouses in the PS and 11 percent of the MDS had been married twice. The frequency of successive marriages has given rise to a dual pattern of marriage, sequential polygamy.[4] This change in the "permanent" character of the marriage contract is a response to the mobility of the population, mass media, and the technological revolution. Our society facilitates divorce without lessening the emotional and physical needs that marriage satisfies.

Until recently, it was a common opinion that the majority of previously married individuals did not remarry. However, Monahan[5] has used population surveys to support his view that about 75 percent of divorcees remarry.[6] The literature on the outcome of a remarriage is equivocal. Bernard[7] and others[8] suggest that remarriages are about as successful as other marriages. On the other hand, Monahan[9] has presented data indicating that sequential marriages have been less stable than first marriages. He assumes that divorce is a repetitive phenomenon. Bergler[10] and recently Giovacchini[11] feel that there is a similarity of psychopathology—remarriages are only a repetition of the first, and only the partner is changed.

Knowledge of previous marriages is of importance in assessing the current conflictual marriage as to prognosis and treatment. In keeping with the theoretical position of GST, all levels of information become valuable for the CDD session. In focusing on the environmental system, it is important to keep in mind that "disturbed families have a deficiency of family boundaries which leads them to involve extended kin in their conflicts and makes them sensitive to influence from extended kin."[12] In Chapter XIII, I described how the extended family can influence a marriage in four possible areas. Thus it is of value to know how the previous marriages were influenced by the extended kin and whether these same forces are now producing conflict. Because many remarriages occur later in life, the kinship networks, particularly in-laws, may by this time have accepted the situation, or they may be distant, and thus their influence now may be minor. Other environmental forces include the attitudes and reactions of children by prior marriages and special custody and support arrangements for them, and the reaction of the new spouse to these children. Difficulties with children were observed in more than 50 percent of the conflicted couple anticipating or following remarriage.[13] The following couple who came for premarital counseling is illustrative:

She: "If I were to marry him, he would like to have his children live with us. They are now living with his former wife, who has custody of them. I like them but am concerned that his primary relationships are with his children instead of me. He has great guilt feelings about being away from them. A parent does not immerse himself in his children as he does. He mentioned to me at one time that some of the women he had gone out with had actually been jealous of his children. I said, it wasn't the children but he who makes them jealous. One time the children didn't want me to come to dinner with them. He had previously asked me to dinner and from the restaurant called me to meet him there. When I got there the children were boiling mad at me. Later, after he had taken his children home, I told him I didn't want to be involved in a situation where the children call the shots. Basically, his children have a way of winding him around their fingers. I think it is hard for him to believe I do love his children. They have been at my house off and on all summer. I do have a good relationship with them. To me, they are kids, like mine."

In this situation, the solicitude of the father for his children of an earlier marriage resulted in frequent quarreling during the courtship, led to counseling where the relationships to his children were clarified, ground rules established about their behavior, and a good marriage ensued.

Other environmental forces influencing the current marriage include direct or indirect intervention by the former spouse through her children. Finally, adverse reactions of friends to the new marital partner can precipitate marital disharmony.

The intrapersonal and interpersonal forces are so intertwined in remarriage that they will be considered together as to their role in marital discord. The psychodynamic forces include guilt feelings. The need for punishment on the part of either spouse may provoke painful retaliation. The guilt may be due to conscious or unconscious death wishes toward the former partner. There may be conscious guilt at having forced a divorce on a partner who is now unhappily married or not married at all. Another force is the repetition of mate choices based on conscious or unconscious homosexual feelings or behavior defended against by marriage, for example, the selection of beautiful, seductive women to conceal inadequate sexual performance by the male. These and many other unconscious forces may be at the root of the current marital discord, and thus knowledge of previous marriages is useful. In several couples involving a remarried widowed person, the deceased spouse was so idealized and the new partner so continuously and unfavorably compared that constant and bitter quarreling occurred. In the next paragraph remarriage will be presented in terms of object choice and relationships, in keeping with psychoanalytic concepts of developmental stages and GST.

Freud's[14] concept of anaclitic and narcissistic object relationships, Anna Freud's[15] phase developmental stages and Benedek's[16] proposals on symbiotic relationships were seminal in psychoanalytic circles. There is a progressive maturation from early physiological unity of infant and mother to a separateness that occurs in a "series of orderly sequential stages."[17] In addition to the mother-child relationship, each infant is born into a family whose intermeshing bonds change through birth, marriage and death. Because of kinship networks, each family is bound to other families. The child's earliest experiences vary in relationship to the kin present, e.g. grandparents living in the same household. Thus during his period of growth, many object relationships become significant, each being reacted to in a specific manner.

Object relationships reflect their historical development as phenomenological voices in the "records" of the individual. We reassess behavior in the adult in the light of antecedent adaptations of the infant, the child and the adolescent. "Every person goes through a series of sequential object relationships. These relationships operate developmentally as well as currently; for example, couplings, intimacies, or antagonisms."[18] The newborn infant progresses from a stage of (narcissistic) parasitism, where it lives off mother, to one of symbiosis. Benedek[19] postulated an early neonatal stage of fusion between mother and child which she called "symbiosis." Husbands and wives are also bound to each other in a symbiotic fashion, but their bond is of a different order from that between mother and child, because the needs of one partner for the other are relatively equal."[20] In the early object relationships, if unsatisfactory mothering occurs, painful "records" are encoded in the individual. These "records," when later projected onto to the partner (via the phenomena of projective identification), can lead to serious problems in marriage. In these couples with marital disharmony, an earlier bad "record" of the mother's "parental" voice is reacted to internally as well as projected onto the spouse, who is then attacked—thus setting off a series of bitter arguments and/or complaints.

Twenty-five years ago, Mittelmann[21] suggested that the neuroses of marital partners complement each other with dovetailing of conflictual and defensive patterns on early developmental levels. Giovacchini[22] recently extended these conclusions and emphasized the mutually adaptive qualities of the marital relationship. In a later presentation he[23] described two types of marital object relationships, which are helpful in understanding both marital discord and sequential marriages. First *a character object relationship,* typified by a total characterological involvement between husband and wife: "The marital partner requires the total personality, including the specific character defenses, of the other partner in order to maintain intrapsychic equilibrium." Second, a *symptom object relationship,* transitory in nature and not having the depth of involvement characteristic of the first type: "The spouse does not require the total personality of the other; he needs only a particular trait or symptom, and the marital involvement seems only a partial one. Other objects with similar traits or symptoms, although differing in many respects, could serve defensive needs as well." The circumscribed meaning of the marital relationship leads to repetitive marriages.

In conclusion, different types of symbiotic ties are present in all marital relationships along a developmental axis. The initial mother-child symbiosis undergoes a series of developments. The elements of the earlier symbiosis continue to operate in all marriages, but in healthy individuals they are expansive rather than constrictive. In marital disharmony we see fixations upon or regression to particular symbiotic states. These constitute the pathological symbiotic states and are attempts to relieve anxiety and deal with conflict.

NOTES

1. Bernard L. Greene: Sequential marriage: repetition or change? in *The Marriage Relationship* (Salo Rosenbaum and Ian Alger, Eds.). New York, Basic Books, 1968, pp. 293–306.
2. Jessie Bernard: *Remarriage: A Study of Marriage*. New York, Dryden Press, 1956.
3. Reuben Hill: Methodological issues in family development research, *Family Process*, 3:186, 1964; and Marian R. Yarrow, John D. Campbell, and R. V. Burton: Reliability of maternal retrospection: A preliminary report, *Family Process*, 3:207, 1964.
4. P. H. Landis: Sequential marriage, *J Home Economics*, 42:625, 1950.
5. Thomas P. Monahan: How stable are remarriages?, *Amer J Sociol*, 58:280, 1952.
6. Landis, *op cit*. Twenty years ago he stated: "At age 30, for example, the chances of remarriage for a divorced woman are 94 in 100; for a widowed woman, 60 in 100. The chances of a spinster of 30 has of eventually marrying are only 48 in 100."
7. Bernard, *op. cit.*, pp. 112–113.
8. W. J. Goode: *After Divorce*. Glencoe, Free Press, 1956; Harvey J. Locke: *Predicting Adjustment in Marriage*. New York, Holt, 1951, p. 302; Harvey J. Locke and W. J. Klausner: Marital adjustment of divorced persons in subsequent marriages, *Sociol Social Res*, 33:97, 1948.
9. Thomas P. Monahan (The changing nature and instability of remarriages *Eugenics Quart*, 5:73, 1958) writes: ". . . A divorce for one party weakens the strength of the marriage bond, and a second divorce experience greatly lessens the chances of survival of the marriage." He gives the following statistics: "Primary marriages (a first marriage for

both parties) show a ratio of only 16.6 per marriages in that category. But where both parties had been divorced *once* before, the figure doubles to 34.9, and where both parties had been divorced *twice or more times*, the ratio climbs to 79.4."

10. Edmund Bergler: *Divorce Won't help.* New York, Harper & Row, 1949, pp. 233–234.
11. Peter L. Giovacchini: Treatment of marital disharmonies: The classical approach, in *The Psychotherapies of Marital Disharmony* (Bernard L. Greene, Ed.). New York, Macmillan, 1965, pp. 39–82.
12. Norman W. Bell: Extended family relations of disturbed and well families, *Family Process, 1*:175, 1962.
13. Bernard L. Greene and Noel Lustig: Remarriage and the physician, *Med Aspects Hum Sexuality*, in press.
14. Sigmund Freud: On Narcissism: An Introduction (1914), in *Collected Papers*, New York, Basic Books, 1959, Vol. IV.
15. Anna Freud: Psychoanalysis and education, *Psychoanal Study Child, 9*:9, 1954; and Anna Freud: Introduction to katya levy's, simultaneous analysis of a mother and her adolescent daughter, *Psychoanal Study Child, 15*:378, 1960.
16. Therese Benedek: The psychosomatic implications of the primary unit: mother-child, *Amer J Orthopsychiat, 19*:642, 1949. See also Margaret S. Mahler and Manuel Furer, who in their book, *On Human Symbiosis and the Vicissitudes of Individuation* (New York, Int. Univs. Press, 1968), suggest that the symbiotic stage begins in the third month after birth, that the peak of the symbiotic phase occurs in the third quarter of the first year and "co-incides with the beginning of the differentiation of the self from the symbiotic object," and that this phase leads into the "separation-individuation phase."
17. George H. Pollock: Transference neurosis: object choice and object relationships: the dyad and triad, *Arch Gen Psychiat, 6*:294, 1962.
18. George H. Pollock: On Symbiosis and Symbiotic Neurosis, *Int J Psychoanal, 45*:1, 1964.
19. Benedek, *op. cit.*
20. Greene: *op. cit.*, p. 298.
21. Bela Mittelmann: Complementary neurotic reactions in intimate relationships, *Psychoanal Quart, 13*:479, 1944.
22. Peter L. Giovacchini: Mutual adaptation in various object relationships, *Int J Psychoanal, 39*:1, 1958. See also his article, Characterological aspects of marital interaction, *Psychoanal Forum, 2*:7, 1967, with discussions by Margaret S. Mahler, Victor H. Rosen, Eric Berne, Martin A. Berezin, Roy R. Grinker, Jr., Clifford J. Sager and David Liberman.
23. Giovacchini: Treatment of marital disharmonies: the classical approach, in *The Psychotherapies of Marital Disharmony.* (Bernard L. Greene, Ed.). New York, Macmillan, 1965.

XV

CHILDHOOD ENVIRONMENT

The family of orientation, as explored under item 14 of the BMQ (see Appendix), exerts an important influence on the couple both before and after marriage. The personality of every individual[1] is a crystallization of cognitive development involving both the "pia" and "inner child" voices, value orientations creating the "parental" voice in the "records," and the effects of the structural arrangements in the family—parental and especially the ordinal position of the person. In Chapter VIII, four ways were discussed in which a married couple could be influenced by their extended kin. In the PS and MDS, four fifths of the parents of both husbands and wives were living at the time the couples were either seeking or undergoing marital therapy. In this chapter the role of the father's and mother's influence upon a marriage will be presented as it pertains to encoding of value orientations, the importance of the ordinal position of each spouse as it can affect a marriage, and lastly, the impact of the parental transactions upon each spouse during their residence at home.

The formation of values, as heard faintly or loudly coming from the "parental" voice of each "record," results from those values we had as children and adolescents. These values come from the interpersonal and environmental systems the individual is transacting with. In childhood these values are primarily the outcome of the parents (or parental surrogates) we had and the type of family we came from. In an excellent article Daniel Cappon[2] has defined values as: "abstract standards which become imbedded in habitual judgements, attitudes, systems and ways of life. Thus values transcend the temporal impulse and even the psychological impetus or motivation which initiated an interest and prompted its attachment to an object, to form a value." He divides the determinants of values into four categories: biological, social, psychological and ecological. The biological determinant of one's values involves the intrapersonal system and is an innate quality of the "inner child." The social determinants involve both the interpersonal and environmental systems, in which parental values play an important role. The psychological determinants of values involve primarily the intrapersonal system in circular causality with components from both the interpersonal and environmental systems and are heard from the "parental" voices of the "records." The ecological determinants of values results from transactions with the environmental system, e.g. "conflict arising from rural upbringing and values clashing with those of the town which supplies the economics for existence."

The encoding of values[3] goes on in an inflexible manner, whether the parents or any element in the interpersonal and environmental systems will it or not. Values are always in relation to other people (interpersonal system) in a given sociocultural milieu in time and space (environmental system). The axiological code of the nature of values and the types of values, whether secular or religious, is in relationships between individuals. The earlier the encoding of "parental" voices, the more forceful their replay in courtship and marriage as a result of projective identification and unconscious collusion.

Until recently little attention in the literature has been given to "father-child relations and the contributory role played by aberrations in these relations in character development."[4] The role of the individual's father is important, e.g. is he charismatic, or was he absent while the person was growing up? We are interested as to the father's age, occupation and whether or not he is living. The occupation of the father gives some clue as to the sociocultural background of the spouse. If the father is self-employed or professional, there may be marital friction resulting from son-in-law or daughter-in-law interference. If this is expressed at this point, the issue is dealt with later when discussing the item of occupational adjustment.

Item 14b on the BMQ (see Appendix) asks about the individual's mother: occupation, whether living or not, and age. A working mother and the type of work she did and does can be important for a diagnostic understanding of the marital discord of the conflicted couple. Most important for the evaluation of the marital disharmony of the couple is the understanding of both the past and the current relationships with their respective parents. Kinship ties often offer many supports for the couple seeking help, financial and otherwise. The many diverse forces influencing a marriage include (1) the model of marriage each spouse was exposed to during his childhood and adolescence in observing the marital relationships of his/her parents, (2) the personalities of individual family members, parents, siblings, as well as other kin living with or influencing the family, (3) the social and cultural values of the family, and so on.

Item 14c on the BMQ asks each spouse to list his siblings, giving first name only, age and sex. Ordinal position among siblings frequently aids in understanding current marital problems. Altus[5] reviewed some of the literature for the past one hundred years and found ordinal position among siblings related to potential eminence and educational learning. He states: ". . . it seems a fairly safe assumption that there is a kind of academic primogeniture operating at the college level." A seminal book by Walter Toman[6] on family constellation should be required reading for all therapists. He presents eight basic sibling positions in his book. He does this in extensive character portraits, comprising the enduring relationships to people and the impact of losses of these people as well as attitudes toward philosophy, religion, death, politics, work, authority, money and property. I have followed his classification in analyzing the 750 couples, using only the five following categories: oldest, youngest, intermediate, only and middle child (see Table XXII).

The intermediate grouping refers to a spouse coming from a family having more than three children and being in any relationship to them as to age. Interestingly, the ordinal position in both series were almost similar. However, the marital combinations were, as to be expected, many and varied. I use the

TABLE XXII
ORDINAL POSITION OF SPOUSES

	PS		MDS	
	Male	*Female*	*Male*	*Female*
Oldest	165	181	95	75
Youngest	130	149	64	70
Intermediate	101	80	45	54
Singleton	80	72	40	35
Middle	24	18	6	16

following figures to represent the ordinal position and place them in the margin of the BMQ opposite item 14 (see Appendix). This method, in my experience, helps to fix the ordinal position in the therapist's mind. Figure 4 shows the nine possible positions for the male.

Toman's studies were based on clinical psychological work and described enduring relationships. The ordinal position may help in understanding how some of the "records" can be projected onto one's spouse or child to produce marital discord. Not infrequently, marital disharmony can occur with pregnancy

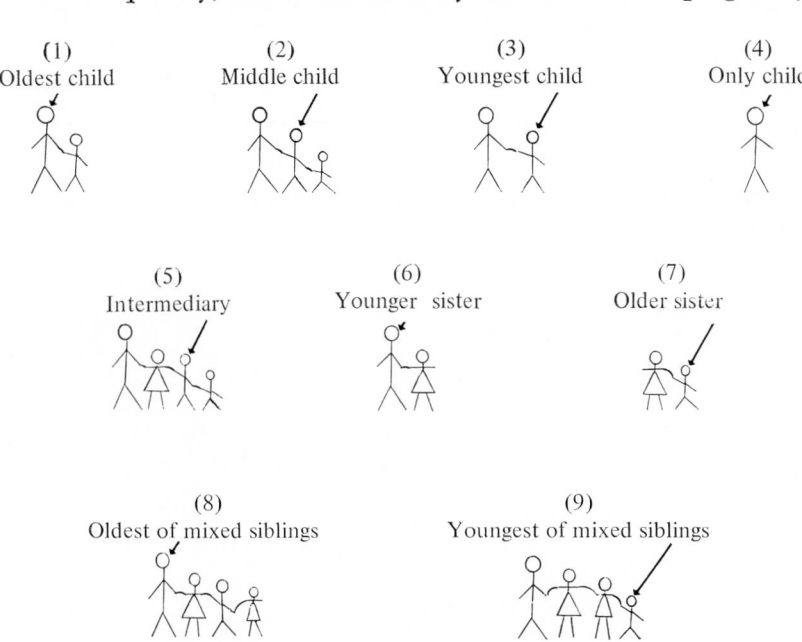

Figure 4. Male ordinal positions.

or birth of the first child. The "record" activated or played will be determined, at times, in the selection of the spouse and co-determined by the kinds of individuals a person has been living with the longest and most intimately. The marriage can duplicate the earliest interpersonal relationships in degrees varying from complete duplication to none at all. Toman hypothecates that the closer the new relationships resemble the earlier ones, the more successful will be the new ones. For example, if an older brother of a sister marries the younger sister of a brother (see figure 5), they are duplicating their childhood relation-

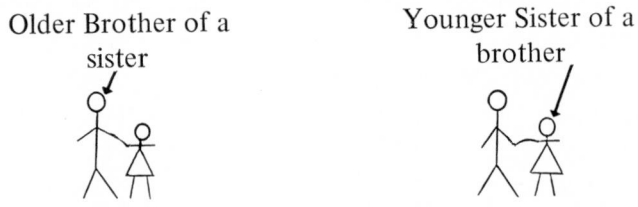

Older Brother of a
sister

Younger Sister of a
brother

Figure 5. Marriage duplicating earlier relationship.

ships regarding seniority rights. In addition, both are used to relating to the other sex and should have no marital conflicts in that area.

In the ninety-five oldest male siblings in the MDS, there was no disharmony when an older brother of a sister married the younger sister of a brother. This surprising finding confirms one of Toman's hypotheses.

There were eight couples in the MDS in which the older brother of a sister married the older sister of a sister (see Fig. 6). Toman notes that this marital arrangement could have con-

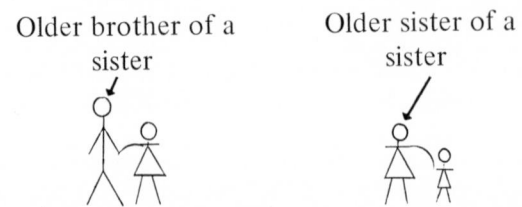

Older brother of a
sister

Older sister of a
sister

Figure 6. Marital combination that can lead to disharmony.

flicts in both the sexual area and in terms of seniority rights. This was illustrated in the following clinical extract:

Mr. Theodosia: "There is little, if any, emotional show in a positive manner on her part. We cannot reach agreement on anything! She is very indifferent to sexual relations, almost none, and then only when she wants it. We disagree on financial disbursements."

Mrs. Theodosia: "We cannot even understand each other's emotional needs. We are both too occupied with our own needs to be giving to each other. If I even try to indicate feelings of unrest, he turns away from me. We have constant arguments. I don't feel my husband is a friend, and I turn away from sexual activity. My husband does not pursue me. We have basically different philosophies about money. He feels if you want something a lot, the heck with whether you have the money; he has confidence that he'll get the money somehow. We seem to be on different wavelengths and in different worlds. What he enjoys, I don't and vice versa."

Another marital combination leading to disharmony in the marriage can occur where the older brother of a brother marries the older sister of a sister (see Fig. 7).

There were four couples of this type in the MDS. Typical of this type of marriage is the following couple where there was both sexual and seniority conflicts:

Mr. Tabitha: "Constant arguments. We have considerable trouble agreeing on many subjects. This is the result of differences on ideas and goals. Sexual dissatisfaction is the result of no activity. My wife has become very passive in this regard and apparently could care less. We seem to have trouble understanding each other. We don't communicate."

Mrs. Tabitha: "Our real problem is lack of communication. Emotional needs are something that must never be acknowledged—feeling deeply, getting excited, or enthused about something, being sad, and crying are things you must never do. Unfortunately, I do all these things, so we have problems. So no sex."

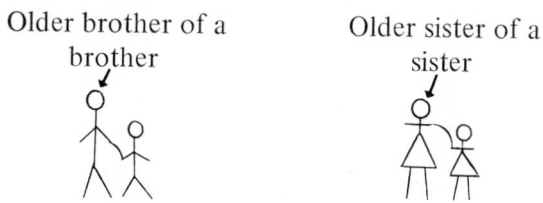

Older brother of a brother   Older sister of a sister

Figure 7. Another combination that can lead to disharmony.

There are other ordinal combinations where the older brother of a sister marries the younger sister of a sister, in which there may be no problem over seniority rights but the woman is not accustomed to having a man about; or the marriage between the younger brother of a sister and the older sister of a brother with the possible reversal of seniority rights where the wife may tend to be controlling and the husband dependent. My experience is in agreement with Toman that the most conflictual of all sixteen possible combinations would be that between the younger brother of a brother and the younger sister of a sister (see Fig. 8).

In this type of marriage I find, as Toman did, sexual problems and conflicts over their unconscious wish to be dependent.

Younger brother of a   Younger sister of a
brother   sister

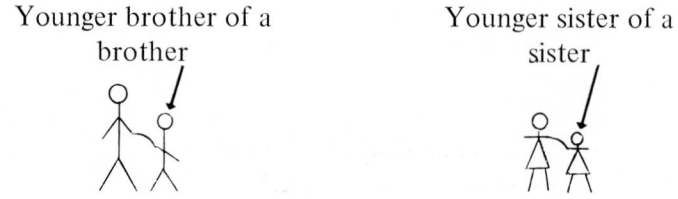

Figure 8. Most conflictual of marital combinations.

Parenthood would interfere with their dependency needs. The following couple is illustrative of this marital situation:

Mrs. Susannah: "I feel my marriage is not a marriage and never has been. I have been living with a very complicated husband. I do not understand him. It seems he doesn't want to be understood. He's indifferent. I do not care for him, my only concern is the effect of a separation on my daughter. I feel very guilty about her. Neither he nor I wanted children. Her conception was unplanned. Now that she is in high school I don't think a divorce would upset her. I believe my husband and I both would be better off separated. My husband does not fulfill my emotional needs. I want someone to love me, and at times I feel he wants to be mothered or taken care of. As to sexual satisfaction, I have had to submit to sexual acts that I hated but submitted to to avoid arguments. At one time, when we were married five years, I was quite taken with a friend of ours. I was lonely, my husband was working almost every night. I did not have any relations with this man, but our mutual feelings toward each other were discovered and of course never forgotten by my husband. I wish we would have divorced then. I have been faithful ever since, but my husband cannot forget or forgive."

Mr. Susannah: "We are constantly arguing, one sided, more in the form of her nagging. I am dissatisfied sexually. Her way or nothing, at her choosing of time. She is always rough on me, and amorous with male partners when she has a number of drinks. If I scold her, she gets insulting in and out of public."

Marital partners come not only from families with two children but also from those with more than two and sometimes with only one child. In families with more than one child,[7] the children have each other to relate to as well as their parents. Siblings are forced not only to compete with each other but also to share. Being an only child usually makes that child extremely important and valuable to his parents, especially if successful impregnation of the mother took a long time. In some families, a single child of unhappily married parents may become the focus of emotional (or even sexual) gratification of the discontented mother or father. Marital disharmony may ensue where a singleton looks for a parent in his/her spouse rather than a partner. Frequently, the singletons want to remain children in their marriage and may even be content without children of their own—often marrying late in life to avoid having children. Occasionally the only child may react in marriage by having many children: "I know what it's like to be an only child, and that is why we have four."

Fifteen percent in both series were singletons. The following is a clinical extract of a couple married ten years, both spouses being only children.

Mr. and Mrs. Stephena came for help because of recent constant quarreling following his job transfer out of state. An executive assistant, he had worked for his present company for fifteen years. The courtship of the Stephenas had been a long one and very smooth. In fact, she had been his secretary. There was a ten-year span between their ages. When she turned thirty, there had been pressure from their mutual friends that they marry and settle down and have a family. They had had premarital sexual relations, and after marriage Mrs. Stephena continued to use contraception without any objection on her husband's part. Both had agreed to have children later. Mrs. Stephena resented the move greatly, since she was very close to her mother, in fact, she called her every evening since her husband's transfer. Previously, before the move, she and her mother spent a great deal of time together while her husband played poker with his friends in the evening or attended lodge meetings. Both had been perfectly happy in their hotel apartment, which was maintained by the management. At the time of the move, he had rented a house, thinking this would make his wife happier in adjusting to the transfer and keep her busy, since she no longer wanted to work. This had only worsened their relationship. Her constant nagging him to keep up the maintenance of the house frequently lead to quarreling. But the main area of arguing centered about her not being close to her mother.

Mrs. Stephena related an incident which happened two years ago, which she can neither forget or forgive. He had sold their stock, the accumulation of both their savings and gifts from their respective families, and bought an expensive sports car against her wishes. She stated they have no practical budget which they follow. This is a problem for both of them, as she dribbles money away on little things, whereas he is more willing to go into debt for big things.

Mr. Stephena stated that his wife associated security with living near her parents. He admitted he is not the easiest person to live with: he never did like to putter around his parent's house and disliked gardening. At times he gets very bored with his job, but his boss overlooks many things. Since moving here, his wife has rejected him sexually, although in the past neither one was oversexed.

When questioned about their sexual relations, Mrs. Stephena had angrily defended herself: "I told him not to move here, and he knew my feelings about it. But he was too lazy to look for another job. I don't feel I'm consciously using sexual relations as a bribe. I don't feel toward him as I once did."

This couple illustrates that the only child is the only one of his kind and frequently remains a child often way into adulthood. He or she is not used to having other children present and is used to being the center of attention, and not infrequently, being the pride and joy of his parents. Frequently, as in this couple, material possessions are of little importance—psychologically they expect their parents or a parental surrogate to come up with the necessary emotional or material needs. Not uncommonly, the female single child tends to be self-centered, extravagant, more capricious, and as one husband complained recently in current avant garde vocabulary: "She is plastic."

In evaluating the role of ordinal position of the spouses as to possible influence in the marital discord, many idiosyncratic factors must be kept in mind. For example, the age differential between siblings, the oldest child may be considerably older than the next child and react like the youngest child; since gender role is assigned by parents or physicians, a child may behave like one of the opposite sex, e.g. a mother may have wanted a girl but gave birth to a boy and influenced the boy to act in an effeminate manner; a frequent complication is loss of a parent by divorce, desertion or death or even being sent away to a boarding school. Toman describes numerous personality configurations related to ordinal position that are frequently found in clinical or environmental situations, e.g. oldest brother of brother(s) is frequently accustomed to be in charge of others, whereas the youngest brother of brother(s) may be capricious and willful and ambivalent in his relationships to his elders.

Item 14d (see Appendix) asks each spouse to describe his parents and how they got along in their marriage.[8] Table XXIII gives some of the data found in the MDS as to the parent's relationships and as to the inidvidual's view of his childhood. In addition, each spouse is asked to described his/her family's circumstances as he was growing up.

The role of projective identification and unconscious collusion in marital discord necessitates exploration of childhood experiences of each spouse. As each mate is able to be confronted with his current behavior and feelings[9] in the marital crisis, as these are related to his earlier unresolved experiences and transactions, he may be able to cope more realistically with his discordant marriage. Reasonable and appropriate values and attitudes by parents are important for the socialization of the child and proscribed by the culture he lives in—his environ-

TABLE XXIII
FAMILY ENVIRONMENT

	Husband %	Wife %
Parents' marriage		
Unhappy	47	57
Average	40	30
Happy	13	13
Divorced	4	10
Desertion	2	3
Death	2	4
Childhood		
Unhappy	52	50
Average	35	26
Happy	13	24

mental system.[10] Unreasonable or excessive attitudes or demands by parents, on the other hand, create "records" that distort the transactions in the marriage. Important to keep in mind is the maturity or immaturity of the perceptual system of the individual that contributes to the encoding of "records." Since parents frequently demand of their own children, consciously or unconsciously, what their own parents demanded of them, in terms of values and attitudes, the next chapter will be developed in this area.

Another valuable finding observed when asking spouses about their early childhood environment and behavior is the information we get about the family setting in which the "inner child" feels most comfortable (the at-home feeling). This is important in understanding how idiosyncratic problems in adults arise and contribute to marital disharmony. I am indebted to Michael Daly's article[11] for his awareness of a book written in 1938 by Levy and Munroe[12] that discusses "how all of us tend to create a home similar to the one we grew up in. We feel most comfortable in a familiar environment. It makes little difference whether this environment is a healthy one." In a similar vein, Missildine[13] speaks of the "child" in every adult seeking constantly the feeling of being "at home" regardless of the peculiarities of the original family. Not infrequently, marital discord results from the clashes of the "inner children" of a couple with different family backgrounds. The following extract is typical:

> Mr. Stella, a gregarious, successful business man, raised in a home where friends neighbors and relatives were coming and going, had married a reserved, quiet woman.
>
> Mrs. Stella remembered her childhood as an average one. Her parents rarely invited guests and spoke to each other in a reserved, dignified manner. She could not invite any playmates to visit without her mother's permission. No one, not even relatives would have thought of dropping in without an invitation. A meticulous housekeeper, she only felt comfortable when her home was neat and orderly. A furious quarrel ensued when Mr. Stella had, on the spur of the moment, invited a business acquaintance to his home for a drink without telling his wife. "I don't have a home, I have a museum. In fact, at times it feels like a mausoleum. At first she said I couldn't have company over until the house was completely finished. It's now two years, and I've yet to have a dinner party. . . ."

When confronted with this complaint, Mrs. Stella at first denied his accusations and then admitted she couldn't run a house like his mother did: "His relatives called his home 'Grand Central Station.' People were always eating there, sleeping there, and partying there, I'm just not that type."

Explaining to both about their "inner child" seeking the security of the past (at-home feeling) and that they were both replaying the past "records" where the "parental" voices had different values and attitudes was most productive therapeutically.

In this chapter I have presented some observations about the role of parental influences as it affects not only the personalities of each spouse but also the marriage. The importance of the ordinal position and family constellation of each spouse was also touched upon. An interesting finding was that almost one half of the spouses reported their parents' marriages to be unhappy. Further one half of the marital partners stated that their own childhood experiences were unhappy. Perhaps a poor marriage in the childhood of a spouse serves as a poor model for later happiness in marriage.

NOTES

1. Leslie Y. Rabkin: The patient's family: research methods, *Family Process*, 4:105, 1965. A stimulating article with a comprehensive bibliography explores the "myriad ways" in which a family exerts its influence on the child "to make the child an extension of itself and of its cultural milieu." See also Stephen Fleck: An approach to family pathology, *Compr Psychiat*, 7:307, 1966; J. Cotter Hirschberg: Today's family: A variable balance of strengths and weaknesses, *Menninger Quart*, 22:16, 1968; Theodore Lidz (*The Family and Human Adaptation*. New York, Int. Univs. Press, 1963), who explores "The critical role of the family in human adaptation and integration." He proposes that "The essential dynamic structure of the family rests upon the parents' ability to form a coalition, maintain boundaries between generations, and adhere to their appropriate sex-linked roles;" Richard L. Jenkins: The varieties of children's behavior problems and family dynamics, *Amer J Psychiat*, 124:1440, 1968; and E. James Anthony (A clinical evaluation of children with psychotic parents, *Amer J Psychiat, 126:* 177, 1969), who found three groups of disturbances: "precursive disturbances—forerunners of later adult psychoses; symbiotic—directly

attributable to the type of relationship between child and sick parent; and induced or parapsychotic—attributable to the environment."

2. Daniel Cappon: Values and value judgement in psychiatry, *Psychiat Quart, 1*, July, 1966. He divides the determinants of values into four categories: "(1) Biological—accounting primarily for perceptual and instrumental values. (2) Social—accounting for cultural, both cognitive and instrumental values. (3) Psychological—accounting for personal preferences. (4) Ecological—accounting primarily for property and quantity as well as for instrumental values."

3. Louis Jolyon West (Ethical psychiatry and biosocial humanism, *Amer J Psychiat, 126:226*, 1969) describes the encoding of the "parental" voices in neuropsychological terms: "Thus it might be said that ethical constructs derive from an integration between digital and analog information that is somehow creatively unified within the brain of individual man. . . . The digital information processing (ego-like) functions of the cerebral lobes, and the analog information processing (id-like) functions of the limbic system or "visceral brain," seem to be interactively modulated by the reticular system through certain septal and hypothalmic connections, whereby (superego-like) emotional meanings and values become related to perceptions and ideas." In psychoanalysis, the encoding process is called internalization. In the process of the internalization, both the figure (father, mother, etc.) and the field are incorporated. A child learns from a model. His values come from the meaningful people in his life. As Jacob A. Arlow points out in The reaches of intrapsychic conflict, *Amer J Psychiat, 121:425*, 1965, "The long period of helplessness at the beginning of life is the biological snare in which the individual is grasped and drawn along the road to socialization. The adults who care for the infant do more than guarantee his survival. . . . A bond of attachment which is specifically human develops towards early objects. . . . By means of this tie, the extraordinary biological endowment of man can be influenced by the human environment. . . . The family unit or its equivalent is the first and main instrumentality through which this process is accomplished. To the family falls the responsibility of causing the distillate, the fundamentals of the experience of the social group, to be incorporated into the mind of the child. . . . The most prominent psychological mechanism by which this transformation is achieved is *identification*." Henry Greenbaum in his chapter on learning behavior (Imitation and identification in learning behavior in *The Etiology of the Neuroses*, Joseph H. Merin, Ed., Palo Alto, Science & Behavior Books, 1966, pp. 69–79) differentiates imitation as a forerunner of and a bridge to identification due to the child's need for social adaptation. "The smiling response, for example, which appears for the first time at the age of three months, is probably learned through the mechanism of imitation. In order for

the capacity to smile to emerge, the child must be exposed to people who smile at him while attending his needs." Greenbaum then proceeds to discuss identification as an unconscious process beginning early in childhood. He states: "Like imitation, it is one of the earliest forms of interpersonal relationships. In identification the connection, the cue and response is strong, *internalized* [italics added], and integrated. Without becoming aware of it, individuals behave as if they were impersonating the people, usually the parents or parent surrogates, with whom they identify." Thus every child imitates what he finds in his world. He tries to be like those he sees—first his parents, other kin, and so on. The more important the figure, the more important that person's code of ethics, values and attitudes becomes to values of the child. Children see through double ethics and adopt the habits rather than the words. See also Arthur M. Bodin: Family Interaction, Coalition, Disagreement, and Compromise in Problem, Normal and Synthetic Family Triads, Technical Report No. 8, Nonr 4374(00), U.S. Government.

4. Robert E. Anderson: Where's dad?, *Arch Gen Psychiat, 18*:641, 1968. See also Marjorie R. Leonard: Fathers, and daughters: the significance of 'fathering' in the psychosexual development of the girl, *Int J Psychoanal, 47*:325, 1966; Ian Gregory: Anterospective data following childhood loss of a parent, I. Delinquency and H. S. dropout. II. Pathology, performance and potential among college students, *Arch Gen Psychiat, 13*:99, 1965, and Retrospective data concerning childhood loss of a parent, *Arch Gen Psychiat, 15*:354, 1966; Milton H. Miller and Leigh M. Roberts: Psychotherapy with the children or disciples of charismatic individuals, *Amer J Psychiat, 123*:1049, 1967; and Gary Jacobson and Robert G. Ryder: Parental loss and some characteristics of the early marriage relationship, *Amer J Orthopsychiat, 39*:779, 1969.

5. William D. Altus: Birth order and its sequelae, *Science, 151*:44, 1966.

6. Walter Toman: *Family Constellation.* New York, Springer, 1961. See also Murray Bowen in a superb article, The use of family theory in clinical practice, *Compr Psychiat, 7*:345, 1966, who writes "There is one other theoretical concept that I have combined with my own work that is used with every family in psychotherapy. These are the personality profiles of the various sibling positions as presented by Toman. . . . I consider his work one of the significant contributions to family knowledge in recent years." On the other hand, George Levenger and Maurice Sonnheim (Complementarity in marital adjustment: Reconsidering Toman's family constellation hypothesis, *J Individ Psychol, 21*: 137, 1965) found no relationship between the birth order of the spouses and their marital adjustment.

7. Jay Haley (Speech sequences of normal and abnormal familities with two children present, *Family Process, 6*:81, 1967) found in his study

that: "normal and abnormal families with two children present no differences between the two groups, in contrast to a previous study where parents and one child were present and *differences were found* [italics added]."

8. Warren M. Brodey in the opening paragraph in his new book (*Changing The Family*. New York, Potter, 1968) succinctly expresses the role of the family of orientation upon children: "A husband and wife in contact speak a million words in every breath. It is this richness that encompasses a family into a living unit and carries on its life into an evolving generation." See also Edward J. Carroll: A Study of Interpersonal Relations Within Families, Research Grant No. MH 05433, NIMH. This 108-page report presents a new model which includes use of the GST.

9. Feelings are either acceptable or unacceptable. Feelings that are acceptable cause no trouble, only unacceptable feelings seem undesirable and are upsetting to the individual. Frequently our feelings are so intense and inappropriate that we may try to consciously suppress them. On the other hand, feelings may be repressed unconsciously—blushing is a common example. Further knowledge about feelings can be found in psychological texts on personality and emotion.

10. Recently there has been a reversal in therapist's attitudes toward parents. Whereas the previous attitude was: "There are no problem children, only problem parents," the current approach is more realistic. As John L. Schmiel (How to help parents of adolescents, *Physician's Panorama*, 5:4, 1967) succinctly puts it: "In recent years parents have come under increasingly severe criticism. Poor parents are accused of neglect and affluent ones of indulgence. Blaming and punishing parents tend to undermine their constructive influence and hence to aggravate the situation. Producing a generation of guilt-ridden parents is not the answer." A recent article by Peter L. Giovacchini (Compulsory happiness, *Arch Gen Psychiat*, 18:650, 1968) describes how some patients ostensibly rebelled against their parents' "compulsion" that they be happy.

11. Michael Joseph Daly: Sexual attitudes in menopausal and postmenopausal women, *Med Aspects Hum Sexuality*, 2:48, 1968.

12. John Levy and Ruth Munroe: *The Happy Family*. New York, Knopf, 1938.

13. W. Hugh Missildine: *Your Inner Child of the Past*. New York, Simon and Schuster, 1963.

XVI

RELATIONSHIP WITH CHILDREN

Item 15 on the BMQ (see Appendix) asks each spouse to describe his children and his relationship with them. This item pertaining to children reveals information from each marital partner as to his "records" as it pertains to the influence of the "parental" voices on the feelings and behavior of the "inner child." Information is obtained as to values, attitudes, feelings and behavior of the respective spouses in the following areas:

1. Discloses the cultural transmission of values between the generations as heard coming from the "parental" voices (see Fig. 9).
2. Offers some correlation about the information obtained under item 14d discussed in the previous chapter (XV) where each spouse is asked to describe his childhood.
3. Reveals further information about item 8h (see Ch. X), which deals with the specific marital complaint of conflicts about children.
4. Divulges the possible scapegoating of a child.
5. Discloses conscious or unconscious relationships with children,[1] e.g. unconscious collusion between parent and child: emotional, incestuous, and so on.

The influence of the "parental" voice, as seen in Figure 9, is both direct and indirect where it contributes to the formation of the "records." Parents exert direct influence by guidance, reassurance, praise, criticism—either overtly or covertly—and indirect influence by their "parental" voices encoded in their children's "records." What a child feels and how he reacts are the reactions of his parents to him. Children have parents who provide positive or negative guidance, whereas adults act as

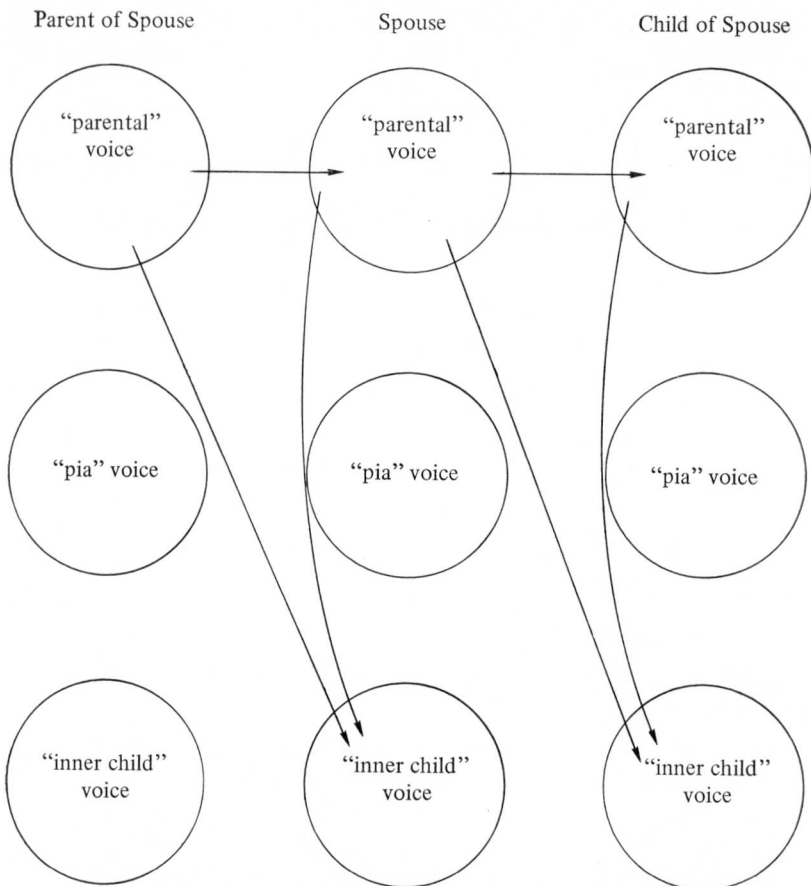

Figure 9. Transmission of values between generations.

parents to themselves by means of their "parental" voices. Thus adults continue the parental values and attitudes that were imposed on them in their childhood, not only toward themselves in adult life but also toward their children. Berne[2] delineates four ways in which a parental figure can influence a child: demeanor, gestures, voice, and vocabulary. Clinically I use his expression of "stroking" to express a positive attitude or action by a spouse and "critical" for an opposite attitude[3] toward another individual.

John P. Spiegel and Normal W. Bell[4] have reviewed and abstracted eighty-five articles published since 1930 on the influence of parent-child relationships on the adjustment of the child, and listed a partial list of pathogenic parental traits, e.g. dependent, domineering, emotionally unstable, fearful, hypochondriacal, inadequate, submissive, controlling, and so on. In reviewing the data of item 15 on the BMQ, the following four pathogenic parental attitudes were found in order of frequency.

OVERCONTROLLING PARENT

A parent who continually supervises, coerces, constrains, and directs the child is overcontrolling. The child may react with compliance or rebel overtly or covertly, e.g. procrastination, dawdling, and so on. Just as the real child may react with compliance or rebel actively or passively, so may the "inner child" of the parent do the same. Not only do we demand of others what we frequently demand of ourselves, but also our "inner child" responds like our real children. Marital disharmony can occur when one spouse attempts to coerce the "inner child" of his partner or in the case of projective identification when one spouse reacts to the coercion of his own "parental" voice as though it were coming from his partner. The following clinical example is illustrative:

Mr. Agnes began the first interview by stating he and his wife had been separated for approximately two months and that both would like to get back together. However, Mrs. Agnes will not permit a reconciliation until some of their problems are worked out. The problem between them primarily is that they do not agree about the discipline of their older teen-age son, a child from her first marriage. She states that he is at the kids all the time, whereas he claims she sticks up for them all the time. Finally, last Christmas he got fed up and left. When he wanted to return, she wouldn't have anything to do with him.

Mr. Agnes stated: "It seems that everything I say to my older son is interpreted by my wife to be picking on him or belittling him. There seems to be no common ground to stand on for the two of us in disciplining out two sons. The children now know this and, I believe, take advantage of it. The older one will stand and argue with me over anything I tell him to do, 'I'll do it in a minute, as soon as I finish reading.' If his mothers hears me arguing with him, she will tell him to do as he wants to. He wasn't that way before he entered high school. He used to be a good student, and we got along fine. Now he doesn't get his homework in on time, and in the past two years my life with him has become one constant argument. Mr. Agnes continued that besides the discipline disagreements, they also argue about other things involving the children. She is always buying clothes for the kids, and he disapproves. He states he is not a permissive parent, and he expects them to toe the line. He adds he says no quite a bit and she says yes about 90 percent of the time. He states, for instance, that he does not approve of the oldest son dancing the twist, and he would not permit it around the house when he was there. However, as soon as he went to work, the mother would let them do the twist. His son used to be well mannered and used to be close to him, but now he is a headstrong punk, and he and his son are now completely opposite. As a matter of fact, the son doesn't want to have anything to do with him. He quotes his wife as stating that if the children want something and it makes them happy, she is going to give it to them. She is very overindulgent, and anything the kids want she tries to get for them. By this, he adds that she had to keep up the Joneses. Mrs. Agnes has a part-time job and lavishes clothes on the two boys. Every weekend she brings home a sweater, shirt, or something else for the children. He states that she is lazy and a poor housewife and that she never had to do much when she was growing up. He adds that part of the trouble between he and his wife is due to his parents never having recognized his wife. He comes from a Lutheran background, Missouri Synod, and states his mother was a very set person, decidedly so, and never changes her mind. She is very old-fashioned and won't accept modern plumbing or modern conveniences. He states his mother was furious when he married a Catholic. His father was the boss in the family and a firm disciplinarian and a man of violent temper. As a youngster he couldn't make a move without his father's permission. Mother was a firm disciplinarian also. He concludes by saying he loves his wife and children, but for some reason the kids seem to be steering them apart, and they very much disagree on how to rear the children.

Mrs. Agnes began by angrily stating: "My husband and I seem to disagree on everything that concerns our two children. He does not leave them alone. He is a constant complainer. He ridicules them. They have never done anything which could be considered seriously wrong. At the dinner table they are told they don't chew right, drink right, sit right, and so on. They are constantly told they are wrong. He never says anything decent to them. Whatever he says is reprimanding. He has a bad temper. He will shout, slam doors, bang cabinets. I am not the best housekeeper there is, and this irritates him. He began to complain more after our first son was born. He complains constantly. Our marriage turned into one constant argument; I could not take it anymore. He expects the kids to be a little better and doesn't let up on them until they do what he says. The problem is that he never lets up. They are either stupid asses, or idiots, and they never have a moment's rest. He never gets off their back, and regardless of what they do, they never do anything right."

The husband in this case illustrates how he plays his "parental" voices toward others as his parents reacted towards him.

Mr. Agnes stated that in his childhood both parents were constantly directing and supervising his actions. Before entering high school, he used to daydream a great deal and procrastinate. Even now at work he occasionally procrastinates. Although he complained about his wife's lack of interest in carrying out her household chores, this did not become a real issue until after his oldest son started to rebel as a teen-ager. This family also illustrates the scapegoating of the older son bearing the brunt of the father's hostility toward his wife.

PERFECTIONISTIC PARENT

This parent demands perfection from his child and gets it by withholding acceptance of the child. In contrast to the controlling parent, who is apt to be tempermental in behavior, the perfectionistic parent is outwardly calm and typically manifests an obsessive-compulsive personality. A good illustration of this type of parent was depicted in a cartoon in the *New Yorker* magazine where a father is looking at his son's report card and calmly states: "A Zimmerman does not get a 'B'." This demand for performance creates in many children a rebellion characterized by underachievement. The "inner child" rebels because he feels he is not loved for what he is but only for what he can do. On the other hand, the withholding of full acceptance by the parent can lead to overachievement by the child in various areas, such as sports, scholarship, or music, but with loss of pleasure in his accomplishments, since the child drives himself with progressive demands of perfection both from outside himself (parents) and internally from the continuously demanding "parental" voices. Later, as an adult he demands perfection, not infrequently from both his children and his wife. This can lead to serious marital difficulties as the following clinical case demonstrates:

Mr. and Mrs. Brigit were referred for therapy by the gynecologist whom Mrs. Brigit had consulted at her husband's insistence that she do something about her frigidity. Complicating the family situation was the underachiever, their only child. Repeated conferences with numerous teachers had elicited the same response: "Your daughter has superior intelligence but is doing mediocre work." Mr. Brigit, a professional man, well endowed intellectually, physically well built, presented the appearance of the successful prototype. His speech was evenly modulated and precisely uttered. Mrs. Brigit was an attractive, intelligent, well-groomed woman.

Mr. Brigit calmly stated: "I believe that we have consistently failed to develop a feeling of mutual understanding. My wife is quite reserved, and while she may feel emotion, she does not show it overtly. Her reserve extends to our lovemaking, where she has never been able to completely abandon herself to the sex act. We have consulted numerous marriage art manuals that I have brought home. Undoubtedly, I have placed too much stress on our sexual relations. . . . I believe that generally I am an easygoing kind of person. . . . I try not to be too critical of others, since this was an early failing. Now I try to be forgiving of faults in others—ironically, except with reference to my wife and daughter. I tend to procrastinate and as often or not will put things off to the last moment. . . . I just don't like to perform badly. . . . Our daughter is exceptionally bright, very perceptive, but not doing well as she could at school. We have a good relationship, but possibly I tend to be too critical and may have set standards to high. . . . My parents have had a basically uneventful marriage. They seem to respect each other but have never appeared particularly attentive or demonstrative to one another. My father is a very capable person and has always demanded that I do everything to the best of my ability, but somehow my best was never good enough. I graduated with honors from high school, second in my class, and his only comment was: "how come wasn't I valedictorian? He never punished me physically as I was growing up, just his even look was sufficient. . . .""

Mrs. Brigit, in an even-tempered voice, stated: "First in point of order from my point of view would come lack of communication caused, I would guess, by sexual dissatisfaction on the part of my husband. Meanwhile, it has colored other aspects of our marriage, so that we no longer adequately fulfill one another's emotional needs. The lines of communication in our marriage, at present, are one-way. I talk and attempt to communicate my feelings, he keeps pretty much to himself. A tendency on his part to be disparaging of me has always been present. No matter what I do, for example, a gourmet meal, will be met with a look of 'It could have been done better.' If I forget to close a drawer completely, he doesn't say anything—but again the same look. From the beginning of our marriage, I resented his mechanical approach to sex. He would bring home these manuals and expect me to read them. It made sex appear like a mechanical thing: you rub the clitoris six times, press each nipple twice and presto— the grand orgasm. So more and more, sex became a ritual instead of the end point of intimacy. He relates to our daughter in the same demanding way. Always expecting perfection from her, so she has given up and is doing average work at school."

The complaints of this woman were beautifully depicted in a dream of another woman married to a perfectionist: she had a solid gold fountain pen that did not work. As Missildine[5] has pointed out in his book, a must reading for therapists, perfectionists are usually very intelligent, well educated and economically better off than most people. Belittling their own accomplishments, they drive themselves, as well as others (in the above couple, both the wife and child) to ever-increasing demands to do better. Mr. Brigit pursued his work methodically, systematically, and with careful attention to details. The exhausted, perfectionistic housewife and overconscientious mother have been described by Berne[6] in the marital game of "Harried." In spite of accomplishment the individual, driven by the demanding "parental" voice, feels little satisfaction in his efforts, since the command of the "parental" voice is to do "still better." Mr. Brigit is typical of this class of persons who have great difficulty in intimate relationships with "significant others." Thus the sexual relationship was focused on performance instead of the exchange of deep feelings. His wife's frigidity was the only area where she could challenge his perfectionism, and he could not make her respond with all his manuals. His perfectionistic demands forced his daughter to rebel by underachievement in school.

SUBMISSIVE PARENT

This parent reverses his parental role, and instead of setting limits to his child's immature demands and behavior, he sacrifices his own prerogatives. He creates a selfish, self-centered child who as an adult is indifferent to the feelings and rights of others. The "parental" voice is so faint that at times it seems to be entirely missing. Usually the voice of the "inner child" sings out as though it was playing an unaccompanied sonata: creative, extremely curious, full of fun and play, and sexual. Without the inhibiting and restraining "parental" voice, these children as adults are attractive, warm people who make friends easily, are impulsive and apt to overindulge in food, alcohol, and women. Their physical attractiveness, spontaneity, creativity, unbounding confidence and charm often attract a spouse who is inhibited, compulsive, controlled and extremely conscientious. The following clinical vignette is typical:

Mr. and Mrs. Almira were referred by their family physician. Recently Mr. Almira had been unable to function as an account executive for an advertising agency because of his increasing alcoholism. He was an attractive, warm, gracious, impeccably dressed man, whose firm was very anxious for his recovery. Mrs. Almira, extremely intelligent, was very quiet and shy in demeanor. Mr. Almira, an only child, was doted on by his parents, who catered to his every wish and whim. He romanced his teachers through his high school years, was very popular with his classmates, and had numerous romances. He was elected class president in his senior year. Called to the dean's office because of driving too fast and under the influence of alcohol, he impulsively quit college at the end of his sophomore year. He began to drink too much as a freshman, but his fraternity brothers had covered up for him. A family friend owned an advertising agency, and he went to work for him. He was soon very successful because of his creativity, confidence and physical attractiveness. He was a natural as an account executive because of his ability to relate quickly and spontaneously with his clients. They liked his charm, ability to come up with creative ideas and his uninhibited manner with women. His secretary idolized him, and like the others in his past, covered up for him, did all the details he detested and never completed, many times even saw that he got to his apartment, undressed him and put him to bed.

Mrs. Almira stated that she knew of his reputation but thought he would change after marriage, settle down, and want a family. But he did not, in fact, his drinking progressively increased. Occasionally the bartender at a local cocktail lounge where he was well known would call her to take her husband home. The only time Mrs. Almira expressed considerable affect in the interview was when she related an incident, early in their marriage, when she was immobilized in bed with a severe back strain, and her husband had gone to the drugstore to get her prescription filled. Instead of returning immediately, he got drunk and did not come home for three days. Although extremely hurt by his inconsiderate behavior, she maintained the marriage, since she did not want to hear her parents say, "We told you so!" They had originally objected to the marriage because of religious differences. Mrs. Almira, the oldest of five children, had been burdened with both the housework and raising of her brothers and sisters during her late childhood and adolescence. Her mother had severe arthritis, which often incapacitated her. Upon finishing high school, she left home because of a male boarder who made a sexual pass at her when he was drunk. When she told her mother of this incident, instead of comforting, she received a scolding.

This couple illustrates how an inhibited individual with considerable unconscious hostility and guilt submits to the narcissistic spouse to achieve closeness and to neutralize her guilt about her hostility—punishment, the currency of guilt. This punishment permeated all areas of their marriage from sexual inconsideration to disregard all of her needs.

OVERINDULGENT PARENT

This parent waits upon the child unceasingly—a cornucopia of presents and attention. Since all the child's needs are anticipated, the "inner child's" creativity, curiosity, creative play and even sensuality may become blunted. Without any incentive to become involved interpersonally or environmentally, the child may display a bored and blasé manner—*enfant gâté*. As an adult, the "parental" voice influences the "inner child" to be bored, passive, disinterested, discontented and unable to establish meaningful relationships, since he always expects others to take care of him. There is lack of initiative and inability at persistent effort. Whereas the "inner child" of an adult with a submissive parent is *active* and demanding, the "inner child" of the overindulged adult is *passive* and bored. Marriage to this type of individual is frustrating, since the partner had originally mistaken her spouse's bored and blasé manner for sophistication. Typical of this type of marriage is the following:

Mr. Antoinette was a tall, handsome, immaculately dressed man, tailored in the newest fashion. He spoke in a somewhat affected manner and nervously puffed on a thin pipe the initial fifteen minutes of the session. He appeared bored and blasé during the interview: "I have some pretty definite ideas on how I want to live. I compromised to some extent. I said to her I would do anything reasonable to reconcile. Our family physician said we should be divorced. In fact, when we had our premarital examination from him, he took me aside and suggested that I should not marry—that I would be happier as a bachelor. My family feels the same way. I think it is a question of two strong-minded persons. With her, I've got courage to do many things. Basically she is unable to go along with my ideas. I have not been happy living in a townhouse after having lived in a mansion. In fact, I still have many of my things in my home. I am pretty much of a traveler. She has strong ideas, and when she doesn't get her way, she throws a fuss. She is not a wife the way I think of a wife. When I was in Europe studying, the women were different, grateful the man is home. I was brought up differently than she was. As a child everything I wanted was immediately obtained. Maybe that spoiled me. My parents were opposed to our marriage. When I suggested we live in a cheaper way so that I would not have to keep running to my parents for money, Jody suggested I go to work. I'm the creative and inventive type but have not gotten around to it yet."

Mrs. Antoinette was a tall, thin, very attractive red-haired woman. Her tight-fitting cashmere sweater complimented her full figure. She appeared depressed, showed very little spontaneous affect and at times appeared on the verge of tears: "I just don't understand it at all. Here I marry the bachelor of the year, and he turns out to be a bust. I thought he would settle down when we married, go to work and want a family. Instead, he still is a playboy. Occasionally he will want to leave to get away by himself. When he does, he calls me after a week and says he misses me and to join him. His folks have been supporting us. My father says he is a spoiled brat. When we are skiing everything is fine. But when we get home, he is bored, listless and continuously complaining that I should anticipate his wants. He had quite a reputation as a lover, but I was disappointed in that I had to be the aggressor. He is a wonderful lover, but I don't get it. I've never met anyone like him before."

The studies of Bowlby[7] on grief and mourning differentiating three phases of protest, despair and detachment resulting from childhood deprivation, Anderson[8] on paternal deprivation and delinquency, Bettelheim[9] on the autistic child, Ehrenwald[10] on patterns of psychosocial defense, Ackerman's[11] seminal book on the psychodynamics of family life, among others,[12] are all valuable in understanding the interplay between child and parent.

In this chapter I have attempted to explain the value of exploring the relationships between the spouses and their children. The music coming from both the children in the family and from the "records" in each adult reflect the values and attitudes of at least three generations.

NOTES

1. Irene Fast and Albert C. Cain: (The stepparent role: potential for disturbances in family functioning, *Amer J Orthypsychiat*, 36:485, 1966) discuss stepparents' role-related difficulties in developing stable patterns of feeling, thinking and acting toward their stepchildren in terms of contradictory pressures on them to act as parent, nonparent, and stepparent. See also Alfred A. Messer: The "Phaedra Complex," *Arch Gen Psychiat*, 21:213, 1969.
2. Eric Berne: *Transactional Analysis in Psychotherapy*. New York, Grove Press, 1961, pp. 72–74.
3. K. Hedges Capers: Spurious and authenic stroking, *Trans Anal Bull*, 6:104, 1967.
4. John P. Spiegel and Norman W. Bell: The family, in *American Handbook of Psychiatry*, (S. Arieti, Ed.). New York, Basic Books, 1959, Vol. I p. 114. See also Richard L. Jenkins: Classification of behavior

problems of children, *Amer J Psychiat*, *21*:1032, 1969; Roy W. Menninger: What values are we giving our children, *Menninger Quart*, *20*:1, 1966–67.

5. W. Hugh Missildine: *Your Inner Child of the Past*. New York, Simon and Schuster, 1963.
6. Eric Berne: *Games People Play*. New York, Grove Press, 1966.
7. John Bowlby, *et al.*: The effects of mother-child separation, *Brit J Med Psychol*, *29*:211, 1956.
8. Robert E. Anderson: Where's dad?, *Arch Gen Psychiat*, *18*:641, 1968. See also Thomas L. Trunnell: The absent father's children's emotional disturbances, *Arch Gen Psychiat*, *19*:180, 1968.
9. Bruno Bettelheim: *The Empty Fortress*. New York, Free Press, 1964.
10. Jan Ehrenwald: *Neurosis in the Family and Patterns of Psychosocial Defense*. New York, Hoeber, 1963.
11. Nathan W. Ackerman: *The Psychodynamics of Family Life*. New York, Basic Books, 1958. See also Gary Jacobson and Robert G. Ryder (Marriage outcome linked to age at death of parent, *Roche Report: Frontiers Clin Psychiat*, *6*:3, 1969) who studied the marital relationships in ninety couples married for two and one-half years and found that those who lost parents during adolescence fared better than those whose loss occurred in childhood.
12. Rene A. Spitz: *The First Year of Life*. New York, Int. Univs. Press, 1965. See also Theodore Lidz: The effects of children on marriage, in *The Marriage Relationship* (Salo Rosenbaum and Ian Alger, Eds.). New York, Basic Books, 1968, pp. 121–131; and Aaron H. Esman: Marital psychopathology its effects on children and their management, in *The Marriage Relationship* (Salo Rosenbaum and Ian Alger, Eds.). New York, Basic Books, 1968, pp. 133–143.

XVII

PERSONALITY AND SCHOOL ADJUSTMENT

This chapter will present some observations on the value of item 16 in the BMQ (see Appendix), which asks each spouse to describe his personality.[1] The three main findings were as follows:

1. Concepts about self-image.
2. Elicitation of feelings, behavior, and psychiatric symptoms.
3. Thumbnail sketches of personality configurations.

It was surprising to find that almost 50 percent of the women and 30 percent of the men complained of a poor self-image. Typical were the following statements:

> I am supersensitive to criticism. I have an inferiority complex. I feel as if I always have to go one better to prove my worth. I feel as if nobody could really want the real me.

> I have feelings of inferiority, feel insecure socially, and immature.

> I am rather primitive in that I am not city bred.

Since my original bias on marriage is clearly stated to the couple in the evaluative phase, namely, that a marriage must be meaningful but cannot be so unless based on mutual respect, which in turn hinges on self-respect, concepts about self-image become very important.[2] What one feels about one's self (jukebox) is intimately involved with the "records" played in that jukebox. The earliest "parental" voices are encoded in childhood and reinforced by further experiences with parental and peer relationshps. Thus the feelings about identity begin in childhood but come into real focus during adolescence.[3] Not only can the jukebox be renovated externally, e.g. by new hair styling, but most important, new music (new "records") can be heard from the jukebox.

Current concepts on normality question what "normal behavior" and "normal self-image" include. Roy Grinker, Sr.'s,[4] studies on homoclites was an early effort in exploring the problem of normal behavior. Offer and Sabshin[5] have presented four perspectives of normality: health, utopia, average and process. GST In a recent article, Sabshin[6] succinctly presents these four functional perspectives. The first perspective, normality as health, is based on the medical model which views health as a reasonable rather than an optimal state, with normality the major portion of a continuum.

The second perspective of normality as utopia looks upon normality as the optimal organization of the psychic apparatus and its mental characteristics "that culminates in optimal functioning." Clinically, I use O. Spurgeon English's[7] utopian philosophy: to entertain one's self, to entertain others—meaningful relationships with "significant others," to entertain a new idea, and to work effectively. This orientation is illustrated in Figure 10.

The third perspective, normality as average, is based on the mathematical principle of the bell-shaped curve. Whereas the perspectives just described visualize normality and abnormality as a straight line continuum, the bell curve view conceives the middle range as normal and both extremes as abnormal.

The fourth concept conceptualizes normality as a process with behavior the end result of transacting systems that change over time. GST understands marriage as continually changing over time and involving the transactions of three systems—a process concept.

PERSONALITY CONFIGURATIONS

Current classifications of psychiatric disorders are based on clinical experience, and their significance is utilitarian rather than scientific. Individuals are infinitely complex and capable of being classified in a variety of ways.[8] Psychoneuroses and

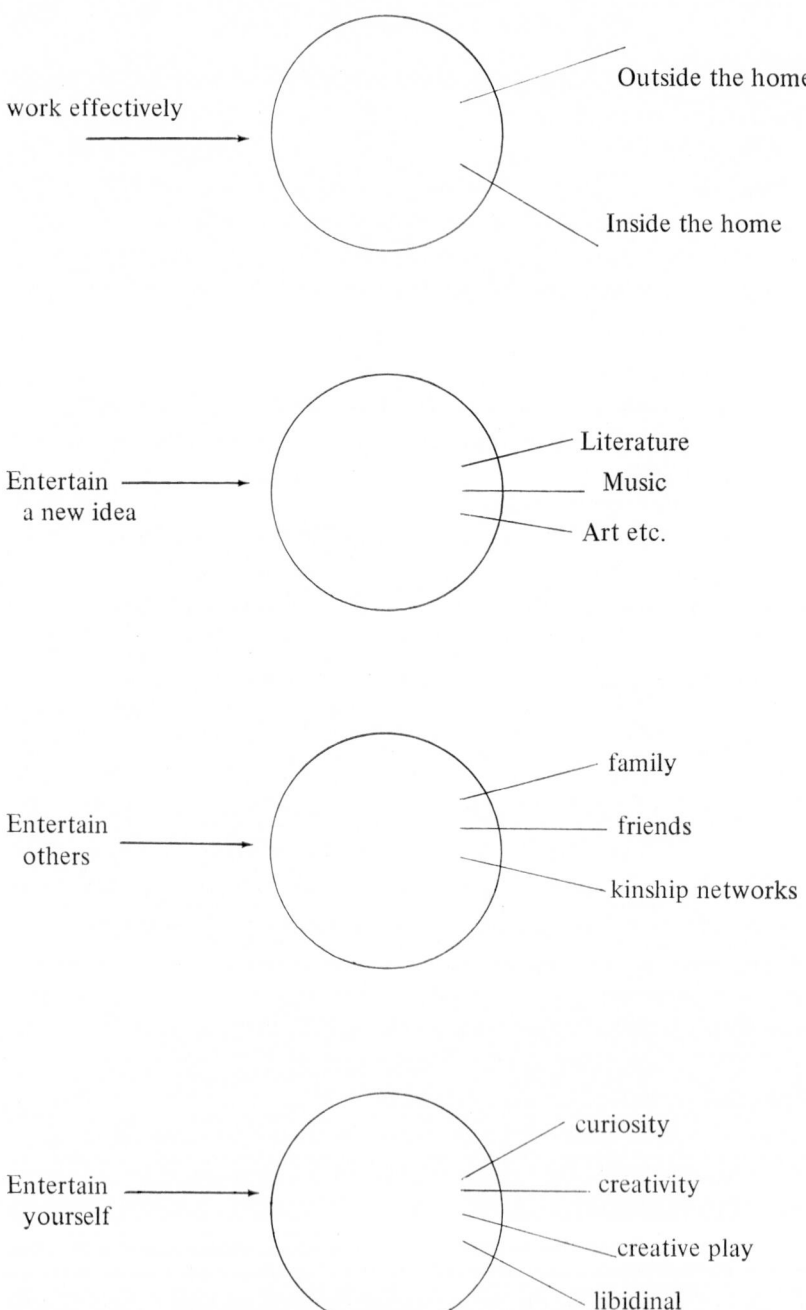

Figure 10. Normality as utopia and process.

psychotic reactions are diagnosed mainly on the basis of intuition and specific symptoms; personality disorders are diagnosed according to patterns of behavior. Psychoneurosis and psychosis do not change the individual's basic personality type. Salzman's[9] presentation of *obsessive-compulsive* defenses, from an adaptive point of view, along a spectrum of severity to classify personality configurations delineates three levels:

1. Obsessive tendencies are present in all persons, e.g. the nightly rituals most people use at bedtime.
2. The obsessive personality has a more congealed set of defenses, but it may produce no noticeable failure in living and may even bring about marked success.

> In one couple with much marital discord, the husband was very successful as a principal. When asked to describe what kind of a person he was, he replied in a staccato manner: I'm opinionated, take charge-type of person, precise, meticulous, methodical, possessive, keep emotions fairly bottled up, patience is not my virtue. I like things done my way if no good reason is advanced for doing it any other way.

3. The behavior patterns of the obsessive-compulsive neurosis often impair the individual's effectiveness and may produce bizarre symptoms. Not infrequently these are described under item 16 of the BMQ.

The obsessive individual is one whose inner "parental" voices demand perfection—the end result of living in an environment where the major emphasis for approval would be the attainment of perfection. As Salzman notes, if one is to be absolutely safe and certain, he has to know everything to predict and prepare for the future. This illusion of perfection for security results in personality compulsivity and rigidity: "one must never make an error or admit a deficiency." Thus, any threat internally from the "parental" voice or externally from spouse results in anxiety of varying degrees. Item 16 on the BMQ showed 10 percent of the spouses to have moderate to severe obsessive-compulsive manifestations.

The next most common configuration observed on the BMQ was that of *depressive* reactions. It occurred in 9 percent of the spouses in the PS and in 20 percent of the MDS. As will be pointed out later in Chapter XX on CDD session, depressive manifestations were present in about one third of the spouses. Frequent complaints listed were the following: tend to be moody, more irritable than usual, do not enjoy the things I did before, do not have the drive and go of my partner; pessimistic, and so on. Cyclothymic reactions in keeping with the concept of "normality as average" form a continuum:

1. Cyclothymic tendencies (i.e. mild mood swings) are present in everyone.
2. A cyclothymic personality is characterized by moderate highs and lows in mood. Questioning the individual during his individual sessions may reveal a past history of several depressive episodes of increasing frequency and duration.
3. Cyclothymic psychosis (manic-depressive psychosis) is characterized by severe mood swings. These depressive reactions were discussed in Chapter XII under suicide.

An awareness of the possibility of an underlying depressive reaction in a spouse, cued in by some notation on item 16 of the BMQ, may be helpful in understanding a current marital crisis. Frequently, a spouse does not understand that his partner is ill, and may regard the depressive withdrawal as a rejection. Occasionally hypomanic behavior with boundless energy may take the form of promiscuity, with resultant severe marital disharmony. The hypomanic individual may reveal his condition by describing the kind of person he is as "full of boundless energy," "my motor seems to be racing," "I want to take care of anything or anyone, small, helpless, or in general," and so on.

The third type of configuration found on item 16, in terms of frequency, was that of *projective* defense reactions. The same continuum of severity can be used to describe projective reactions. We all use projection to deal with painful experiences: "I got a ticket for speeding because the traffic cop was hiding behind a fence." The paranoid personality disorder is a more serious condition, and one common form was described in Chapter X under the label of "the district attorney syndrome." Last on the spectrum is the paranoid psychotic reaction with distortion of reality and bizarre complaints. The therapist should be alerted to the projective defense reactions by comments on item 16 such as, "I'm very jealous," "I feel people try to take advantage of me."

The fourth type of configuration was related to *character disorders*. Character or personality is made up of the repetitive patterns of behavior which a person has adapted to his inner beliefs and values and to those of the prevailing cultural milieu. The "normal" person's behavior is in harmony with his value system. In character disorders, behavior is "abnormal" primarily as judged by the value systems of others. Since the individual is unaware of this, he does not experience anxiety or guilt. The diagnosis of character disorder is based on antisocial behavior—his psychopathic actions are inappropriate to his educational background and to the values and behavior of his parents or authorities. He is usually indifferent to the impact of his behavior on others.[10] On occasion he may suddenly react violently. He is a great rationalizer and convincing in his excuses. He is often unable to form lasting relationships. Frequently, there is a long history of dyssocial behavior. Many of these individuals describe themselves as "impulsive" with an inability to endure delays in need satisfaction. Others describe themselves as "loners," "on the outside looking in," in describing their sense of isolation. Still other types of character disorders, in addition to the borderline states[11] just mentioned, include the addictions—alcohol or drugs.

In this section of this chapter, I have concentrated on the value and observations of the sixteenth item on the BMQ, which asks each spouse to describe the kind of person he is. Concepts of self-image were presented as well as current perspectives on normality, namely, health, utopia, average and process. Finally, some comments on personality configurations were presented.

SCHOOL ADJUSTMENT

Item 17 on the BMQ (see Appendix) asks each spouse to describe his school adjustment. The "records" encoded during an individual's schooling may at times be valuable in estimating the intensity of the three different voices, especially an approximation of the innate intellectual capacity of the individual. When one begins schooling, two new main invariables appear: the demands of school authorities in terms of performance academically and behaviorally, and relationships with peers. Not infrequently some individuals focus on intellectual pursuits in order to escape their anxiety about their object relationships to their peers. On the other hand, since each person matures at different rates, and since the environmental influences change, various modes of adjustment manifest themselves. The following clinical excerpt shows adjustments at different time intervals:

Mrs. Adeline answered item 17 as follows: "I learned to read before I entered first grade at the age of five. Though bright I was not mature enough for first grade and was tense. I often wet my pants, for example, because I was afraid to ask to be excused. My first two years of schooling was at a parochial school, run by rather formidable nuns who operated on a gold star or slap across the knuckles with a ruler basis. As time went by, in the public school I later attended, I became more relaxed and was a good student. I liked school and have been an avid reader since the age of four. I read everything in sight at home, where there was a good, varied supply of reading matter and nothing was proscribed, and everything at the library. I had a few good friends but was somewhat off-beat and aroused antagonism in some of my classmates, particularly the kids who came from families of conservative background, of which there were many in our neighborhood. I had what I felt to be an extremely large and ugly nose (in reality Mrs. Adeline was extremely pretty with a normal size nose), and of course my "enemies" soon found this tender spot and would tease me about it. In general, however, I had enough friends and was respected even by those who didn't like me because I was smart.

"After grade school I attended a large high school with excellent facilities for its 5000 students. I went right into honor classes because of my high IQ. I did not maintain my potential. The school was enormous and at the time overcrowded, and though there was counseling available, I did not use it. My parents were not sophisticated in the ways of getting the best out of a school for their children, and I did not know how either, so I became lost in the shuffle, maintaining a barely adequate average to enter college, which I intended to do. Socially, I had my own group of friends, was very interested in boys, but generally alienated any that were vaguely interested in me by my "wit," which failed to captivate them. I had very few dates but my friends and I had parties with boys, and we did things together like going horseback riding, to the beach, and such.

"After high school I announced that I wanted to go away to college. I felt superior to the city's public colleges to consider them, and my grades were shaky. My parents said, 'with what?' So I got a job for a year, saved all my money, and went away to college, a small college, which accepted my grades. I felt it second-rate and would have preferred Radcliffe. This college proved perfect for me. My talents were appreciated. I was editor of everything, I maintained highest honors through my time there, and in general, was sailing high. All that I read seemed to fall happily together, and I developed a good, thirsty approach to knowledge which I have never lost. It was a fruitful time of my life and I was thoroughly happy."

This woman illustrates different academic and social adjustments from grade through high school and college.

The next individual is typical of a different type of adjustment:

"I had good grades in grammar school, but I was very shy and always felt inferior. I feared and sometimes detested my teachers. In high school I was an honor student for the first two years, but in the last two years I barely passed. I was shy and had a strong inferiority complex. As a result I participated in no extracurricular activities and never dated. Part of this was due to financial problems; I had a part-time job after school. In addition, I had started to study music just before entering high school and this kept me busy. My parents were very strict, and I was never allowed to have friends at home."

The following two individuals illustrate good adjustment in all areas during their school years:

"I always loved school. I was the teacher's favorite in grammar school. In high school I was co-editor of the school magazine and in the upper 3 percent of my class. I was on the honor roll. In college I made National Honor Society. I studied hard during the week and dated like mad on weekends. I was selected campus beauty queen and was active in my sorority, president in my senior year."

"I was always a very good student. I was valedictorian of my high school class. My college career was full of fun. I did well academically, participated in all sports and lead an active social life."

An evaluation of the couples in the MDS revealed some interesting findings. The overall picture showed the men to have an average social adjustment (45%), to be excellent to outstanding academically (54%), to have average participation in extracurricular activities (51%), and a better than average self-image (60%). On the other hand, the women in the MDS had a poor social adjustment (52%), did excellently to outstandingly scholastically (57%), participated poorly in extracurricular activities (60%) and almost half (46%) had a poor self-image (see Table XXIV).

In our Western culture, especially at the college level, women's roles emphasize social participation, especially per-

TABLE XXIV
SCHOOL ADJUSTMENT

	Male %	Female %
Social		
Poor	25	52
Average	45	35
Excellent	30	13
Academic		
Poor	14	5
Average	32	38
Excellent	54	57
Extracurricular		
Poor	26	60
Average	51	19
Excellent	23	21
Self-image		
Poor	15	46
Average	60	39
Excellent	25	15

formance in dating and covert marriage marketability. Many girls get the wrong degree, a bachelor in arts or sciences instead of the coveted bachelor—the MRS degree. Perhaps the poor self-image (46%) may account for the poor marital adjustments later and perhaps for overcompensation scholastically— 57 percent had excellent to outstanding academic achievements. On the other hand, men market their athletic and extracurricular abilities as well as their functionally specific aptitudes—this could account for both the average to excellent self-image (85%) and about average to excellent (75%) showing in the social, academic and extracurricular areas. Perhaps, in addition to the above, emotional problems already present during the school period may enhance scholastic performance to avoid participation in social activities—the complaint of poor self-image can be an indicator of an emotional problem.

In this second section of the chapter, I have attempted to point out how information about an individual's adjustment during his school years can be of aid in evaluating the positive and negative forces a spouse can add to the resolution of a marital crisis.

NOTES

1. It is essential that the clergy particularly be familiar with the common personality types, as well as the common manifestations of mental illness, in order to detect these symptoms even when camouflaged by religious content. See William D. Sharpe: *Medicine and the Ministry*. New York, Appleton-Century, 1966. As E. Mansell Pattison points out in his article, Clergymen's role in community health clinics (*JAMA, 203:902,* 1968), "Although the clergy often see people in early stages of distress, we have not capitalized on their contacts to implement effective early treatment. The clergy make very few referrals (1% to 8%) to mental health centers. This paradox highlights a problem for preventive intervention where we seek to encourage early identification and referral of the mentally ill to treatment centers."

2. Warren L. Jones (Marriage—growth or disaster? *Amer J Psychiat, 125:*1115, 1969) writes: "Marriage remains a creative act and there are many strong, productive, happy marriages . . . (where) each spouse has a strong sense of personal *identity* [italics added], and each seeks intimacy with the other. These couples always have an active dialogue, see each other as allies, and respect each other's autonomy."

3. Erik H. Erikson: The problem of ego identity, *J Amer Psychoanal Assn, 4:*56, 1956. See also Theodore R. Sarbin: On the distinction between social roles and social types, with special reference to the hippie, *Amer J Psychiat, 125:*1024, 1969.

4. Roy R. Grinker, Sr.: A dynamic story of the 'Homoclite.' In *Science and Psychoanalysis* (Jules H. Masserman, Ed.). New York, Grune & Stratton, 1963, p. 128.

5. Daniel Offer and Melvin Sabshin: *Normality: Theoretical and Clinical Concepts of Mental Health.* New York, Basic Books, 1966.

6. Melvin Sabshin: Psychiatric perspectives on normality, *Arch Gen Psychiat, 17:*258, 1967.

7. O. Spurgeon English: Changing techniques of psychotherapy, *Voices*, 2:91, 1966.

8. Kenneth M. Colby succinctly describes the current status of psychiatric typology when he states: "A majestic absurdity characterizes the classification system in psychiatry. Since there is such poor agreement among diagnosticians, the categories of classification are unreliable. And since there is little correlation between diagnosis, signs and symptoms, the categories are of doubtful validity. Problems of classification are shunned by clinicians who confuse classification (forming classes in a collection of objects) with identification (identifying an object as a member of a class). Yet a more satisfactory taxonomy is crucial for clinical practice, and in particular for future research designed to yield dependable knowledge." (Computer-aided language development in nonspeaking children, *Arch Gen Psychiat*, *19*:641, 1968). In the discussion of configuration, I suggest a cluster of symptoms and behaviors that tend to occur together with marked frequency.

9. Leon Salzman: The therapy of obsessional states, *Amer J Psychiat*, *122*:1139, 1966. In his excellent book, *The Obsessive Personality* (New York: Science House, 1968), Salzman begins with a description of traits and attitudes that characterize all obsessive persons to the predicament of our contemporary culture. In Part II of this book, he relates the obsessive mechanisms to abnormal states. This book is an outstanding descriptive work and a "major theoretical statement by an author whose mind is at once flexible and rigorous, philosophical and scientific." Highly recommended to every therapist. See also Martin G. Blinder (The pragmatic classification of depression, *Amer J Psychiat*, *123*:259, 1966), who describes "five types of patients frequently encountered who together constitute the greater part of the depressive continuum." Also the scholarly article by Dennis Hill (Depression: disease, reaction, or posture?, *Amer J Psychiat*, *125*:445, 1968), who concludes that "depressive illness can be seen as disease in the sense that its manifestations are deviations from normal biological functions, and as reaction in the sense that it is a response to a crisis situation, resulting in a catastrophic lowering of self-esteem. But the therapeutic skill of the psychiatrist is best displayed when he understands the patient's depression as posture, the symptoms of which are forms of communication."

10. Jeannette P. Maas: Cathexes toward significant others by sociopathic women, *Arch Gen Psychiat*, *15*:259, 1966. An excellent study which explores certain perceptions of the self and significant others, held by a group of sociopathic women. See also Peter E. Nathan, Albert Samaraweera, Marcia M. Andberg, and Vernon D. Patch (Syndromes of psychosis and psychoneurosis, *Arch Gen Psychiat*, *19*:704, 1968). who conclude: "These results indicate that current diagnostic pro-

cedures permit the reliable differentiation of psychosis and psychoneurosis. They also emphasize the nature and extent of the inability of these procedures to enable diagnostic differentiation between the psychoneurosis and the personality disorders." They found "almost half the personality disorder patients were mislabeled (by calling them either psychotic or psychoneurotic)"; and Walter Bromberg: Psychopathic personality concept evaluated and reevaluated, *Arch Gen Psychiat, 17:*641, 1967.

11. Norman S. Litowitz and Kenneth M. Newman: Borderline personality and the theatre of the absurd, *Arch Gen Psychiat, 16:*268, 1967. They present a superb review of the literature on the borderline personality from the point of view of ego functions and conflicts and used two contemporary plays, Samuel Beckett's, *Waiting for Godot* and Edward Albee's, *The Zoo Story* to illustrate their concepts.

XVIII

MEDICAL HISTORY

The eighteenth item on the BMQ (see Appendix) asks each spouse six questions pertaining to his past and current medical history. This brief medical history is important for the nonmedical therapist. The first question asks for the name and address of the family physician who can be called to help in a medical emergency, e.g. acute delirium tremens due to alcoholism, acute drug poisoning, and so on.

The second question concerning the patient's medical history inquires about his present state of health, e.g. insommia with early rising in the morning or a recent onset of numerous physical complaints may mask an early depression. Some replies are short and curt:

"I'm healthy as an ox but plagued by beastly headaches." Other replies are longer and informative:

"I have some abnormal changes on my electrocardiogram. I have had infrequent, short spells of tachycardia [rapid heart rate—author's note] since the age of ten. I learned to stop and control this. Exercise helps prevent occurrences. I am conscious of my heart, and as my father died of a coronary, I have had some concern about developing coronary disease. On orders of my physician I quit smoking after having the habit for twenty years, and lost weight. I have also cut down on dietary fats, and so on."

Usually this question is answered briefly as excellent, good, poor, nervous, and so on. Table XXV shows how the spouses in the MDS rated their present state of health.

In our culture it is not manly to complain about one's health. Thus twice as many women as men stated their health was poor, and three times as many stated they were nervous. Interestingly, 5 percent stated they were pregnant.

The third question on medical history asks each spouse when

TABLE XXV
PRESENT STATE OF HEALTH (MDS)

	Males %	Females %
Excellent	23	13
Good	63	54
Poor	6	13
Nervous	8	20
Pregnant		5

he had his last medical checkup. This is the first attempt by the therapist to practice prevention.

The fourth question on the medical history asks each spouse what serious illnesses he has had and when. Although current research has shown that there is no specificity of personality configuration in psychosomatic diseases, clinically many individuals do show specificity, e.g. there were seven spouses with past and/or current asthma with sensitivity to separation (separation anxiety), fifteen spouses with peptic ulcer (most of them hard-driving and ambitious), and so on. Three spouses stated they were epileptics and on anticonvulsant therapy. Two men had poliomyelitis with moderate atrophy of one leg, which was not visible in their gait, and helped me understand their violent reaction to their wive's request for divorce. There were eight women who had had a severe nervous breakdown necessitating hospitalization—three of them having received electroconvulsive therapy. Among other conditions mentioned were pulmonary tuberculosis (3), diabetes (3), cancer and multiple sclerosis. One woman in her late thirties answered the question on medical illnesses as follows:

"I am a chronic complainer, I have duodenal ulcer, a faulty gallbladder, am a latent diabetic, have beginning arthritis and impaired hearing." (In addition, she listed six abdominal operations).

Some current illnesses affect the marital relationship.[1] Since there were seven spouses (6 males and 1 female) who had diabetes, I should like to discuss this condition as it may affect the marital relationship.

Rubin,[2] as a result of detailed inquiry into the reproductive capacity of diabetic men, showed diabetes to be associated with impotence. He noted: "Indeed, impotence occasionally is the symptom for which the patient first seeks medical aid; the diabetes is then discovered." One of the two diabetic men in this series (MDS) was impotent and his wife's chief marital complaint was sexual dissatisfaction. Rubin further comments: "Impotence that arises while the diabetes is poorly controlled usually disappears when good control is established. If impotence develops when the diabetes is under adequate control, it is much more likely to be permanent." His figures for impotence were roughly 25 percent for men in their thirties, 40 percent for men in their forties, and 50 percent for men in their fifties. He adds that the impotence associated with diabetes does not appear to be psychic in origin. My observations on the five diabetic women in my private series (PS) were equivocal as to their sexual behavior. However, they were aware of the possible complications during their pregnancies: increased difficulty in control of their blood sugar, and possible termination of pregnancy before the due date by cesarean section (3 had cesareans). Thus diabetes is one important reason for asking each spouse about his last medical checkup.

A glance at Table XXV shows that one fifth of the spouses complained of poor health (13% females and 6% males). Clinical experience indicates that the patient in poor health, contrary to what one would expect, still is quite interested in sex, although the frequency and the length of sexual performance is reduced. Even the woman presented as a "chronic complainer" with duodenal ulcer, faulty gallbladder and arthritis was described by her husband as sexually demanding. Two patients in this series had had a "mild stroke." Both were in their fifties and with different sexual reactions—in one there was no further interest in sex, much to the annoyance of his spouse, and in the other, his sexual behavior was unchanged. Kalliomaki[3] *et al.* studied the sexual interest and behavior of 105 patients below the age of sixty following a "stroke." They found that in about 30 percent of the individuals, there was loss of interest in sex, but that in 60 percent it was unchanged or increased. In the same group, the rate of intercourse was decreased for 43 percent and was unchanged or increased for about 25 percent.

Another important medical condition involving the vascular system pertains to the coronary arteries. There were no women in the MDS with any coronary disease, but four of the men had involvement—two had had acute coronary occlusions and two were having anginal attacks. The studies of Masters and Johnson[4] are helpful in managing individuals with coronary disease. When possible, the therapist should refer the responsibility to a physician. An excellent article by Ford and Orfirer[5] has been written on the sexual behavior and the chronically ill patient. One of their comments is especially pertinent for therapists: "The physician's first task is to take stock of his own attitudes and feelings about sex in general and the sexual function of disabled people in particular." Their comments are valid for spouses complaining of poor health or with residuals of serious medical illnesses.

The fifth question asked each spouse about his medical history as it relates to surgical operations. Excluding tonsillectomies, women had three times as many operations as the men in the MDS. Operations on the female reproductive system, as well as the breast and thyroid, accounted for the difference in the figures. Information on surgery performed can be valuable in assessing both conscious and unconscious forces operating in the spouses and their possible role in the marital disharmony, e.g. vasectomies in men and "gridiron abdomen" (multiple postsurgical scars) in women. Obviously there are many valid medical reasons for surgery, e.g. appendectomy for an acute appendicitis. In PS and MDS, three types of women were observed who used surgery for psychological purposes:

1. To alleviate unconscious guilt (so-called neurotic guilt based on fantasy—sexual, murderous impulses, etc.).
2. To gain attention from spouse.
3. As a manifestation of the hysterical personality—the so-called "gridiron abdomen."

The hysterical personality is characterized by a "belle indifference" as she relates her story. Usually there is a histrionic manner, as though she was on the stage instead of really living in her relationships. Many are overly made up—false eyelashes, excessive cosmetics, miniskirts, and so on. There is a "little girl" appearance, yet in a seductive manner. The chronicity of their medical complaints frequently produce unnecessary operations. The majority of today's surgeons know of this type of woman and refuse to operate without psychiatric clearance. A clinical example of this type of personality follows:

Mr. and Mrs. Hilaria were referred by their respective lawyers for counseling. Mr. Hilaria was angry at his wife for their financial difficulties due to excessive medical expenditures and clothes-buying splurges. Mrs. Hilaria was annoyed with her husband for his unfaithfulness, especially since it was with her best girl friend, when she was convalescing in the hospital from her last operation. She related the following surgical history on the BMQ: (1) appendectomy at twenty-one, two years after marriage, for a chronic appendicitis of one-year duration, (2) exploratory laparotomy at twenty-three at which adhesions (?) were found (a laporatomy is an abdominal operation for an undiagnosed medical condition), (3) suspension of the uterus (abdominal operation) for chronic low back pain at age thirty, (4) gallbladder removed at age thirty-five because of upper abdominal pains, and (5) hysterectomy (uterus removed) at age thirty-eight. It was during this last operation that husband's infidelity occurred.

Occasionally hospitalizations, both for medical and surgical conditions, is a bid for attention from the partner, and/or avoidance of the daily household chores. The woman previously cited as the "chronic complainer" with ulcer, gallbladder and arthritic pains frankly stated: "The only time my husband and family pay any attention to me is when I am in the hospital." In addition to numerous hospitalizations for nonsurgical conditions, she also had been hospitalized for four major surgical operations. Her numerous abdominal scars made her abdomen look like a football field ("gridiron abdomen").

Another type of woman characterized by repeated surgery revealed on intensive therapy marked guilt complexes due to unconscious guilt about sexual and/or murderous impulses.

Hysterectomy was the second most common surgical condition—appendectomies were three times as often. Many women react strongly and often irrationally to the removal of their uterus. I recommend Trainer's[6] book on the physiologic foundations for marriage counseling. Written in his humorous style, it covers not only physiology but pertinent anatomic and surgical knowledge. Many women regard the uterus as a necessary organ for the successful enactment of their feminine roles, childbearing function, general body health and feminine attractiveness. As Drellich[7] has shown, many women fear that "after hysterectomy they will not be able to carry out their everyday activities at home and at work." This fear can contribute to marital discord. Especially in relation to sexuality, he states there is no evidence that hysterectomy, with or without the removal of the ovaries, produces any change in sexual desire or performance. In his article he discusses the ambivalence about loss of menstruation, fear of sexual unacceptability, belief that the hysterectomy was punishment for sin, and so on.

The importance of inquiring about surgical operations in the male was highlighted by finding that one in seventy-five of the men had had a vasectomy. Interestingly, on BMQ one man did not state that he had this operation, but his wife reported it on her BMQ. Vasectomy for sterilizing the male can be done as a simple office procedure. As one reviewer of a study by Ziegler[8] and his associates on the effects of vasectomy commented: "Vasectomy could prove the 'Unkindest Cut of All.'" A spouse's voluntary sterilization can result in unsuspected emotional problems for him and his partner. In my experience with ten couples there were a variety of reactions. Some women suspected their husbands of infidelity. In some, the men responded to the sterilization as a demasculinizing effect, and the wives reacted to changes in the spouses' behavior with anxiety and anger. As one husband stated:

"I had this operation done at the suggestion of her psychiatrist. It was his opinion that her mental health could not stand another child. She consented, but ever since, I have been angry at her. I don't feel as masculine as I did before. Our relationship has deteriorated; we argue frequently and as a result the frequency of our sex has decreased."

In another couple, referred for counseling because of repeated games of "Uproar," all the quarrels resulted from his excessive sexual demands. He had wanted frequent sex before his vasectomy, like twice a night, and she had rejected him by stating she was afraid of further pregnancies (they had four children). So he had a vasectomy done on his own accord so that she would have no further excuses. To her dismay, he now wanted sex at all times. When she refused, he would get violent and beat her.

Landis[9] studied the attitudes of individual physicians on the use of vasectomy for birth control. He notes that 100,000 American males obtain voluntary sterilization for birth control reasons each year. Recently the Ferbers[10] stated that vasectomy can have a favorable effect on sexual behavior. On the other hand, they also observed that vasectomy is not a magic solution to marital conflict, even when both partners think it might be.

The sixth and last question on the medical history asks each spouse as to drugs presently taken, smoking and alcohol intake. Certain medications can give clues as to an underlying psychiatric condition, e.g. Thorazine® in schizophrenia, energizers in depression, and so on. Not infrequently, some persons have been taking medications for many years without medical supervision, e.g. thyroid tablets, which could cause marital disharmony by increased irritability, low threshold for patience with children, and so on. The question of smoking habits is in itself unimportant but enabels the counselor to lead into the question of alcoholic intake. Occasionally one spouse will admit being an alcoholic, to the surprise of the partner. Ask specifically the amount of alcohol taken, e.g. one man stated he only drank two bottles of beer each night when asked how much, in response to a complaint by his wife in her individual session. This did not seem unreasonable to the interviewer, so it was not further discussed. When this was related to his wife, she bitterly asked: "Did you ask what size bottle?" To his chagrin, he had not. It turned out they were half-gallon size bottles. Similarly, with alcoholic beverages, one drink may be an ounce or a tumbler-full. Table XXVI shows the six most frequent drugs taken by the spouses in the MDS.

An interesting finding was that only 15 percent of the women

TABLE XXVI
DRUGS TAKEN BY THE SPOUSES (MDS)

	Female %	*Male* %
None	15	50
Tranquilizers	38	7
Contraceptive pill	13	
Sedatives	11	5
Diet pills	10	4
Thyroid tablets	7	2

did not use any drugs compared to 50 percent of the men. In most categories, the women used twice as much medication as the men. Conspicuous was the finding that women used tranquilizers more than five times as often as the men.

It is unwise to generalize about the correlation about drugs and behavior, considering the large number of drugs currently obtainable, the varied motivations for the use of any specific drug, and most important, the idiosyncratic response of many individuals to any specific drug. Since about 50 percent of the spouses were on tranquilizers, the therapist should be concerned about their role in the marital complaint of sexual dissatisfaction. In some individuals there is a decreased sexual desire with phenothiazines (a strong tranquilizer). Bartholomew[11] has even reported some success with this drug in reducing sexual drive and performance in controlling deviant sexual behavior. Some physicians have reported that the "pill" (oral contraceptive) can drive libido away. At a talk given in 1966 before the American Academy of Psychoanalysis, Masters stated unequivocally that when consulted by a woman for secondary frigidity (failure to reach an orgasm after previously satisfactory responsiveness), his first question asked is whether she has been taking the "pill" for more than eighteen months. If the response is yes, he insists that the woman discontinue the "pill" for six months before seeing him again, and further added that in some instances further steps proved unnecessary. On the other hand, Wallach and Celso-Ramon Garcia,[12] in a review of the literature on the psychodynamic aspects of oral contraception, have reported depression in association with their use but not lessening of libido. Sturgis[13] comments that most married couples report greater frequency, spontaneity, and enjoyment of intercourse. Recently marijuana (pot) has become popular with an appreciable number of young people[14] in the middle and upper socioeconomic classes. I highly recommend Jordan Scher's[15] article on patterns and profiles of addiction and drug abuse. The therapist should maintain an attitude of "watchful expectancy" regarding drugs.

In studying the findings on the BMQ regarding alcoholic intake, 12 percent of both the men and women in the MDS stated that they were teetotalers. On the other hand, twice as many men as women stated they were alcoholics—10 percent vis-à-vis 5 percent. Thus 83 percent of the females and 78 percent of the males drank in varying amounts, ranging from occasionally to moderately. In a thought-provoking article, Max Hayman[16,17] casts doubt on the myth of social drinking. He casts doubts on three well-accepted myths: that social drinking is a definable entity, that it is not harmful, and that it is helpful.

In this chapter I have attempted to stress the value of six questions in taking a medical history by the therapist.

NOTES

1. W.W. Meissner in an excellent article with a good bibliography points out that to understand human disease, a knowledge of pathology, as well as ecology, has become necessary: Family dynamics and psychosomatic processes, *Family Process*, 5:142, 1966. See also Mortimer D. Gross: Marital stress and psychosomatic disorders, *Med Aspects Hum Sexuality*, 3:22, 1969.
2. Alan Rubin: Sexual behavior in diabetes mellitus, *Med Aspects Hum Sexuality*, 2:23, 1967.
3. J.L. Kalliomaki, T.K. Markkanen, and V.A. Mustonen: Sexual behavior after cerebral vascular accident: a study on patients below the age of 60 years, *Fertil Steril*, 12:156, 1961.
4. William H. Masters and Virginia E. Johnson: *Human Sexual Response*. Boston, Little, Brown, 1966.
5. Amasa B. Ford and Alexander P. Orfirer: Sexual behavior and the chronically ill patient, *Med Aspects Hum Sexuality*, 1:51, 1967. See also David Scherf, Edward Massie, Albert S. Hyman, and Maurice S. Rawlings: Viewpoints on sex activity for postcoronary patients,

Med Aspects Hum Sexuality, 2:22, 1968; Barney M. Dlin, H. Keith Fischer, and Benjamin Huddell (Psychologic adaptation to pacemaker and open heart surgery, *Arch Gen Psychiat, 19*:599, 1968) comment on the individual's reactions to heart surgery are equally applicable to coronary heart attacks; and Herman K. Hellerstein and Ernest H. Friedman: Sexual activity and the postcoronary patient, *Med Aspects Hum Sexuality*, 3:70, 1969.

6. Joseph B. Trainer: *Physiologic Foundations For Marriage Counseling.* St. Louis, Mosby, 1965. See also Bernice C. Sachs (This bosom business, *Med Aspects Hum Sexuality*, 3:14, 1969) for comments on mastectomy.

7. Marvin G. Drellich: Sex after hysterectomy, *Med Aspects Hum Sexuality, 1*:62, 1967. See also Marc H. Hollender: Hysterectomy and feelings of femininity, *Med Aspects Hum Sexuality*, 3:6, 1969.

8. Frederick J. Ziegler, David A. Rodgers, and Sali Kriegsman: Effect of vasectomy on psychologic functioning, *Psychosom Med, 28*:50, 1966. In their study the marriage partners' average age was near thirty, had been married about seven years and had intecouse about eight to ten times a month. The husbands were not under pressure to have the operation from their wives. Although effects were not prominent, previous findings of negative changes following vasectomy were confirmed. A contradictory emotional pattern was found when the vasectomized men and their spouses were interviewed and tested one to two years after the operation. The picture that emerges then of the men is one of mild but definite anxiety with counterphobic behavior to the fear of being nonmasculine. They become less flexible generally (doing fewer household chores, working harder at his job, etc.). In some instances, the men reacted in a positive manner to the operation: more mature, more decisive and with improvement in their roles occupationally, parentally and as a husband. On the other hand, some showed decreased personal effectiveness, heightened personal anxiety and marital discord. See also Ziegler, Rodgers, and Robert J. Prentiss: Psychosocial response to vasectomy, *Arch Gen Psychiat, 21*:46, 1969.

9. Judson T. Landis: Attitudes of individual California physicians and policies of state medical societies on vasectomy for birth control, *J Marriage Fam, 277*, August, 1966.

10. Andrew Ferber and William L. Ferber: Vasectomy, *Med Aspects Hum Sexuality*, 2:29, 1968. They discuss the medical effects and complications; sexual, psychological, marital and social effects; cultural attitudes; contraindications; and the proper use of vasectomy as a contraceptive procedure.

11. A.A. Bartholomew: A long-acting phenothiazine as a possible agent to control deviant sexual behavior, *Amer J Psychiat, 124*:917, 1968.

12. Edward E. Wallach: and Celso-Ramon Garcia: Psychodynamic aspects of oral contraception, *JAMA*, *203*:927, 1968. In this article they state: "Emotional response to the use of oral contraceptives results from numerous factors, basic among them are the attitudes of patient and husband towards (1) contraception, (2) pregnancy, and (3) sexuality." See also Rudolph H.ι Moos: Psychological aspects of oral contraceptives, *Arch Gen Psychiat*, *19*:87, 1968; and Frederick J. Ziegler, David A. Rodgers, Sali Ann Kriegsman, and Purvis L. Martin: Ovulation suppressors, psychological functioning and marital adjustment, *JAMA*, *204*:849, 1968.

13. Somers H. Sturgis: Oral contraceptives and their effect on sex behavior, *Med Aspects Hum Sexuality*, *2*:4, 1968.

14. Joel Fort (Marijuana: the real problems and the responsibilities of the professions in solving them, *Psychiatric Opinion*, *5*:9, 1968) gives the following figures . . ." it is estimated that in the United States fifteen to twenty percent of the college students and 20–40% of urban high school students use or have used it. Many more have experimented with it in the past, including 10% of a recent representative sample of adults surveyed in the San Francisco metropolitan area. As significant as the numbers involved is the spread to all socio-economic classes and occupational groups." His surveys conducted over the past year showed that in one large urban school district 18 percent of the seventh grade boys and 12 percent of the girls had used marijuana. In the twelfth grade, 41 percent of the boys and 43 percent of the girls had used the drug, the majority with some regularity. See also Daniel Offer, David Marcus, and Judith L. Offer (A longitudinal study of normal adolescent boys, *Amer J Psychiat*, *126*:919, 1970) comments of drug experiences: "Smoking marijuana was not a norm for this group. Twenty-two percent of the subjects had smoked marijuana at least once. Of those who had, half had tried it once or twice and then abandoned its use. . . . No subject reported having taken LSD or any other drug."

15. Jordan Scher: Patterns and profiles of addiction and drug abuse, *Arch Gen Psychiat*, *15*:539, 1966. See also Daniel X. Freedman: On the use and abuse of LSD, *Arch Gen Psychiat*, *18*:330, 1968; and Alfred M. Freedman: Drugs and sexual behavior, *Med Aspects Hum Sexuality*, *1*:25, 1967.

16. Max Hayman: The myth of social drinking, *Amer J Psychiat*, *124*:585, 1967.

17. John E. Ewing: Alcohol, sex, and marriage, *Med Aspects Hum Sexuality*, *2*:43, 1968.

XIX
THE ROLE OF SOCIAL ACTIVITIES, OCCUPATION AND RELIGION

The nineteenth item on the BMQ (see Appendix) asks each spouse to describe his participation in social and civic activities. In addition, each is asked to describe his personal hobbies and interests. This item gives added insights into the voices of the "inner child"—curiosity, creativity, play and libidinal feelings. In keeping with the GST, the alteration of any component in any system will cause changes in the other systems. For example, a spouse (intrapersonal system) who changes his relationships with his friends, e.g. giving up his weekly card or golf game in order to spend more time with his newly married wife (interpersonal system) will alter the friendship ties of others as well (environmental and interpersonal systems). As a result of this change, his friends will react toward him, e.g. anger at disrupting a previous long-established golf foursome.

The concept of "togetherness" in marriage can lead to what Cox[1] calls the "loner" marriage. He comments that statistics show that married couples with many social contacts tend to have more stable marriages. "When an argument occurs in the 'loner' marriage, the spouse tends to react to it in light of his prior limited heterosexual experiences. . . . If these are not appropriate to the new reality, he then has no place to turn to correct this reaction because of the private quality of his marriage (it is no one else's business)."

The voice of the "inner child" frequently overshadows the other two "voices" when a "record" involving recreation is played. Recreation in many ways resembles the happy days of childhood. Because of different childhood experiences, recreation can be an area of bitter conflict in marriage, e.g. arguments on the honeymoon where the brides were pressured into fishing trips or where the newly married husband was very unhappy at a plush resort. In some marriages conflicts can arise over being a "golf widow" or where the husband resents being a baby-sitter while his wife is gone for hours playing Mah-Jongg with her girl friends. Marital discord can spiral when the husband or wife compete bitterly in tennis, golf or in bowling. Instead of the "inner children" playing for fun, "parental" voices stress performance.

Considerable research has been done on the social and cultural forces operating in the production of marital disharmony. Apparently, the pressure to participate in civic activities is so great that not one single spouse left unanswered some participation. Table XXVII shows the spouses' (MDS) participation in community activities.

TABLE XXVII
PARTICIPATION IN COMMUNITY ACTIVITIES (MDS)

	Men %	Women %
Religious organizations	30	35
Professional organizations	25	10
Fraternal and political organizations	18	8
Social organizations	16	20
PTA	5	19
Country club	4	5
School board	2	3

The spouses in the MDS tended to participate about equally in religious organizations. Men tended to be twice as active as women in professional, fraternal and political organizations. A marked difference was that women were about four times as active in Parent-Teachers Association as the men.

OCCUPATION

The twentieth item on the BMQ (see Appendix) asks each spouse to describe his job or occupation.[2] Next, each is asked to discuss his feelings about his work and how he gets along with his co-workers and employer. Finally, each is asked whether he has changed jobs frequently, and if so, to give details. All these questions can give important dimensions of information about the individual and frequently about his marriage, especially if the kinship networks are involved. Just as industrial medicine has recently recognized that many of its patients have overtly emotional problems or covertly disguised psychosomatic reactions due to work problems, so must the marriage therapist be aware of the role of his patient's occupation in the current marital crisis. Some of the factors to be considered include fulfillment of the person in his work setting, identification with the organization—the man in the blue flannel suit, identification with one's labors, the "accident prone" person with severe emotional or marital problems, the reaction of the individual to authoritative figures, and so on.

One not uncommon source of marital friction was observed in couples where there was an overlap of occupational and kinship roles. Thirty percent (30%) of the husbands in my PS indicated that they were presently or had at some time been involved in a business with relatives. In most of these couples, the husbands were no longer associated with the business. Thus, the couple involved in a family business can lead to serious marital discord as the following clinical excerpts illustrate.

Mr. and Mrs. Honoris came for marital counseling following his request for divorce. Married fifteen years and having fathered three children with Mrs. Honoris, he had suddenly confronted her with his request for a separation. He had met his wife while working for her father. After marriage she never let him forget that he married the boss's daughter. He liked his father-in-law and had tolerated his wife's depreciating, belittling, and "castrating" behavior until he became financially independent in other business ventures.

On the other hand, the next couple, Mr. and Mrs. Hortense, came for counseling following Mrs. Hortense's request for a divorce:

Mr. and Mrs. Hortense had met at college. Mrs. Hortense fell madly in love with the campus athletic star and after six months of a romantic courtship was pinned. A year later they were engaged against the furious anger of her father, who wanted his only daughter to enter his successful business. Mr. Hortense was amazed at his future father-in-law's behavior. President of his fraternity, an outstanding athlete and popular with his classmates, this was his first rebuff in life. The engaged couple were happy, mutually enjoyed sexual intercourse, and married when they graduated. Her father grudgingly accepted the marriage (they had eloped) and in an abrupt turnabout in his previous position, offered his son-in-law a position in his firm. After the first month of employment, a drastic change occurred in his relationship with his son-in-law. He began to belittle him in front of the other employees, assigned him to the most menial tasks, and in general made life miserable for him. Mr. Hortense reacted with severe headaches, was very irritable at home, furious at his wife whenever she defended her father—not believing he could act in that manner. It was at this point that a change occurred in the couple's sexual relations. Mr. Hortense began to have premature ejaculations. After working one year for his father-in-law, he left to take a position at a friend's firm. Within a short time there was a marked change in his feelings and behavior, no longer did he have excruciating headaches, became pleasant again, and was the same as in the period before his marriage, but with one exception, he still had premature ejaculations, but only with his wife who was still in close contact with her father. When his father-in-law died of a sudden heart attack, he felt great pleasure but he still was unable to perform adequately with his wife— ignored her at social functions, was impervious to her feelings, and rejected her openly. Things were brought to a head when she returned from a visit with a girl friend in Las Vegas and told her husband she had fallen in love with another man and wanted a divorce.

Other sources on kinship difficulties between couples occur when external circumstances create a need to go out of business but emotional problems prevent it:

The Huldahs had frequent bitter arguments about his father. The elder Huldah had been in business at the same location for many years. When the younger Huldah got out of service, he reentered his father's business. Gradually the neighborhood deteriorated, the old customers moved away, and the new ones had different tastes. The income of the firm was insufficient for two families. The young Mrs. Huldah harassed her husband to liquidate the business, that it was time the other children participated in some arrangements for their father.

Mr. Huldah endlessly repeated: What was Father going to do at his age, it would kill him to give up his business.

Thus the environmental system has not only social and cultural components but also interpersonal elements. The marital transactions cannot be understood without knowledge of the ways in which a spouse's occupation impinges on his marriage. In turn the spouse's occupational role is part of a broader environmental system and is influenced by that system.

In Chapter I, the *perceptive-integrative-adaptive* ("pia") voice of the "record" was presented as purely data processing and nonemotional. In Chapter III, the clinical observation was noted that an individual's occupation sometimes parallels his mode of relating to others. Thus the manner in which a person describes his relationships with his fellow employees or employer may mirror his relationship with his wife. One's occupation usually does not involve intimacy, but a good marriage does. In the following couple, Mr. and Mrs. Inez, his description of his occupation as an accountant—cool, methodical, completely logical mirrored Mrs. Inez's complaints about her unsatisfactory marriage.

Mr. and Mrs. Inez had been married for ten years, Mrs. Inez described her husband as: dull, staid, uncreative and "resents my friends and activities." He is very logical, nonemotional, and when he comes home he first reads his mail, then the whole family lines up in front of him and reports their day's activities like he has his subordinates do at his office. He is nonargumentative and provides no strength so that I could "lean" on him at times.

Mr. Inez appeared very well dressed in a business suit, took out his completed BMQ from his attaché case, and immediately began to talk of his marital problem. He seemed to be under a great deal of pressure to convey all minute facts as quickly as possible. He presented his complaints as a lawyer would before a judge. He held a piece of paper, read off his complaints, and then elaborated at length. He presented love letters (evidence) from his wife's close boyfriend. He stated he loved his wife but wanted the marriage without the triangle boyfriend involvement.

Mr. Inez filled out the item on the BMQ dealing with his work in the same methodical, logical manner, listing the name of his firm, his position as chief accountant, his relationship with his employer which was friendly, proper and without any personal discussions, his proper but distant ways of relating to his subordinates. "If they try to tell me about their personal problems, I quietly but firmly let them know that we have a job to do."

Thus all of Mr. Inez's interpersonal relationships were characterized by "records" in which the "pia" was mechanically dealt with, where the "parental" voices were firm and no nonsense, and where the voice of the "inner child" was faintly heard.

RELIGION

Item 21 on the BMQ (see Appendix) raises the issue of religion.[3] Every individual has some attitude toward his religion:

faith, disbelief, or reluctance to commit himself. Furthermore, he may be militant, casual, or indifferent about his attitude. The attitude of one's parents ("parental") voices is often crucial in determining an individual's attitude to religion. The person's attitude ranges along a continuum from compliance at one pole to rebellion at the other end. These attitudes are clearly stated in the biblical story where the first "parental" voice was from God to Adam and Eve—not to eat the fruit of the tree of knowledge. At first they complied, then rebelled and ate the fruit. Sometimes couples bring religious difficulties to therapy as a cloak for problems in other areas of their marriage. Thus the therapist must not be maneuvered into theologic controversy as seen in the following couple:

Mr. and Mrs. Irene were referred for marital counseling by the industrial surgeon at the factory where Mr. Irene is a highly skilled maintenance man with fifteen years of uninterrupted work. For the past two years there had been no sexual intercourse between the couple because Mrs. Irene's refusal of sex unless she could take the "pill." In the past ten years Mr. Irene had joined three different small churches, in which he became very active. Then after some disagreement with the preacher he would abruptly leave and join another group. The last church was very fundamentalist and insisted there be sex only for procreation. This had resulted in marital problems at home. At the CDD session Mr. Irene was found to be suffering from a very severe paranoid delusional system with auditory hallucinations. This condition apparently had been present for a number of years and did not interfere with his work, which was of solo nature and done at night when all the workers were gone. Religion in this specific individual enabled ego-syntonic behavior, and it was felt best to leave his psychiatric condition alone.

In reviewing the answers to item 21 on the BMQ, I found it difficult to trace definite lines of acculturation and change. There was an extreme diversification in the religious beliefs and practices of the spouses. This diversification was so complex that I found it impossible to compare marriages. However, there was a definite trend away from orthodoxy between the older and younger generations. Occasionally, there was a reversal, with the younger generation being more religious than the older.

ADDITIONAL COMMENTS ABOUT YOUR MARRIAGE

The last item (22) on the BMQ (see Appendix) is unstructured and asks each spouse to make any additional comments about their marriage. Not infrequently this question elicits several pages of important data about the marital transactions and some surprising confidential material. In addition, since this question is vaguely worded, each spouse can "freely associate" and relate material not previously reported. Furthermore, the previous items of the BMQ may have mobilized anxieties and/or hostilities or raised issues in need of clarification. Occasionally the real areas of marital conflict may be expressed under this heading.

Free association, a controversial concept, can lead the individual into unconscious layers by using conscious and preconscious elements. Marmor,[4] in a thought-provoking article, has succinctly presented the limitations of free association. Clinically, free association has provided unexpected insights into both the individual's fantasies and current situations. The following example illustrates an unconscious recall by a patient during his third year of therapy:

The patient, while discussing his current difficulty with his superior at work, suddenly began to talk about his venerable ninety-three-year-old patriarchal grandfather. This grandfather was a learned, respected scholar, who demanded strict obedience from his children, wore a religious skull cap, and none could enter his bedroom unless invited in.

The patient related visiting his grandparents' home and being invited into their bedroom when he was four years old. Upon entering the room, he recalled being blessed by his grandfather. In relating this incident, the patient raised his left hand spontaneously. Since he was right handed, I commented on this, and he gave the "aha" reaction (where something meaningful or of insight is recalled by the patient).

He replied: I haven't thought of this in thirty-five years but Grandfather was left-handed. To escape induction into the Russian army, he put his hand in a loaf of bread and courageously cut off the trigger finger on his left hand. I've never told you this before.

Free association works on the principle of psychic continuity and determinism. According to this concept, every psychic phenomenon, conscious or unconscious, is determined by pre-

ceding ones and becomes itself a determinant of the future.
The associations of the determinants effect the psychic continuity. Often this continuity appears interrupted or ended.
Such seeming discontinuities correspond to unconscious areas
of psychic continuity. This continuity has limits, since it exists
only within the person's mind and is based on the individual's
own past history, i.e. its repertoire of "records" in its jukebox.
You cannot recall a "record" unless it was previously encoded.[5]
Freud's important discovery of psychic determinism remains
relatively unchanged and continues to be a basic construct of
most psychiatrists.

NOTES

1. Frank D. Cox: The honeymoon is over, *Voices*, 2:86, 1966.
2. Robert Rapoport and Rhona Rapoport: Work and family in contemporary society, *Amer Sociol Rev*, 30:381, 1965. An excellent article
   about the relationships of work vis-à-vis the family. See also Frank S.
   Pittman III, Donald G. Langsley, and Carol D. DeYoung (Work and
   school phobias: a family approach to treatment, *Amer J Psychiat*,
   124:1535, 1968), who differentiate between work phobia, work inhibition and success neurosis. They define work phobia as an acute,
   episodic anxiety state associated with leaving home and going to work
   due to fear of separation from the mother, later the wife, and to be
   the adult counterpart of school phobia. Work inhibition is described
   as a chronic, diffuse, characterologic disturbance of performance due
   to a variety of nonspecific conflicts. The individual often abhors work
   because he considers it the opposite of play. Success neurosis often
   is directly related to a specific situation—often a promotion. The
   individual fails at work because of fear of success. The symptom may
   result from fear of displeasing, competing with, or threatening authority.
3. Esther Oshiver Fisher: *Help For Today's Troubled Marriages.* New
   York, Hawthorn Books, 1968.
4. Judd Marmor (Limitations of free association, *Arch Gen Psychiat*,
   22:160, 1970) writes: ". . . my basic theme . . . is that material
   of which the patient is unconscious does not necessarily always reside
   in the patient's '*unconscious.*' There are many aspects of a patient
   and his character structure that he has never repressed because he
   has never been aware of them, even subliminally."
5. About two decades ago the neurosurgeon Dr. Wilder Penfield was

performing brain surgery under local anesthesia on a patient. When he stimulated the exposed cortex with an electrode, the patient immediately reported: "I hear music." When the electrode was removed, the music stopped abruptly and began again whenever the contact was made. The patient heard the same tune each time, reported it was in such realistic detail as though she was reliving a past experience. Subsequent experiments by others has suggested there exists in the brain a master recording which can be brought to the surface in the original form in which it was recorded.

XX

THE CONJOINT DIAGNOSTIC AND DISPOSITION SESSION (CDD)

The routine CDD in couples with marital discord is the end point of the evaluative phase. After the individual sessions with each spouse, unless conjoint sessions were begun at the outset, the couple is seen together for both diagnostic and planning purposes. The therapist must constantly be on the alert as to the varied ways marital disharmony may masquerade or express itself in vocational ineffectiveness, alcoholism, psychosomatic complaints,[1] neurosis, and so on. These phenomena are related either with the intrinsic needs and psychological motivations of the spouses or with the demands made upon them by their culture. As one describes a person's needs and motivations, the implication is often made that these patterns of behavior are pathological per se. Thus it is easy to talk of a man's need to be mothered, or of his need to dominate, or of his need to escape reality. But none of these needs are necessarily pathological, and many are worthwhile. Emotionally healthy people have such needs too. In evaluating a marriage, we observe whether the husband wants to be mastered while his wife likes to dominate. This does not mean the marriage is conflictual in that area. What is important is the totality of the transactions between the couple and not to condemn overtly or covertly such transactions in psychological terms. It is essential that we recognize the feelings and biases that each of us have.

Interviewing the husband and wife together, the conjoint session, has long been a technique utilized in social work family service agencies. It is only recently that psychiatrists have used the conjoint session for both the diagnosis and treatment of marital conflicts.[2] Draper,[3] experienced and well trained in both theology and psychiatry, emphasizes in his excellent book that: "Before the student becomes a therapist he must first become a diagnostician. . . . Proper treatment depends upon correct diagnosis. . . . It is my conviction that the pastor no less than the doctor has the responsibility of performing diagnostic duties and reaching a decision before he begins therapeutic action." This is born out by a study of 250 CDD's that I, personally, have performed (see Table XXVIII).

TABLE XXVIII
A STUDY OF 250 CONJOINT DIAGNOSTIC AND DISPOSITION SESSIONS

Marital Disharmony due to Interpersonal Problems	%
Therapy recommended	
Accepted	58
Not accepted	11
And couple to remain separated	2
Total	71
Marital Disharmony due to Psychiatric Problems	
Severe psychoneurosis	8
Manic-depressive psychosis	
Depressed	5
Hypomanic	1
Schizophrenia	4
Borderline state	3
Paranoid reaction	3
Severe alcoholism	3
Psychopathic personality	2
Total	29

Marital diagnosis continues to remain a postulate.[4] There is as yet no generally accepted classification of marital disharmony. In keeping with the GST, all three systems (intrapersonal, interpersonal and environmental) are considered in marital diagnosis. Otto Pollak's[5] observations are valuable in understanding the dynamics of marital diagnosis. The concepts of Dicks[6] (projective identification and unconscious collusion) are also helpful in arriving at a marital diagnosis. Further, communicational clarification, involving the interpersonal system particularly, is of value, especially the observations of Jurgen Ruesch,[7] Virginia Satir[8] and Watzlawick[9] and co-workers. In the CDD, I occasionally discuss Watzlawick's concepts of both content and relationship and complementary closure vis-à-vis mutual escalation. I sometimes illustrate the latter by asking the couple if they have ever seen the play or movie by Albee,[10] *Who's Afraid of Virginia Wolff?* This play beautifully depicts not only mutual escalation but also the game of "Uproar." This leads to the value of "games" in making a marital diagnosis. Games analysis[11] adds a valuable parameter in understanding the interpersonal system.

SOCIOLOGICAL AND PSYCHOANALYTIC CONCEPTS IN MARRIAGE

Otto Pollak uses sociological and psychoanalytic concepts to characterize marital relationships in terms of secondary gains in the realm of psychodynamics and of unresolved problems created by social change. He[12] writes: "Sociological concern with interaction patterns, small-group analysis, and role theory provides a safeguard against concentrating on a specific and thereby becoming involved in the intrapsychic conflicts of one individual only." Concentrating on one spouse in therapy assumes that solution of the intrapsychic conflicts in one spouse (intrapersonal system) in marriage will benefit the partner. Although this may occur, it cannot be taken for granted. Not infrequently, as pointed out in Chapter I, clinical improvement of one spouse can result in decompensation of the partner. For this reason, concepts like the GST force the therapist to consider the interplay of all elements in the various systems. This point of view is in agreement with Otto Pollak's observation that "the interaction patterns of healthy marital relationships in the various phases of family development are based on the assumption of satisfactory exchange of relationships, in which marriage partners function at the same time as sources and recipients of marital need satisfaction."

Otto Pollak has described how a marriage may be disturbed by failure of need complementarity between the spouses in the areas of interpersonal reorientation, sexuality, finances, and ego strengthening as the family passes from one developmental phase to another. Thus an awareness of the different phases of the marriage cycle and the tasks involved may be of diagnostic import.

PROJECTIVE IDENTIFICATION

Another dimension of information in the CDD relates to the concepts of projective identification and unconscious collusion. We are indebted to some members of the English school of psychoanalysts for these concepts.[13] At times it is necessary to describe these phenomena to the spouses in the CDD. They are specifically told about the jukeboxes and permanent library of "records." This is described simply and told how one area of their marital disharmony is due to one spouse playing a "record" no longer applicable to the present, and responding to the music coming from within as well as responding to the same "record" as though it were coming from his partner, i.e. the phenomena of projective identification. It is surprising how readily this metaphor is grasped by some spouses and responded to positively in the CDD—their first conjoint session.

The following clinical example is illustrative of the phenomenon of projective identification:

Mrs. Joyce, a young, intelligent, attractive, and professional woman, stated in her first appointment that her husband no longer cared for her, although he says he still loves her.

"I have become morose, insecure, and generally miserable. He is very distant. Shuts me out of his emotional life almost entirely. Any gesture I make seems to bear intrusion, and he admits to simply not being affectionate, enthusiastic and loving."

She was at a loss to explain this behavior in her husband, which began about six months ago when she had raised the issue of having a baby.

Mr. Joyce, a handsome, well-dressed, professional man in his late twenties, seemed perplexed as to his change in his feelings toward his wife. He too dated the beginning of their difficulty to the past six months.

"I feel that my wife and I have not been happy with each other. We have grown farther apart, and today we barely speak to each other. I do not feel affection toward my wife, and I do not believe that she feels affection for me, although she professes to. A year and a half ago my wife was firmly against having children, and I felt the same way. Recently she has changed her mind, but I have not. This is a major problem in our marriage today. She wants children very much, but I will not have them. We rarely argue about anything and have always until this year gotten along very well. Today we just don't seem to like each other very much." When Mrs. Joyce was seen again, she stated that she had some information to tell me that might throw light on their difficulty.

"I had a talk with his mother, who is a strong person as I am. She related that she resented her first baby being a boy but that she did not express it outwardly. When his sister was born two years later, she was very happy."

Although Mr. Joyce's mother did not outwardly express her dissatisfaction, the child was aware of it. With the birth of his sister, not only was he dethroned, but a rival entered the scene. What love he had been getting was now even less. His unconscious anger toward his mother (an old "record") had gathered dust in his jukebox until his wife strongly raised the issue of having a baby. Now all the rage originally felt toward mother was heard again internally as well as externally from the music coming from the same "record" projected onto his wife, as well as her real request for a baby.

The concept of projective identification helped understand the acute marital crisis in this couple.

COMMUNICATIONAL CLARIFICATION

The third dimension of information relates to pragmatic communication. As so often observed in conjoint sessions, what one spouse relates about a happening and what the partner says about the same incident and what really happened are very often three different things. Thus the conjoint session is valuable in the clarification of communications. An important observation is that spouses many times play their "records" as though no one was watching or listening. The so-called contamination of the transference that Freud was so concerned about frequently does not appear. A pyrotechnical verbal CDD is not uncommon, and occasionally the therapist may have to prevent physical battle between the spouses. I use two axioms of Watzlawick[14] and his co-workers' in the CDD: (1) that of content and relationship, and (2) complementary closure vis-à-vis mutual escalation. The first axiom helps the couple understand that the variant complaints each is voicing are purely content, and the real issue causing their disharmony is their discordant relationship underlying their complaints. The second axiom is stated in terms of the seesaw, and that since each is seated at one end of the seesaw, both are responsible for the discord and its resolution. Thus both are determining in different degrees the closure (complementarity) or escalation of their relationships. Another helpful tool for the therapist in the clarification of communication between the spouses occurring in the CDD are Satir's[15] concepts on communication theory.

MARITAL GAMES

Knowledge of the Bernean[16] games married people play can be helpful both in the CDD session and in therapy. When I use a "game" in the CDD, I specifically tell the couple that a game should not be taken to have any playful implication but that it refers to sequences of behavior which are governed by rules. A game of whatever category follows the various abstractions that define a system, e.g. time, openness and feedback. A marital game involves husband and wife in the process of, or at the level of, clarifying the nature of their relationship. Relationship patterns exist independently from content, e.g. the game of "Uproar," where the content can vary from a new hat to a visit by a mother-in-law. You cannot have a marital game unless there are two people seated on a seesaw. As soon as one gets off the seesaw (actually or figuratively), the game stops.

In 1966[17] I reviewed Berne's fourteen marital games played by my most recent three hundred conflicted couples. I find that the spouses find it easier to understand the metaphor of stereophonic "records" using the tripartite blending of the three voices— "parental," "pia" and "inner child" than the Bernean description of the parental, adult and child ego states. Berne, in his concept of games, attempts to abstract the formal relations between communication and behavior. Table XXIX shows the six most common games played by the couples. The other games described by Berne occurred with a frequency of less than 3 percent.

Games involve all three systems (intrapersonal, interpersonal and environmental) in varying degrees. Games, as Berne rightly points out, are both desirable and necessary if they are

TABLE XXIX
GAMES MARRIED PEOPLE PLAY *of 300 couples*

	PS	MDS
Projection—"If It Weren't For You"	110	98
Indoor Commando—"Uproar"	104	92
I can't or won't play—"Frigid Woman"	34	31
Game of one-up—"Now I've Got You, You S.O.B."	28	18
Obsessive-compulsive—"Harried"	12	8
"Alcoholic"	12	9

The totals do not represent addition of figures in each column but are cumulative, as one couple may play several games.

some games directed toward useful and constructive ends. Berne describes seven major categories of games. In the following paragraphs some of the most common marital games are discussed.

The Game of Projection

The most common marital game is that of projection[18] or as Berne calls it—"If It Weren't For You." This game occurred in two-thirds of the couples (110 in the PS and 98 in the MDS). As a clergyman pointed out in one of my seminars, the first time this game was played was in the Garden of Eden when Adam said, "If it weren't for Eve," and Eve said, "If it weren't for the Serpent." Berne feels that this game is frequently used as a counterphobic mechanism—to avoid doing something that causes fear by blaming another as the one responsible for the avoidance. The following couple is illustrative:

Mr. and Mrs. Jacqueline were referred by the child psychiatrist who was treating their son for underachievement at school. Mrs. Jacqueline had no complaints about the marriage, but Mr. Jacqueline did. He said, that as president of his corporation his business demanded that he entertain prospective customers and their wives. Since his wife was afraid of social gatherings—deluxe restaurants, their country club, and so on, he had missed some deals because he had to send his sales manager and his wife. This man was very competent, but some customers resented his absence, which they mistook for snobbishness on his part.

Mr. Jacqueline was a well-dressed handsome man, who had graduated with honors from a leading Eastern college. Upon graduating, he had entered the family business. When his father was made chairman of the board, he was promoted to president. He had met his wife through his father. She was the daughter of his father's best friend. He had been impressed with her intelligence, good looks, and the fact that she preferred to spend a quiet evening at home rather than the activities of the jet set.

Shortly after marriage her shyness among people increased to fears of being in closed places, especially social gatherings. Gradually their social relationships constricted, and more and more they remained home.

Since Mrs. Jacqueline had an obvious phobia, she was started on intensive psychotherapy, and Mr. Jacqueline was seen bimonthly. As Mrs. Jacqueline began to improve and expressed a desire to entertain, Mr. Jacqueline began to evidence marked anxiety. For the first time he expressed phobias almost identical to those of his wife: fear of board meetings, avoidance of the usual luncheons with his executives, and fear of social gatherings. Mr. Jacqueline too was started in intensive therapy.

This couple is interesting in that Mr. Jacqueline played the game "If It Weren't For Her," in which his wife's symptoms enabled him to avoid anxiety-producing situations. Thus Mr. Jacqueline never had to experience his phobias or even to admit their existence. The "records" his wife's jukebox played served to help him mute his "records" so that he was able to function occupationally. However, with the changing forces on the seesaw due to his wife's improvement, his own fears emerged. Mrs. Jacqueline's symptoms served to maintain his own self-image and self-respect. Thus, later, after marriage, he could complain that he could do better businesswise "if it weren't for her."

"Uproar" and "Frigid Woman"

The "indoor commando" game of "Uproar" was the second most common game observed. Since "Uproar" is frequently the terminal phase of the game of "Frigid Woman," both games will be discussed together. "Frigid Woman" was the third most frequent marital game occurring in approximately one fifth of the couples. The unconscious, and sometimes conscious, purpose of these two games is the avoidance of intimacy between two individuals. Occasionally it occurs between a seductive or domineering father and a teen-age daughter, especially when there is a sexually inhibited mother in the family. This is shown in an excerpt from a conjoint family session:

Mr. and Mrs. Jane and teen-age daughter have adjoining bedrooms with intervening door. Mr. Jane tells his daughter to leave the door open at bedtime to protect her should a prowler enter their apartment.

Daughter: "Daddy! We live on the thirtieth floor!"
Mr. Jane: "Do as I say!"
Daughter: "Mother! This is ridiculous. I want the door closed!"
Mrs. Jane does not answer.
Daughter: "I am going to close the door."
Mr. Jane: "I'm only thinking of you."
Daughter: "This is silly, you are acting like an old woman."
Both get angry at each other and daughter slams the door shut.

Anger can be expressed in at least four ways. It can be *repressed* unconsciously, *expressed* consciously, *suppressed* consciously, or even *denied* that it exists. The following incidents related by Mrs. Janet are informative:

"I was thinking over our last session, and I told John I couldn't get over the fact I had to practice new "records" reaching my goals, just as he did. I mentioned it was like when we learned how to dance, we had to count the dance steps until it became automatic. John turned up the radio as I was speaking. That was rude, to say the least, and it made me mad. I knew he didn't want to hear what I had to say so I shut up (suppression). I claim that he took me up wrong. He didn't let me finish my thought. If I sounded like a broken record to him, why couldn't he put me in my place instead of being rude?

"He stopped the car, and we went into the restaurant. There was a line waiting to be seated. John placed himself at the end of the line and waited there too. I became perturbed because I should think John would know the score by now. In a situation of this sort, you seek out the attendant who is doing the seating, and you give him your name and number of people in your party. It seems to me John is extremely self-conscious and doesn't like to make a spectacle of himself, so he stays in the background. By walking to the front of the line and telling the hostess your name does not make a person a public show. We waited too long, and we had a big argument going home (expression). We didn't talk the rest of the evening."

(Mr. Janet didn't recall turning up the car radio or that he was particularly annoyed that evening (denial), but he recalled a dream he had that night in which he had just dropped an atom bomb on some enemies (repression).

This couple, being treated concurrently (individually but synchronously) with John receiving analytic therapy for his nonpassionate relationship with his wife as well as for premature ejaculation (the "Frigid Man" game), were in a game of "Uproar" unconsciously set up by Mr. Janet as the following incident reveals:

Mrs. Janet: "We were in bed watching TV. I was loving and cuddly. John said to me: You smell of kitchen odors that I find distasteful. I blew up. I'm tired of his rejections. How can I feel his love when he tells me I stink. Perhaps he can't allow a close relationship. Is it possible that he ejaculates prematurely at times because he won't let himself experience a union besides his anger toward me. I am looking for the answer to why he reacts this way. I can't believe it's because he doesn't think. When I cooled down, and we spoke about it, he said, after denying his attack, that kitchen odors remind him of his mother. Actually, I didn't cook that day. Later on, he said he didn't detect that same odor. I did nothing for it. But I was no longer interested in him or sex."

This couple illustrates several methods, conscious and unconscious, of dealing with anger as well as the game of "Uproar."

As pointed out previously, the game of "Frigid Woman" occurred in about one fifth of the couples. The crucial point of "Frigid Woman" is the terminal phase of "Uproar." Once this phase is reached, sexual intimacy, or for that matter, intimacy of any sort, is out of the question. The converse game, "Frigid Man" is less common but takes the same general direction as pointed out in the previous couple, the Janets. Usually the husband makes the sexual advance to his wife and is rejected.

The following couple shows how the game was played for fifteen years before seeking marital counseling:

Mr. and Mrs. Josephine began their first conjoint session with Mrs. Josephine doing the talking and preempting the session. Mrs. Josephine: "It seems to me that my husband's not fulfilling my emotional needs is the circular pattern to the rut of this marriage and me. Everytime a decision was made by my husband, it didn't seem to meet my requirements. An argument would begin and I'd put sex out of my mind. He says I'm strong-willed, I say, I'm being realistic. Sex seemed all right, although I've never had an orgasm until I discovered I was trying to do what he wanted me to do and found he really wasn't doing any of the things I asked him to do: protect me from babies, we have three; be prepared to have intercourse—first arouse me, then leave me freezing in bed while he floundered in the dresser drawer looking for a condom, forget the lubrication, spend five minutes in the bathroom looking for it, and then expect me to be warm and receptive when he returned. He truly found me disappointed and angry when he returned. Sometimes I've made up my mind against letting this pathetic idiot arouse me again. I feel like this is a failure on his part, possibly it's all the arguments ("Uproar") of the years that fail to allow me to participate. I can't help but think that any normal man would give me these considerations if I had asked. When I have asked for them from my husband, he calls me crazy, stupid or demanding. I call it equality."

Mr. Josephine: "Our arguments are somewhat constant and sometimes a daily thing, mostly stemming from her opinion of me as being a perpetual liar. If I were to describe her, I would have to say she is a perfectionist. Our house is a museum, look but don't touch or sit down. She demands and expects no mistakes in any avenue: basement cleaning, garage, lawn care, you name it. If it isn't to her specifications, a big argument ensues. She is worse than the first sergeant I had in the army. Sexually, I feel it is far below par, once a month or so. I have always found her very frigid. Now I am told I am a poor bed partner: not preparing with precaution, towel, Vaseline and the like. We would reach a point or arousal and I would get up for the necessary articles and upon my return everything would be gone. Frustration from her, disgust from me. I was the bungler! If we did have sex, she would insist we both take a shower immediately and change the linens. Cleanliness is her God, and any spot of dirt and the house is a turmoil. I think she actually would start the arguments so as to avoid sex."

This is a good example of both the games of "Uproar" and "Frigid Woman."

THE USE OF DREAMS IN THE CDD

The use of dreams in the CDD has been found helpful in understanding the psychodynamics of the spouses. Dreaming involves primarily the intrapersonal system of each spouse. The use of dreams in therapy is contingent upon the therapist's training and clinical experience. Freud[19] reawakened attention about dreams in the understanding of the intrapsychic processes of the individual in his external relationships. His famous book on dream interpretation was published at the beginning of the century. Not until over fifty years later did Boss[20] and Bonime[21] publish their books on dreams. Dreams, related by one partner, and sometimes associated to by the other spouse, can serve as a dynamic force in bringing to view concealed feelings and attitudes which effect the partners. It is a frequent clinical observation that a day's experiences may be included in that night's dreams. Thus the activities and thoughts of a spouse the night before the CDD may be more revealing than verbal communications. The following dream is illustrative:

"I dreamt last night that I was to appear before a bankruptcy hearing. I was telling the referee about my assets but was concealing some information. I was smiling inwardly at putting one over him."

This man was aware that he was only going through the gestures of the therapy process. Although he had stated he was willing to do anything to save the marriage, in reality he had decided on a divorce (bankruptcy). He was going through the marital evaluation and perhaps therapy to mollify his wife. He was playing the game described by Berne,[22] "Look How Hard I've Tried," in which one spouse is bucking for a divorce but outwardly cooperating in the therapeutic process.

INTRAPERSONAL SYSTEM IN THE CDD

As pointed out at the beginning of this chapter, 29 percent of the 250 couples in the MDS had psychiatric problems that in addition to personal problems also produced marital discord. Thus in addition to the marital diagnosis, the second task of the CDD is to assess the individual personality makeup of each spouse: intellectually, perceptually, defensively, and so on. The personality is dependent upon the perceptual apparatus of each person, his retrieval of units of past information, his integrative capacity, his defensive maneuverings and, finally, his executive abilities.

At this point I would like to amplify my comments on the projective defense reactions stated in Chapter XVII. A common area of marital complaint expressed in the CDD revolves around the accusation of infidelity that may be real, suspected or delusional. I have been influenced by Abroms and his co-workers.[23] They present some challenging ideas on percept assimilation and paranoid severity that may be helpful in assessing the complaint of unfaithfulness. They suggest a phenomenological assessment of projective defense reactions along a continuum: ". . . mild paranoids are primarily *suspicious* [italics added], moderate paranoids show projection, guardedness, and *fluid delusions* [italics added], and severe paranoids differ from the milder cases by having *fixed delusions* [italics added]." My clinical experience is in agreement with theirs that paranoid people are hypervigilant. If one of the spouses during the evaluation is hypervigilant, the therapist should carefully weigh the spouse's words and actions.

Another dimension of the intrapersonal system of each spouse to be evaluated in the CDD is the assessment of a spouse's potential to enter therapy, which will allow for the establishment of a "working alliance."[24] In a previous article, we[25] differentiated five foci of transference phenomena: "In the development of the transference, we see first, the *relationship to the therapist as a real person* and a new object." The transactional relationships in the development of a working alliance depend primarily on the capacity of the spouse to relate to the therapist as a real person and a new object and on empathic activity on the part of the therapist. Another important factor in the establishment of a working alliance is the assessment of motivation of a spouse. As Robbins and Simon[26] point out:

. . . positive motivation (for psychoanalysis but equally applicable to psychotherapy) is described in terms of suffering from symptoms, recognizing the internal nature of the problems, and wishing to change . . . the implication is that the ability to recognize the internal nature of a problem requires that one truly has been able to differentiate from the object and that there is a mature degree of reality testing. The fact that one suffers and at the same time recognizes the internal sources of the suffering could imply a potential to tolerate suffering while observing it.

After the diagnostic survey of both partners and their marital transactions, the final step is to determine the tentative goals and to plan the operational approach of therapy. This is done routinely in the CDD, and it prevents misconceptions and distortions if stated in the individual session. In addition, the statement by the therapist of his concept of the marriage as the patient helps clarify the marital crisis. I have previously presented[27] the four possible outcomes of the CDD:

1. The couple is *accepted* for treatment.
2. The couple is *rejected* for treatment, since the marital malfunction may be a symptom of a severe dysfunction in the intrapersonal system of the spouse, or the marriage is beyond repair.

3. One or both spouses may *refuse* my suggestions.
4. The couple may be referred elsewhere (financial or individual reasons, e.g. lack of time, specific type of intervention needed—religious, psychoanalytic, etc.).

If referral is indicated, this can be done with the facts and tact.

In order to formulate a treatment plan, it is necessary to contrast the evaluation of marital disharmony with the ideal type of marriage for goal direction as well as the available treatment resources for goal limitation.[28] The therapist tentatively decides on the best possible marital adjustment within the range of each spouse's current situation, needs, present strengths of ego, and motivation. In the CDD, the various therapeutic techniques are briefly outlined, and the couple is told that they will be utilized to individualize therapy according to the changing marital problems and the needs of the couple.

The final point I make in the CDD is the setting of a *target date* for the couple accepted for therapy. I usually give an arbitrary figure of three months and tell the couple that their rate of therapeutic progress, at the end of this date will be evaluated as to further disposition, e.g. continuance or discharge. The use of a target date is an influence of Freud's[29] proposal of trial analysis as the only type of preliminary examination by which to determine suitability of the patient-analyst relationship.

In this chapter some of the relevant dimensions of the CDD have been presented. First, I have pointed out that the opportunity to see both spouses together enables a shaping up of what has transpired in the individual conferences, recapitulating the importance of individual patterns as to how they merge into the marriage. Secondly, I have elaborated on how marital disharmony may be due to either transactional marital discord or may be a manifestation of an individual psychiatric problem. The latter, a psychiatric problem in a spouse, first needs individual help. Thirdly, I presented the use of the GST conceptual frame in making a marital diagnosis. Thus the use of Pollak's blend of sociological and psychoanalytic concepts to characterize various forms of marital relationships, the use of projective identification and unconscious collusion, communicational clarification, and games married people play have been elaborated upon as to their value in the CDD. The CDD permits the identification of patterns of communication that are diagnostically important and enables the planning of therapy. My therapy procedures are a fusion of both treatment and management. Treatment aims to encode new "records" inside the individual (jukebox). Management is guided first by general probabilities based on data observed by the therapist in the acquisition of his clinical experience. Later, management focuses on the ongoing action between the couple and its environment and is guided by specific step-by-step probabilities.[30] Management is the prerogative of the therapist, who is in a position to reorganize kinship networks, to introduce new rules and roles, and finally, to reformulate goals.

NOTES

1. W.W. Meissner: Family dynamics and psychosomatic processes, *Family Process*, 5:142, 1966.
2. Clifford J. Sager: The diagnosis and treatment of marital conflicts, *Amer J Psychoanal*, 27:139, 1967. See also John P. Spiegel: Classificacation of body messages, *Arch Gen Psychiat*, 17:298, 1967; Carlos E. Sluzki, Janet H. Beavin, Alejandro Tarnopolsky, and Eliseo Veron: Transactional disqualification-research on the double bind, *Arch Gen Psychiat*, 16:494, 1967; Norman A. Polansky: On duplicity in the interview, *Amer J Orthopsychiat*, 37:568, 1967; Peter G.S. Beckett, James Grisell, Gordon Crandall, and Roger Gudobba: A method of formalizing psychiatric study, *Arch Gen Psychiat*, 16:407, 1967; and George W. Brown and Michael Rutter: The measurement of family activities and relationships, *Hum Relations*, 19:241, 1966. I was unaware of Henry V. Dicks' (*Marital Tensions*. New York, Basic Books, 1967, pp. 196–206) use of the "Joint interview," which he described in 1953, which parallels my experiences with the CDD. He writes: "I have indicated that this instrument for *marital diagnosis* [italics added] and therapy is a central feature of my work, though I claim no priority in its invention."
3. Edgar Draper: *Psychiatry and Pastoral Care*. Englewood Cliffs, Prentice Hall, 1965; and Granger E. Westberg and Edgar Draper: *Community Psychiatry and the Clergyman*. Springfield, Thomas, 1966.

4. Enid Balint (Marital conflicts and their treatment, *Compr Psychiat,* 7:403, 1966) tries to answer five questions in making a diagnosis about the marriage and to plan treatment.
5. Otto Pollak: Sociological and psychoanalytic concepts in family diagnosis, in the *Psychotherapies of Marital Disharmony* (B.L. Greene, Ed.). New York, Free Press, 1965, pp. 15–26.
6. Henry V. Dicks: Object relations theory and marital studies, *Brit J Med Psychol,* 37:125, 1963.
7. Jurgeon Ruesch: see Chapter III, see notes 3 to 6.
8. Virginia Satir: *Conjoint Family Therapy. Palo Alto,* Science and Behavior Books, 1964.
9. Paul Watzlawick, Janet H. Beavin, and Don D. Jackson: *Pragmatics of Human Communication.* New York, Norton, 1967.
10. Edward Albee: *Who's Afraid of Virginia Woolf?* New York, Atheneum, 1962. Albee is one of the great contemporary writers of the American marital institution.
11. Eric Berne: *Games People Play.* New York, Grove Press, 1966.
12. Otto Pollak: *Integrating Sociological and Psychoanalytic Concepts: An Exploration in Child Psychotherapy.* New York, Russell Sage Foundation, 1956.
13. The phenomena of *projective identification* in object relationships was first introduced by Melanie Klein (On identification, In Melanie Klein, Paula Heiman, and Roger Money-Kryle (Eds.): *New Directions in Psychoanalysis.* New York, Basic Books, 1954). Elliott Jacques in the same book agrees with Melanie Klein that Freud was aware of the process of identification by projection, although he was mainly interested in the process of identification by introjection.

The valuable phenomena of projective identification in marriage is highlighted by Dicks and his co-workers. (Mental hygiene of marital interaction, Proceedings of International Congress on Mental Health, Paris 1961, Group XVI, pp. 216–219; and Henry V. Dicks: Object relations theory and marital studies, *Brit J Med Psychol,* 36:125, 1963.) They pointed out that such identifications are the basis for an unconscious collusive process in the marital transactions. Their statements on marital disharmony are equally applicable to courtship:" . . . in marital disharmony one or both partners often fail to confirm the other's personality or identity. Instead they require the other to conform to an inner role mode, and punish them if the expectation is disappointed." I agree with Dicks that much marital conflict stems from efforts to coerce or mold the partner by very rigid and stereotyped tactics to these inner models and " . . . although these techniques arouse resistance and frustrations of the other spouse's ego, needs at a deeper level are part of a collusive process." I am in accord with these observations and with his comment that, where projective identifications have taken place, ". . . hate is felt both inside the self and towards object, and towards the self in the object from the outside."

Ronald D. Laing, Herbert Phillipson and A. Russell Lee in their book (*Interpersonal Perception,* New York, Springer, 1966, pp. 16–17) succinctly describe the phenomena of projective identification: "Projection refers to a mode of experiencing the other in which one experiences one's outer world in terms of one's inner world. Another way of putting this is that one experiences the perceptual world in terms of one's phantasy system, *without realizing that one is doing this* [italics added]." See also Henry V. Dicks (*Marital Tensions.* New York, Basic Books, 1967), where a number of comments on projective identification occur throughout the book. A descriptive vignette from my clinical practice follows: "The realization came to me that basically this (marital discord) was my doing. The things I have done to her and made her feel were barbaric. I made her feel inadequate. I did everything to annoy her. Basically I set her up as my mother and then destroyed her. Mother is not a warm, giving person. She is brilliant, dynamic, strong and substantial. She doesn't have maternal attributes. She is the opposite of my wife. What I have done is set her up as my mother, many times *I was unaware I was doing* this, and then destroyed her. I feel I put my wife in this position. The blocks she set against me—it's amazing they didn't come sooner."

14. Watzlawick *et al., op. cit.*
15. Satir, *op. cit.*
16. Berne, *op. cit.*
17. Bernard L. Greene: Panel of Transactional Analysis in Marital Therapy—Eric Berne, moderator, annual meeting, American Psychiatric Association, Atlantic City, New Jersey, May 10, 1966.
18. James L. Tichener (The problem of interpretation in marital therapy, *Compr Psychiat,* 7:333, 1966) finds as I did that "Projective and Introjective mechanisms and their allied processes lead the list (in marital interaction systems)."
19. Sigmund Freud: *The Interpretation of Dreams.* New York, Basic Books, 1958.
20. Medard Boss: *The Analysis of Dreams.* London, Rider, 1957.
21. Walter Bonime: *The Clinical Use of Dreams.* New York, Basic Books, 1962. See also Milton Kramer: Manifest dream content in normal and psychopathologic states, *Arch Gen Psychiat,* 22:149, 1970. This excellent article contains a comprehensive bibliography.
22. Eric Berne, *Games People Play.* New York, Grove Press, 1966.
23. Gene M. Abroms, Zebulon C. Taintor and William T. Lhamon: Percept assimilation and paranoid severity, *Arch Gen Psychiat,* 14:491, 1966. They find experimental confirmation of their hypotheses in an

experimental study by J. Silverman (The scanning control mechanism and cognitive filtering in paranoid and non-paranoid schizophrenia, *J Consult Psychol, 28:*385, 1964) which shows paranoid schizophrenics to be high scanners of the visual field. They further state: "Whatever the origins of this scanning attitude, whether initially an adaptive, coping strategy or the manifestation of a constitutionally high level of arousal (R. Lynn: Russian theory and research in schizophrenia, *Psychol Bull, 60:*486, 1963), the paranoid subject thereby provides himself with a large quantity of novel, potentially thereatening experiences which cannot always be neutralized by conventional denial and distortion mechanisms. . . . In the face of new experiences, a perceiver has the option of formulating new hypotheses to assimilate them or of leaving them unexplained pending the collection of more data, i.e., suspending judgment. The tendency to take the latter option, when circumstances permit, is commonly called open-mindedness or tolerance of ambiguity." Abroms *et al.* continue that it is their hypothesis that suspicious individuals find it "difficult to be open-minded or tolerant of ambiguity. Confronted with a large quantity of anxiety-provoking percepts, the products of his *hyper-vigilance* [italics added], the paranoid has developed a strategy of urgently forming assimilatory hypotheses."

Clinically, one finds this visual hypervigilance reported by comments from a spouse such as: "I carefully examined his suit and found some blonde hairs on his jacket," or, "I carefully inspected his shorts (or her panties) and found some suspicious spots. I brought them along for you to see." Comments of this nature should alert the counselor in the CDD. Finally, Abroms *et al.* conclude: "Suspicions, fluid delusions, and fixed delusions are differentiated by the tenacity with which their contents are subscribed to or, conversely, by the ease with which they are given up in the face of disconfirming evidence. Suspicions stop short of becoming firm beliefs; they are constantly modulated by reality contact. Fluid delusions, less open to experience, can be modified, perhaps temporarily, only after an impressive marshalling of counterevidence. Fixed delusions, *easily aroused in any situation* [italics added], are virtually uninfluenced by negative experience. . . . Thus it can be said that suspicions, fluid delusions, and fixed delusions represent three degrees of hypothesis strength."

24. Ralph R. Greenson: *The Technique and Practice of Psychoanalysis.* New York, Int. Univs. Press, 1968, p. 29. He writes: "A word should be added at this point about the relatively non-neurotic, rational, and realistic attitudes of the patient toward the analyst: the *working alliance.*" This working alliance is the foundation of all therapeutic efforts.

25. Bernard L. Greene and Alfred P. Solomon: Marital Disharmony: concurrent psychoanalytic therapy of husband and wife by the same

psychiatrist—the triangular transference transactions, *Amer J Psychotherapy, 17:*443, 1963.
26. Fred P. Robbins and Joy Simon: Research On Criteria For Analyzability. Reported to Staff of Institute for Psychoanalysis, February 15, 1967. Their presentations of self-object is helpful in understanding how the voice of the "pia" separates from the voice of the "inner child." "This differentiation is a complex process derived from primive conflicts and are responses to frustration and separation. It is in relation to these experiences of internal and external dangers that the child first becomes aware of his own identity as separate from others, the major step in this differentiation of self from object. The degree to which this is successful will depend upon many things." They then point out that this self-object differentiation is contingent on the development of trust, confidence, ability to distinguish between needs and wishes, relatively consistent reality testing, and so on.
27. Bernard L. Greene: (Discussion of paper by Marc H. Hollender) Marital Problems: The Selection of therapy. In *Current Trends in Psychiatry.* Des Plaines, The Forest Hosp. Foundation, 1968, pp. 41–44.
28. Roy R. Grinker, Sr., Helen MacGregor, Kate Selan, Annette Klein, and Janet Kohrman in their book (*Psychiatric Social Work. A Transactional Case Book.* New York, Basic Books, 1961, p. 118) express my views on treatment goals.
29. Sigmund Freud: Further recommendations on the techniques of psychoanalysis, Standard Edition, *12:*157, London: Hogarth Press, 1958.
30. Morris Gelfman (A post-Freudian comment on sexuality, *Amer J Psychiat, 126:*651, 1969) suggests that it is more realistic where there is rapprochement to accept the neurotic person on his terms which may result in adequate functioning.

Part Two
Management of Marital Problems

XXI

A MULTIOPERATIONAL APPROACH TO MARITAL PROBLEMS

Marriage can't be lovable if it isn't livable.

——Joseph B. Trainer[1]

The complexity of our society results in great variations in marital patterns and greater flexibility in therapeutic techniques. Clinical necessity, therapeutic failures and advancing knowledge require further flexibility in technique. Psychotherapy is replete with rigidly held but widely varied doctrines.[2] It is not unusual for experienced therapists to have difficulty in understanding colleagues trained in different schools. Franz Alexander[3] observes: "Instead of progressive improvements of knowledge and practice, the tendency to rest on the laurels of the past appears in the form of dogmatism . . . re-evaluation (of knowledge) necessarily leads to changes and requires constant revision of techniques of treatment and *steady experimentation* [italics added]." Psychotherapies differ only in methods for achieving the same goals.

The therapist must evaluate the problem of each couple and decide intuitively which technique or combination of techniques is most applicable at any particular moment. He must be able to tailor his approach to the couple's individual, as well as mutual, needs—custom-tailored therapy.[4] From personal experience[5] with all the operational approaches to be discussed in the following chapters (see Table XXX), from communications, and from culling the literature,[6] I have proposed a "six C" classification of therapeutic modalities.

I. Supportive therapy.

    A. Crisis counseling—an orientation stressing sociocultural

TABLE XXX

514 COUPLES (PS) WITH MARITAL DISHARMONY EVALUATED AND/OR
TREATED IN THE PAST FIFTEEN YEARS

Year	Rejects-refusals	Counseling	Concurrent	Conjoint	Combined	Collaborative	Classical analysis
1954*	0	0	0	0	0	3	1
1955	3	4	3	0	0	4	1
1956	1	4	3	0	0	4	1
1957	1	3	3	0	0	2	2
1958	1	2	8	0	0	2	6
1959	2	4	12	0	0	1	6
1960	5	4	17	0	0	1	3
1961	5	4	17	0	0	0	3
1962	6	10	12	3	2	1	2
1963	8	12	16	7	10	4	4
1964	20	29	13	18	20	5	6
1965	20	30	12	4	15	3	6
1966	16	16	11	10	11	4	10
1967	18	17	15	20	24	3	11
1968	15	23	5	12	9	2	6
1969†	13	15	10	6	12	4	8
Totals	134	144	78	50	50	25	33

* Figure given is for six-month period only.
† Figure given is for nine-month period only.
The totals do not represent addition of figures in each column but are cumulative, as therapy may overlap from one year to another. Only 312 of the above couples received intensive therapy.

forces and explicitly acknowledging the implications of the "here and now" situation.

II. Intensive therapy.
   A. Classical psychoanalysis—an individually oriented approach.
   B. Collaborative therapy—the marital partners are treated by different therapists, who communicate with the permission of the spouses, for the purpose of maintaining the marriage.
   C. Concurrent therapy—both spouses are treated individually but synchronously by the same therapist.
   D. Conjoint marital therapy—both partners are seen together in the same session by the same therapist.
   E. Combined therapy.
      1. Simple—a combination of individual, concurrent, and conjoint sessions in various purposeful combinations.
      2. Conjoint family therapy.[7]

3. Combined-collaborative therapy.[8]
4. Marital group psychotherapy.[9]

In the evolution of therapeutic techniques, I began by focusing upon the individual, on the dyadic one-to-one relationship. I investigated the patient's environment only to the extent necessary for achieving my therapeutic aim of intrapsychic changes. Treatment failures necessitated the inclusion of the relationship between husband and wife as well as their individual personalities. The triadic approaches, including concurrent, conjoint marital, and combined techniques were thus utilized. Finally, because of therapeutic impasses with certain couples, I had to move beyond the marital relationship to include children, who were contributing to the marital discord. Treatment can thus be visualized, in terms of a spectrum of therapeutic settings, with the dyadic approaches of classical and collaborative techniques at one end, the triadic approaches of concurrent, conjoint marital and combined therapies in the middle, and conjoint family therapy and marital group therapy at the other end. The spectrum concept offers a guide to the available techniques for helping conflicted couples. Furthermore, this spectrum concept does not imply that any one therapist can be talented in or interested in all the varied techniques. But it is expected that the couple's needs be given prime consideration and, furthermore, that the therapist be prepared to identify the optimum mode of therapy, even though he himself cannot continue with that form of treatment.

PRINCIPLES OF MANAGEMENT OF MARITAL DISCORD

Mutual Responsibility

The mutual responsibility of both spouses for their marital disharmony and its solution is emphasized. I point out that since both are seated on the seesaw, the ride they get is the one each wants, either consciously or unconsciously. However, I stress that the patient is the seesaw.

Marriage Contract

The marriage contract is again reviewed with the couple. In addition to the sexual aspects of the contract, the nonsexual collaborative relationships are stated—voluntary, permanent, exclusive[10] and goal oriented. I specifically emphasize that the past behavior is a "historical necessity"[11] but that each spouse will be responsible for current behavior. The contract I present is a biased one, and after the marriage is reequilibrated, it is the couple's prerogative to change the contract if mutually acceptable. In many couples where infidelity was a major source of conflict, the stress on exclusiveness in the marital relationship often alleviates anxiety and hastens the therapeutic process. In effect, I am actively setting limits. Clinical experience indicates that a therapist cannot avoid communicating his values, even if he tries to avoid giving directives. By his verbal and nonverbal cues and metacommunications, he directly or indirectly persuades, suggests, and controls the behavior of his patients. I point out that setting limits to behavior produces anxiety and helps in uncovering the motivations behind the behavior. Abroms[12] has written an excellent article on setting limits, in which he outlines five types of behavior which may call for explicit limit setting by a therapist: destructive behavior, disorganized behavior, deviant behavior, withdrawn behavior, and dependent behavior.

Target Date

The target date is twelve sessions of therapy—usually a therapeutic trial of three months. The couple is told that at that time the progress of the therapy will be assessed by the therapist and couple as to continuance or interruption. Should the couple feel that they are ready to interrupt the therapy before the three months and work their problems out by themselves, this will be satisfactory to the therapist.

Nuclear Model

The nuclear dynamic model[13,14] is presented to the couple in terms of the possible outcome of their marriage. This nuclear model can be visualized as a circle containing an enclosed smaller circle and thus having an internal and external boundary (see Fig. 11).

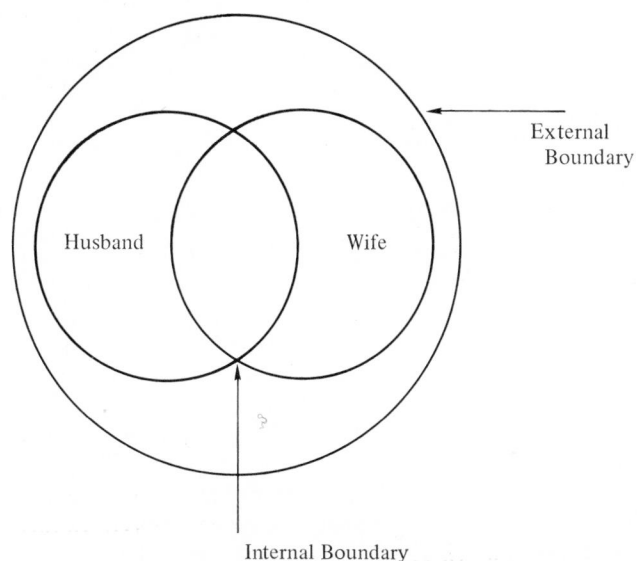

Figure 11. Nuclear dynamic model of the family.

The external environmental factors influencing the outcome of a marriage are outside the external boundary and consist of sociocultural forces. The internal environmental forces influencing the outcome of a marriage are within the external boundary. Four stages occur in the progressive dissolution of a marriage.

Durable Incompatible Marriage

This has both internal and external boundaries intact. The conflicting partners constantly take advantage of one another, playing the marital games previously described.

Emotional Divorce

This has the external boundary intact, while the internal boundary is disrupted (see Fig. 12).

Each spouse goes his separate way but maintains the facade of his marriage. The partners make neither psychological nor physiological demands upon one another and preserve their marriage only for economic, religious, or social reasons, e.g. "for the sake of the children." The following clinical extract is typical:

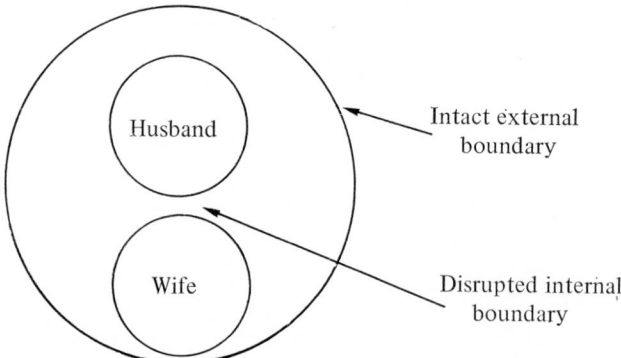

Figure 12. Nuclear dynamic model in emotional divorce.

Mr. Justina, a lean, muscular man with cold, grey eyes, who appears older than his stated age of forty-five, relates in a composed, poised, and self-insulating fashion. So insulated, he describes his early years on the farm as the oldest of two children, emotionally abandoned by a cold, disinterested farmer father to the tyranical control of a suspicious, religious, moralistic and socially self-isolating mother. He believes his parents' marriage was entered into because of mutual loneliness and mutual convenience: "Mother did not love my father, only respected him. Before I entered grammar school, there were constant protracted arguments between them. After I started school, the arguments ceased as Father tolerated Mother with resignation for the sake of us children. As the years passed, they settled into a condition of cold coexistence. There ceased to be any affection of any kind between them; they went their separate ways and slept in separate bedrooms."

Separation

Separation disrupts the internal boundary and fragments the external boundary. While the couple live in separate house-

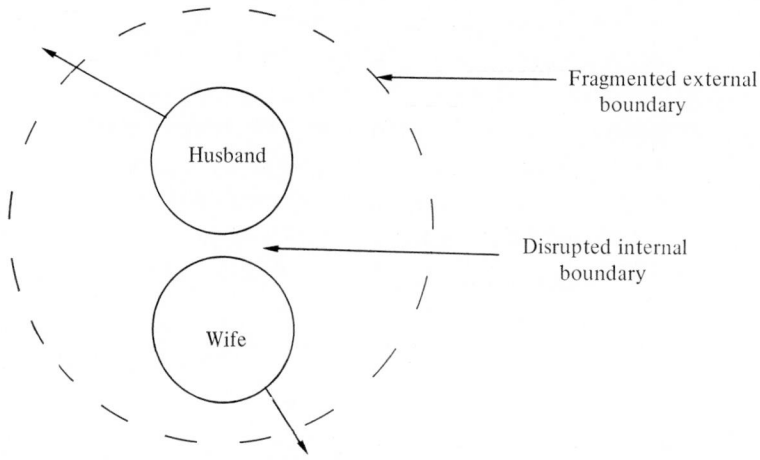

Fragmented external boundary

Husband

Disrupted internal boundary

Wife

Figure 13. Nuclear dynamic model of family in separation.

holds, they maintain the marriage for economic, social, societal, or legal purposes (see Fig. 13).

Divorce

Divorce disrupts both external and internal boundaries, dissolves the marriage legally, and returns the couple to their single status.

Transient Structured Distance (TSD)

TSD carefully delineates rules and roles in certain couples with marital disharmony.[15] This distancing maneuver may be structured either at the beginning or during the therapeutic process. This sociopsychological maneuver of environmental structuring, whereby certain rules are set up by the therapist to establish rights of and maintain a certain distance between marital partners, has been found to be both diagnostic and therapeutic. Rules are based on conflict areas that, in the opinion of the therapist, require the introduction of distance between the partners. They include all or some of the following:

1. Intercourse can be initiated only by the spouse who com-

plains of a too demanding partner; the latter has the choice of accepting or rejecting the advance.

2. Either partner may ask the other to participate in a social function, and the partner need not acquiesce.
3. Specified roles are assigned and carefully spelled out in a conjoint session to avoid later arguments.
4. Separate bedrooms are at times indicated for each spouse.
5. Partners can go their own way without accounting to each other. However, this is not intended to imply that either has the right to break existing secular or sacred laws governing the marriage.

In three fifths of the couples where this distancing maneuver was introduced, one or both spouses had reached the conclusion that separation or divorce was inevitable. For some of the couples, TSD has become a periodic living arrangement, utilized as a cooling-off maneuver for neutralizing mounting hostility. In some it has been used as a holding operation, where one of the spouses was about to engage in an irreversible, impulsive act, and the TSD was an attempt to allow adequate time to involve the symptomatic partner more deeply into therapy.

As a diagnostic tool, the TSD is used to clarify the status of the marriage, to determine the readiness of a spouse for separation, and to ascertain the spouses' motivation for help. As a therapeutic tool, it can be used to neutralize pyramiding hostility and/or anxiety that threatens to prematurely disrupt the marriage. Occasionally the TSD provides a means for overcoming therapeutic impasses during treatment. Before initiating the TSD (or any kind of action by the therapist), an attempt should be made to evaluate the risks involved, such as a rage reaction or homosexual panic reaction from the partner. When in doubt, decrease one's therapeutic ambition.

GST Principles

Two therapeutic principles in keeping with the GST should be kept in mind:

1. It is impossible to alter significantly one element in any of the three systems (intrapersonal, interpersonal or environmental) without producing changes in the entire system.
2. It is futile to select one element for attention and action while ignoring and disregarding the others.

Confidentiality

Finally, I stress to the couple my insistence on confidentiality in terms of our relationship. Before we continue, it is to be clearly understood that under no circumstances will I be called to testify in court at a later date should their relationship encounter legal problems. It is explained that my value as a marriage counselor would be undermined if either spouse would not feel completely free to relate his feelings and experiences could these be held against him later in court. Henry V. Dicks, with his extensive experience in marital disharmony writes as follows in his book (*Marital Tensions.* New York, Basic Books, 1967, p. 188): "On similar grounds we *categorically refuse* [italics added] to give evidence in any divorce proceedings that our clients, past or present, may become involved in. We cannot later appear in court for one side when we have worked with both. Only by this being clear can any sense of security be created in potential clients' minds that we shall respect their confidences in all circumstances."

CUSTOM-TAILORED CRISIS COUNSELING

The therapist must be able to tailor his therapeutic approach to the couple's individual, as well as mutual, needs—custom-tailored crisis counseling.[16] The counseling approaches to be presented are based upon personal experience with 144 couples (see Table XXX). In addition, the therapy of more than 100 couples has been evaluated indirectly through supervision of their therapists.

The application of the von Bertalanffy model of GST to marital counseling enables a spouse to form his judgements about himself and others more in terms of objective evidence and less on the basis of distortions, misconceptions or biased assumptions. This approach is a phenomenological one that "rings a bell" in both spouses, since the observations are current and replicable in the therapeutic procedures. This approach consists of a precise description of the three main voices in each "record"—"parental," "pia" and "inner child." The interplay of the voices of the spouses in the marital transactions is pointed out, and distortions and illogical conclusions are highlighted in both the individual and/or conjoint sessions. By focusing on the voices and their interplay, the couple is enabled to proceed from a more realistic basis in attempting to modify this marital discord and reestablish a more meaningful relationship. At all times the attitude of the therapist must be analytic and non-judgmental[17]—easily said but difficult to do!

The cutting of new "records" in each spouse resulting in new behavior involves learning (intrapersonal system), communication (interpersonal system) and the concept of social field interdependence (environmental system). In one of his last papers, Franz Alexander[18] stressed the importance of learning theories in the dynamics of psychotherapy. He suggested that psychodynamic therapy be reexamined from a learning point of view derived from experimental psychology. Brady[19] correctly states: "The object of such a reformulation (about learning theory) is not the reduction of dynamic concepts to learning or conditioning terms. Rather, the expectation is that viewing therapy in this *additional* and *complementing* [italics added] frame of reference may clarify some basic therapeutic issues."

The word *counseling* has been used to describe a wide variety of activities, and accordingly, carries different connotations to persons of different backgrounds and experience.[20] Professional counseling contains certain definite attributes (see Ch. XXVII). It is a learned art in which a professionally trained person has acquired basic knowledges, attitudes, and skills, and has integrated these into a disciplined capacity to use himself therapeutically with the person seeking help within the immediate experience of the interview. In addition, the therapist should have a disciplined awareness of his own biases and attitudes, as these affect the counseling situation. Counseling denotes a supportive and abbreviated form of therapy that sets no limits on the number of sessions. However, an attempt is made by the therapist to terminate the counseling process as soon as feasible.

I have used my own ongoing therapeutic experiential development as a model for training therapists, based on a graduated series of clinical settings which replicates my own development from a psychoanalyst to a marital therapist. For the beginning therapist, the counseling of one spouse (the dyadic one-to-one relationship) is less anxiety producing. In this technique the therapeutic focus varies from internal psychodynamics and how patterns of behavior develop to how the partner reacts to these patterns. In the collaborative technique both spouses are treated by separate therapists who communicate with each other. This approach is still a dyadic one-to-one relationship but introduces the therapist to a better understanding of the marital transactions. This increased awareness of marital transactions is due to another dimension of information about the marriage that the collaborating therapist brings to the collaborative session. For the collaborative sessions to be effective, they should be regularly scheduled. In the concurrent technique the therapist now shifts from the dyadic to the triadic relationships with the troubled couple. In this method both spouses are treated individually but synchronously by the same therapist. With both partners involved in therapy, not only can the therapist avoid unnecessary anxieties and interference from the partner (not uncommon in the classic dyadic relationships), but the therapist is in the unique position to evaluate communications and behavior as observed and reported from both spouses. With increasing clinical experience, the therapist will feel more confident to attempt the conjoint technique. In this approach both spouses are seen together in the same session by the same therapist. This approach is the one most commonly employed by counselors. Seeing both partners together gives heightened perception of the marital relationships. Thus direct observation facilitates more objective evaluation of the spouses' behavior and limits the need to judge distortion from more indirect data. With increasing clinical experience the therapist is now prepared to utilize the combined approaches. The combined approaches use individual, concurrent and conjoint sessions in various purposeful combinations. The two most common arrangements are the simple method—which is a combination of dyadic and triadic sessions, and the conjoint family therapy. In the latter method the children of the couple are included in the therapeutic sessions when they are either being used as scapegoats or are producing an impasse in the treatment of their parents. Recently I began to use another approach which I have found useful, the combined-collaborative technique. In this method two therapists meet once a week together with the couple. In addition to this session, each therapist sees his patient in individual dyadic sessions. The last approach the therapist may want to utilize is that of marital group psychotherapy. In this method usually four couples are treated together. Depending upon circumstances the therapist may wish to employ individual sessions as well as the group approach. This "integrated" approach is used by some therapists.

Counseling techniques were utilized in the treatment of 144 couples or 38 percent of the total couples treated privately. The most common counseling approach was the conjoint marital technique (see Table XXXI).

Since the indications and contradictions for the various techniques are the same in counseling and in intensive therapy with conflicted couples, each treatment modality will be dealt with in a separate chapter. Each treatment approach will be pre-

TABLE XXXI
COUNSELING TECHNIQUES WITH 144 COUPLES

Technique	*Percentage*
Conjoint Marital	44
Concurrent	26
Combined	14
Classic	10
Collaborative	6

sented along a continuum for the moderately skilled, skilled, and very skilled therapist. The clinical extracts will be used to help clarify the treatment goals and treatment process.

NOTES

1. Joseph B. Trainer: *Physiologic Foundations For Marriage Counseling.* St. Louis, Mosby, 1965, p. 216.
2. W.W. Meissner, in an excellent comprehensive survey of the literature on the family, has pinpointed the "issues and problems which must be thought through in working toward an understanding of the family" (Thinking about the family-psychiatric aspects, *Family Process,* 3:1, 1964); Gregory Bateson, Don D. Jackson, Jay Haley, and John H. Weakland describe the "double bind" situation (Toward a theory of schizophrenia, *Behav Sci, 1:*151, 1956); Edward J. Carroll and Aldo W. Mell: An Assessment of Family Interviewing. Paper presented at the panel, Family Interaction Tests, at the annual meeting of the American Orthopsychiatric Association, Chicago, 1964; Robert J. Drechsler and Marvin I. Shapiro: A procedure for direct observation of family interaction in a child guidance clinic, *Psychiatry,* 24:163, 1961; Antonio J. Ferriera: Family myth and homeostasis, *Arch Gen Psychiat,* 9:457, 1963; Don D. Jackson, Jules Riskin, and Virginia M. Satir: A method of analysis of a family interview, *Arch Gen Psychiat,* 5:321, 1961; Jan Ehrenwald: *Neurosis in the Family and Patterns of Psychosocial Defense,* New York, Hoeber, Ed., Harper & Row, 1963; Irene M. Josselyn: The family as a psychological unit, *Soc Casework,* 34:336, 1953; Cora Kasius: *Social Casework in the Fifties: Selected Articles, 1951–1960.* New York, Family Service Association of America, 1962; Gardner Murphy: New knowledge about family dynamics, *Soc Casework,* 40:363, 1959; Herbert A. Otto: The Family Resource Development Program: The Production of Criteria for Assessing Family Strength. Paper presented at the National Conference on Social Welfare, New York City, 1962; Howard J. Parad and Roger R. Miller (Eds.): *Ego-Oriented Casework: Problems and Perspectives.* New York, Family Service Association of America, 1963; John P. Spiegel: Homeostatic Mechanisms Within the Family, in *The Family in Contemporary Society* (Iago Galdston, Ed.) New York, Int. Univs. Press, 1958, pp. 73–89; Fred L. Strodtbeck: Instruments Used in the Study of Family Interaction by the Revealed Difference Method, Social Psychology Laboratory, Univ. Chicago, 1962; James L. Tichener, Thomas D'Zmura, Myra Golden, and Richard Emerson: Family transaction and derivation of individuality, *Family Process,* 2:95, 1963; Francis J. Turner: A comparison of procedures in the treatment of clients with

two different value orientations, *Soc Casework, 45:*273, 1964; Ferdinand van der Veen, B. Huebner, Barbara Jorgens, and P. Neja: Relationships between the parents concept of the family and family adjustment, *Amer J Orthopsychiat, 34:*45, 1964.

3. Franz Alexander: *The Scope of Psychoanalysis.* New York, Basic Books, 1961, pp. 541–544.

4. Bernard L. Greene: Training clergymen in marriage counseling, *Pastoral Counselor, 5:*42, 1967. Recently Harold I. Lief, in his presidential message, Psychoanalysis 1948–1968, at the annual meeting of the American Academy of Psychoanalysis, Boston, Massachusettes, May, 1968, stated: "As an illustration of the increasing flexibility demanded of a modern day psychoanalyst, the last role listed, that of marriage counselor, deserves special mention. Clinical evidence demonstrates that at least half the patients seen in psychoanalysis have significant marital problems. Often enough, these problems are due to the difficulties in interaction between husband and wife, rather than to the psychopathology of one or the other partner. The psychoanalysis of one partner is an inadequate way to treat the marital interactional pathology. Conjoint methods are necessary to replace or at least to augment individual treatment."

5. Bernard L. Greene: Marital disharmony: concurrent analysis of husband and wife. I. Preliminary Report, *Dis Nerv System, 21:*1, 1960. In a recent Franz Alexander lecture, Hans H. Strupp (Toward a specification of teaching and learning in psychotherapy, *Arch Gen Psychiat, 21:*203, 1969) comments: "Hence, advances in psychotherapy are not likely to come from theoreticians or researchers but from therapists engaged in clinical pursuits."

6. Ian Alger and Peter Hogan: Enduring effects of videotape playback experience on family and marital relationships, *Amer J Orthopsychiat, 39:*86, 1969; D. R. Bardill and J. J. Bevilacqua: Family interviewing by two caseworkers, *Soc Casework, 45:*278, 1964; Frances L. Beatman: Family interaction: its significance for diagnosis and treatment, in *Social Casework in the Fifties* (Cora Kasius, Ed.). New York, Family Service Association of America, 1962, pp. 212–225; John E. Bell: *Family Group Therapy.* U.S. Dept. of Health, Education and Welfare, Pub. Health Monograph 64; H. Waldo Bird and Peter A. Martin: Countertransference in psychotherapy of marriage partners, *Psychiatry, 19:*353, 1956; Martin G. Blinder and Martin Kirschenbaum: The Technique of married couple group therapy, *Arch Gen Psychiat, 19:*44, 1967; Murray Bowen: Family psychotherapy, *Amer J Orthopsychiat, 31:*40, 1961; Selwyn Brody: Simultaneous psychotherapy of married couples, *Psychoanal Psychoanal Rev, 48:*94, 1961–1962; Edward J. Carroll: Family therapy—some observations and comparisons, *Family Process, 3:*178, 1964; Ed-

ward J. Carroll, C. Glenn Cambor, Jay V. Leopold, Miles D. Miller, and Walter J. Reis: Psychotherapy of marital couples, *Family Process*, 2:25, 1963; Erika Chance: *Families in Treatment*. New York, Basic Books, 1959; James L. Curtis, Melly Simon, Frances L. Boykin, and Emma R. Noe: Observations on 29 multiproblem families, *Amer J Orthopsychiat*, 34:510, 1964; Rudolph Dreikurs: Techniques and dynamics of multiple psychotherapy, *Psychiat Quart*, 24:788, 1950; Meyer Elkin: Short-contact counseling in a conciliation court, *Soc Casework*, 43:1, 1962; Emily C. Faucett: Multiple-client interviewing: a means of assessing family processes, *Soc Casework*, 43:114, 1962; Regina Flesch: Treatment goals and techniques in marital discord, *J Soc Casework* pp. 382–388, 1949; Alfred S. Friedman: Family therapy as conducted in the home, *Family Process*, 1:132, 1962; Joanne Geist and Norman M. Gerber: Joint interviewing: A treatment technique with marital partners, *Soc Casework*, 41:76, 1960; Alexander Gralnick: Family psychotherapy: general and specific considerations, *Amer J Orthopsychiat*, 32:515, 1962; Richard Green: Collaborative and conjoint therapy combined, *Family Process*, 3:90, 1964; Irwin M. Greenberg, Ira Glick, Sandra Match, and Sylvia S. Riback: Family therapy: indications and rationale, *Arch Gen Psychiat*, 10:7, 1964; Roy R. Grinker, Jr.: Complementary psychotherapy: treatment of "associated pairs," *Amer J Psychiat*, 123:633, 1966; Martin Grotjahn: *Psychoanalysis and the Family Neurosis*. New York, Norton, 1960; David Hallowitz, Robert G. Clement, and Albert V. Cutter: The treatment process with both parents together, *Amer J Orthopsychiat*, 27:587, 1957; David Hallowitz and Albert V. Cutter: Collaborative diagnostic and treatment process with parents, *Social Work*, 39:90, 1958; C. Herndon Nash and Ethel M. Nash: Premarriage and marriage counseling, *JAMA*, 180:395, 1062; Richard N. Hey and Emily H. Mudd: Recurring problems in marriage counseling, *Marriage Fam Living*, 21:127, 1959; Florence Hollis: *Casework—A Psychosocial Therapy*. New York, Random House, 1964; Don D. Jackson and John H. Weakland: Conjoint family therapy, *Psychiatry*, 24:30, 1061; James Jackson and Martin Grotjahn: The concurrent psychotherapy of a latent schizophrenic and his wife, *Psychiatry*, 22:153, 1959; Miriam Jolesch: Casework treatment of young married couples, *Soc Casework*, 43:245, 1962; Warren L. Jones: The villain and the victim: group therapy for married couples, *Amer J Psychiat*, 124:351, 1967; Aaron Krich: A Reluctant Counselee: A Specimen Case, in (*Emily H. Mudd and Aaron Krich, Eds.*). *Man and Wife*. New York, Norton, 1957, pp. 258–275; Robert L. Laidlaw: Marriage Counseling, in *Understanding Your Patient* (Samuel Liebman, Ed.). Philadelphia, Lippincott, 1957, p. 132; Robert L. Laidlaw: The Psychotherapy of Marital Problems, in *Progress in Psychotherapy*. New

York, Grune & Stratton, 1960, Vol. V pp. 140–147; Arthur L. Leader: The role of intervention in family-goup treatment, *Soc Casework, 45:* 327, 1964; Nathaniel S. Lehrman: The joint interview: an aid to psychotherapy and family stability, *Amer J Psychotherapy, 17:*83, 1963; Robert K. Liek and L.K. Northwood: The Classification of Family Interaction Problems for Treatment Purposes. Paper read at the National Council on Family Relations, August, 1963; Robert Mac-Gregor: Multiple impact psychotherapy with families, *Family Process, 1:*15, 1962; Peter A. Martin and H. Waldo Bird: An approach to the psychotherapy of marriage partners, *Psychiatry, 16:*123, 1953; Salvador Minuchin, Edgar H. Auerswald, Charles H. King, and Clara Rabinowitz: The study and treatment of families that produce multiple acting-out boys, *Amer J Orthopsychiat, 34:*125, 1964; Bela Mittlemann: The concurrent analysis of married couples, *Psychoanal Quart, 17:*182, 1948; Emily H. Mudd: *The Practice of Marriage Counseling.* New York, Association Press, 1951; Emily H. Mudd and Martin Goldberg: How to help your patients with marital problems, *Consultant S K & F Laboratories,* 1961; Emily H. Mudd and Hilda M. Goodwin: Counseling Couples in Conflicted Marriages, in *The Psychotherapies of Marital Disharmony* (Bernard L. Greene, Ed.). New York, Free Press, 1965, pp. 27–37; Clarence P. Oberndorf: Psychoanalysis of married couples, *Psychoanal Rev, 25:*453, 1938; Howard J. Parad: Brief Ego-oriented Casework With Families in Crisis, in *Ego-Oriented Casework* (Howard J. Parad and Roger R. Miller, Eds.). New York, Family Service Association of America, 1963 pp. 145–64; Morris B. Parloff: The family in psychotherapy, *Arch Gen Psychiat, 45:*445, 1961; Jane E. Patterson and Florence E. Cyr: The use of the home visit in present-day social work, *Soc Casework, 41:*184, 1960; William L. Peltz: Practical Aspects of Marriage Counseling, in *Man and Wife* (Emily H. Mudd and Aaron Krich, Eds.). New York, Norton, 1957, pp. 242–57; Morton S. Perlmutter, Dorothy G. Loeb, Gary Gumpert, Frank O'Hara, and Imogene S. Higbie: Family diagnosis and therapy using videotape playback, *Amer J Orthopsychiat, 37:*900, 1967; Jeannette Regensburg: Application of psychoanalytic concepts to casework treatment of marital problems, *Soc Casework, 35:*424, 1954; Joseph J. Reidy: Family treatment approaches, *Amer J Orthopsychiat, 32:* 133, 1962; Clifford J. Sager: Concurrent individual and group analytic psychotherapy, *Amer J Orthopsychiat, 30:*225, 1960, and, The development of marriage therapy: a historical review, *Amer J Orthopsychiat, 36:*458, 1966; Leon J. Saul, Robert W. Laidlaw, Janet F. Nelson, Ralph Ormsby, Abraham Stone, Sidney Eisenberg, Kenneth E. Appel, and Emily H. Mudd: Can one partner be successfully counseled without the other?, *Marriage Fam Living, 15:*61, 1953; David S. Shapiro and Leonard T. Maholick: A systematic approach to mental health assessment and counseling, *Ment Hyg*, 46:393, 1962; Robert S. Shellow, Bertram S. Brown, and James W. Osberg: Family group therapy in retrospect: four years and sixty families, *Family Process*, 2:52, 1963; Sanford N. Sherman: Joint interviews in casework practice, *Social Work*, 4:20, 1959; Phillip H. Starr: The "triangular treatment" approach in child therapy: complementary psychotherapy of mother and child, *Amer J Psychotherapy*, 10:40, 1956; John Warkentin and Carl A. Whitaker: Preliminary working paper. Serial impasses in marriage. Personal communication, Feb. 26, 1965; Miriam Weisberg: Joint interviewing with marital partners, *Soc Casework*, 45:221, 1964; Viola W. Weiss and Russell R. Monroe: A Framework for Understanding Family Dynamics, in *Social Casework in the Fifties* (Cora Kasius, Ed.). New York, Family Service Association of America, 1962, pp. 175–198; Lyman C. Wynne: The Study of Intrafamilial Alignments and Splits in Exploratory Family Therapy, in Exploring the Base for Family Therapy (Nathan W. Ackerman, Frances L. Beatman, and Sanford H. Sherman, Eds.). New York, Family Service Association of America, 1961, pp. 95–115; Irvin D. Yalom and Kenneth Rand: Compatibility and cohesiveness in therapy groups, *Arch Gen Psychiat*, 15:267, 1966; and Robert Liberman: Behavior approaches to family and couple therapy, *Amer J Orthopsychiat*, 40:106. 1970.

7. Recent literature on conjoint family therapy, in addition to that listed in note 6, includes: John G. Howells: *Family Psychiatry*. Springfield, Thomas, 1963; Ivan Boszormenyi-Nagy and James L. Framo (Eds.): *Intensive Family Therapy*. New York, Harper & Row, 1965; Theodore Lidz, Stephen Fleck and Alice Cornelison (Eds.): *Schizophrenia and the Family*. New York, Int. Univs. Press, 1965; Special Issue: Family Treatment and Marriage Counseling: Why, When, How and by Whom (New York: Grune & Stratton), *Compr Psychiat*, 7:307, 1966; Alfred S. Friedman, Ivan Boszormenyi-Nagy, Jerome E. Jungreis, Geraldine Lincoln, Howard E. Mitchell, John C. Sonne, Ross V. Speck, and George Spivack: *Psychotherapy For the Whole Family*. New York, Springer, 1965; Nathan W. Ackerman: Family Therapy, in *American Handbook of Psychiatry* (Silvano Arieti, Ed.). New York, Basic Books, 1966, Vol. III, pp. 201–212; Clifford J. Sager: The Treatment of Married Couples, in *American Handbook of Psychiatry* (Silvano Arieti, Ed.). New York, Basic Books, 1966, Vol. III, pp. 213–224; Martin Grotjahn: Indications for Psychoanalytic Family Therapy, in *The Marriage Relationship* (Salo Rosenbaum and Ian Alger, Eds.). New York, Basic Books, 1968, pp. 283–292; Gerald H. Zuk: The Side-taking function in family therapy, *Amer J Orthopsychiat*, 38:553, 1968; Nathan W. Ackerman: *Treating The Troubled Family*. New York, Basic Books, 1968; Jay Haley and Lynn Hoffman: *Tech-*

niques of Family Therapy. New York, Basic Books, 1968; and Henry V. Dicks: *Marital Tensions.* New York, Basic Books, 1968.

8. See Chapter XXVI for bibliography.

9. I have not done group psychotherapy in recent years because of time limitation. This valuable approach was available at the Marital Department of the Forest Hospital while I was its director. For partial bibliography see note 2, Chapter XXVI.

10. Abram Kardiner: A Psychoanalytic Understanding of Monogamy, in *The Marriage Relationship* (Salo Rosenbaum and Ian Alger, Eds.). New York, Basic Books, 1968, pp. 21–30, surveys "the institution of monogamy from the point of view of social evolution" and concludes "that monogamy has been one of the lucky strikes of humanity. A million and a half years of social evolution can't go wrong."

11. Erik H. Erikson: *Identity (Youth and Crises).* New York, Norton, 1968, p. 74. "The individual's mastery over his neurosis begins where he is put in a position to accept the historical necessity which made him what he is."

12. Gene N. Abroms: Setting limits, *Arch Gen Psychiat, 19:*113, 1968.

13. Bernard L. Greene: Sequential marriage, in *The Marriage Relationship* (Salo Rosenbaum and Ian Alger, Eds.). New York, Basic Books, 1968, pp. 295–300.

14. Eric Berne: *The Structure and Dynamics of Organizations and Groups.* Philadelphia, Lippincott, 1963. In an excellent article on kinship, Joan Aldous (Intergenerational visiting patterns: variation in boundary maintenance as an explanation, *Family Process, 6:*235, 1967) presents some interesting comments on boundaries. See also Frederick C. Redlich and Boris Astrachan: Group dynamics training, *Amer J Psychiat, 125:*1501, 1969.

15. Bernard L. Greene, Alfred P. Solomon, and Noel Lustig: Transient Structured Distance as a Therapeutic Activity in Marital Crises. Paper presented August 31, 1965, at the Seventh Western Divisional meeting, American Psychiatric Association, Honolulu, Hawaii. For some interesting concepts on distancing, read Brechtain theatre as a model for conjoint family therapy, *Family Process, 5:*218, 1966, by Robert E. Kantor and Lynn Hoffman. Also see Clifford S. Briggin and Norman E. Zinberg: Manipulation and its clinical application, *Amer J Psychotherapy, 23:*198, 1969; William Lederer and Don D. Jackson, *Mirages of Marriage,* New York, Norton, 1968, pp. 356–357), present some of the dynamics observed in the TSD.

16. To paraphrase Samuel C. Klagsbrun (In search of an identity, *Arch Gen Psychiat, 16:*286, 1967), I call the various operational counseling procedures custom-tailored counseling.

17. The issue here is an ancient and moral one. "And why beholdst thou the mote that is in thy brother's eye but considerest not the beam

that is in thine own eye?" Marvin J. Feldman correctly points out in his article, Privacy and conjoint family therapy, *Family Process, 6:1,* 1967, "that psychotherapy is far from the neutral, nonjudgmental procedure so often stated to be the therapeutic ideology. Evidence can readily be adduced to support a contrary view, namely, that personal preferences and values play a pervasive part in the process." He quotes references from the literature that therapists like the patients who they rate improved and vice-versa, that patients who rate positive self-improvement also liked their therapists, that liking precedes improvements, and finally, that the values and preferences are linked.

18. Franz Alexander: The dynamics of psychotherapy in light of learning theory, *Amer J Psychiat, 120:440,* 1963.

19. John Paul Brady: Psychotherapy, learning theory, and insight, *Arch Gen Psychiat, 16:304,* 1967. He defines learning as the " . . . process by which changes occur in an individual's behavior as a consequence of his reacting to encountered situations, excluding, of course, those changes directly attributable to maturational processes and physical causes (toxins, drugs, injuries, etc.)." He describes clearly and briefly four clinical levels of insight: (1) the patient's awareness that he is ill to degree that he recognizes his feelings, thoughts, and/or behavior are abnormal. (2) the patient's recognition of the nature of his disorder—in particular, the consequences it has for his own satisfactions and adjustments and its effect on others (*what I include in the interpersonal system,* author's note) (3) self-awareness of dynamic factors which gave rise to various symptoms and now operate to maintain them, (4) self-awareness into the unconscious roots of the *original* conflict, that is, the inadequately resolved. Brady next points out what every experienced therapist has observed, that the old differentiation between intellectual versus emotional insight is no longer warranted.

The level of insight obtained by the spouses, irrespective of the therapist's conceptual framework, is not as important as the relationship between the therapist and the patients. This observation is also expressed by Judd Marmor (Psychoanalytic Therapy as an Educational Process. In *Science and Psychoanalysis,* (Jules H. Masserman, Ed.). New York, Grune & Stratton, 1962, Vol. 5, p. 290, who writes that it is this relationship which persuades individuals to accept the model of more "mature" or "healthy behavior." See also Arnold M. Ludwig: The formal characteristics of therapeutic insight, *Amer J Psychotherapy, 20:305,* 1966.

The cutting of new "records," leading to improved patterns of relating, requires time. As with the learning of any new techniques, e.g. musical, time is of great importance. One cannot learn efficient and effective techniques without practicing. This practicing oils the mechanism in the jukebox, permitting easier selection of "records," which manifests itself in altered behavior and personality trait configurations. Brady succinctly states: "Time is required to translate the newly acquired perceptions and attitudes into more healthy patterns of behavior." Since all jukeboxes are unique in their existence, I have found it difficult to predict the time needed in any particular couple. Most important is that the two jukeboxes seated at either end of the seesaw are in a dynamic relationship with circular feedback amplification—the process of action-reaction, reaction to the reaction and reaction to that. Or as Brady puts it: "Thus, a measure of insight into some current difficulty may facilitate improved functioning in this area. This in return may permit further or deeper insight into related problem areas, which brings about further improved functioning, and so forth."

The interested reader will find a brief but concise description of various theories of learning from Pavlov to the Tote hypothesis (G.A. Miller, E. Galanter, and K.H. Pribram: *Plans and the Structure of Behavior.* New York, Henry Holt, 1960) in this article by Brady. My concept on the jukebox corresponds to what Miller *et al.* define as the organism's image ". . . everything the organism has learned—his values as well as his facts—organized by whatever concepts, images, or relations he has been able to master." Our "records" correspond to their repertoire of plans which complement their image. They define a plan as "any hierarchical process in the organism that can control the order in which a sequence of operations is to be performed." See also Monroe S. Arlen (Conjoint therapy and the corrective emotional experience, *Family Process,* 5:91, 1966), who makes a suggestion as to why some individuals play the wrong "records" as it perhaps pertains to the mechanism in the jukebox. "The patient's maladaptive behavior patterns operate subtly and repetitiously in ways that tend to evoke expected reactions of rejection, hostility and resentment in the significant people around him. This vicious cycle or *error activated system* [italics added] tends to sustain both the interpersonal and intrapsychic disturbance." See also Yasuhiko Taketomo: The application of imprinting to psychodynamics, in *Animal and Human, Science and Psychoanalysis* (Jules H. Masserman, Ed.). New York, Grune & Stratton, 1968, Vol. XII, pp. 166–183.

20. In addition to the articles and books previously mentioned in this book, other descriptions of counseling include: Rollo May: *The Art of Counseling.* New York and Nashville, Abingdon Press, 1949; Seward Hiltner: *The Counselor in Counseling.* New York, and Nashville, Abingdon Press, 1950; Carroll A. Wise: *Pastoral Counseling. Its Theory & Practice.* New York, Harper & Brothers, 1951; Douglass W. Orr: *Professional Counseling on Human Behavior: Its Principles*

and Practices. New York, Franklin Watts, 1965; Richard H. Klemer: *Counseling In Marital and Sexual Problems. A Physician's Handbook.* Baltimore, Williams & Wilkins, 1965; Howard J. Clinebell, Jr.: *Basic Types of Pastoral Counseling.* New York and Nashville, Abingdon Press, 1966; Peter E. Sifneos: Two Different kinds of psychotherapy of short duration, *Amer J Psychiat, 123:*1069, 1967; Gerald F. Jacobson: Brief intervention in acute emotional crises, *Psychiat Progr,* Dec., 1965; Glen E. Whitlock: Counseling in crisis situations, *Pastoral Counselor,* 5:37, 1967; Walter Kempler. (Experiential psychotherapy with families, *Family Process,* 7:88, 1968) describes his therapy as "attention to the current interaction as the pivotal point for all awareness and interventions; involvement of the total therapist-person bringing overtly and richly his full personal impact on the families with whom he works . . . the extant interaction—the current encounter—demands constant vigil. It means attention to the here and now, not to the exclusion of the past and future but to the extent that any pertinent deviation from the here and now be considered a transient, though necessary diversion, and that each detour be succinct and promptly returned and integrated into the current interaction." Hilda M. Goodwin and Emily H. Mudd: Indication for marriage counseling: methods and goals, *Compr Psychiat,* 7:450, 1966. This is an outstanding article with an excellent bibliography. C. Knight Aldrich and Carl Nighswonger: *A Pastoral Counseling Casebook* Philadelphia, Westminister Press, 1968, is an outstanding book that actually tells how an experienced therapist gives pastors specific guidance in counseling; *The Handbook of Marriage Counseling* (Palo Alto, California: Science and Behavior Books, 1969), edited by Ben N. Ard, Jr., and Constance C. Ard, is a good primary textbook for classes in marriage counseling and includes an excellent chapter on Basic Books for the Marriage Counselor pp. 444–449; and, Lester A. Kirkendall: *Marriage and Family Relations—a reading and study guide for students.* W.C. Brown Co., 135 So. Locust St., Dubuque, Iowa, (3rd ed.) may be correlated with Ards' textbook and is composed of thirty-nine study guides.

XXII

THE CLASSIC TECHNIQUE IN MARITAL DISHARMONY

The classic approach[1] in counseling and in-depth therapy be defined as a dyadic one-to-one relationship between the therapist and his patient. In this type of treatment the therapists of each spouse do not communicate. Thus confidentiality of all the transactions between the therapist and patient is crucial.[2] The classic approach was used in 10 percent of the couples receiving counseling, and in about 9 percent of the couples where one or both spouses received intensive psychotherapy.

The question is often raised as to what criteria exist for selecting individual or multiperson approaches. In the classic approach, therapy is focused on the problems of the individual within himself or in his relationship to the world outside himself. The focus is on individual psychodynamics with the marriage as the backdrop. How patterns of behavior develop receives selective focus over how spouses react to these patterns.

The indications for the classic approach in counseling include the following:

1. Therapist's knowledge of acting-out behavior[3] by one partner of which the other is unaware, e.g. continuous infidelity or homosexuality.[4] These so-called family secrets are known, either consciously or unconsciously, by the partner. However, premature discussion of the secret could disrupt the marriage if the therapist was confronted with the secret by the partner.
2. Personal preference of one or both spouses.
3. An emotional immaturity exists in a spouse which precludes sharing the therapist.

4. One spouse feels he has to figure out his own way irrespective of the consequences to his partner.
5. Where it is evident that the husband and wife have widely differing goals in terms of their marriage problem.

The following clinical vignettes illustrate indications for the classic approach in marital disharmony.

Below is an example of the first indication, therapist's knowledge of acting-out behavior by one partner of which the other is unaware, for the classic approach.

The Lavinas came at the insistence of Mr. Lavina, as he was unable to understand the recent change in his wife's feelings toward him. Their courtship was smooth. One year after marriage they had their first child, two years later, their second. When the youngest was three, Mrs. Lavina had gone to work to save money for a down payment on a home. They had been very happy for the next two years when Mr. Lavina gradually noticed that his wife, seemed preoccupied and disinterested in their sexual relations which previously were enjoyable. Repeated questioning on his part as to this change brought no satisfactory answer except that 'it will go away.' Mrs. Lavina agreed with her husband, and stated that she did not know what had gone wrong.

An entirely different story was told at her first individual diagnostic session: "This October will be three years that I have been working for Bob, my boss, as his personal secretary. Bob has always been very polite and considerate. I admired the way he dressed, his brilliant mind, and his executive ability. But he was my boss, lived in a different world than I, and was happily married.

"Last Christmas eve we had to work until noon. The other girls in the office were fixing up the office for our annual Christmas party. Two of the girls brought in a drink at 9:30 to our office. They insisted I have it. I overslept that morning and had little for breakfast and the one drink made me woozy. I made several errors in a letter that I overlooked and Bob started teasing me. Then he went out and had a drink. I went out and had another drink. We were both teasing each other now.

"At noon we finished our work and joined the rest of the office at the party. I deliberately avoided him. I had a funny premonition of danger. On one hand I felt some anxiety, and on the other hand I was tingling with excitement. I was talking to Bob's boss when he asked me if I had kissed Bob, Happy Christmas. I blushed and said, No! So he took me over to Bob and told him to kiss his secretary—that it was necessary for office morale. Bob kissed me so hard that I was trembling. Shortly after that I went home.

"When I went back to work, I couldn't look at Bob. He was his usual self, but I was anxious and trembling even though it was three days after Christmas. My anxiety increased when Bob told me how much he had enjoyed kissing me. From then on I noticed a change in his attitude toward me—more considerate, more complimentary about my clothes and appearance. Occasionally when I would glance up from my work, I would find him staring at me. Three months later, he asked me for a date after we had worked late in the evening on a special report he had to get out. He kept asking me after that, but I kept telling him we were both married. So he stopped and things were as before Christmas, except occasionally I would bring a rose and put it in a vase on his desk. He would thank me and that was that.

"Then it happened. Two months later he went on a vacation and that was when I really started to miss him. Here I was a married woman, until now happily married, religious but suddenly in love with another man. I was determined to end this situation. I thought of transfering to another branch. It was this indecision that caused a change in my relationships at home. When Jim (Mr. Lavina) would ask me what was wrong, I kept telling him nothing. When he suggested that I stop working, that perhaps holding down two jobs was too much for me, I said, No.

"Then it happened. It was raining and Bob offered to drive me home. I accepted. He stopped before we reached my apartment. He told me that he was unable to forget about me since that kiss on Christmas, and we began to kiss each other. I was trembling so. He told me that for some unknown reason his wife was rejecting him sexually. He thought a vacation would help the relationship between them, but it hadn't—she was more interested in skiing than in him. I told him I had missed him so, but that we were both married and should not see each other. But I really didn't mean what I was saying because I kissed him very hard. That Sunday I went to confessional and afterwards resolved not to see him again outside of the office. A month later, when we were working overtime and everyone had gone home, he stated how unhappy he was about his marriage—his wife was still rejecting him, and now he was in love with me. And so it happened.

"A real love relationship developed between us. I couldn't help thinking about him all the time. I felt guilty and so did he, but each time we wanted to stop, we couldn't.

"But then Bob said he was feeling very guilty. Somehow his wife had changed. That we both loved our children and this wasn't fair to everyone concerned. He kept saying we've got to end it. So we stopped seeing each other for a month. But it all began again. I said, perhaps I should quit working with him. He said, I don't want you to leave. He said: I will divorce my wife and marry you. I said: how could I, I am a Catholic. Besides, I love my children and would lose them, since I have no grounds for a divorce. Furthermore, I had been in love with Jim until he came along. We agreed not to see each other again outside of the office. But all week he talked about marriage. I could see how upset he was, and in love with me. He couldn't concentrate on his work. He kept telling me how guilty he felt about what had happened. That he loved me so much and wanted to marry me. I thought I could not love my husband again. I love my children. My husband is a wonderful person. I thought of suicide and took ten aspirin tablets. All it did was upset my stomach. I don't know how I got into this mess. Please help me."

This interview is an excellent example of a so-called family secret. (For Mrs. Lavina's therapy, see end of this chapter.)

The following is an example of the second indication for a classical approach, personal preference of one or both spouses.

The Lenas had come for marital counseling at the request of their minister. In his first individual diagnostic session, Mr. Lena stated: "The basic complaint is that Alice is selfish and self-centered to the point of excluding everyone else. Her basic orientation is "me first" without any regard for the needs or feelings of me or anyone else. Our marriage has been marked by five years of Alice's inability to be concerned over anyone or anything but herself. It's true that during the first two years, when I first began my practice, she suffered and was forced to do a good deal for me because of the demands on my time and no money. But even then it was forced and strained, and this too took its toll.

"In the past two years, since she started her psychotherapy, she has been more bitchy and nasty. Her self-centered attitude manifests itself in many different ways. Primarily her unwillingness to participate in social affairs. Alice spends 90 percent of her time at home in bed reading, or watching TV, or eating. Most exasperating, is her "Wooden Leg" game—Alice is always a little bit ill with lower back pain or stomach pains. Her "migraine headache" is common as long as there is nothing Alice wants to do. All this results in frequent games of "Uproar." Finally, I am very angry about our infrequent sex.

Mrs. Lena was cooperative for her interviews but appeared to be bored and annoyed. Her main complaints centered on her sexual dissatisfaction with her husband. Also, that he did not meet her emotional needs. "There is no meeting of the minds. There used to be. Now there is a lack of communication and no sharing of interests. Things we had in common before marriage no longer exist—skiing, music, golf, opera.

"Sexually, I am dissatisfied. I have structured things so that there is no pleasure on my part in the act. At times I am close to being repelled by him, and at times, completely frigid with him. There has always been a sexual problem in our marriage."

The CDD was so stormy that I suggested a "star boarder arrangement" (TSD) to lower the level of hostility between the couple. I further suggested a three-month trial of conjoint therapy.

Mr. Lena appeared alone at the next session. He stated: "After you made the suggestion of star boarder routine, Alice's reaction was marked when we got home. What a game of "Uproar." She got more depressed and disabled. She spent the next four days in bed and finally called up her former therapist and returned to him. She felt that you wouldn't be objective and would side with me. She laced into you as being a cold fish. She said to tell you that she prefers to see her own therapist."

This vignette illustrates the third indication for the classic approach, an emotional immaturity in a spouse exists which precludes sharing the therapist.

The Letitias were referred by a friend for marital counseling. Mrs. Letitia, a petite blonde receptionist, had met her husband at work where he was a junior executive. She was in her early twenties, her husband was ten years older and the boss's son.

In her individual diagnostic sessions, Mrs. Letitia gave the following information. "I can't come during intercourse. Nothing is wrong with me physically. I get to a certain point, and it stops. I've been putting off my husband. We've talked about it frequently. In all other areas we get along fabulously. But I dread going to bed. We've been married nine months. Last night I dreamt our minister, who is like a second father to me, was telling me to go ahead and have intercourse. I woke up my husband and we tried so hard, but it was most frustrating."

Mrs. Letitia stated she was an only child: "My parents are happily married. My father is very wonderful. I'm very dependent on him, even now. I was always very close to him. He is a pharmacist and a genius with figures. It took him a long time to permit me to drive the car. Instead, he would drive me anyplace, day or night. Dad was against me marrying. That I was too young to get married at twenty-two. He wasn't about to lose a daughter."

Mrs. Letitia described her mother as very warm and affectionate, "I never thought she understood me. She never explained the facts of life to me. Both my parents are very religious people. Sex was taboo in the house. You don't talk about your period in the home. She never wanted me to shave my legs or use deodorant.

"It was always hard for me to share my father. Both of my parents were extremely protective of me. Never allowed me in anyone's house to play. I couldn't leave the lawn in front of the house until I was much older than the other children in the neighborhood."

She described her first date at sixteen with a boy in her church group. "I was quite wound up in church activities, three or four nights a week for years. I hung around with this church youth group. I always was afraid of petting until I started going steady with Jack. I would date three or four boys, but if they got interested, I would break up with them. I couldn't stand to be mauled or petted.

"Our courtship was uneventful, smooth, and of one-year duration. When I went to work, I noticed this tall man. I was told he was the boss's son. He was handsome, well built and I fell for him from the beginning. I've always liked older men but not that old. Imagine my surprise when six months later he asked for a date. Our parents knew each other. We dated quite a bit. He was always a gentleman. He danced like a dream, which I have always loved to. After a while we decided we were in love and decided to marry. We had much in common: good music, the same kind of movies, and even the same kind of foods."

Mr. Letitia at his first interview presented the same picture that his wife had described. He was a serious male, very much in love with his wife, and completely at a loss to understand his wife's reaction to sex: "She has a certain tenseness and fear. The anticipation of the climax. What to expect. She reaches a certain point and automatically wants to stop. She has never experienced a climax. We have only had one good sexual experience since we married. She feels she can't function as a woman. That she is really not a woman unless she has a climax.

"Her father is a rather domineering man but very personable. I couldn't get close to either of her parents. Aloof. I never felt they approved of our relationship, which they didn't. We were very seriously considering eloping. I had asked his permission to marry his daughter, and he felt I was too old for her. Sometime shortly after that, she was home alone, they had a big discussion, and it ended up that they hadn't communicated about what she wanted. Everyone cried and it was accepted. We get along pretty well now."

In the CDD it was obvious that Mr. Letitia was very protective toward his wife, who acted like a little girl throughout the session. At one point she attempted to set up a coalition with the therapist and tried to exclude her husband. Mr. Letitia appeared fairly well adjusted. I suggested treating Mrs. Letitia first and call Mr. Letitia later if necessary. Her treatment will be described later in the chapter.

Next is an example of the fourth reason indicating the classical technique, one spouse feels he has to figure out his own way irrespective of the consequences to his partner.

The Livias were referred for counseling by her parents. Both were in their early thirties, had been married ten years and had three children, the youngest two years old.

Mrs. Livia, attractive, attractively dressed and well groomed, tearfully stated her complaints: "He does not desire me sexually anymore. He goes out by himself all of the time. He doesn't enjoy being with the family. He has no tolerance for my family either. We were getting along fine until three months before our youngest child was born. Since his birth, two years ago, we have had sex about six times. We separated about one year ago, but he returned home after being gone three months. During that time he had an affair, about which he carries guilt feelings, since he promised to marry the girl after she got a divorce. She did and then he decided to come home. I don't understand what has happened, but I want to make a go of our marriage."

Mr. Livia appeared nervous and tense at his first individual diagnostic session. "I don't love her anymore. I resent her. She seems to be pushing. She is the type who is always wondering what will the neighbors think. I find her repulsive. I respect and love her in some ways. She is faithful, a good mother and housewife. But it's always, 'What will the neighbors think?'

"She is just like her mother who knows everything. I told her many times to shut her mouth. A few months ago we were visiting a couple and the discussion centered on a Japanese family that had moved near them. They said they tried to make them comfortable. I raised the issue of real estate values. Not against the Japs, not prejudice, but an economic fact. Right away she became very upset. That I was sounding like a bigot, making an ass of myself, or shaming her. All I tried was to point out the economic facts to this couple. She said these things in front of our friends!

"Just before our boy was born, two years ago, I did something I wanted to do all my life. Buy a foreign sports car and join a sports car club. I bought an Austin-Healy. I loved it, and it became an addiction. Soon I was leaving her alone quite often on the weekends. She resented this. Things got farther and farther apart. I felt no love for her. Occasionally I would put my arm around her. I feel lonesome without her. Yet when I'm with her, I feel nothing.

"We had a big fight about her mother a year ago, and I left home for three months. But I kept thinking about the children. They kept pulling at me. Not my feelings about my wife. I was ready to go out of my mind. For a period of time I thought if I had the guts, I would kill myself. Between my three children and ten years of marriage and Mabel on the other side, I still haven't been able to make a decision. I don't want to lose Mabel. I love her. She is the other woman that my wife thinks I have given up. She got a divorce to marry me.

"I had a most unhappy childhood. My parents quarreled continuously. Father left home repeatedly for short periods, just like I'm doing. Much of the arguing was blamed on my bad behavior. Father was intolerant and impatient. Mother was nagging and both were headstrong. Mother, at times, went into rages and struck me with anything available. There were many times when I came so close to striking her. Once I d'd strike her, moved out, and shortly after, I got married. When my wife nags me, she sounds like my mother.

"I need a psychiatrist and know it. I'm confused about Mabel. I've got to come to terms with myself regardless of how it affects my wife. Will you please treat me!"

I told him I would, and would send his wife to another therapist.

Mrs. Livia gave the following additional information at her next appointment: "My husband seemed better after he talked to you. I've been thinking of his lack of sexual desire for me. For the past seven years he has not been adequate sexually. He refused to do anything about it. He went his way, and I went my way. One day he said he was fed up, and he left. While separated he met another woman. He said, 'With this woman I feel like a man. If you could only treat me like this woman does. She doesn't nag, is kind and considerate.' I can be that way with other people but not with my husband. He is so good looking. He would never approach me for sex. I said, 'See a doctor.' He said, 'Other people have worse problems.' He wants me and the children. This is the first other woman he has ever had. It started after our first child was born.

Before that he was all right. He says he wants to make a go of it but that he still hasn't the feeling for me.

"When we were first married, we had sex at least three times a week. But when I became pregnant, he seemed to change. After our first child was born, I had to make all the approaches. For two years he didn't touch me after he couldn't reach a climax. This shook him up completely.

"Two weeks ago he said, 'Let's go on a trip together.' He tried again but no orgasm after fifteen minutes. Yet, with this other woman, he said, he had no trouble at all, he even had a climax with her three times in one night. So now I feel it's his feelings toward me. He told me detail by detail the way the other girl made him feel. He only told me this to help me.

"I was always interested in the opposite sex, so hungry for affection. I have a good idea why he feels this way about me. I'm a very giving person to everyone except him. I never put myself out for him. I didn't realize that until he told me. I suddenly realized that I did everything for others but not for him. He took up the hobby of sports cars, and I showed no interest in it at all. I refused to go on the races they had. He met this girl at one of their meets. She showed him consideration, kindness, and just being a nice person. Two weeks before he came back, I started to change my ways.

"But I wonder if we should remain married. He has no respect for my parents. He is selfish. He calls me very filthy names when we argue."

I suggested the classic approach for him and referred her to another therapist.

The fifth reason for the classical approach, where it is evident that husband and wife have widely differing goals in terms of their marriage problems, is illustrated below.

From the very onset, both Mr. and Mrs. Louisa approached the matter in a very intellectualized, cold, and highly unemotional manner. Mr. Louisa's opening comment was that their problem is that they are both angry at each other and neither one knows wholly why it is this way. He said his wife insisted on coming with him for his first interview as she did not think he would accept counseling and keep his appointment.

"Materially, we have everything we need, yet, we are both unhappy people, within ourselves not necessarily with the marriage. I don't think I am essentially a happy person. I'm restless but with a lot of drive for what I want. I'm not a joyful person. I have difficulty relating to people, but not because I'm not verbal. Basically I have difficulty relating to females. All these things lead to difficulties with my wife. At times our relationship is excellent. We have three wonderful children, whom I enjoy greatly, plus the mechanical things, a place to hang your hat, and sleep. I expect to go to the closet and find my suits clean, my shoes heeled. She objects to taking care of these things. I don't take particular pride in dressing or apparel, but like to be neat and clean. I have a poor self-image of myself."

Mrs. Louisa stated her complaint that he would not talk, that he dismisses any subject that she brings up because she supposedly can't understand and resents how he totally categorizes anything she states by, "I never," or "I always."

She stated, what he wants and expects in marriage just does not exist. As a result, we have had very explosive arguments in all areas, and recently they have become more vehement and frequent. I don't know why I am afraid of him, but when I do get frightened, I just shut up.

"I take my marriage on a day-to-day basis. We have our children. Jim is exceedingly involved in his business and proud of its success. He has very little else. Next he is most interested in his reading. His business is a great challenge to Jim. He says, 'My family is more important to me than my business,' but he doesn't live it. Our marriage is based on a 'potential.' We live in hopes of what Jim could be. But that isn't reality.

"Usually he is lazy around the house, but when he does the things that need to be done, he goes at it hammer and tong. If he could be less serious. The other day our oldest child, ten years old, wouldn't listen and he called it insubordinate, like when I don't obey him or they don't obey him. He is very unrealistic in regards to sex; Jim feels I am frigid, and this is not so. I do enjoy sex with him when he is tender and we have not argued earlier over something trivial." Mrs. Louisa delivered the above comments in an academic manner that sounded like a dull lecture.

Mr. Louisa replied that he would cooperate in any manner that would help the marriage. "I love my wife and children. She says she loves me too. Marriage is a sacred thing, and it is very unfair to place the children in a home with only one parent. We have created the children, and we have a parental responsibility to provide a family for them. Besides I have a certain type of ego that can never admit failure. I belong with the family and the children. Neither one of us wants a divorce."

At the end of the evaluation and the CDD, it was suggested that each have his individual therapist. This suggestion was offered, since both had had deprived childhoods and each needed the intense dyadic relationship with his own therapist to clarify his expectations of marriage and explore his inner world of thoughts, fantasies, and feelings.

The contradiction to the classic approach in marital disharmony is when a spouse has moderate to severe paranoid reactions to being "told on" or being influenced by the other spouse. This suspicious behavior by a spouse leads to repeated questioning as to what went on in the partner's individual session and frequent distortion. This type of situation is best handled in the triadic clinical setting.

I shall now present several cases illustrating the techniques of the classic approach along a spectrum of therapeutic experience. The spouse can be treated by a moderately skilled therapist, by a skilled therapist, and, finally, by a very skilled therapist.

CLASSIC APPROACH FOR MODERATELY SKILLED THERAPIST

At the beginning of this chapter I presented a clinical extract of a couple with a family secret—the Lavinas. The following is a condensation of Mrs. Lavina's therapy, which consisted of six sessions and covered a period of three months:

In her first therapeutic session, Mrs. Lavina looked well. She stated that she was feeling much better. She wanted to know why this had happened and would like to save her marriage. Praying has not helped.

In her second session, eleven days later, she reported a few weepy spells but on the whole she was feeling better: "I have hope now that something can be done. I have handed in my resignation at work and will leave as soon as an adequate replacement is found. I love my husband, but at times he treats me like a baby. He is very serious most of the time. He would like to give me and our children all possible advantages. Besides, he is never at home. He works all day and goes to school at night to earn more money so we can have new furniture when we move into our home. Sexually we have always been very compatible. Since I got involved with Bob, I have been disinterested in sex with Jim. There is nothing wrong with Jim. He is a skilled serviceman. He is mad at me at times because I'm not interested in what he does. There is nothing romantic about servicing an appliance. If we fight, it's over money. I had a nightmare last night. My husband said he heard me screaming: 'Jim, don't! Jim, don't!' I woke up screaming. I was at a picnic. Sitting on this blanket. I wanted so badly to have Jim like me. He put ants down my back and I was screaming: "Don't! Don't! Jim, don't!"

Her associations dealt with inability to feel toward Jim as she once did and recalled a time shortly after marriage when they had gone on a picnic and both became sexually aroused and wandered off into the woods and had sex. When they returned to the group, they found ants on their food.

She was given the interpretation that she felt very guilty about her recent behavior and was punishing herself in the dream by putting ants on her back—for lying on her back with Bob, and secondly, by not permitting her husband to relate to her. Furthermore, unconsciously she still had some guilt about her earlier sexual behavior when, shortly after marriage, she and her husband left the group and wandered off into the woods because she had "ants in her pants."

In an attempt to alleviate her guilt, past and present, she was told that mortals make mistakes and she need no longer punish herself. Only saints are pure.

In her third session, two weeks later, she related a dream about being in a dungeon and being punished by the devil. Her boss was not pressuring her, as she told him that she was now seeing a marriage counselor. The session dealt mostly with how much she would give up if she divorced her husband—her religion, her children, her family and friends. It was suggested to her that perhaps she was still putting ants on her back.

In her fourth session, three weeks later, she said she had given a lot of thought to our last meeting: "I went to see my priest. We talked for hours. I was scared to see Bob after work but did. He had gone to see a psychiatrist with his wife about their marriage. His wife was hysterical for the next twenty-four hours. He told me he was going to get a divorce and marry me. Not wait until I finish seeing you. When I got home Jim asked me where I was. I told him I had talked to Father Ireland about our marriage, about leaving him. He was shocked. He changed so the next day. He didn't go to school, doing all the things I had complained about—not so critical, spending more time with me, and so forth.

"The next day Bob didn't show up for work until noon. His face down to the ground. He had spent all morning with his children. He kept thinking how he could have me and his children. That night we met after work. He said he was going to marry me. I said: 'Bob this isn't the first time you have this guilty feeling about your children. You can't have both!' He said: 'Maybe your counselor is right—that you should first work out your problems about your own marriage independently of me.' We talked and talked. I made up my mind to give him up.

"When I got home from work, I decided to tell Jim everything and ask his forgiveness. But there was Jim with a mischievous grin on his face. Flowers on the table. Then I decided I can't tell him. We made love that night and I was tender and accepting—the first time in months. Afterwards we talked for hours, and it was like old times."

When seen again, two weeks later, Mrs. Lavina reported that she and her boss (Bob) were real businesslike towards each other. That as soon as they could get a replacement for her, she was leaving. "I cannot now stand Jim touching me again. I try to bluff that I am. Yet I reach a climax each time. I don't know what is happening to me."

She was told that she was again punishing herself and that it was time to get rid of the ants on her back, that she was a wonderful person and would be all right.

In her sixth and last session, two weeks later, she stated: "I almost didn't come today. I know I will have to solve this myself. But I wanted to talk to you once more to tell you how grateful I am for your efforts. I am leaving the job tomorrow. They finally found a replacement for me. Bob is gone all the time now, traveling. He is really going to try to make his marriage work. His wife is acting differently toward him. At home with Jim everything is OK. We are getting along fine in all areas.

I have made up my mind to solve my problem alone. I had a dream last night that I don't understand, except that I feel it tells me to forget about Bob: I was in a telephone booth with Bob. He had a yomulka on. He was calling his wife from the the booth to ask how his youngest daughter was feeling. She had been ill during the night. In the center of the yomulka are two blue balls. We were running away. Next, his wife is in the booth with us. I had the feeling the two blue balls had something to do with his children."

This dream deals with the problem of the role Bob's children would play in a new marriage as well as the difference in their religions. She was told that the dream indicated her awareness that his two children are like balls and chains around his neck. That he could not give up his children. Further, their respective religions would interfere with their remarriage. She was told that the course of action she had selected was a good one, that I would see her again if she needed me. A year later I received an announcement of the arrival of a new baby and a note expressing her gratitude for saving her marriage. She and her husband were getting along very well.

CLASSIC APPROACH FOR THE SKILLED THERAPIST

In the middle of this chapter I presented a clinical extract of the Letitias in which I had decided that the classic approach was the correct one for Mrs. Letitia because of her immaturity. The following material highlights her therapeutic course.

Mrs. Letitia began her second session by commenting: "I don't really understand it. Before we were married I really wanted sex, but on our wedding night I said: 'Let's go at it slowly.' We have had sex once since our visit with you three weeks ago. I had a little more reaction. When I had my premarital examination, the doctor was unable to put the speculuum in because I was so tensed up.

"I wonder how my father would feel if he were to find out I am going for psychotherapy because I was so tied to his apron strings. I feel guilty that I am taking the 'pill.' Mother told me 'Don't try to prevent pregnancy.' I've kept a lot of things from them, my smoking. Father was always worried about who I would marry. I would always be too young to marry if Father had his way. I've always enjoyed dancing with Father, he is a fabulous dancer."

In the next session, Mrs. Letitia continued to talk about her close relationship with her parents: "Father and Mother have called me a great deal recently because of the weather. He would never let me drive when there was snow. Mother doesn't drive. She really gives me to my father or my father to me. I really don't know how to state it."

I comment: "Perhaps his closeness to you has encouraged you not to give him up?"

"I don't want to give him up. Does that sound terrible. Mother will still say to me after we visit them that it is so hard to see you go away with Jack and not coming home. We have a very close family. In some ways I'm quite a child and soon to be twenty-three. I have to cut out seeing them as often, like three times a week."

In the following six sessions, her dreams and associations dealt with feelings about her father plus a new theme—her fear of losing control of her feelings, e.g. in a dream everyone in the neighborhood went psychotic. She was the only one who was calm.

When asked, what psychotic could symbolize, she replied: "Letting go completely, not in control. I really remain quite calm during the whole sexual act. I hold back in every area."

In her twelfth session, she reported having sex for the first time in a month: We had sex last night. I was pleased with myself that I did it, for Jack's sake. It hurt something fierce, but I told him to continue. I feel suddenly I am taking my marriage seriously."

In her fourteenth session, three months after starting therapy, Mrs. Letitia related the following dream: "Jack and a friend organizing some kind of a dance. We invited all kinds of couples and they came. Jack and friend were to teach the dance. The couples formed a circle. Then I am on a real high stool, but I was scared because I couldn't figure how to get down. Then some giant came along and helped me down. I woke up scared. I couldn't figure how I would get down from the stool. This giant helped me.

"I could remember the sensation going down. You and my husband are organizing my life. The dance represents something a couple do, that two people do, sex? When I sat on the real high stool, I thought of a dunce's stool."

When I asked her how a little girl views her father, she replied: "Like a giant. I felt a sensation of an elevator coming down too fast. Like butterflies in the stomach. The feeling was real. I remembered the feeling when I awoke."

When asked what problem she was trying to solve in the dream, she replied: "Being a woman and trying to join the circle of couples. I don't want to see my husband as a father. For if I do, I will never grow up and will keep sitting on the dunce's stool."

In the next two months Mrs. Letitia reported increasing sexual tension, more frequent sex with her husband that she would occasionally initiate, and awareness of some pleasure in the act itself. Concomitant with her increased sexual behavior were dreams expressing fears of becoming promiscuous and erotic transference phenomena toward me, disguised in her dreams as reacting to her gynecologist. Upon a return from a vacation, she stated: "Jack is very pleased with the change in me. Once we had intercourse twice in one night. Once I woke him up. I get on top of him now. I get more sensation that way. Sex is no longer painful but I still haven't reached an orgasm." In her twenty-fifth session, she related how all her girl friends had one or two babies now, but that she wasn't interested in having one. She concluded her session by commenting: "My parents said I was a pleasure as a child, no problem. They could take me anyplace, lay me down and I would immediately fall asleep. I had so many relatives taking care of me and making such a fuss over me. Perhaps I don't want a baby because that would make me a mother, and I would have to relinquish my position as baby!"

In her next session she reported: "We had sex last night. It didn't hurt. But nothing special. I was a little more relaxed and for the first time I wasn't depressed; usually I cry afterwards."

The four following sessions revealed the slow development of the negative transference: her dreams showed me as a depreciated person, displaced anger onto her mother-in-law (therapist) with open arguments and for the first time forgot to pay for her therapy.

"We've been getting along fine. I'm reacting better sexually. Intercourse four times in the past two weeks. Once two nights in a row that shocked both of us. I wonder if I'm hypersexed."

In her thirty-fourth session Mrs. Letitia reported that she was doing better in many areas of her behavior. She commented: "It is ten months since I first started seeing you. We had intercourse once this week. For the first time I felt sensation inside my vagina. Before I only enjoyed the clitoral stimulation."

In her thirty-ninth session she stated she was feeling so much better and asked whether she could come every other week. She reported: "Our marriage seems much better. My mother-in-law aggravates me less. Jack keeps commenting on how I have improved."

In her next session she commented that she felt better, even though her last session was two weeks ago: "I had a dream: I'm walking with my gynecologist. We had to separate. We were walking very close. We separate. I took it in stride.

I felt OK, that you were the gynecologist and I was accepting the fact of coming every other week. Jack and I have been getting along fine. We had sex three times since I was here, more excitement and much better."

In her forty-first session (one year after the onset of therapy) she reported being very aggravated with her husband over little things. On the other hand, they have been having sex twice a week.

In her forty-third session she reported a dream in which she was getting married again but felt sad at leaving her home. Her material indicated an awareness of her improvement and her depression at the approaching end of her treatment.

In her forty-fifth session (her final one and fourteen months after the onset of therapy) she reported everything was fine and that twice in the past week she had reached an orgasm. "I had a dream last night: I'm on an airplane. Lots of people. In the back the people are decrepit. But I am seated in the first-class compartment.'"

In her associations she stated: "I wasn't part of the decrepit group. I was separated from the sick people. I felt secure and sure of myself."

I comment: "This dream is a far cry from your dream in which you are seated on a tall high stool with a dunce cap on."

She replied that it was and that in the past week she had been thinking about stopping her therapy. I don't feel I have that many things to say either. Sexually I'm OK.

I suggested that I still keep her next appointment four weeks hence but that she could cancel at the last moment if things were going satisfactory. Three weeks later she called to state that everything was fine and that she and her husband felt satisfied. Thirteen months later I received a brief note announcing the birth of her first child.

CLASSIC APPROACH FOR THE VERY SKILLED THERAPIST

In about 9 percent of the couples, one or both spouses received classical psychoanalysis. However, the very skilled therapist can use any approach that he is successful with. I find that I get best results with psychoanalysis when this modality is indicated. The following situation is illustrative:

Mr. and Mrs. Lucinda were referred for marital counseling by her parents—former patients of mine. Both were extremely attractive in appearance and college graduates. Mrs. Lucinda stated that for the past six months their marriage had shown progressive deterioration, and that unless something was done, a divorce was in the offing. For the past six months her husband had insisted on being gone one night a week without questions asked. She suspected that perhaps another woman was involved, but this was only a vague possibility since they were very compatible sexually.

Mr. Lucinda, when seen individually, stated he loved his wife and children but that his wife did not understand him. During his freshman year at college he had a homosexual relationship. He had then met his wife and was able to stop that relationship. Their courtship was smooth and wonderful with excellent premarital sex. About one year ago, following an important promotion at work, he became extremely anxious and found relief by seeking out transient homosexual partners. Then he met Bob and a different type of relationship began. Bob opened up a new world of music, art, ballet, and so on. On the other hand, he realized that he was not cut out for the "gay world" and wanted to stop seeing Bob but could not, although their relationship was no longer sexual but intellectual. It was these evenings out that he spent with Bob and his friends. His wife knew nothing about his behavior. He loved his wife and wanted to save his marriage.

Mr. Lucinda was started on intensive therapy, receiving a total of 450 hours over the next three years—a classical analysis with therapy three times a week on the couch. Gradually he changed, and a good marriage ensued.

Currently, when there is no family secret and the spouse knows of the homosexuality, I prefer to treat both spouses.

NOTES

1. Peter L. Giovacchini (Treatment of Marital Disharmonies: The Classical Approach, in *The Psychotherapies of Marital Disharmony* (B.L. Greene, Ed.). New York, Free Press, 1965, pp. 39–82) prefers the classic psychoanalytic approach in marital disharmony. A similar position is presented by Marvin G. Drellich: Psychoanalysis of marital partners by separate analysts. In *The Marriage Relationship* (Salo Rosenbaum and Ian Alger, Eds.). New York, Basic Books, 1968, pp. 237–250. These two articles raise issues that must be considered in the combined-collaborative approach (see Ch. XXVI).

2. Marvin J. Feldman: Privacy and conjoint family therapy, *Family Process*, 6:1, 1967. In this paper the author examines the effects of privacy on treatment by contrasting certain aspects of individual and conjoint family therapy. "It is a basic assumption of most forms of psychotherapy that the success of the endeavor is contingent upon a considerable degree of self-exploration. In turn, there is an implicit assumption that intensive exploration is aided by a high degree of privacy . . . it is an open question whether this form of therapy (one-to-one psychotherapeutic relationship) is a prerequisite for meaningful self-exploration at this time. In fact, the highly private nature of individual psychotherapy may contain latent dysfunctional aspects for both the therapist and the client. Such possibilities might be examined with profit for our general understanding of psychotherapy." Theoretically, the issues raised by the author are valid, but clinically many situations occur where privacy and confidentiality are necessary for successfully treating a disturbed marriage.

3. For a discussion of acting-out behavior, see Chapter XXVII.

4. Alfred H. Rifkin: Homosexuality in Marriage, in *The Marriage Relationship* (Salo Rosenbaum and Ian Alger, Eds.). New York, Basic Books, 1968, p. 206. He writes: "My experience with this group of patients suggests that it may be desirable to insist that the spouse enter treatment along with the primary patient." See also Lionel Ovesey and Willard Gaylin (Psychotherapy of male homosexuality, *Amer J Psychotherapy*, 19:382, 1965), who describe a psychodynamic formulation for male homosexuality. "The homosexual flees from women and seeks genital contact with other males not only for sexual reasons, but for nonsexual reasons as well . . . dependency, and power." The latter two motivations have nonsexual goals, although involving the genital organs, are designated by them as pseudohomosexual. On the other hand, Bieber and his associates (Irving Bieber, H.J. Dain, P.R. Dinch, M.G. Drellich, H.G. Grand, R.H. Gundlach, Malvina W. Kremer, A.H. Rifkin, Cornelia B. Wilbur, and Toby B. Bieber: *Homosexuality—A Psychoanalytic Study of Male*

Homosexuals. New York, Basic Books, 1962) stress that homosexuals are driven by fear, fostered within the family constellation, to sexual inversion. They point out a basic psychopathology centering about erroneous fantasies about fear of reprisal from aggressive, punitive men (hostile father or frightening older brother) for acts of success (self-enhancement, assertiveness, and masculinity). Usually there is a lack of identification with a hostile, rejecting, detached father, and the presence of a controlling, dominating, seductive mother. See also Stanley E. Willis II: *Understanding and Counseling the Male Homosexual.* Boston, Little, Brown, 1967. He postulates that homosexuality is an experientially determined pattern of adaptation—the outgrowth of occurrences in the individuals formative years. He emphasizes that the psychodynamics in each individual are different. Judd Marmor (Ed.): *Sexual Inversion—The Multiple Roots of Homosexuality,* New York, Basic Books, 1965. Marmor presents a group of experts focusing on aspects of homosexuality from the perspective of their own specialties. In spite of intellectual understanding, there is considerable anxiety about homosexuality in many individuals. The spector of "latent homosexuality" remains a source of considerable anxiety to many persons. I differentiate between the normal positive feelings of the individual toward the parent of the same sex (autonomous aspect of the ego) and defensive homosexuality.

XXIII

THE COLLABORATIVE TECHNIQUE IN MARITAL DISHARMONY

In the collaborative approach in marital disharmony, both spouses are treated individually but currently by separate therapists who communicate with the knowledge and permission of each marital partner. The collaborative approach, a dyadic one-to-one therapeutic relationship, was used in 10 percent of the couples receiving counseling and in about 8 percent of couples where one or both spouses received intensive psychotherapy. The collaborative approach enables the therapist-in-training to enhance his knowledge about marital transactions as he gradually acquires the experience to treat two or more individuals in the same clinical setting. Martin and Bird[1] were pioneers in 1948 in the development of the collaborative approach in marital disharmony. In 1952 they first reported on their technique, which they called the "stereoscopic technique."[2] Initially Martin and Bird met only occasionally about their patients, but soon they developed their occasional meetings into a regularly scheduled program. I also found that collaborative therapy requires regular scheduled meetings between the therapists.

The following are indications for the collaborative approach:

1. Opposition of one spouse to being treated by the same therapist as his partner.
2. Initial hostility of one spouse toward the therapist.
3. Referral from another therapist because of his personal reasons, e.g. uncomfortable in the triadic situation, inexperience with the triadic approach, and/or nonacceptance of the frame of reference of triadic techniques.

4. Referral from another therapist because the partner has created therapeutic complications, and it is evident to the referring therapist that the husband and wife have widely differing goals in terms of their marriage problem. Should divorce or separation ensue, it may be necessary for the two therapists not only to supply ongoing emotional support to each spouse but also to help in structuring the various family arrangements.

The contraindications for collaborative technique are the same as for the classic dyadic one-to-one approach as outlined in Chapter XXII.

Although the first patients treated had spouses who originally were in therapy for severe emotional disturbances, for example, severe depressions, it soon became obvious that the collaborative approach was valuable as a primary approach for certain conflicted couples. The following clinical vignettes are illustrative:

The following illustrates the first reason, opposition of one spouse to being treated by the same therapist as his partner, for collaborative therapy.

Mr. and Mrs. Myra were referred by their physician for marital therapy. Mr. Myra was seen first and stated: "This blowup has been building up for several years. Ann has a great drive for excitement. I am the quiet sort of person, and she is just the opposite. She has a great amount of personal drive and is extremely vocal and social. Many of these things I have not. I realized this after the first years of our marriage, that I would have to change a lot to please her. She has always leaned to extremes. I have been the conservative one. I had hoped that when she went back to work, it would have helped her. She reads rapidly and a great deal. I have been trying to read more. She is so adamant about being free of me. She is very affectionate to our son. At times a little more self-centered than other mothers I have seen. But she is very interested in the boy and his welfare. I will do anything to save this marriage."

Mrs. Myra, an attractive, vivacious woman, appeared much younger than her stated age of twenty-seven. She stated that they married while they were in college because she wanted to settle down. She was not in love with him when they married, but she felt quiet with him and content.

"There is no communication and no challenge to my growth. He doesn't perceive my needs or reactions. He is a marvelous father. But I want out— a divorce. I want to live, to see and be with people. I'm in no great rush to remarry. Six months ago I told him I couldn't make love to him anymore. First, I got pregnant, but it ended in a miscarriage. Secondly, I went back to work. Being at work only increased my unhappiness. I told him I wanted a divorce. He agreed on the condition that I see a psychiatrist for six months.

"John reacted very positively to his session with you. But I am not going to see you again. I feel you will try to brainwash me into staying married to him. I want you to send me to another therapist. He will be my therapist, and you two can cooperate."

When I next saw Mr. Myra, he agreed to collaborative therapy. When seen a week later, he angrily stated: "I am very irritated at my wife. She wants to sell the house and move into an apartment with our child. I do not feel it is fair to uproot the boy." I told him that I would get together with her therapist to discuss the situation.

(Comment: At our first collaborative session it was decided that Mrs. Myra could move out as she wished, and her husband remain in the home, and that I would attempt to help him improve his self-image. In the interim an attempt would be made to understand the psychodynamics of Mrs. Myra. Two months later Mrs. Myra moved back into their home, having reestablished a meaningful relationship with her husband. Since there had been a strong therapeutic alliance between Mrs. Myra and her therapist, I suggested that the Myras both continue with him conjointly. Six months later he reported they were doing well and he had discontinued their treatment.)

Initial hostility of one spouse toward the therapist, the second reason for collaborative therapy, is illustrated below.

Mr. Miranda, a tall, thin male in his late thirties stated he was at his wit's end in coping with his wife's extravagant spending. When he would remonstrate with her, she would get furiously angry at him and throw things. Finally, in desperation he moved out of their apartment into a nearby motel. A week later she had reached him at work and agreed to psychiatric help, provided he also went.

Mrs. Miranda was an exotic-looking woman, who came for her first interview wearing black, tight toreador pants with a gray sweater. She looked older than her stated age of twenty-nine and wore heavy makeup and thick false eyelashes. She spoke in a very precise fashion. Her main complaint was about her husband being so penurious: "He has turned out to be like my father. My parents were always arguing about money. Father was always ranting and raving in the home about Mother's spending and that we would all end up in the poorhouse."

At one point in the interview she became annoyed with me when I inquired about how she met her husband. Her answer was evasive, and she quickly changed the subject.

When Mr. Miranda came for his next interview, he stated that his wife felt that I did not like her and was not going to return but that she would see someone else, preferably a woman doctor who understands women.

An illustration of the third reason for collaborative therapy, referral from another therapist because of his personal reasons, e.g. inexperience with the triadic marital approach, is below:

Mr. Mildred was referred by the psychiatrist who was treating his wife for a reactive depression. Dr. —— felt Mrs. Mildred's emotional state was due principally to marital disharmony. He had referred Mr. Mildred, since he was inexperienced in treating couples. The Mildreds were in their late twenties and worked at the same factory where she was a nurse and he, a skilled maintenance worker.

Mr. Mildred began his first session by commenting: "We are not getting along. Worse since our honeymoon two years ago. She acts neurotic with a lot of anxiety. We met at a party four years ago. I was going to night school, taking electronics. I noticed her but didn't call her until a month later. She responded to things I said. She is very intelligent.

"We are both very athletic and enjoy skiing. She reads a lot and is interested in accomplishing things. We first ran into problems during our courtship. I couldn't find the right kind of job. She would get very upset when I wouldn't look for two days. I got a job I liked but the place burned down in a month. I looked around again. She would give me ultimatums: If you don't get a job in two weeks, I'm calling off the engagement. We had arguments. I tried to pacify her. One night she said let's break it off. I was undecided but said maybe it's a good idea. I told her I wasn't ready to settle down. She got emotional and blew up. I figured I would forget the deal.

"Prior to this I had received a call from a former Army buddy. He wanted me to go into business with him in California. I had told her about his call. The next day she called and suggested that we get married. I told her I wasn't sure. I was thinking about California. I was undecided, and she was superpositive. She told me she was really in love with me. I felt I was getting involved sooner than I wanted. I quit my job. I felt I met her too early, I was only twenty-seven, that I wasn't mature enough for marriage. Also, I wanted to get California out of my system. She didn't like this at all. I took a plane and asked her if she would wait. She said, Yes. I wrote her factual letters, but that I missed her. I didn't like California and knew I would be happier in Chicago. I called Jane and told her I was coming home. She was happy.

"It seemed like I was a bad employment risk. I started working at this place as a mechanic but didn't like my boss, so quit. When I told Jane this, it was like an atom bomb. I told my father and he said: Don't feel so bad, start thinking positively, get married. So I went out and bought a ring. I asked her to marry me. I didn't tell her that I wasn't working. Later I began to feel guilty and decided to tell her. She gave the ring back to me and told me not to bother her anymore, but the next night she called me and said she thought it over and would marry me. But we kept having arguments. We would be in a movie, and she would say something to me. I wouldn't hear her and she would storm out. She was continually mad over nothing. Finally the arguments stopped and we got married.

"Our honeymoon was a fizzle. The first night she was a little nervous. We were both tired from the wedding, so when we got into bed, she said she was tired and maybe it would be a good thing to get some sleep. I felt I didn't have a good erection so it didn't bother me. The next day we left for Niagara Falls. We drove 150 miles. I felt I wanted to sweep her off her feet. I had never had intercourse before. I had read quite a bit about it. I had trouble finding the entrance. But before I got that far, I had an ejaculation. The same thing happened the next night. She started getting emotional and didn't like it.

"We had sexual problems for a year. During this time she was getting disgusted with me and sleeping in another bed. Finally she began to feel extremely nervous and went to see a psychiatrist. He suggested I see you, that my sex drive is not as it should be—that I need some help. So here I am."

At the first collaborative session, Dr. —— reported that Mrs. Mildred was very happy that her husband was receiving help, and that she would like her marriage to be successful but had her doubts. If she could control her emotions and accept things the way they were, there would be no problems to consider. She made many demands on Jim and he, very few. All he wanted was that she be calm and good natured. She didn't feel useful, needed or married. There was little communication with her husband, and his procrastination in all areas was most frustrating.

Dr. —— also stated that Mrs. Mildred complained that her husband was very inhibited sexually, and that some of her sexual aggressive behavior had shocked him and embarrassed her to passivity. He quoted her as follows: The low level of communication, understanding, sex activity, social and intellectual activity, planning together, acting on problems, and above all, his procrastination has had its effect. It's what Jim does not do. I imagine his complaints concern what I do.

Jim was seen twice weekly for six months with considerable improvement in his total behavior at work and in his sexual performance. He had regained his sexual adequacy but discovered his wife to be frigid. Weekly collaborative sessions with Dr. —— confirmed my clinical impression of Jane as a very controlling obsessive-compulsive personality. Six months after the onset of therapy, with Jane's continually questioning her husband as to everything discussed in his sessions, I suggested to Dr. —— that he try to conjoint therapy with the couple.

Referral from another therapist because the partner is complicating the therapy of his spouse is the fourth reason for collaborative therapy. The following clinical extract is illustrative.

Mr. Melissa, a handsome, intelligent executive, was referred by his wife's therapist. She had gone for marital counseling, but her husband refused to cooperate until threatened by the possibility of divorce. Mrs. Melissa's therapist was pessimistic about the marriage and wanted the collaborative technique, both as a last attempt to salvage the marriage and to help structure the various family arrangements should the couple separate.

At the first collaborative session, Dr. —— stated that he had been treating Mrs. Melissa for the past six months with considerable improvement in her depressed moods. However, Mrs. Melissa had been increasingly angry at her husband for not wanting to work on the marriage. Her main complaint was unfulfilled emotional needs. He quoted her as saying: "I feel that I would like to know, to understand, to be totally intimate with the person who is going to share my life. He does not possess the same needs for a relationship in depth. We do not communicate. We have a superficially compatible pattern of dealing with each other, and frankly I'm tired of my role."

Dr. —— described Mrs. Melissa as very intelligent, very attractive and an extrovert.

In his first session, Mr. Melissa stated that he was at a loss to understand what has happened to his marriage: "Everything had been fine until a year ago when Ann began to complain that I was insensitive to her needs as a woman: I make too few gestures of love, am not spontaneous enough, and show little in the way of tokens of affection. Under different circumstances my ego would be hurt. However, three years after we were married, Ann and I got this irritation out into the open, and I discovered that her needs are excessive. Not that I could not fulfill her needs, but I resented her incessant reminding me about her emotional needs and my not fulfilling them. Somehow when my wife reminded me to bring home something cute or funny or just surprise her, I would balk. I can't be creative by manifesto. Then we got along fine, until a year ago when the same bit started up again. The friction and continuous reminding me was most irritating, and I began to withdraw from her. We now virtually have separate lives, which I can live with but do not like.

"I would like my marriage to last. Both Dr. —— and my wife have pushed me to see you. I don't feel I have been remiss and have really worked hard to be better in the marriage situation. I've tried to meet the excessive needs of my wife."

In the next six sessions, Mr. Melissa expressed rage at his wife's demands and recalled how his parents continually stressed performance in everything he did, e.g. if he got 95 on an exam, why didn't he get 100.

It was pointed out to him that perhaps he was overreacting to his wife's demands with the anger he could not express toward his parents, who kept making increasing demands on him. That he was reacting, not only with anger to his wife, but also projecting onto her an old performance 'record' in his jukebox—an angry one from his "inner child" voice to the perfectionistic demands of the "parental" voices (an excellent example of projective identification).

In the next collaborative session with Dr. ——, the role of projective identification in the marital disharmony of the Melissa's was discussed, and it was suggested that Ann keep her demands and criticisms to a minimum, and how her husband was overreacting to them.

In his next session, Mr. Melissa commented: "You have helped me to see myself differently. I'm easier with people now. Now I see myself acting more strongly as a man. For years I've tried not to react to other women. But now I could. That's something I'm concerned about. Ann doesn't feel the same way about moral behavior as I do. I have been very faithful since I got married. I know many men who step out on their wives. Ann says, if you step out on a convention, it's OK—unless you fall in love. My parents told me otherwise. It bothers me that Ann doesn't think that way. The one thing I have been hanging onto morally is weakening. We had sex last night, the first in over two months.

"Ann has had extreme lows and extreme highs this week. I see things now that I don't like, that I didn't see before. She was screaming at the kid and me. I called her aside in the bedroom and said, 'Don't talk to me that way again.' I never was that firm with her before. She was surprised.

"I keep not delivering. Her theory is that if everything is swell in bed, you can manage anything. But sex is something you lead up to. I can't turn it on that easy. When we had sex the other night, she was not too responsive. She feels she is not capable of responding to me. She feels I am losing my desire for her. She is right. She doesn't make me feel virile lately."

At the next collaborative session, Dr. —— stated that Mrs. Melissa was frustrated with her husband, especially sexually. She likes to be free-wheeling and allow her "inner child" to play. He puts a damper on it. Most of the time she has had to initiate sex. At times she rebuffs him. Sex is not satisfactory for her. She has noticed an improvement in her husband in terms of communication. I raised the issue of whether Ann was insatiable in her needs and demands. Also, whether we were dealing with a cyclothymic personality because of her marked mood swings.

Mr. Melissa reported that things had been going very nicely for the past three weeks. "It's scary. She is trying. I think she is enjoying making a meal for me now. She did a lot of nice things for me."

At the next collaborative session, Dr. —— reported that Ann was again angry at her husband. She had gone out of her way to do all the things he likes, e.g. gourmet meals. All she got was a lot of nice compliments but no display of affection. Dr. —— related these incidents with considerable annoyance at Mr. Melissa but was unaware of his counter-transference. When this was pointed out, at first he was annoyed at me then laughingly pointed out how protective I was about Mr. Melissa. We both discussed our respective feelings and cleared the atmosphere.

In his fifth month of therapy, Mr. Melissa was depressed: "The knowledge that whatever I do won't pay off. I think she is turned off, intellectually and sexually. I don't have anyone to talk to. She does not inquire about my work. Absolutely scintillating when we get out of our environment. I am preparing myself for separation from Ann. Something originally I could not have been prepared to do six months ago. The other night we had a slight argument and she said: 'This stalemate. When the hell is it all going to end.' She has tuned me out because of my noninvolvement with her. Yet, you tell me that we could make a go of our marriage if I could be emotionally involved with her again. When she tries, I move away, and when I try, she doesn't respond. We are caught in a vicious cycle."

In the collaborative session, both therapists agreed that, although their respective patients were developing in their personal behavior, the marriage was coming apart. Paradoxically, as Mr. Melissa showed increased aggressivity at home and at work, where he had just received a promotion, Mrs. Melissa was becoming depressed and not so sure she wanted a separation now. She knew she was rejecting her husband but couldn't react to him in a positive manner. We decided to tell each spouse that if there was no improvement within two months, we would discontinue collaborative sessions.

Mr. Melissa reported that Ann had reacted to the two-month target date with another attempt at trying to make the marriage work: "She was seductive and sat on my lap. I said, 'Let's go to bed.' She said, 'Do you remember how?' but not in a sarcastic manner. I said, 'It is you who has been avoiding it.' We had a good sexual experience. First time in several months. I've changed since coming here. Ann is no longer the physical pursuer as she has been for years. I am going to have to initiate it. I've never been emotionally built like that. I didn't know she was going to run out of steam. I've never seen my parents embrace. Mother is an absolutely frigid person. Ann coming into my life with this open display of affection."

At the next collaborative session, Dr. —— stated that Mrs. Melissa noticed no change in her husband's sexual patterns. He quoted her as follows: "Dick has been nice enough to me lately. I can tell he is trying, but he's so inhibited in his ability to show love that I can only feel sorry for him. I am an affectionate, romantic, feminine person. He turned me into someone who sought professional help because I began to think I was frigid. I have since experienced profoundly beautiful sexual love and I no longer have any reason to assume any guilt of an unsuccessful sexual relationship. Love for him, especially sexual love, if it exists at all, and strangely I think he does love me, is not comprehensible to me in my terms of expression. In such an environment my love has died. At this point in the marriage, I don't inspire him, I don't nag him and the wall grows." Dr. —— had taken down her comments verbatim. It was decided that the marriage was no longer meaningful, that we should stop our sessions, and that we would tell our patients and focus on them instead of the marriage.

Mr. Melissa at his next appointment commented: "I never realized how distant Ann is. I was out of town for a week at our New York branch. I missed Ann and the boy. But when I returned, such blankness. She is a master at turning me off. We are in bed. She said, 'Rub my back.' I was rubbing her back when she said, 'What was the weather like in New York?' It turned off my sexual desire. I felt certain that we are mismated. I laid back in misbelief. A week later I told her that the only level of communication was in terms of our child, that she was distant and that physically she turned me off when I came back from New York. She didn't say anything. I said I want to make a go of our marriage. I said

I hope it's only a phase. She said, 'It's just two people finding out how different they are.' It turned off my hope. I said it's been a bad six months. She said it's been two years. She keeps pushing me farther and farther away."

I told Mr. Melissa that Dr. —— and I had discontinued our collaborative sessions. I suggested he and his wife separate but start dating each other again to see if they could play the old "records" of their courtship. Also I set a target date of three months, and if there is no change in their relationship, to consider divorce.

He replied: "Three months ago I could not have accepted this. Now I can. She isn't interested in being with me anymore. She is just a social vehicle, not an intimate companion."

Mr. Melissa began his ninth month of therapy and his forty-fifth session by looking very unhappy and concerned. For the past two weeks he and his wife had gone their separate ways and slept in separate bedrooms. They were friendly with each other but treated each other as strangers (emotional divorce).

"My unhappiness is getting oppressive. Two weeks ago Ann and I had a talk. No arguments. But we are not making it. Socially each going separate ways. Ann is right, we are not communicating. I told her my thinking about moving out of our house. Then she began to cry. "I am now absolutely and totally turned off toward her. The saddest thing I feel is about our child. I'm not in love with her. She can't motivate me to anything. We have had this emotional divorce you have been talking about for the past year or two."

I suggested that perhaps he should move out. That sometimes distance is necessary to clarify a marital relationship and frequently the meaning of the partner. Either they draw farther apart or move closer to each other.

He replied: "Everyone I know is having other outlets. I never had. Maybe if I did, the marriage would be better. She said maybe I should have an affair. Maybe I need to get my ego or organs reinforced. It might give me more tolerance with Ann's needs and demands. I think Ann thinks it is all right. That is the most palatable solution to my marriage. To have two women in my life: my wife to run the house, take care of our child, and to go out with socially, and another woman to turn me on sexually. There is nothing in her behavior to send me or to indicate that I send her. Something I used to do with other women—five or six times in an evening."

In his next session he continued to be depressed: I've been looking around for an apartment. We are not on the same wavelength. If Ann was sitting here she would say, 'All I have allowed you the past ten years is to indulge your needs.' I've been brought up differently. Wait and see things a bit longer. It was her idea to see Dr. ——. She is more expressive. She then got me to go. She made an honest attempt. In doing this she accelerated the breakdown, the inequities in our marriage."

It took Mr. Melissa five weeks before he could move out: "I had the most traumatic week. I moved out a week ago. It was a terrible week.

Moving out of my house and from my child. Being uprooted was a terrible, upsetting thing to me. I can hardly sleep. I am closer to my son now. At one o'clock we are seeing the lawyers. I saw this girl last night. A total explosion of chemistry. She felt the same way about me. I've regained my self-respect."

An amiable settlement was worked out between the couple without any problems. Two months later, during which Mr. Melissa received divorce counseling, he asked to discontinue treatment. He was advised to take at least two years before he remarried and to call for remarital counseling. Through referrals over the past few years from both Melissas I heard that they are both doing well in their separate ways.

In the collaborative approach, both spouses are treated concurrently by different therapists who communicate at regular, scheduled intervals. The collaboration of the therapists permits the spouses to gain some understanding of their partner's psychodynamics as it influences the marital transactions, thus enabling some containment of excessive anxiety and/or hostility. Experience has shown difficulties of communication between therapists with this technique. Mutual trust and confidence does not prevent cross-transference difficulties between the therapists. Each therapist identifies with the viewpoint of his patient and gets a biased picture of the real situation at home. Most important in this technique is the loss of the strategical center for integrating all relevant observations of the marriage, when the events and perceptions are parceled out between two therapists.

NOTES

1. Peter A. Martin: Treatment of marital disharmony by collaborative therapy. In *The Psychotherapies of Marital Disharmony* (Bernard L. Greene, Ed.), New York, Free Press, 1965, pp. 83–101.
2. Peter A. Martin and H. Waldo Bird: An approach to the psychotherapy of marriage partners—the stereoscopic technique, *Psychiatry*, 16:123, 1953. At about the same time Henry V. Dicks in England (*Marital Tensions*. New York, Basic Books, 1967, pp. 53–54) began to experiment with new techniques including the combined-collaborative and collaborative approaches and wrote: "For therapy, we took on a small proportion of cases, each of us treating the partner we had interviewed on our familiar lines, with periodic conferencing to coordinate findings and policy."

XXIV

THE CONCURRENT APPROACH IN MARITAL DISHARMONY

In the concurrent approach in marital disharmony, both spouses are treated individually but synchronously by the same therapist. This technique begins the first triadic clinical setting for the therapist. This technique is of value in treating marital discord, when a therapy must deal with elements of the intrapersonal system and with family transactions as well. Bela Mittlemann[1] pioneered in the use of analytic concurrent therapy for married couples. The concurrent technique was used in counseling about one fourth of the couples and with one fourth of the couples receiving intensive therapy.

The indications[2] for the concurrent approach in marital discord include the following:

1. Where the mental status of one spouse has overwhelmed his partner.
2. Where insight into their behavior patterns as they affect each partner is needed to produce changes in behavior.
3. A test of counseling procedures has indicated that one or both spouses could profit from a deeper understanding of the components of their three systems (intrapersonal, interpersonal and environmental).

The current contraindications for concurrent therapy exist in some spouses with the following:

1. Severe psychoses or severe character disorders.
2. Paranoid reactions.
3. Suspicious attitudes toward the communications of the spouses.

4. Excessive sibling-rivalry attitudes that preclude sharing the therapist.
5. Family secrets.
6. Very rigid defenses which, if broken, might produce a severe psychoneurosis, a psychosomatic crisis, or a psychosis.

THERAPEUTIC ELEMENTS AND THERAPEUTIC ACTION

Concurrent therapy contains specific therapeutic elements and a therapeutic action inherent in its design. A couple that is under considerable stress reacts to concurrent therapy with feelings of emotional support and with relief of their anxiety. We are reminded here of Alexander's[3] comment that the supportive effects of the psychoanalytic process (as well as other therapeutic processes) have not been sufficiently recognized as one of the main factors favoring both insight and the emergence of new behavioral patterns. There is another important therapeutic gain in a technical procedure that extends the integrative force of hope for the restoration of equilibrium in a marital relationship.

Another therapeutic element in concurrent therapy is the multidimensional view of the marriage transactions gained by the therapist from the communications, often contradictory and constantly changing, of the spouses. Through this triadic communication system, knowledge is gained in minimal time of both the nuclear and kinship transactions and of the immediate and peripheral environmental situations and influences (environmental system). The therapist hears both sides of long-standing controversies, and each spouse is aware that the therapist is hearing two sides of a complaint. As the concurrent therapy proceeds, partners frequently discuss between themselves ideas gained through insights. Particularly in the later phases of the therapy, this type of communication may become an extension of the learning process. On the other hand, these incidents often reveal to the therapist additional information about his patients' resistances or about the significance of the resentments, frustrations, or projections produced by these interspouse communications. The communication of unconscious sibling-rivalry attitudes or oedipal feelings, as highlighted in the triangular representation of the original family constellation, is a further therapeutic element.

I direct the spouses to report their dreams.[4] I find that dream material enables me to grasp important preoccupations behind the behavioral facades. This knowledge aids me in planning therapeutic maneuvers. Further, dreams furnish many important clues about the spouses' coping maneuvers and bring freely into focus the precise nature of their projective identifications and their feedbacks. Not infrequently having one spouse report his dream to his partner as interpreted in his session may relieve anxiety and/or hostility of the partner.

Another distinctive therapeutic element in concurrent therapy is the triangular transference transactions. We[5] have differentiated five foci of transactions in the transference relationships. The first focus of transaction involves the relationship to the therapist as a real person, and subsequently, as a new object as well. The second focus of transaction pertains to those situations where the therapist is experienced as a symbolic figure endowed with qualities of existing fantasies, as those involved in projections and displacements. The regressive phenomena manifested in the dyadic, one-to-one, transference neurosis[6] comprise the third focus of transaction. These three foci of transactions between patient and therapist are fundamental in all therapeutic relationships. In concurrent therapy, because the transference reactions of both spouses are directed toward the same therapist, as well as toward each other, two other foci of transaction related to the triangular transactions are introduced. The first of these is the *triangular transference neurosis*, such as the reproduction of the oedipal constellation. The second, the *triangular transference transactions*, concern the production of adaptive feedbacks, not only toward the therapist but also to the other spouse, who in turn feeds back to his spouse, to the therapist or to both. Interpretations of the transference phenomena in concurrent therapy are made from the frame of reference of both the dyadic and triangular aspects of the transference. The additional foci of transaction favor the increased production of emotional and intellectual insights, which is conducive to the learning process.[7]

In the following pages I shall present three clinical vignettes illustrating the concurrent approach that could be utilized by a moderately skilled, skilled, and very skilled therapist.

CONCURRENT APPROACH WITH A MODERATELY SKILLED THERAPIST

The following couple illustrates the concurrent approach by a moderately skilled therapist:

The Marcellas were referred for marital counseling. Mr. Marcella chose his words carefully and frequently paused for short periods while searching for the precise word to express his thoughts. His manner was pleasant, and he seemed to be searching for answers to what may be causing the problems between him and his wife. Although Mr. Marcella almost casually expressed the belief that he might be in error in his actions toward his wife, it was felt that this was more superficial than he could admit to himself. He spontaneously excluded sex or extramarital interests as being elements of their problem and preferred to label the discontent as related to his resentment to having seen his wife drunk on several occasions. Here, too, he was able to state that he was aware that there must be some underlying reason for his reaction, since he had lost respect for her. The preciseness in his language structure was most apparent when talking of his reactions to his wife and family members. His essential circumlocution was evidence by such remarks as: "We've talked about it and never concluded that we should," in reply to his feelings toward having children during their fifteen years of marriage.

Mrs. Marcella was a petite, plump, bespectacled woman in her mid-thirties with an intense business like demeanor. While openly pleasant, her reserve and anxiety were obviously just beneath the surface. She spoke of the difficulties which had arisen between her and her husband over the past two years. Her answers displayed an extreme dearth of psychological sophistication and an emotional naiveté. Her chief complaint was that her husband tended to criticize her household operations like an efficiency expert. This, as well as several other criticisms and suspicions he had leveled at her, had given rise to an increasing tension and decreasing communication within the home. Mrs. Marcella was also concerned over her own perceived increased reliance on alcohol, and her own and her husband's fears that she might become an alcoholic. She seemed quite sincere in her desire to seek help to obviate the difficulties between her husband and her.

"Neither John nor I seem to communicate with each other. One or the other gets angry. We are both highly critical of the other. He feels everything I do should be perfect. In the kitchen he will stand and count my steps and correct me if I'm not logical and precise. He can't stand doors left ajar. I think John has secret ways of doing things. Until the other day I didn't know we had two safety boxes. I asked him what's in it, and he said nothing. When he talks to me I'm supposed to tell him everything, but he won't tell me. His family was very strict about telling things outside the home. I knew his folks were going to separate before they told him" (an excellent example of suspicious "parental" voices present in their son's "records").

"John has certain people he thinks are just right and that I should be like them. He thinks I should run a house like his aunt, who is sixty and has no children, and has nothing to do but run the house. I hold down a full-time job. He is just like the professor in "My Fair Lady." When I am in the kitchen, he watches the way I prepare the food. This makes me nervous. I feel more emotions than I show. I think I show him more of my feelings than anyone else, but he doesn't think I am as affectionate as he is. I drink too much at times. I don't know why. Then I can tell John things that normally I couldn't say. He thinks I am becoming an alcoholic. I drink too much but not consistently. I once gave my folks some money. Ever since, he has the idea that I give my parents money on the side. He has accused me of this. Although I have denied this, he says that I have. I don't say anything but take a couple of drinks and feel better."

In the next two sessions, Mr. Marcella discussed their courtship, which went very smoothly: "No premarital relations, although we had plenty of opportunities. It was mutual. Our first night on our honeymoon was like amateur night. She was relatively frigid but got better and she seemed more relaxed. She would want a drink or two prior to sex. About five years ago she began to enjoy it. Not a hell of lot of frequency but satisfactory. She is on the shy side. No problem as far as I am concerned. Never been a source of argument. Occasionally she would complain I didn't satisfy her, that I was too fast.

"I have been accused of being a perfectionist. In my mind, No! But everything has to be just right. I want her to be immaculately dressed, as I am.

"Last Christmas Lil came home from her office party drunk. In my opinion she was drunk. I lit into her. Then six months later she got sick at a party, and it teed me off. Another incident three months later when she came home from bowling and I felt she had too much to drink. I got mad. I object to her getting drunk. She becomes belligerent and independent."

In her second interview, Mrs. Marcella talked about her courtship: "I knew him from high school. I liked him right from the beginning. He was very quiet and bashful when I first met him, but he soon got over that. We went together four years. I was engaged for two years before marriage. At times he would be affectionate. At that time he was more of a gentle person that he is now, and kindhearted. He doesn't seem to be that way now. He is more cold about everything now. If it doesn't involve him personally, he is not interested. After we married, we seemed to see eye to eye on everything. He always made me feel I was being a help to him, that he needed me. But now I don't feel that's true. He rarely ever asks my advice. He has gone beyond me. He has advanced to a very good position in his company. He is so self-sufficient."

When asked what she meant by he had "gone beyond" her, she replied: "Yes, he has. When I first met him, he was shy and bashful and had no self-confidence. Now he is overly confident that everything he says and does is right. In some instances I disagree."

When asked about her sexual adjustment, she answered: "I had never had any affairs before marriage. John was very clean-cut. Four out of the six girls I went with did. John and I had many opportunities to. I might have. I think I am average or even undersexed. I enjoy it more now than previously. Within two weeks after we married I had my first orgasm. John is very gentle and fine during sex. Most of the time he satisfies me. I am slower and at times he is too fast. That doesn't annoy me. No problem sexually.

"There is something that does bother John! This neighbor once grabbed me and kissed me. We were having a party at our house. I was walking down the stairs with a tray full of hors d'oeuvres when this neighbor grabbed me and kissed me. John just came in. That has disturbed John. This same neighbor was doing that to other girls at the party. He had had to much to drink. This happened five years ago, and he keeps asking me about it. Cross-examines me regularly. He always jokes about it. This is something that bothers him because he keeps bringing it up. There has been absolutely nothing between us. But he keeps questioning me about it, and this makes me mad. He is the jealous and suspicious type. He never appeared to be before this incident. And this is his best friend. I know his mother is extremely jealous (mother's "parental" voice in his "records"). I really don't understand it. I'm just an average-looking woman, in fact, on the plain side. I get angry and explode, take a few drinks, and forget it. But John plans and plots his revenge, like his family."

In her third session, Mrs. Marcella said: "I've felt so much better since my first visit with you two weeks ago. Like someone lifted the weight of the world off my back. I had never told anyone else about John's suspicions and questioning me. I haven't had a drink since I first saw you. I just feel that I can now have one drink and that is it."

She was told that if she felt the need to drink, we would explore the underlying reasons, otherwise I saw no need for further treatments, since her husband's only complaint was her drinking. But that I would see her a few more times.

Mrs. Marcella began her fourth session by stating: "I have been thinking about what you said the last hour. I don't think I need to go deeper in treatment. I feel much better now. I've stopped my drinking completely. If I were to do it again, I wouldn't get married. I haven't been particularly happy. Mainly disagreements John and I have had. I've been happy with the material things. But my emotional needs have not been met. Sexually, yes. But his lack of understanding. His criticism has made me unhappy. And it has always been present since the first year of marriage. The only bad feature is his continual criticism of me. He gets it from his father. The only thing is his watching and criticizing me. He is not jealous of me when we are out in a group. I will admit that this neighbor does pay attention to me, like light my cigarette. Maybe that is what makes John suspicious."

In his fourth session, Mr. Marcella commented: "Everything was fine for two days and then an argument and all hell broke loose. I said, 'Is the episode with Bob (the neighbor) all over?' and that started it. The one thing that bothers me is the explanation. That she said 'nothing' when I asked her what was going on. I don't think anything went on. I am inclined to think that it's her reaction to it. She says she has explained it to me. In my own mind I do not recall her going into detail. The mere fact it bounces in and out of my mind. This could be the crux of the whole thing. I saw nothing."

She said you saw her kissing him.

"That's right. He came back to the landing on the second floor of our house—it's like a mezzanine off our kitchen—and checked to see the traffic. We had a party for about six couples. That's where the suspicion begins. Explain to me why she refuses to talk about it. I know when I forget about it I feel better, it happened a long time ago, but it keeps cropping up in my thoughts. Let's assume it's a figment of my imagination, then how can I stop thinking about it. Saturday and Sunday we were getting along fine. She has stopped drinking since she first saw you. It was like a second honeymoon. Then when I talked about it and pushed, she got upset. Logically, I know it's impossible. I am pretty well convinced that nothing did go on. This doesn't bother me a bit (sic). I had a dream last night. A silly damn thing: I had flown my plane and parked it at Meigs Field. I was coming here for my appointment. A fellow took my plane and did something with it and collected twenty dollars. He refused to split the money with me. Here I had set my plane in a public airport and this man had used it. And, without my permission. Made twenty dollars and didn't even want to give me part of it. Strictly a sense of distrust."

The hour had ended and no interpretation of the dream was given. The dream suggests someone is out to take advantage of him. I made the suggestion that he ask his wife about the incident with the neighbor, telling her it was my idea and that she was to answer all his questions without anger.

In her fifth and last session, Mrs. Marcella commented: "We were able to communicate after his last session with you, and talk quietly about that incident. I explained fully to him that nothing had happened sexually, that he kissed me while I had my arms full with a tray of hors d'oeuvres, that nothing had ever happened before or since, and that I was not interested in any other man. I feel very good and am happy since I started coming here a month ago. He has been sleeping very well since his last visit with you and is in good spirits. I would like to stop treatment but be able to see you only when something comes up that I can't handle with John."

Mr. Marcella opened his fifth and last appointment by stating: "I feel great. She has answered all my questions. She feels that you have helped her a great deal. I would like to discontinue treatment also."

I discussed our sessions, and I told him that I was a little concerned about his dream in which he felt a man was trying to take advantage of him financially. But since the marriage had stabilized, this would be our last session. However, should his suspicious thoughts return, to immediately phone for an appointment.

CONCURRENT APPROACH WITH A SKILLED THERAPIST

The following couple illustrates the concurrent approach by a skilled therapist:

The Zeldas, both in their late twenties, were extremely intelligent and made a handsome couple. After six years of marriage, they were divorced for the past three months. They both came for their first interview and stated they were unhappy at their separation. Their two main complaints were lack of communication and periodic arguments.

Mr. Zelda stated that after an argument he would crawl into his shell because he felt that she should apologize.

Mrs. Zelda commented that she had a great deal of personal pride, and that each waited for the other to do the apologizing. "After an argument I would be wishing I were dead. I would be lonely and crying and he would not speak to me for several days."

Mr. Zelda interrupted: "After we divorced I felt so miserable I couldn't concentrate and neglected my work, but I couldn't pick up the phone and tell her how much I missed her. I felt it was her place to call me."

I felt the prognosis was excellent and that the usual diagnostic workup was unnecessary and suggested the concurrent approach. Both readily agreed. The therapy lasted three months, each seen once a week. On Mrs. Zelda's birthday they remarried: three years later they were getting along very well. The following illustrates the course of therapy.

Mr. Zelda began his first individual session by stating: "After our session with you I gave considerable thought about why we argued, and I find myself laughing about how foolish the arguments were. We would argue about the things she would say to her parents or family. Then, many of the times I would feel that Jill was just looking for an argument for the sake of trying to see how far she can go without my reacting. After an argument I would be hurt and unwilling to make up, but Jill was ready just after a few minutes.

"Our courtship was wonderful. Doing things together, going to the theatre, shows, meeting our relatives, and just getting to know each other. Our honeymoon was a new experience for both of us. I felt we were adjusting to each other emotionally and physically without much hesitation. Everything fell into place and was so natural."

He described himself as very competitive and determined to be successful. Thus he was captain of the basketball team in college, and rapidly promoted at work. His father was a quiet man, an accountant, but a strict disciplinarian. He was fair but unforgiving and would hold a grudge for years: "I am like him. Once one of my aunts slapped me over a small argument. I didn't talk to her for three years" (an excellent example of "parental" voice projection in his "records").

He further comments: "If I did something wrong, my father would not speak to me for days." His parents were very religious Mormons.

The precipitating reason for their separation was a minor incident, but neither would make the first overture of apologizing. Thus the chasm between the two widened and finally led to divorce: "Sometimes I get angry, but by time I get over it, I don't know what it was about. We were in bed and Jill lightly pinched me. For some reason this irritated me and I retaliated by pinching her severely. She cried but I couldn't apologize for some reason. She didn't talk the next day, so I didn't talk to her. Later we talked but had no sex relations at all for two months. Things got worse, and she left like I did twice before. Although I missed her, I made no effort to talk to her. I felt a man does not do that sort of thing, since she was the one who left. Both of us are very proud and so we divorced."

He related his first dream as the hour ended: "I am back in Salt Lake City. Jill is with me. We are at a night club. A man comes up to me and hands me a note written by Jill: 'Don't wait for me. I will come home with this man.' I leave alone. I am driving ninety miles an hour when I realized I was speeding and woke up."

His interview ended before he could associate to the dream. But the dream reveals a wish to be back with his wife. But time is fast running out and he is afraid his wife will become interested in another man.

Mrs. Zelda began her first individual session by stating: "I'm a little confused about my emotions. Your idea that we start dating again as though we had just met was wonderful. I missed him so and am happier since I have been seeing him. I think we have both profited from our separation. We have had some sexual dissatisfaction. He gets aroused too soon. He said everything had to be sexually the way I want. He doesn't realize that women are slower to be aroused than men. For him, the act itself was it. He didn't realize what sex was closeness, kissing, tenderness. To him, I'm selfish.

"Living with Tom can be compared to living with a keg of dynamite. You never know when or what may set him off. Insignificant comments or actions done on my part seem to be significant enough to cause him to explode when I least expect it, for instance, teasing or an affectionate gesture. Sometimes reference to my family or upbringing is interpreted on his part as bragging in comparison to his background. We are of different family and economic backgrounds. I come from an old well-established New England family. I would not have married him if I didn't respect his values, morals and character more than his economic position. These are often causes of our arguments. Then I become extremely unsatisfied emotionally for I am forced to endure long periods of silence and lack of affection for periods as long as three and four weeks. Communication is impossible unless you are able to beg for it day after day. It is as if he hates me so much he receives pleasure from my loneliness and tears. I did not ever want a divorce. I am very much in love with my husband, and I know he loves me. However, twice before he got angry after long silences and left, 'calling it quits.' Because I knew we were both miserable, I eventually called him, and we reconciled. The last time I left after we quarreled. I had to go through with his request for divorce for fear I would spend the rest of my life in long, lonely silences and separations. I want more than anything for him to receive help in communicating his feelings instead of harboring them and running away. In spite of all the misery I often underwent, and so did he, I was happy in our marriage and I still want to be his wife, but only if you can help me deal with our problems more maturely. This time he called me!"

In his second session we discussed the clash of cultural values that was playing a factor in the arguments between them. It was pointed out that he was demanding of his wife's "inner child" what he demanded of his "inner child," that a meaningful marriage was based on mutual respect.

He next reported a dream of the previous night: "I am in a cocktail lounge with Jill. Some man walks in and tries to butt into our conversation. I was going to object and hit him. Then I decide it's not worth it. So we go about our business. The scene changes. I'm on top of a hill. Below is a big valley. Large mountains surrounding the valley. The Viet Cong are taking over the valley and digging in. Then suddenly see the Green Berets chop them to pieces."

In his associations he stated that someone is trying to help him but that he began by rejecting the help, but then decided to accept this man.

When I asked him who the man could be, he answered, "probably you." I replied, this was a normal reaction to the invasion of his privacy and that he was quite angry about it—"You chop me to pieces."

He commented: "I'm strongly dug in and someone really shattered it— things I need to hold on, my very conservative values and ideas about marriage, just like my father. My wife could perhaps represent the Green Berets chopping those values to pieces." (This is a good example of the triangular transference neurosis, both oedipal and sibling rivalry, a common reaction to triadic therapy—two is company and three is a crowd).

In her second session, Mrs. Zelda stated things were going well between them. But she was still concerned whether he would get angry at her and stop talking.

This had first happened shortly after their engagement. They were playing golf, and when he paid the caddy, she had asked him if he tipped him sufficiently. He didn't answer but had both a hurt and angry look. Just silence on his part. This occurred later—these periods of silence.

It was pointed out to her that when she acts in a manner to question his masculinity, he counterattacks by withdrawing into silence. Actually she was playing a "record" in which her "parental" voice was loud and clear, telling him his "inner child" was stupid.

In his third session, Mr. Zelda stated: "We are getting along better. The things you have pointed out to me have been most helpful. Before I wanted things my way, instead of seeing her side of the picture. I am honestly trying to solve this problem. I'm very grateful to you."

With the positive dyadic transference to me as a real object as well as the dyadic transference neurosis—the omnipotent and omniscient powers of father—I asked him about his sexual relationship with his wife.

"We had sex for the first time, twice over the week-end. In many ways I am confused about it. That it is not right. We are no longer married. I was brought up to wait until you were married. I always had such a strong guilt complex when I was single and had intercourse. She could be someone's sister. But sex was very enjoyable this past weekend. Much more than previously. The last time was one of the best and longest I ever had. In the past there were times I would come very fast. A feeling to get it over with as rapidly as possible. At times she is aggressive, verbally, she would make a few hints; I felt it was a man's job to do all the advances. This made me angry at times."

He was praised at his improvement and given some of the basic facts about sexuality, e.g. that both partners are on the seesaw and both can be aggressive in the sexual act. Secondly, his "parental" voice comes on too strongly when he is having sex, making him feel guilty and thus to get sex over as quickly as possible (there was no need to raise the issue of other psychodynamic forces).

In her third session, Mrs. Zelda stated that for the first time she and Tom were able to sit down and communicate about how they managed their finances in the past, and how they would handle their money if they remarried. "I'm apt to be more impulsive than he is, but he is much too conservative. He doesn't want to buy things on credit. Although it ended in a slight argument, we really talked.

In his fourth session, Mr. Zelda commented: "She is trying to counsel me as to the way I should spend my earnings. She said, if we go back, we should each give a little—I should be less conservative and she, more restraining. It got a little heated toward the end. I started to retaliate by becoming silent, then realized this was an old "record" and said, let's talk about it further at another time."

Mrs. Zelda opened her fourth session by commenting: "We had a very nice week. No longer any of the silent treatment when we argue. You are helping both of us. He looks forward to his sessions with you."

When I saw Mr. Zelda at his fifth session a few days later, I told him Jill said everything was coming along fine. Mr. Zelda seemed very pleased and stated: "I've been seeing her every day. We've been getting along fine. We went to a dance, and for the first time I didn't react when she was doing a Charleston step. I know what she is afraid of—that I'll revert back to my previous behavior. I have no intention of doing that."

Mrs. Zelda began her fifth session by relating the following dream: "I came to your home for an appointment. I was greeted by a bevy of fine and lovely daughters. You were friendly. One of your daughters and I are sneaking cake off the table.

"The dream was full of fun and happiness. I had a nice, warm feeling toward you, as though I was one of your family. Tom and I are getting along fine. I have a sense of pride in voicing every thought I have up here. I have never disciplined myself. You mentioned why fight over little things. The cake was a special cake we used to have on special occasions in the sorority house."

(Comment: Instead of dealing with the dyadic transference level—she has become one of my daughters—I focused on her current marital situation by asking: "In your marriage you would like to have your cake and eat it too?")

Mrs. Zelda replied: "Yes, on two levels. I would like it to be "we," but Tom is such a strong personality. I was competing with him. I was afraid he would take complete control of me and turn me into a passive, submissive nonentity."

In her sixth and seventh sessions, Mrs. Zelda reported increasing harmony and love in her relationship to Tom. "We are getting along fine. My birthday is in three weeks, and we would like to get remarried on that day. He was elated but said he would like to get your opinion."

In his sixth and last session, Mr. Zelda said: "We are getting along fine. Sexually it has been great. I had a dream: I'm with this person I work with. We are at Harvard—the school of business administration. He passes and I failed. We are co-workers. He is only interested in one phase of the operation, bonds, whereas I am interested in all types of securities."

I asked him why he thought his marriage had failed. He replied that he had not really understood himself, his wife, and what marriage entailed. I commented: "You focused on one area in your marriage and missed the total picture, like your co-worker who is only interested in one phase. I see no reason why you and Jill cannot remarry. If a major problem arises, call for an appointment."

In her eighth and final session, Mrs. Zelda stated: "We are getting along fine. We are getting married on my birthday. I think I have grown up and so has he. Like he enjoys me more as I am, not as he wants me to be. I have no complaints in my relationship to him now. If we have any future problems, this will be the first place we will come to. Tom planned to come in with me today but had an emergency meeting. He said to thank you for everything."

THE CONCURRENT APPROACH WITH A VERY SKILLED THERAPIST

The following couple, the Mathildas, received the concurrent approach because of marital as well as individual problems. Because of the wealth of clinical material, only the high points of the first six sessions will be presented. Each spouse was seen three times weekly—the entire therapy lasting three years for both individuals.

The Mathildas were referred by the school counselor who was treating their only child for academic underachievement. Mrs. Mathilda was a beautiful, well-dressed woman in her mid-twenties, who had worked as a model prior to her marriage eight years ago. Mr. Mathilda was fifteen years older than his wife. A wealthy executive, college graduate, of serious mien. He was quite concerned about his wife and child. He was well dressed and appeared to be the typical executive in his grey flannel suit, grey hair, and dark horn-rimmed glasses. He stated that he had been very upset for the past month when his wife told him that she loved another man—a neighbor. He blamed himself because his work involved considerable out-of-state traveling.

Mrs. Mathilda's main complaint was her husband's sexual rejection of her for long periods of time.

Mr. Mathilda first tended to maintain that the marriage was satisfactory; he did admit her complaint about infrequent sex was valid. But that now that he was approaching her sexually, she was rejecting him.

Mrs. Mathilda, an only child, graduated from high school, won a beauty contest and became a model. Her parents had wanted her to go on to college and were very unhappy at her becoming a model. Her father, a skilled tradesman and deeply religious, worked hard to support his family. Her mother returned to work as a telephone operator when she began high school. Mrs. Mathilda frequently was told by her teachers that she did not work up to her capacity. She got average grades but was very active in the drama group and had wanted to go on the stage. Her father would have none of that but agreed to her becoming a model and living at home.

She met her husband while modeling at a convention. "Maybe our courtship was too smooth. A kiss goodnight was a peck on the cheek. He wasn't a passionate lover during our courtship, even after we got engaged. He never tried to get fresh with me. I was impressed that he was different in this respect to my other experiences with men who think every model goes to bed. I interpreted his "coolness" as hard to get, and this made him even more desirable. I fell in love with him. She next described a wonderful honeymoon in Europe, at which time she became pregnant—both had wanted a baby.

"We both got along wonderfully until my sixth month of pregnancy when I began to show that I was pregnant. It was then when he began to change. He no longer approached me sexually and began to drink excessively at social functions. Later his drinking became embarrassing to me. After the baby was born, his sexual attention dropped considerably to an average of about once in four months. I was so busy nursing the baby and enjoying this that at first I didn't mind. Later, this sexual rejection was hard to take, but now I have grown used to it. With the way I feel now, I am rejecting him. Last New Year's Eve at our country club dance,

I met this neighbor. When he danced with me I could sense he was deeply attracted to me. The way he held me. I felt strongly attracted to him and did my best to put him out of my mind. He doesn't know how I feel about him. I told my husband about this, but he says it will go away. This plus the way I feel about my husband has me in a depressed state. It is fortunate for us that the counselor recommended seeing you, otherwise my husband would not have consented."

Mr. Mathilda was pleasant and cooperative as he spoke: "I have a beautiful wife whom I love. I feel she has problems for which I am responsible. I have no complaints about my marriage. At times I feel my wife is selfish. Also, and again, only at times she seems to have little interest in the job of being a housewife. All in all I'm not unhappy with our marriage and hope our troubles can be straightened out."

He described their courtship as being very smooth and uneventful. "Our honeymoon was very nice and no problems. She was a virgin. I felt marriage was the best thing that could have happened to me. I had a young and beautiful wife, whom I loved and who loved me." He described himself as rather stable but sensitive. "I don't have any feelings of inferiority. I either do it good or I don't try." Upon graduation he went into the family business.

Mrs. Mathilda began her second session by stating: "I was tempted not to see you again but am glad I did. At this point I don't think I love Jim (Mr. Mathilda) anymore. The tension is getting greater each day between us, and I know it is my fault. Before he was rejecting me, now I am rejecting him. His excuse was that he only wanted one child and refused to use a contraceptive, but I would not have objected to him using them. He approached me after his visit with you but I rejected him. I am still angry. The last time we had sex was three months ago. He has always been too fast. I've never let him know it. Recently he said he has always felt inadequate sexually."

In his second session Mr. Mathilda was asked about his wife's complaint of infrequent sex. "She has a valid argument there. Off and on she has complained about my lack of interest sexually. I'm afraid to have more than one child because I travel a good deal and felt I could not be a good father to more than one. I was very surprised when Donna told me she was in love with this man and me. This man doesn't know about Donna's feelings about him. Donna is willing to do anything to save our marriage. I had a dream last night: In bed with my wife, I reach over to touch her. She refused me. The scene changes. I am walking in the country and am surprised to see I am carrying Donna's purse."

In his associations he stated that "this has happened in reality too—the sexual rejection—my fault previously. For some reason I didn't have much of a sexual drive after the boy was born. Once every two months was sufficient. Recently she has refused me. We had sex quite frequently, two or three times a week, until she got quite pregnant. We didn't have any sex before marriage. I knew she was a virgin. I don't understand my carrying her purse. On our farm I usually carry a rifle. I'm afraid to get angry." When asked whether he had ever lost his temper, he replied: "At age seven the neighbor kid and I got into an argument about something. I began to hit him with a shovel. I don't know what would have happened if the other children hadn't stopped me."

In her third session Mrs. Mathilda brought in her first dream which she was hesitant to tell me: "Jim and I are at a resort. A couple is in a room. It was her birthday. She had cake with a very long candle on it. We had previously visited them. We leave and Jim goes to our room alone. I am sitting in the lobby waiting for the other man to come out. I waited and waited, then I woke up. "In the dream this man was spending the night in this woman's room. The candle was very high. I was fascinated by its size. I was a tomboy as a child. I played baseball with the boys. I loved drama and was always in the school plays. I enjoyed being on the stage. No stage fright."

I comment that in the dream her husband leaves her alone in the lobby and goes to their room.

She replied: "In Canada we were at this resort and there was this dance. He went to bed early so that he could arise early to go fishing. He left me alone, although he knew there was a man who was very interested in me and danced with me most of the time. Jim doesn't care to dance and I love to. Was it unconscious, to see how much he could trust me with that man. He hardly ever set his foot down and set limits. He dislikes fights and arguments."

(Comment: In this dream we see two important levels: her first hint at penis envy—boys have long candles; and the unconscious awareness that her husband sets her up to act out his anxiety about his unconscious passive defense. She becomes the vehicle for this. This is her first dream, and no interpretation was given.)

In his third session, Mr. Mathilda stated that he had been drinking more recently. I suggest that this should be explored as to its meanings and that he lie on the couch so that he would find it easier to associate.

He readily accepted and commented: "What is this going to lead to? I am quite jealous of her. I felt jealous of her when she danced with someone at the country club party last night." His associations were all about his jealousy. At the end of the session I asked how he would proceed if he were to woo his wife again.

Thus in the fourth session he commented: "The roses and candy worked beautifully. An hour later we embraced and we both cried. We went to sleep, and we awoke early in the morning. I reached over and made a gesture, and we had sex. The first time in three months. It was wonderful."

(Comment: This is an example of a triangular transactional feed back. His reaction to being put on the couch mobilizing his anxiety about his passive defenses which was neutralized by his having sex and proving he was a man. On the other hand, there could be other reasons: a three-month abstinence, a receptive wife responding to his gift of roses and candy, her reaction to me, and so on.)

"I had a dream last night: Someone had a plastic gun, but shooting real bullets. I was shooting at people but only to wound. I was afraid Donna would get the gun and shoot to kill. She ran terrified. First I bury the gun, but then I dig it up.

"The gun was rather complicated. It didn't look like a gun, but functioned like one. I first buried it then later dug it up. When I dug it up it was a model plane. Beautiful. I find myself wondering what Donna's reaction was last night. I felt rather anxious coming here this morning and annoyed. I try to keep from prying into other people's business. I don't like to hear gossip."

(Comment: The usual reaction to invasion of privacy).

Mrs. Mathilda in her fifth session and seen the same day commented: "Lot of funny things have happened. Jim is beginning to bite back at me. He was in a gay mood yesterday—with a dozen roses and two boxes of candy. He is changing. He seems so nice and different last night. Did he tell you his dream this morning. It was about a plastic gun that shot real bullets. He buried it, and later dug it up. It was a model plane. Something that changed from something deadly to something that was not. Jim has changed. Why the gun?"

I asked what a gun could represent in a dream.

"In this case it was a toy. It is a child's weapon. All of a sudden he has become an opposite person. About four this morning he reached over. I responded (begins to cry). I had no feeling for him at all. He hasn't acted like much of a man sexually in the last few years."

I ask: "What do you expect in a man?"

"One who won't take any guff from me. I am spoiled and I know it. I need someone who can be strong with me. Jim has permitted me to do things as I wanted. Someone who won't take me to a dance and sit and talk business and let me dance with someone else's husband. Jim is his mother's favorite son. The night before we were married she said to me, 'Nice to have you in the family,' but she said to Jim, 'Why don't you wait.'

In her sixth session she stated: "He thinks things are improving. If anything, each day is a little worse. Yesterday I was jumping at our son. When I called you I was very upset (she had called me on the phone very depressed and given reassurance). I didn't want him near me. Yet I don't want to reject him. Now he wants to know why. We got into a big fight the other night. He started to scream at me! 'You are going to listen to me.' I started to laugh. I didn't care that he was mad, I was glad. He said, 'I have kept this inside of me for years.'"

(Comment: I gave her the interpretation that Jim was as much a man as anyone else, but that he was afraid of his anger—he does not get just angry but unconsciously murderous. So he holds it back. But in doing that he also inhibits all his other emotions. So he "buries his gun." This interpretation shows an aspect of the concurrent approach where the partner's dream is used to help the spouse understand the behavior of her partner. Another important element is that the concurrent approach opens up avenues of communication between the couple. They discuss their dreams, contents of their hours, and so on.)

Mr. Mathilda began his sixth session by commenting that things at home were very relaxed and friendly. "I had a dream: I am walking to work with a full field pack. I get tired and wind up in a room just left by a pint-sized officer. I lay down in his bed and fall asleep. When he returns I get up to leave. I start to dress and find stones in my socks. I

seem to remember the man from another dream in which he was a guide.
"This pint-sized officer was a guide. But where was my rifle? I woke up
feeling very annoyed. Am I trying to punish myself?"
(Comment: He was given the interpretation that he was angry at me.
That the analysis involves a lot of "work" and is not only slow—"walking"
but also painful—"full field pack" and "stones in his socks." So he depre-
ciates me as a "pint-sized guide" but that on the other hand I am going to
"guide" him to a better type of marriage and a better self-image—all
therapy involves suggestion.)

This couple illustrates the utilization of the concurrent approach in a couple having both individual and marital problems.
Intensive therapy was necessary to solve their problems.

NOTES

1. Bela Mittlemann: The concurrent analysis of married couples, *Psychoanal Quart*, 17:182, 1948.
2. Bernard L. Greene; Marital disharmony: concurrent analysis of husband and wife. I. Preliminary report, *Dis Nerv System*, 21:1, 1960;
   Alfred P. Solomon and Bernard L. Greene: Marital disharmony: concurrent analysis of husband and wife by the same psychiatrist, An
   analysis of the therapeutic elements and action, *Dis Nerv System*,
   24:105, 1963; Bernard L. Greene and Alfred P. Solomon: Marital
   disharmony: concurrent psychoanalytic therapy of husband and wife
   by the same psychiatrist, the triangular transference transactions,
   Amer J Psychotherapy, 17:443, 1963; and Alfred P. Solomon and
   Bernard L. Greene: Concurrent Psychoanalytic Therapy in Marital
   Disharmony, in *The Psychotherapies of Marital Disharmony* (Bernard
   L. Greene, Ed.). New York, Free Press, 1965, pp. 103–120. In these
   articles, for purposes of clarifying indications, we divided our patients
   into two groups. The first group included those couples who spontaneously sought help primarily because of marital problems, often
   because of the threat of impending divorce. In the second group,
   concurrent treatment was recommended to the partners of spouses
   already in individual office or hospital therapy because of clinical
   indications for the improvement of the marriage relationships or for
   overcoming therapeutic impasses.
3. Franz Alexander: Psychoanalysis and Psychotherapy, In *Science and
   Psychoanalysis, III. Psychoanalysis and Human Values* (Jules H.
   Masserman, Ed.). New York, Grune & Stratton, 1960, 250–259.
4. Clifford J. Sager: The diagnosis and treatment of marital conflicts,
   Amer J Psychoanal, 27:142, 1967.

5. Bernard L. Greene and Alfred P. Solomon: Triangular transference transactions, *Amer J Psychotherapy, 17:*443, 1963.
6. The transference neurosis is a Freudian psychoanalytic term to describe a symbolic reaction to the therapist, in which the feelings and re-actions of the patient or analysand toward important people of child-hood are currently projected onto the therapist.
7. Franz Alexander: The psychodynamics of psychotherapy in light of the learning theory, *Amer J Psychiat, 120:*440, 1963.

XXV

THE CONJOINT APPROACH IN MARITAL DISHARMONY

For many years, the literature of social workers has been replete with references to joint interviewing of couples with marital problems. It was not until 1959, however, that Don D. Jackson[1] first introduced the term *conjoint therapy* in psychiatric circles. In 1962, Watson[2] succinctly described this approach. Recently Satir[3] has written about the conjoint approach. In the conjoint approach both marital partners are seen together by the same therapist in the same session.[4] The conjoint technique was used in counseling about one half (44%) of the conflicted couples and is the most commonly used approach. The conjoint technique was used in the intensive treatment of marital discord in one sixth of the couples.

The indications for conjoint therapy in marital discord are the same as we previously described in 1964:[5]

1. Therapeutic impasse[6] with the concurrent approach.
2. Paranoid or suspicious behavior of one spouse who reacts with anxiety and distortion of the comments which either the therapist or the partner are reputed to have stated in the individual session.
3. Economic—the cost of the treatment is halved. (There is ample evidence that the decision as to which spouse gets therapy depends to a large extent on economic considerations.)
4. Explosiveness of the marital situation demands speed in bringing order to the family environment.
5. Couples in which the problems in marriage are largely of an acting-out nature.

6. Need to foster communication between the partners.
7. Couples who perceive relationships between events and their own responses only when confronted with them acutely. These couples lack capacity to traverse time and space, which is necessary for gaining appreciation and conviction about such experiences and their meaning.[7]
8. To point out not merely the differences but the possibility of complementation in the transactions between the couple.

The contraindications for conjoint therapy in marital disharmony occur in some spouses with severe psychoses, with excessive sibling rivalry attitudes, and with family secrets.

In indicated couples I found that seeing both partners together in the same session provided more access to the marital dynamics.[8] This increased awareness will be presented later in this chapter in the clinical extract of Mr. and Mrs. Joyce, where the conjoint sessions revealed that the couple on a deeper psychological level had mutual strivings and interdependent needs, although on a conscious level their distrust was quite deep and their hostility violently expressed.

In some couples, conjoint sessions gives the advantage of heightened perception. "There is the immediate advantage of direct observation of the participants in the family problem. This facilitates more objective evaluation of the partners' behavior and limits the need to judge distortion from more indirect data."[9] Witnessing the marital relationships in action affords an opportunity to observe the nonverbal transactions between the partners. With both partners in the session, the therapist can observe the healthier side of the marriage—the positive strivings and values. Where and how the couple join in healthy strivings is more difficult to perceive or infer from individual interviews and easier in the conjoint sessions.

An important advantage of conjoint treatment is the opportunity afforded the partners via the therapist to receive a lesson in how to communicate. Not infrequently one spouse is more verbal than the other, and the therapist can turn to the silent partner and ask his reactions to his partner's comments.

This enables a spouse to express how he really feels when his spouse speaks or behaves in a certain manner.

At times, the couple may appear harmonious during the sessions, but disharmony prevails shortly after leaving the session. When this occurs, it is suggested that they express their conflicts in the office where they can be explored. Similarly, in conjoint sessions, a couple can work out reality problems which they have not been able to solve at home, e.g. financial or management of the children. The dynamics of the conflict which preclude a solution at home can be brought into the open for efforts at a solution while in the office. Further, the setting of limits in the marriage enables the therapist to structure the marriage for the exploration of the variables underlying the disharmony.

Another advantage of the conjoint technique is the leverage it places on the couple to reexamine their reality testing. When an interpretation of feelings or behavior, frequently in terms of content and relationships in their transactions, is made to one partner, the other spouse also hears it and may further discuss it outside the sessions. Not only does this improve communication between the spouses, but in effect, each spouse indirectly provides the therapist with a "co-therapist," who may reinforce the interpretations made during the session. As Watson[10] notes: "While there is a possibility and even a probability that interpretations will be used for nontherapeutic purposes, the general summation-effect is reinforcement of, and mounting pressure toward, reality testing by both spouses. . . . The speed with which conjoint therapy improves reality testing is a distinct advantage." A clinical observation I have repeatedly observed. I shall now present the conjoint approach to marital problems as can be utilized by therapists of varying clinical experience.

THE CONJOINT APPROACH WITH A MODERATELY SKILLED THERAPIST

The following couple with marital disharmony had seven conjoint sessions over a period of three months. The husband had called in an acute crisis saying that he came home unexpectedly from work and found his wife entertaining Jack, an old boyfriend of hers. Jack appeared flustered, embarrassed, and after making some flimsy excuse left. After some questioning, his wife admitted that nothing had happened, but that it could have.

The Jacquelines were a young attractive couple in their mid-twenties, married three years and had one child. Mr. Jacqueline opened the session by stating he had had a premonition about something like this happening for the past two years. "I felt we were not responding sexually to each other. I found my wife with Jack, and only because I arrived early can I say we have a chance to save our marriage. Nothing happened and I believe her. She has never lied to me. We have had a sexual problem. My wife is very attractive and excites me easily. The problem is that I have failed to help her reach a climax. She feels inadequate in that there is something wrong with her because she doesn't want to continue sex. In every other way our marriage is what we want, except sex; perhaps this has driven her to look elsewhere. We want to try to solve our problem now before anything else happens. Our problem is that Joy wants everything perfect. She expects romantic love and sex to be a Hollywood production. We go to bed as though we've been married for twenty years. I'm tired one night, she is tired the next, and therefore we rarely are on the same wavelength. Joy says she alternates between being satisfied and dissatisfied about our marriage."

Mrs. Jacqueline appeared straightforward and honest as she said "nothing had happened with this other man, but it could have, had Bob not come home early. I guess I always wanted, as most girls, to have an ideal marriage, but after the first year I began to have doubts. I knew I cared for and respected Bob very much for his business success. But since we had to get married, as I was pregnant, I never felt I had chosen Bob. I became unsure of making love. I didn't enjoy having sex, but I tried to conceal my true feelings. I thought I could do that, but Bob told me he was aware of the true situation. Anyway, I tried to keep it inside, but I became more and more confused. I loved Bob, but when it came to sex, most of the time he didn't excite me. So I wondered whether someone else could arouse me. It so happened that Jack called. He was in town for a convention and called to say hello. Bob was working late, but I invited him over for a drink after I put our son to sleep. When he arrived I put some records on and he only kissed me a few times. Then Bob came home earlier than he planned. After Jack left we talked for hours and our minister came over and talked to us. It was an embarrassing incident. I know it hurt Bob, but since the affair didn't really materialize, Bob was pretty understanding. We started to talk everything out. Our minister thought we needed more help than he could give."

(Comment: The parental backgrounds of both the Jacquelines were upper middle class. Both fathers were successful executives, very religious and well respected in their communities. The Jacquelines had met at a sorority-fraternity dance, he was a sophomore and she, a freshman. Since my clinical impression was that the marriage was basically a good one, no further evaluation was deemed necessary and conjoint therapy recommended.)

In the second session, the Jacquelines commented how much better both felt, although Bob stated he still finds himself angry at what happened and thinking, suppose he had not come home early that evening. Joy then related the following dream: "It was about my girl friend. She was crying because her husband wouldn't forgive her. She had unjustly accused him of infidelity. The scene changes, I met an old boyfriend. He was sad that I had gotten pregnant and married Bob."

In her associations she stated she had the feeling that she had disappointed her parents by getting pregnant; and disappointed Bob in her recent behavior (cries).

Bob interrupted to comment: "When she told her parents she was pregnant, her father was very unhappy, even though our parents are very good friends."

I asked how he felt about impregnating her.

"I had planned it that way. I was very angry when she didn't want to marry me. I had previously proposed to her, and she turned me down. She was enjoying college and didn't want to settle down. I asked her to meet me at a friend's apartment, as he had gone home for the weekend."

I pointed out to both of them that, although he had planned to impregnate her, she was not an unwilling victim. "You can talk in other places than in an apartment. Apparently, part of you wanted to have sex, and no precautions were taken. Thus both of you are responsible for the pregnancy." I suggested that since both had been tied down too much without taking a vacation since marriage, they go away for a week.

Upon their return from their vacation, they both reported they had had a wonderful time. "It was like a second honeymoon. Everything worked out fine in every area." Mr. Jacqueline reported a dream he had last night: "Mother tells me we should separate. That she would raise our son as Joy is an unfit mother."

Mr. Jacqueline commented that he was still disturbed about what had happened. Even on the vacation he kept thinking, what would have happened if he had not come home early. "My mother was very jealous of my father for years, and without reason. The same suspicions I have had the last two years. That's why I came home early that night. I have on other occasions too that Joy doesn't know about." (An excellent example of the introjection of the "parental" voices in his "records.")

Mrs. Jacqueline opened the fourth conjoint session by stating that they were both getting along very well. "It is five weeks since we started coming here. I had a dream last night where Bob goes over to have a neighborly chat and is gone all afternoon helping the man paint his garage. When he returns I am very angry and say: You always do more than required."

I ask, what is the message in the dream.

Joy replies, she doesn't know.

Bob comments: "That I am always doing something extra. Like I impregnated her (laughs)."

Joy then relates how she had never had intercourse until the night she was impregnated. "I knew I should not have gone to the apartment. I knew what he had in mind. But I thought he would have known what precautions to take. I didn't know he planned to impregnate me. I was furious with him when I missed my period. I did not want to get married at that time."

Mrs. Jacqueline opened the fifth session by stating that she had been very angry since our last meeting. In fact, she was dreaming all night and woke up very angry.

There were two themes running through all the dreams: her stupidity at not protecting herself against impregnation, and a series of obstacles in reaching her destination—many detours on a road. She was given the interpretation that she had never fully worked through her original anger at her impregnation, plus her guilt; that was why she was punishing herself by creating all obstacles in her path.

In the last two sessions (sixth and seventh) both reported that things were very much better. Mrs. Jacqueline stated that "Bob still needles me, but less and less." Mr. Jacqueline commented that he felt things had been settled and that they felt they could work out their problem themselves. "I still play that old 'record,' but not as often."

Both seemed happy and therapy was interrupted. They were told to call me should any further problems arise that they could not handle by themselves.

THE CONJOINT APPROACH WITH A SKILLED THERAPIST

The following couple with marital disharmony illustrates both an indication for the conjoint approach by a skilled therapist as well as the need to change therapeutic technique because of a treatment impasse with the concurrent approach.

Mrs. Joyce was originally referred twelve years ago for psychoanalysis because of an intractable peptic ulcer that had resisted medical treatment. After two years of therapy, her pain was gone, only to return in six months. She strongly felt this was due to the continuous frustration of her emotional needs by her husband. He reluctantly agreed to see another psychiatrist because she put severe pressure upon him. After a brief period of therapy, both he and his therapist agreed that nothing was being accomplished and further therapeutic efforts discontinued. Mrs. Joyce reacted with great anger and, after considerable quarreling, left home. After a week's absence, Mr. Joyce was finally able to locate her. He pleaded with her to return home, promising he would do anything she requested. At this time both spouses were started on concurrent therapy. At the end of six months, because of a therapeutic impasse, the conjoint was attempted.

The first conjoint session started quietly, but it quickly changed when Mrs. Joyce turned on her spouse with a vituperative attack reducing him to a nonentity. (In conjoint sessions, one can expect stormy sessions quite often.)

In the next session, Mrs. Joyce reported that her husband's nightmare had awakened her. I woke him up and asked him what he was dreaming about, and he told me this dream: "Walking somewhere with an Indian woman. I had a five dollar bill in my hand. See a boarded-up church. She said: You got to pray. I said: You cannot, pointing to the boarded-up condition of the church. With that she grabbed my money, and I tried to keep her away."

Mr. Joyce interrupted by commenting that he was asleep when his wife tried to awaken him. He had struck out, hitting the nightstand so hard his hand was black and blue. "Lucky, I did not strike her. She asked me my dream and wrote it down."

Both were asked to associate to the dream. The associations were mostly of two themes, firstly, whether the conjoint approach would be helpful, although both were curious as to how the other felt about it, and secondly, mutual recriminations about their lack of communication.

Mr. Joyce felt his wife was like the squaw, who gave little emotionally and was out for his money.

Mrs. Joyce angrily retorted that this was not so and proceeded to relate an incident that she felt refuted this. "I had called him to come home from the neighbors to do something with his children and me. I said: 'Do you realize why I called you to come home?' He replied: 'Yes! To get them off your back so you can take a nap.' I was so angry, but I contained myself. I feel sorry for myself. He has no sensitivity to life at all. He thinks everybody is out for himself, like he is, that everyone is out to steal his measly five dollars. He doesn't realize that there are some people who give of themselves. And when I confront him with the truth, he fights back. Besides, he calls me a screwball."

During this recitation Mr. Joyce was silent but his eyes were cold with rage. When asked if he was angry, he denied he was.

When it was pointed out that his facial expressions denied this, he angrily replied: "Yes, I am. A series of unjust accusations. I feel she exaggerates, and her interpretations of my behavior are not true. With her we live not only today, but twenty years ago."

It was pointed out that the purpose of the joint sessions was to improve communications between both in an atmosphere where both could express their feelings. The tone of each gradually reached normal qualities and both left in a pleasant mood. This session was most informative in the interplay and display of nonverbal expressions of feelings that are not usually present in the one-to-one dyadic therapeutic situations.

Gradually the home situation became progressively more peaceful.

Mrs. Joyce began the sixth month of conjoint therapy by stating: "He is beginning to control himself much better. Sunday, for the first time in our marriage he was so relaxed around the house. He was pleasant. I told him how pleased I was, but that night he had a nightmare. I asked him about it. He said a woman was making love to him but was smothering him. Then he said he was sitting in a chair, and a woman in back of him was trying to choke him."

Mr. Joyce related that he did not remember the dream at all. The dream was used as a point of departure to explore his reactions when he felt closeness to his wife. Mrs. Joyce gained additional insight into her husband's reaction patterns. There was gradual improvement in communication and interaction between the couple; and, six months later therapy was discontinued.

THE CONJOINT APPROACH WITH A VERY SKILLED THERAPIST

The following couple with marital disharmony illustrates an indication for the conjoint approach by a very skilled therapist.

The Jacquettes, married ten years, came in together for their first interview at the insistence of Mrs. Jacquette. The Jacquettes concurred in their respective beliefs that there is virtually no communication in their marriage: Neither one tells the other what each is doing, and Agnes states this condition has produced extreme tension between them and has spilled over onto the children. She says that she wants to feel that when she suggests something, that she has Jim's wholehearted approval. She feels that while he is making some attempt at supporting her in this direction, that these efforts at best are superficial.

Jim concurred with his wife's complaints and stated: "We see things quite differently. There is no mutual understanding between us, and this void has been present right from the start of our marriage. It has always been very hard for me to express what I feel."

He is convinced that the marital problem arises from the fact that they have never gotten to the basic problems surrounding the marriage. The decision for seeking help was mutually decided upon. Jim comments that he has his own successful business that he himself started just before his marriage. He has a good relationship with his employees and customers.

The Jacquettes agree that there is "no warmth" in the home, with either themselves or between them and the children. Their social life has been maintained somewhat. Agnes states that she really felt she loved Jim until three years ago. For the past three years there has been total avoidance of any sexual relationship between them. Both spouses indicate that there hasn't been any real personal gratification in sexual relations. They both agreed that their wedding night was a "complete disaster." Jim had been unable to complete the act, and this initial experience resulted in a great lack of self-confidence which has never really left him. Since then, he has hardly ever initiated sexual activity for fear always that he would not be able to follow through in the completion of the act.

Agnes stated that she had sensed Jim's inability to obtain or give sexual gratification at the beginning of their marriage and on the wedding night. (It was obvious during the interview that she was really challenging his manliness.) She hoped that whatever his problem was in this regard, it would be resolved. This was communicated with real anger and disgust.

Jim added that he had had a classical psychoanalysis for four years with four visits weekly. It was terminated after they had "reached an impasse." Although the decision to terminate was mutual, for the past two years he has had sporadic visits with his analyst. In assessing his period of analysis, Jim stated that for as long as he could remember he has been "role playing." He indicated that he has always had difficulty in being able to judge people's reactions and that because of this he has found it difficult to judge how he should act in relation to them. He said the reason for undergoing analysis was fear he would act out his homosexual fantasies. Agnes interrupted that she hated his analyst, since he would never talk to her, and she resented this!

I outlined my procedure: two individual diagnostic sessions and a conjoint diagnostic and disposition session at which time I would tell them both my impressions and recommendations.

In her diagnostic sessions, Agnes indicated that she suspected infidelity. Jim has a sustained pattern of being away from home Friday or Saturday evenings, ostensibly to go to the movies, but that movies don't let out at two or three in the morning. I have never asked what he does because perhaps I am a coward. So many things have been going wrong that I guess I didn't want to add to the already existing complications.

We also have financial disagreements. Jim's idea of success is having a nice home, a maid and extensive vacations. I feel he needs material things to bolster his ego because he is not big enough inside to fulfill his role as husband and father adequately.

During their two-year courtship, Agnes stated that they saw each other practically every day. She described their courtship as having been a very happy period in their lives. There had not been any premarital sex. Both were very moral and religious, and both their respective fathers were ministers. However, Jim had appeared pretty aggressive, and there had been extensive petting. They enjoyed each other's company and had the same cultural interests. During their courtship there had been no evidence of Jim's inability to adequately fulfill her emotional needs and gratifications.

An only child for the first six years, she had been overindulged not only by her parents but by all the relatives. All this attention was shattered by the arrival of her twin brothers. At first she was angry and jealous, but after a few years she got over this feeling. Conspicuous in both sessions was the theme of anger at Jim's former analyst, not only the effect he had on Jim, but also his excluding her from any discussion about the lack of progress in their marriage.

In his individual sessions, Jim was much more verbal in his concerns regarding his marriage than he had been in the initial conjoint. He reported that Agnes did not fulfill his emotional needs. He had sought and needed warmth and affection for a very long period in his life which he had never received. Though he did not think so at the time, he feels now that his marriage to Agnes was basically not borne out of love but because it was the thing to do. He stated that Agnes had never really actively shown any degree of warmth or affection to him after their marriage as she did during their courtship. When she did now, he shied away from response because of his concern and inability to know how to react.

With regard to a complaint made by his wife about "financial disagreement" that he was preoccupied with material things, he stated he guessed she was right, since this was an easier way to demonstrate manliness—father and provider. Likewise, in regard to his wife's concern over possible infidelity, he stated that this was certainly not true. His excursions from home on Friday or Saturday nights were to go to the movies as a form of running away, though he did indicate later that these occasions also were in pursuit of homosexual fantasies which were never carried out.

His childhood centered about a strong, seductive but rejecting mother and a nonexistent father who was always buried in his study. He described his social life in high school as having been virtually nil. His relationships were basically centered among five schoolmates—all identified as being top academically but all of whom were having "dating problems." His few female dates were "adolescent disasters." His first homosexual fantasy began in his senior year when he was elected class president.

At the CDD, the Jacquettes appeared extremely receptive to treatment. I felt the prognosis, ego strength, and motivation to change were good. Since there was no family secret, I suggested a trial period of conjoint sessions with a target date of three months.

The Jacquettes received forty conjoint sessions, once weekly, over a period of eighteen months, with marked improvement in their marriage in all areas.

In the first conjoint session, Mrs. Jacquette reported one dream: "I was climbing a very steep cliff. Found it very difficult. People watching me struggle and no one offering assistance. Finally, a man gives me his hand and assists me."

In her associations she identified the man as her family physician, the personification of a solid, compassionate, helpful man, a solid person. "The opposite of my husband" (note the needle!).

When Jim was asked what he saw in his wife's dream, he replied: "The steep hill is the therapy and it is going to be difficult." (Jim has had four years of psychoanalysis and is more sophisticated psychologically.)

I agree, but also comment that she is very angry at her husband and needles him, he withdraws, then she complains that he rejects her. In the dream she sees me as the man who offers her a helping hand. I wonder out loud why she makes things so difficult for herself, climbing a steep hill.

Jim was next asked whether he had had any dreams.

He replied all week he had recurring dreams which were full of hostility and anger. All evidenced an underlying struggle, a battle of some kind and there was both, danger and great anger.

I posed a question to Agnes: "Are you aware of the tremendous rage in your husband?"

To this she replied: Not always because I don't think it shows, he has rarely shouted at me in our ten years of marriage.

I comment that Jim is afraid of the tremendous emotions within himself. When he curbs it in one area, it's curbed in other areas as well. I suggest that in my approach I encourage the couple to reach out to the limit of their anxieties. On this note, I ask when was the last time they had a date.

Mrs. Jacquette replied that not for several months. I ask her, what she would like to do? She replied: "Go out for dinner and then to a play." Since this was acceptable to Jim, it was agreed upon.

He closed the session by adding: "I've always been aware of my anger. When I was a kid I hit my brother on the neck with a stick after an argument. When he died ten years later from cancer, I vividly recall his mentioning this incident to me prior to his death. I've had an awful long history of controlling not only my emotions but anger as well, and this has included embarrassment, a propensity to cry, and feelings of love."

In the second conjoint session, both reported a good week and their date had been a lot of fun. The following three sessions dealt with two themes, hostility on the part of Mrs. Jacquette toward her mother in relation to the twins and guilt about these hostile impulses, and anxiety dreams on the part of Jim in which he is seeking something and unable to find it.

In the sixth session, Mrs. Jacquette reported that the past week Jim had been cold and rejecting and preoccupied. I had a dream last night: "I am engaged to Ted Kennedy. I am at their mansion. We were always together, but he always moved away. His whole family disapproved of me. A relative arrives. He makes some remarks—heckling me. Saying that I wasn't good enough for him.

"I woke up feeling very sad. I've never felt accepted by my friends or relatives. Yet I know they all liked me. Jim was the first person I really dated. I always expected him to stop seeing me. People have always told me I was very attractive, yet, I don't feel that way."

I ask why she expects to be rejected.

Jim commented that he always felt he had married a very attractive wife, but somehow he couldn't express his feelings to her. "I've been dreaming every night, the same theme. It's not easy to tell you the dream: I am attending a convention. Some conversation that one of the men, prominent in the field, was a homosexual. Most of the dream was spent in trying to find out if he really was. I had sympathy for him. Also some desires on my part toward him."

In his associations he talked about how he was trying to overcome his problem but finding it difficult.

(Comment: I told him the problem is not love for men but a defense against his hostile, competitive feelings with them—the prominent man was perhaps the therapist and on a deeper level his father. As a little boy he wanted to displace his father and have all of mothers love and affection. But to a little boy, father is a giant and the little boy fears severe retaliation—so he runs away, just as in Jack and the Bean Stalk, where Jack wants to steal the hen that lays the golden egg (mother) and runs away from the frightening giant. "I don't hate you father, I love you." Thus homosexuality is nothing more than a defense against hostile competitive feelings. Every child has to solve this problem in one way or another. (A good example of the triangular transference neurosis—his wife has previously equated me with Ted Kennedy and mobilized his competitive feelings toward me.) I actively suggest that since it is now six months since the onset of our therapy, they begin to attempt sex. For him to make an attempt to reach her to the level of his anxiety. No matter how little the reaching out to her, she was not to react with anger but to encourage him.

In the next session, Jim proudly reported that they had sexual relations, the first in three years.

Mrs. Jacquette, smiling happily, concurred that their sex was most enjoyable. "We have had a better week. Jim has not been as cross. More freedom in talking. Not so critical toward the children. The entire atmosphere in the home has changed. The children are happy now. I had a dream: You and another man here. Your office is dimly lit. Before I could sit down I had to move a bunch of papers off your couch. I felt warmly toward you. In the dream I was disgusted that I had to move all the things before I could sit down. Perhaps I am rearranging my thoughts and feelings."

Mr. Jacquette added: "I've been thinking about what you said at the last session. Finally I gathered up courage and approached Agnes, and we had sex. That night I had a highly charged dream: I am visiting you at your home office. I was told to take notes, since you were moving out. You asked me to check to see if all your things had been moved. This bothered me, since I didn't want to let you down. I walk down to the pool. A fish pool. The water is low and slimy."

In his associations he commented: "The dream had strong sexual connotations. I had a strong erection and discharge during the dream. I was surprised when I woke up, since we had had sex that night. That night we had sex again. Excellent sex."

I ask Mrs. Jacquette how she felt during the act.

She replied: "The best sex we ever had."

He interrupted and commented: "The first night especially. I was so surprised to want sex two nights in a row."

I ask about the pool in the dream.

Jim: "My soul. Basically I am pretty rotten inside. But perhaps not altogether. It was the accumulation of all past sins and inadequacies. I am going to Bermuda and am taking Agnes along. It's both business and pleasure. I have never invited her to come along before."

Upon their return, after two weeks in Bermuda, both commented on the wonderful time they had, like a second honeymoon. Unfortunately Jim's reaction a week later was progressive anxiety and sexual withdrawal from his wife. Mrs. Jacquette became depressed, and her dreams revealed increasing sexual frustration and, finally, fantasies of promiscuity. Repeated interpretations were made of her reacting to his withdrawal as rejection instead of seeing his behavior resulting from severe anxiety due to remobilization of his hostile competitive feelings (with the therapist) and fear of retaliation. Gradually his anxiety decreased and sexual relations resumed. Six months later both reported a good relationship, not only between themselves, but also in the general atmosphere of the family.

Bieber,[11] a psychiatrist with extensive experience treating male homosexuals, recommends encouraging wives to enter therapy parallel with their husbands. A recent study[12] indicates that about one out of six male homosexuals have been or are married. Thus conjoint marital therapy, when there is no family secret should be considered if indicated.

In this chapter the value[13] of conjoint marital therapy in marital disharmony was presented.

NOTES

1. For an excellent presentation on the history of family diagnosis and therapy, see Don D. Jackson and Virginia M. Satir: A review of psychiatric developments in family diagnosis and family therapy, in *Exploring the Base For Family Therapy* (Nathan W. Ackerman, Frances L. Beatman and Sanford N. Sherman, Eds.). New York, Family Service Association of America, 1961, pp. 29–51.
2. Andrew S. Watson: The conjoint psychotherapy of marriage partners, *Amer J Orthopsychiat*, 33:912, 1963.
3. Virginia M. Satir: Conjoint marital therapy, in *The Psychotherapies of Marital Disharmony* (Bernard L. Greene, Ed.). New York, Free Press, 1965, pp. 121–134; and *Conjoint Family Therapy*, Palo Alto, Science and Behavior Books, 1964. See also Jay Haley: Marriage therapy, *Arch Gen Psychiat*, 8:213, 1963.
4. Maxwell Jones (Therapeutic community practice, *Amer J Psychiat*, 122:1275, 1966) describes the "living-learning situation" which is pertinent to what frequently happens in the conjoint sessions. "A living-learning situation implies the analysis of a current interpersonal problem and the immediate face-to-face confrontation of all relevant personnel. Each individual is helped to become aware of the thinking and feeling of the other, and this leads to a more comprehensive and holistic view of the situation as it affects each of the people involved. The term as it is used here applies mainly to conscious awareness of previously unconscious factors." In the same vein Saul L. Brown (personal communication) writes that "the conjoint sessions represent an effort to reduce the 'field resistance' to therapeutic progress. The conjoint session then would reflect the recognition that the patient's inability to change constructively is a function of the psychological field of the patient and his spouse." See also Clifford Sager: Transference in conjoint treatment of married couples, *Arch Gen Psychiat*, 16:185, 1967; Robert A. Ravich: Short-term, intensive treatment of marital discord, *Voices*, 2:42, 1966.

5. Bernard L. Greene and Noel Lustig: Multi-operational Psychotherapies of Marital Disharmony. Paper presented at the annual meeting of the American Psychiatric Association, May 7, 1964, in Los Angeles, California.

6. Ernst Kris has presented many interesting ideas on the subject of impasse in therapy in his article, The recovery of childhood memories in psychoanalysis, *Psychoanal Study Child*, 9:54, 1956. He comments: "The closer we approach the area where repression has lost its power as central defense, the less can the transition from the past to the present become one of the indicators of the progress in analytic work and the less significant will it turn out to be in the recovery of memories and the emergence of a biographical picture." He continues: "The full investment of the casual connections established by the insight into the personal history protects in turn the preconsciously available memories against disappearance from the realm of the ego. Without this protection they can once more become part of the id by repression and by other defense mechanisms (isolation and denial) which will draw them back into the whirl of the primary process." This protection he speaks of can be supplied by conjoint sessions. There the patient has less opportunity to associate freely to the traumatizing experience of the past. Rather, he is induced emotionally to utilize gained and loosely kept insights in a more total, integrated and real context—that of the here-and-now relationships. The dyadic one-to-one relationship, whether in the classic, collaborative or concurrent modalities, is more one-dimensional and one-directional, more persistent, anchored and interlocked with distortions of the therapist-patient interpersonal transactions. The dyadic relationship is more inducive to fantasies and regressive projective indentifications of childhood in which the old "records" are being heard as coming from the therapist. Thus, instead of progressive improvement in the spouse, he seems to circle slowly about an impasse.

7. Arthur A. Miller and Melvin Sabshin: Psychotherapy in psychiatric hospitals, *Arch Gen Psychiat*, 9, 56, 1963.

8. John E. Bell (Contrasting approaches in marital counseling, *Family Process*, 6:16, 1967) has written an excellent article describing the advantages and disadvantages of the individual vis-à-vis the conjoint modalities.

9. Andrew S. Watson, *op. cit.*

10. Andrew S. Watson, *op. cit.*

11. I agree with Irving Bieber (The married male homosexual, *Med Aspects Hum Sexuality*, 3:76, 1969), who states: "In those instances where the married homosexual is oriented toward psychotherapy and inclined toward restoring heterosexuality and preserving his marriage,

the wife (if she is aware of her husband's condition) should also be encouraged to enter treatment. . . ."

12. Marcel T. Saghir, Eli Robbins, and Bonnie Walbran (Homosexuality, *Arch Gen Psychiat*, *21*:219, 1969) in a recent study of eighty-nine male homosexuals found that 14 percent were divorced, 2 percent separated or widowed, and 2 percent were married.
13. R.V. Fitzgerald: Conjoint marital psychotherapy: an outcome and follow-up study, *Family Process*, *8*:261, 1969.

XXVI
THE COMBINED TECHNIQUES IN MARITAL DISHARMONY

In the combined approach in marital disharmony, the conflicted couple is seen in a variety of dyadic and triadic clinical settings. The three types of clinical settings to be described in this chapter include the following:

1. Simple—a combination of individual, concurrent, and conjoint sessions in various purposeful combinations.
2. Conjoint family therapy—where one or more of the children of the couple are included in the therapeutic setting.
3. Combined-collaborative—where each spouse is treated individually by separate therapists and all four individuals meet together at regular intervals.

The combined approach was used in 14 percent of the couples undergoing counseling and in about one sixth of the couples receiving intensive therapy.

The variability in marital patterns and the unpredictable therapeutic course necessitated the technical variations found in the combined approaches. The treatment process in the combined techniques is based on a plan of active support, including environmental manipulation, complementary goals, clarification of role expectations and enactments, redirection of intrapersonal energies, and evocation of "healthier" communication.

An increasing number of therapists[1] are beginning to devote more attention to multipersonal approaches to the treatment of marital disharmony. The work of some group therapists[2] has much to offer the student of the "combined approach." As more and more therapists use multiperson interviews, one notices the gradual development of new therapeutic techniques shared by all of them. Should this process continue, a broader range of treatment possibilities and greater acceptance of multipersonal approaches may ensue. This possibility does not mean that the dyadic one-to-one therapy is to be replaced in marital disharmony, but it does promise greater latitude for therapists in the choice of treatment methods.

A combined approach to therapy differs in many ways from the approaches previously described. When the dyadic and triadic sessions are combined, the interview takes on additional meanings for the participants. The form of the "combined" approach represents various aspects of functioning in the marital relationship. As previously described in the GST (see Ch. I), a human being may be regarded as incorporating three separate systems: an intrapersonal system (the library of "records" in the jukebox), an interpersonal system involving transactions with significant others, and an environmental system responding to an interplay of forces between the individual and society. The three systems are reflected in the combined approach through the use of dyadic and triadic sessions, which alternately focus on the individual, the spouse and the marriage. The process of treatment demonstrates the therapist's dual concern with understanding the origin of feelings in the past and their reenactment in current marital transactions.

The combined technique increases the perceptive awareness of all participants—the couple's as well as the therapist's.[3] In triadic interviews, the aim is to eliminate incongruity and distortions from communication so that covert and overt meanings and messages become identical. The opportunity to experience different environments points up the contrast between individual and multipersonal relationships and brings out different sides of the personality that could well be lost in dyadic treatment. There is a tendency for therapists to make the mistake of assuming that a person will behave in the same way in all situations.[4] The opportunity for feedback through the use of dyadic and triadic sessions furnishes a corrective for the therapist's misperceptions and misinterpretations.

The dyadic and triadic treatment settings deal with different clinical material of the couple. The dyadic sessions reflect the importance of the intrapersonal system of each partner. In the dyadic session, what comes to the fore is the individual's more deeply rooted (unconscious) personality components, whereas in the triadic setting, the "intersocial reality" comes into focus. These two settings offer opportunities to work through different clinical material more adequately material that is complementary. The utilization of multifocal transference phenomena is a cornerstone in the combined approach.

The experience of the triadic session is an important phenomenon. Experiencing the difference between the dyadic and triadic situations being reacted to differently and observing the repercussions of one's behavior and verbalizations on two or more individuals or its interpretations stimulate a desire to understand one's reactions. The triadic interviews thus promote tolerance for the other person's uniqueness and integrity and represent a shift from "ego centered private fields to fields of mutual orientation."[5]

In the triadic session, the healthy and unhealthy transactions can be experienced by the couple. Inappropriate behavior can be clarified on the spot. Failures of the individual partners in perception, interpretation of perceptions, communication, and interpersonal behavior become the material that is dealt with in the sessions. In the triangular setting, the therapist witnesses the unfolding of the conflicts *in situ*, which enables him to understand the dynamics much better. Anger may be expressed, but the presence of the therapist helps to soften as well as to exploit these feelings for understanding and tolerance.

The triangular setting activates the childhood conflicts of each partner, who tends to act them out in the therapeutic situation. The therapist can see more clearly the unfolding projection of these conflictual situations onto both he and the partners (projective identification). Furthermore, one can observe the manner in which each partner provokes his spouse to play unconscious roles. The couple reexperience the original family conflicts, but in a different atmosphere, one conducive to learning and "growing up."

Each spouse must be moderately secure in his own identity

if he is to accept appropriate roles, to complement and support the partner, to evolve a workable communication system, and to operate flexibly under changing conditions to achieve common goals. The dyadic sessions provide opportunities to trace the development of the self-image from reflected appraisals by significant adults, principally parents ("parental" voices in the "records"), a concept expertly stated by Sullivan[6] and others. If the parents' appraisals are based on their own neurotic distortions and are derogatory rather than accepting, the child, lacking experience and judgement, will incorporate these appraisals and develop a negative self-image. In the triadic sessions, the impact of the negative self-image on the interpersonal relationship of couple is pointed out.[7] Interpretations to both that this factor is disturbing the marital relationship can be valuable in improving the marriage. Furthermore, as both spouses begin to understand the ways in which they operate toward each other because of their poor self-images, pressure for change develops. The next step involves bringing into focus the positive and creative aspects of the partners.

The indications for the combined approach in marital disharmony (simple and combined-collaborative types) include the following:

1. Initial evaluation indicates triadic sessions to manage the marital relationship in order to achieve harmony, and dyadic sessions for entrenched personal conflicts.
2. Therapeutic impasse with other techniques.
3. Acting out by one or both spouses that cannot be dealt with by the other techniques.
4. A patient's obsessive-compulsive personality pattern that makes it necessary to enlist the cooperation of the partner.
5. A spouse's relationship with a single parent introjected to the degree that he is threatened by a dyadic setting (sexual, hostile, or oral dependent needs).
6. An impasse in concurrent therapy because of transference difficulties: either too intense (libidinal or aggressive)

or involving insufficient emotional involvement of the patient.

7. A therapeutic impasse occurs in dyadic interviews because the dyadic transference neurosis can be activated and interpreted only in the triadic sessions.[8]

The indications for the conjoint family therapy include those of conjoint marital therapy (see Ch. XXV) plus the following:

1. A child contributing to marital discord by acting out parental unconscious impulses or being used as a pawn in the struggle with another family member.[9]

2. When the child is being used as a scapegoat[10] in the marital conflicts, and this is producing increasing marital friction.

The contraindications for the combined approach are similar to those listed under conjoint therapy (see Ch. XXV).

THE SIMPLE COMBINED APPROACH CONSISTING OF INDIVIDUAL AND CONJOINT SESSIONS

The simple form of the combined approach in marital disharmony—a combination of single and conjoint sessions—was used in fifty-two couples (32 in the PS and 20 in the MDS). The number of interviews with each couple ranged from a minimum of sixteen sessions (the Octavias) over a period of three months to a maximum of 1,743 sessions (the Olympias) over a period of nine years (see Table XXXII).

TABLE XXXII
THE COMBINED APPROACH WITH THE OLYMPIAS

| Year | Individual Sessions | | Conjoint Sessions | Home Visit | Hospitalization |
	Husband	Wife			
1960	146	44	1	1	
1961	146	159			1 (8 sessions)
1962	156	180			
1963	154	172	1		
1964	51	86	53		
1965	36	83	20		1 (4 sessions)
1966	0	82	2		
1967	1	90			
1968	0	57	10		
Totals	690	953	87	1	2 (12 sessions)

The following clinical material highlights the therapy of first the Octavias and next the Olympias.

The Octavias received a total of sixteen sessions, Mrs. Octavia had three individual sessions, Dr. Octavia had five individual sessions, and both had eight conjoint sessions. The Octavias were a handsome couple in their late twenties, married five years. Dr. Octavia is a physician and Mrs. Octavia, a schoolteacher.

In his first individual session, Dr. Octavia stated: "I love my wife very much, but recently we have been arguing constantly. These center primarily about my wish for children, and her desire for a career. She wants to become principal. I feel if we don't have children now, we never will. As a physician I know the risks involved in having children after she reaches thirty. This incessant drive toward a career has had our marriage on the rocks many times, besides, my friends and colleagues rib me about "shooting blanks," as if I am not virile enough. Another point of dissatisfaction is our sexual problem. She has a difficult time reaching a climax. I want her to reach a climax when I do. I will work fifteen or more minutes until she does. Further, she complains about my overdominance.

Mrs. Octavia, a beautiful and extremely intelligent woman, was dressed seductively and acted so in her first session. She began the interview stating: "I will not even try to become a mother while my husband and I cannot communicate. I am unable to express my feelings or thoughts because he gets hurt and pouts. I keep things inside, and my only outlet has been my career.

When we got married, Jack felt strongly that a woman's place is in the home—cooking, cleaning and children. It has been a constant struggle for me to complete my B.A. degree, and he finally gave me his permission. The past two years of our marriage have been stormy because he has tried to dominate my behavior and to control my thoughts and actions.

Jack is not a lover. While we are making love, he will ask if I have reached my climax. This turns me off. He is very offended when I don't respond. Sometimes we would have intercourse for what seems hours before I reach an orgasm. It's not love, but performance that seems to be important to him. I resent his attitude."

Dr. Octavia began his second session by commenting that he and his wife had a bitter quarrel the previous night. He felt badly when she accused him of treating her like an object instead of a woman. A year ago, after a similar quarrel about his desire for chilren, he had decided he was through with the marriage and was walking out when she blurted out in tears that she was afraid of having a baby—that perhaps she would not make a good mother, and that she was afraid of childbirth. So he had remained.

Since the argument had been over his demand for sex, I suggested to him not to approach her, and to wait until she made the initial overtures. That I would explore this complaint with his wife.

In her second session, Mrs. Octavia was deeply disturbed about her ambivalence toward her marriage and marriage counseling. "I feel very screwed up. I come from a very close family. I want a family but I don't want it with Jack. All he talks about are his patients. I need mental stimulation. Jack thinks that having a baby is the panacea. Otherwise we should split."

I suggested that perhaps we should change to the classic approach where the individual's needs are primary and the marriage secondary. To think it over and let me know—and I would send her to another therapist whose primary focus would be her welfare. The next night she called to state that she had decided upon working on her marriage.

Dr. Octavia seemed very happy as he began his third session. "It was quite a session you had with Ann last Friday. She was on the verge of tears when she came home. She was very quiet and moody. Later in the evening she broke down, not completely, and presented herself to me very passionately. Lovemaking ensued. Then she broke down and said, you inferred she see another therapist. Separate therapists, who would concentrate on the individual with the marriage secondary. I said, if there is a divorce, I would do whatever was the gentlemanly thing to do for her.

"I've never seen her so completely spent after her session with you. I have a different attitude since talking to you. I was emotionally confused. At the hospital I make many important decisions each day and stick with it. I would like to save our marriage. But if it's to be a divorce, perhaps it is best now while there are no children involved. Later she said she called you to save the marriage. I was floored. The next night we had nothing planned. So we stayed home, watched a play on TV—a very enjoyable evening on both our parts. That night she asked for sex. Two nights in a row! I could not believe my ears. She reached a climax on her own, and exclaimed happily, 'I feel like a woman.'

"When I came home that evening, she kissed me and said: 'Guess what? I love you!' I don't know what to make of it. We are now able to talk. I do have a different attitude. I feel now that we both have indulged in some soul searching."

I commented that in our last session one of her main complaints about the marriage was that he was too controlling of her behavior.

"When we first started out I was. But not now. I want to wear the pants in the family. I know she feels I control her, but it is not so. She had such a dominating home. Her parents are very dominating. Any slight suggestion on my part later set her off. This is where the root of the problem comes from."

(Excellent example of projective identification—this was pointed out to him, how his wife overreacts to his suggestions not only by hearing old "records" from her parents but also by projecting these "records" onto him and doubly reacting as though her "records" were coming from him. That he was to consider his words before he addressed them to her.)

Dr. Octavia commented: "It makes sense to me, and I will try not to be critical of her behavior. I think another problem is her fear of pregnancy. Her mother and her aunt had difficult labors."

In his fourth individual session Dr. Octavia came in upset that his wife had reverted back to her old patterns: "No change. When am I going to be treated like her husband. My ulcer pain returned. No tenderness, no concern, no asking 'Can I get you something?' I think she needs help in finding out whether she wants marriage or a career. If she wants a career then it is no marriage, not with me."

Mrs. Octavia opened her third session as follows: "We have really been working together, trying very hard and enjoying each other."

I ask about the last few days which were very tense according to her husband.

"It was very tense. He has been nagging at me. He is too possessive. He makes lists of things each morning for me to do. I really resent this. He is like a child about illness—and he is a doctor. I had a dream: My mother, sister and I are all going up a tall ladder. They fell off. I don't know what the dream means."

I inquire about her hostile feelings toward her mother and sister? "They do fall off!"

"I knew you were going to ask me about this. They are always telling me how much they love Jack, and want the marriage to work. Her wonderful son-in-law—just because he gives them free medical advice and samples. My mother and sister are very close. Mother keeps telling me that I should have children before it is too late."

In his fifth and last individual session, Dr. Octavia reported things were going well again at home. I suggest that we now have conjoint sessions to further open the channels of communication between them. His wife had cued me in to his recent extensive quizzing her about her individual sessions with me. He readily agreed to conjoint sessions.

In the first conjoint session Dr. Octavia opened the session with a dream in which the focus was on an event in which he performs in an outstanding manner.

He was asked if performance was so important. He replied: "I don't think so."

Ann interrupted to comment: "Performance is very important to him. He wants his friends to know how much he does at the hospital—the way he handles emergencies. We have many arguments about using his standards. I had worked all day. I didn't have time to have his car greased. He tore into me and embarrassed me in front of my girl friend who was visiting me."

Jack replied: "I'm not interested in performance. I'm only efficient. It is easier to do things the right way. She is always procrastinating."

It was pointed out that a big source of argument was his demand of her "inner child" to act on the same level of performance that he demanded of his "inner child." When he did this, she rebelled by a "sit-down strike."

After two good weeks, both the second and third sessions dealt with the preceding theme of performance, the Octavias left for a three-week vacation. Dr. Octavia began the fourth conjoint session as follows: Just before we left, she said she has been thinking of separation frequently. We slept in separate beds. Now everything is going smoothly. I can't understand why one week is fine and the next week horrible.

"He makes me feel inadequate, that I don't show enough affection toward him. I feel very badly and guilty about it. Yet once we arrived in Hawaii, we had a wonderful time. He was sweet, romantic, entertaining. I could not have asked for a better husband. What really gets me mad now is when he says publicly, 'things will be different with my second wife.' Nothing I do seems to satisfy him."

In the fifth session both reported a good two weeks. Mrs. Octavia stated: "We are starting to verbally express ourselves instead of holding back and sulking. I have been very happy these two past weeks."

He replied: "What little disagreements we had later seemed nonsensical. She wants to cut down our visits here to every other week. I think we should explore the area of children first."

In the sixth session, Mrs. Octavia opened: "We had a wonderful first week then, a week later, Jack said he wanted a divorce. I was shocked! The next morning we had sexual intercourse. That night we made love again. The next night we had a little quarrel, and he said he wanted a separation. I said, what do you want? (crying) I'll give up my teaching, if this will make you happy. I don't know what he wants. When he says these things I get colder and colder inside of me."

Dr. Octavia: "I've accidentally discovered what is wrong with our marriage. I've hit on one word. Need. You don't need me. I want to be needed."

Two nights later the Octavias called for an emergency appointment, that they had had a breakthrough in their marriage. When seen that evening they came in looking very happy.

"I saw things in my wife I didn't see before—compassion, tears, never seen before in here. A deep feeling for me. She looked up and said she loved me and doesn't want to live without me. I love her, too, I told her."

Mrs. Octavia replied that it was her idea for this appointment. That, perhaps, this could be their last session. I suggested, they keep their next appointment, two weeks hence, and, if everything was going satisfactorily, we would stop therapy.

In their eighth and final session, Mrs. Octavia began by stating: "We have been getting along beautifully. No complaints. Not a single one, except, I'm dreaming like crazy. Jack and I are developing a very good relationship. For the first time we are communicating. I'm trying very hard. We are starting to work out our problems. He was the one who threw me for a loop, asking for a divorce. I have tremendous guilt feelings about what my role is, career versus motherhood. We really are getting along fine now. Yes, we are. No arguments. No fights. Really trying to please each other."

He commented: "What she has said is also what I feel. We are getting along beautifully. How do you feel about discontinuing and our trying to work out our problems alone?"

She added: "There have been no periods before where we have been able to talk things out without explosion. You have opened the avenues of communication."

I suggested that I schedule an appointment one month later but, to cancel if things were working out satisfactorily. Three weeks later she called to say that the marriage was fine and cancelled the appointment.

The following couple, the Olympias, who had 1,743 sessions, demonstrates the great flexibility necessary in the use of the simple form of the combined approach in marital disharmony. The excellent result with this couple warranted the tremendous time and effort expanded by the two spouses and the therapist.

Mr. Olympia was referred by his family physician for therapy. His main complaint was alcoholism. After he stopped drinking completely for ten years, he recently began to drink excessively again. As a result, both his business and marriage were threatened. A brilliant, creative, gregarious individual, he had developed his own very successful advertising agency with the help of his wife who was the office manager. The complete material on this couple consists of over fifteen hundred typed pages, and only the highlights will be presented. Mrs. Olympia was an attractive, petite, reserved woman, whose quiet manner concealed a mind more brilliant than her husband's. At the time of the initial visit, they were living alone. Both of their children had completed college and married.

Mr. Olympia described his parents as happily married. "Everybody liked my father. Well respected by his fellow workers. People would come to him with their problems. Rough guy on me as a kid, very strict with me. I had to get good grades, no excuse. He was a firm disciplinarian. Mother was a very devout fundamentalist, fear ridden about sinning and going to Hell. Very loving, buxom, perfectly clean but scared to death of her shadow."

The oldest of two children, he had a younger sister. Popular in high school, a top student, he had always been interested in art and drama. His drinking began in his freshman year in college with his fraternity brothers. After graduation he went into sales and eventually into advertising. Before he married, he drank too much and chased too many women. At thirty he decided to get married and settle down.

"What I saw in her that I didn't have, were principles. She was ten years younger, very reserved, very straight-laced, idealistic, with a tremendous sense of loyalty. She is the best thing that ever happened to me. Till I stopped drinking ten years ago, I was pretty interested in myself, unfaithful; I knew it was wrong, and it always happened when I was drinking. And you do a lot of entertaining and drinking with your clients."

In his fourth hour (being seen four times a week) I explained the basic rule in psychoanalysis and placed him on the couch.

"I have often wondered if my alcoholism was a penalty for stepping out. I have the highest regard for my wife's integrity, the highest regard for her. My wife is the exact opposite of me. She doesn't enjoy socializing.

She is puritanical and straight-laced. I feel strongly at times, am impulsive, and impetuous."

During the next four months of analysis, he talked about his behavior as being a rebellion against his father, but that ten years ago after a very close friend of his died in an acute alcoholic delirium tremens, he joined AA and went on the wagon. Then recently because of severe business pressures, he began to drink again. At first his wife was understanding of his drinking but in the last few months began to nag him considerably. His pattern of drinking was generally in the evening—then a few drinks in the morning "to shake the fuzz out of my head."

In his fifth week of therapy he related the following dream: "I had a feeling of rectal pain. I'm in the shower. I put my hand there and suddenly realize that I have feces all over my hand. The scene changes. Several people around a table. Some man I knew came in with a jar of pills. He wanted me to take a handful. After I took them I felt badly. I didn't want to take them. In the process of returning them when Elizabeth (Mrs. Olympia) enters. Greatest concern was whether she had seen the jar of pills."

In his associations he stated that he had definitely made up his mind to stop drinking completely. Elizabeth is getting very depressed about my drinking.

I comment that he is feeling very guilty about something—his hands are soiled. I ask whether he is also taking pills.

He stated, he used to take Dexedrine® to get started in the morning after a night of drinking, but he doesn't anymore. He then expressed considerable concern about his wife's depression. I ask if he objected to my talking to her. He replied, he would be grateful if I did.

Mrs. Olympia was first seen five weeks after her husband's first visit. She was very depressed about his drinking. She felt the problem was the pressures at the office and his rage at his chief account executive, who he felt was ungrateful, since her husband had taught him all he knew in his work.

During the first four months of analysis, considerable rage was expressed toward his father, who said one thing but did another, yet wanted his son to do as told and not as he did. Considerable rage was also expressed toward his mother, who was both seductive yet rejecting and also did not protect him from Father's controlling, demanding behavior toward him.

At the beginning of the fifth month of his analysis, Mrs. Olympia called in an acute panic state, that her husband was drunk and pugnacious and threatening to leave town and "that no one was going to tell him what to do!" When I asked to talk to him he refused to come to the telephone so I told her that I would come to their apartment (the first home visit[11]). When I reached their apartment, an hour later—a distance of thirty miles—the situation had calmed down. I suggested that he stay home for a few days and then return for his analysis. At his next appointment, he was extremely grateful and promised that he would stop drinking completely. I suggested instead that we face each day as it arose.

A month later I saw the Olympias together for their first conjoint session. It was an emergency appointment that lasted two hours and followed another alcoholic crisis. Mrs. Olympia was very nervous and was started on Librium® (tranquilizer), given an appointment for the next day after he had expressed considerable anxiety about his wife having a possible nervous breakdown. She was to be seen once weekly to begin with and more frequently as time became available (concurrent approach). She stated tearfully that his behavior was threatening their business—his slurring speech when drunk had caused a disruption of the morale of their employees and loss of respect of all concerned.

Mr. Olympia stated that this time he would definitely stop drinking. He stopped drinking ten years ago, and he could do it again.

I suggested that he enter a hospital for dauerschlaf (sleep treatment) for two weeks. Then to be on an open ward for two weeks until he was his old self.

He reacted with controlled anger, saying that he would agree to go in the hospital but when he would be released, he would *really start drinking*. It was decided he should have another chance.

In the ensuing months Mr. Olympia stopped drinking. He said that he had also stopped taking pills. He was concerned about becoming like his father. "So many things I saw in my Dad I see in myself. This rebellion and resentment got me."

Mrs. Olympia had established a strong positive transference (to me as a real object as well as the omnipotent, omniscient level of the dyadic transference neurosis). "You seem my only touch with reality and sanity. Last weekend was the nicest one in many months."

Mr. Olympia related the following dream that had awakened him with an excruciating headache at three in the morning: "The director of our art work is driving my car. Elizabeth is in the front seat next to him. I am in the back seat. I said: 'Please keep your eyes on the road or you will run into the ditch.'

"I woke up with a severe headache in the back of my neck. I don't understand the dream except that this art director looks like you."

It was pointed out to him that he was reacting to his wife seeing me and that he felt I was in the driver's seat and he was in the back seat. That I was a severe pain in the neck to him in the dream (excellent example of the triangular transference neurosis).

Mrs. Olympia in her session told of a childhood of complete rejection: "Father was unhappy and didn't want me when I was born; my sister was the beautiful one and wouldn't want me to be ever seen with her; my relatives didn't like me except my grandmother; and Mother blamed me for her illness which followed my birth. I couldn't believe it when my husband became interested in me. I had just finished college and was working in his office. After we were married I suffered. Holidays always meant an occasion to get drunk. All my life it seems, for the first fifteen years of our marriage all this drinking. Then for the ten years he stopped drinking, everything seemed so nice. Although he irritated me with his infidelity a lot of times, and although I felt anger and humiliation, it seemed worth it until his drinking all started again." Typical of her expectation of rejection was the following dream: "I was on my way to keep an appointment with you. I stumble and fall into a hole and get all full of mud. I called you on the telephone. I said, the girls in the office wouldn't recognize me. You said, come down anyhow."

Her associations dealt with her first sexual experience at the age of nine when a man exposed himself in front of her and considerable guilt about her first sexual experience (petting) at fourteen. Recalling her mother telling her when she was sixteen that if she got into trouble not to bother coming home.

During the second year of psychoanalysis (concurrent), the Olympias were each seen four times a week. The only unusual occurrence that year was in the fourteenth month of therapy when Mr. Olympia had his first hospitalization following an alcoholic spree. He was given sleep treatment for two weeks, and this was followed by psychotherapy every other day for two weeks. Upon discharge from the hospital, the Olympias left for a three-week vacation in Acapulco, their first real vacation in years.

Upon their return Mr. Olympia looked very happy: "Our first honeymoon. Ann looks wonderful. I've only had six aspirin since I saw you last. I had a dream last night: I was with a fellow. We go into a gin mill. He had a drink. They poured one for me. I got so mad I threw it against the glass bar and shattered it. I woke up shaking.

"I suppose I am both fellows and fighting against taking a drink."

Mrs. Olympia looked very happy at her first session. They just returned from Mexico. We actually enjoyed every minute. Mexico is very beautiful. We had sex. The first time in several years. I really enjoyed it, especially after all the hatred I felt toward Jack. Afterwards I felt so promiscuous. I kept thinking about you while I was on vacation. How you have helped both of us." (An example of the triangular transference transaction.)

Mr. Olympia described his first week back at work as excellent. He looked very well. "I had a dream last night: I was back in Milwaukee. Visiting an old friend, Jim. He was telling me about a girl he was going to marry but wasn't sure. He puts on a red scarlet robe. He is immaculately clothed. She comes in.

"In reality, Jim has let himself go. He used to be a perfectionist. Then regressed so badly. In the dream he is immaculate. The color of the robe is identical to one I had years ago. He looked sharp, very happy and confident. I hope it's me."

I noted that this had been a rough week for him, having to face everybody.

"It was: everyone in the office, at the club, the elevator starter, and so on.

I comment: "You came through with flying colors. This is your new self-image."

However, in his session the next day, he reported a dream in which he is embarrassed that his mother (analyst) discovers he has a hole in his sock. When asked his fear of discovery and the achilles spot in his heel, he replied, "three things: women, pills and alcohol." The dream indicated that he was still on alcohol and taking pills. He denied this but added his hospitalization was a very frightening experience. Not only these alcoholics who had been there several times, but those poor people getting shock treatment.

Mrs. Olympia, in her next session, reported that her husband was doing very well in the office but the last hour had really stirred him up. Her material in the following months dealt with her poor self-image: depreciatory comments from relatives, few playmates and rejection from her mother. "Our family physician meant a great deal to me as I was growing up. He was the only one who was sure I wouldn't grow up to be a monstrosity. I feel the same way about you. [The dyadic transference neurosis.] Yet in one way or another I get burned when I get close to people. If I let my guard down, I end up letting people take advantage of me."

As she began to see herself in a more positive light, her transference material changed from the omnipotent father figure to a disguised erotic transference, as shown in the following dream: "I am in your office. Your receptionist took me to an inner office and gave me a toothbrush and paste. She asked, 'Are your gums hot?' I said, 'No!' but they began to get hot."

In her associations she commented she had another dream where she is looking into a bakery window. "That bakery could be all the things I would like to taste and experience. Perhaps sex. I never was very comfortable about it. I think I have had everything neatly packed, and you broke the string, and I can't put things back together. I think I've been a past master at everything I couldn't handle. I know my old pattern is not to feel anything and then I don't have problems. You are probably the first person who has not let me down, remained stable—probably a combination of God, my father, my doctor and a friend" (again primarily the dyadic transference neurosis.)

In the seventeenth month of therapy, Mr. Olympia reported he was almost back to his old self (as confirmed by his wife) but was concerned about both discovery and conflict between individualism and conformity. "I have been concerned that the analysis will make me into a conformist instead of a creative individualist. I long for conformity, but am afraid it will destroy me."

In his eighteenth month of therapy Mr. Olympia reported: "I had an amusing dream last night: I wandered into a rundown neighborhood. Saw a beautiful new house—two story and sixteen rooms, set back on a big plot of land but with a small barn on the front lawn. House was not painted yet. The ground not seeded. Some people thought the barn was out of place. I defended vigorously that this was an improvement. I went inside and met some friends."

His associations: "So I built a new house. No wonder I woke up tired. I've started to build a new spacious house. The house is up. Not finished. But the barn is in front of the house not in back of it. (Laughs.) Backwards."

I comment that perhaps although he is building a new, spacious house, he is still resisting conformity: You are going to keep the barn in front of the house.

He replied: "A new twist in our house. Ann is reading like mad. For years I couldn't get her to read. It used to make me mad."

In the last three months of her second year of analysis (203 sessions), Mrs. Olympia began to deal with both a slowly improving self-image and the relationship between her murderous feelings toward her parents, sibling and husband and her masochistic behavior. With acceptance of all her feelings (both positive and negative) by her therapist, she worked through her masochistic behavior (punishment as expiation for murderous fantasies) in understanding her over solicitous behavior toward her relatives and passive acceptance of her husband's drinking and extramarital affairs.

In the final three months of his second year of analysis, Mr. Olympia reacted to his wife's transference feelings toward me with increasing unconscious anger but was performing well in his work and without alcohol. Both attended a convention in Las Vegas. Mrs. Olympia commented that Jack passed the Las Vegas test with flying colors. We had an excellent time.

Mr. Olympia reported a dream he had in Las Vegas which was symbolic of his changing self-image: "I am on a platform. I see this diesel engine. The longest one I have ever seen. Tremendous. Really a power house. I am with the engineer inspecting this big unit."

In his associations he stated: "I feel better than I have felt in years. I did an excellent job in Las Vegas. You are the engineer but it's my engine. I feel very optimistic now.

"Before we left for the convention I had a dream: Ann and I in a war area. I recall one man trying to overpower me. I had him by the head but he wiggled away. Then I booted him under the neck and knocked him out. It was so violent that it woke me up—the booting. It was as though this man was trying to take Ann from me."

In his associations he stated: "I am growing more and more sure of myself. I've had a series of dreams in which someone is trying to overpower me" (triangular transference neurosis).

During the third year of their concurrent analysis, the Olympias showed slow but continuous improvement. Mr. Olympia was seen four times a week until the eighth month of the year, when his sessions were decreased to three times weekly. At the end of the year he had completed 448 sessions. Mrs. Olympia was seen four times per week for the entire year. At the end of the year she had completed 180 sessions with a grand total of 383.

Mrs. Olympia opened her first session of the year by stating: "We had a pretty good holiday season. We exchanged viewpoints. Jack has been doing fine. I had a nightmare last night: Our parakeet was out of the cage. Jack got up and opened the window without thinking. That frightened me. I couldn't get Jack's attention. I tried to get out of the bed but was entangled in the covers. I was just frozen and didn't know what to do. I awakened screaming with fear.

Holidays cause me anxiety. You had gone on a vacation and Christmas time is when everyone drinks. I try to be tactful with Jack. I can't slink back into the corner like I used to do and bottle it all up. Here I speak freely. I want to change my personality, and yet I am afraid. I've never liked what I have been."

I point out that her dream is an excellent example of the phenomenon Freud described as resistance. It is the tremendous anxiety that accompanies the fear of change. You know what you are, and don't know what you will become. You are still a bird, poor self-image, out of your cage, the imprisonment of your neurosis, and terrified of the outside world, the opened window.

Six weeks later she reported: "Everything is fine and quiet now. As it was during the lull of the years before Jack got ill again. Now Jack and I are able to talk to each other."

At the beginning of the fourth month (third year) she stated: "I felt that what he was saying was that I made him feel boxed in, that he needs excitement. He says he knows that he throws himself into a project completely. If he felt like working all night, he wants to, but that he will try to pace himself. I felt last night that he is not satisfied. That some rebellion is brewing. I can't let this cause him to go back to where he was. Nothing is that important. On the other hand, I don't think I can take what happens and be that mouse in the alley as before. We are on a friendly basis. Yet I feel there is some trouble brewing."

Mrs. Olympia continued developing her potential by buying a high fidelity set: "Got our stereo yesterday. Really enjoyed it."

Two weeks later I told her to expect some hostile behavior on the part of her husband, that he was very upset and might be provocative toward her. (This is one advantage of the triadic therapy—it enables the partner to be tuned into the spouse's emotional condition and thus prepared to cope with the ensuing anxiety and/or hostility.)

Mrs. Olympia continued to improve in all aspects of her behavior and slowly began to develop repressed anger at the analyst for not meeting her emotional needs. The following dream at the beginning of the sixth month (third year) was typical: "Lying on a slab of cement. Hard and cold. When I woke up it was in a strange place. Many couches without backs. A lot of water on the floor.

When I woke up I thought you would say it's only anxiety and binding your anger. It seemed like things were getting out of control."

I asked: "What could the slab of cement represent?"

She replied: "That you are cold, unfeeling."

I replied: "Yes, you complain that I am cold, as a 'slab of cement.' You are angry—all that 'water on the floor.' The little girl in you wants comfort and warmth, instead of distance. This is a normal feeling. You also resent that I have other patients—too many couches (triangular transference neurosis). And it is normal to be angry about these thoughts."

In the following month Mrs. Olympia continued to struggle with both her erotic and dependent feeling toward the analyst. The marriage relationship had improved. Jack said: "It is great the way we are now able to communicate with each other. There has been a big improvement on both our parts. Saturday night, for the first time, we went to a concert at Ravinia."

"It was like being with a different person," stated Mrs. Olympia. "Jack was so relaxed, not self-centered, and really nice to be with."

In Mrs. Olympia's ninth month (third year) she reported that it had been a very rough weekend. "You have decreased Jack's sessions to three times a week and it has caused him to feel rejected, and he expressed a lot of anger although consciously, he said he was very happy about it."

Mrs. Olympia was told that this was to be expected. His "inner child" felt rejected and rightly angry.

A month later she was saying: "I feel I am able to control my anger better. I painted until 1:30 in the morning. It took the pressure off."

In her eleventh month (third year) of therapy, she stated: "Jack is doing very well. Whatever you talked about with him as to his procrastination worked. We are almost all caught up at the office. I had a dream: Birds again. Two of them. In a dark room. Out of their cage. I wanted to get the birds back in the cage. There is a light switch with four buttons. The switch doesn't work. I pick up the first bird in the dark. I had a hard time getting him into the cage. I go back for the other bird, which was small and frail. He bit me when I picked him up. The scene changed: Jack and I in your office. You were busy, active and preoccupied with something else. You ask me a question but didn't care what I said. I seemed to want to talk to you before the session was up. You walk out of the door and your nurse said you would be traveling with your wife. I looked at myself and saw that my hair was coming down and that I was in pajamas.

"When I awoke I felt that you had gone on your vacation already. The birds must be me and the conflict about being out of the cage, frightened and out of control, the two parts of me. Even when I got them back in the cage the door was still open. The four buttons could be the four appointments. No lights went on. I feel muddled up. Long periods of anger. Now a different type of anger. I'm still in the dark. I didn't seem worth your time—rejection. My hair was falling down. I wasn't in very good order, not dressed. Poor image, I guess. I was uncertain about being on the outside, unfamiliar, that I could make mistakes and be rejected."

I asked: "What new element is introduced in the second sequence of the dream?"

"No new ones. Your nurse has been there before and so has Jack."

I asked: "What about my wife?"

"I don't know why I put her in. I don't see that it means anything. You always have a good reason for going away. A convention or something."

I asked: "What new element could be introduced that you would just as soon be in the dark about?"

"Your family?" (A very long pause!)

I asked: "What about your competitive feelings?"

"I'm not very competitive in anything."

My comment: "This is a big step forward for you. To compete means that you are developing a better self-image!"

In her next session Mrs. Olympia commented: "I don't know why I was that angry the other day. Yesterday I thought of my being so prim and proper on the outside and promiscuous on the inside in my dream."

Mrs. Olympia's remaining sessions that year dealt with her competitive feelings and her final dream of the year shows she is no longer a bird but a woman pushing a baby carriage after leaving my office.

During Mr. Olympia's third year of therapy, there was slow but gradual improvement. In his second month of analysis (third year), he had a dream in which he had been awarded a plaque as the most valuable player. My comment: If he continues to improve, perhaps next month we would decrease his sessions to three times weekly. However, his reaction was repressed anger in his dreams, and verbal anger to his wife that I was rushing things (an indirect message to me!). A dream two months later was typical: "I was with my father. Something he said made me terribly mad. I made a run at him. Backed him into a corner. I was bending his leg up. I was so damned mad. Then I noticed perspiration running down his face. His eyes looked so hurt and shocked.

"I awakened thinking about this. All next day I kept seeing those eyes. So hurt and surprised. Several times in the last thirty days I have been in a state of rebellion. I don't like to be boxed in, told that I have to do something or be regimented."

I pointed out to him that he was angry at me for suggesting decreasing his sessions. He reacted emotionally and tearfully said: "You have saved my life."

This was followed by a period of time in which he complained in dreams that I was telling him what coat to wear, that he was being sold shoes that were too tight, that he was forced to listen to me play the violin and didn't like the music.

In his sixth month (third year) he reported: "Three rough days with somatic symptoms. I was so jittery yesterday. I feel much calmer this morning. I had a sick headache yesterday. I didn't want to eat. I had the feeling if I got over this hump I would hit a home run. The most miserable I've felt in a year. It would have been so easy to reach for a drink or pill. Yesterday I had a big fight with myself. I could smell those gin mills a thousand miles away. But I won out."

The next month he was productive at work and stated that he and his wife were relating and communicating the best they have ever in their marriage. With continued improvement at the beginning of his ninth month of analysis (third year) his sessions were decreased to three times weekly—seven months after the initial suggestion was made!

In his tenth month (third year) he reported a dream in which there was a team of horses in harness. "One was high powered and the other steady. The dream has to do with me, about pacing myself, and that the driver was using bad judgement. About the team of horses—I was the high-powered one on the left side that was bolting and couldn't be paced, Ann was the steady one on the right and dependable. The one on the left had a mind of its own."

I commented: "If you and Ann are going to stay in the harness, both of you will have to pace and work together."

He replied: "I felt that someone could help them work together and not beat them."

Mr. Olympia continued to improve, and in his last month of analysis (third year) he stated: "Yesterday I had a full day. I was able to work smoothly and nicely. I paced myself. I had a dream: I ran into a gal I knew. We chit-chat about old times. I run into her again three days later. She is suggestive and we end up having sex.

"I have feelings of going to be caught and guilt. I have more energy these days. In prior dreams I really didn't get my old trigger working. This time I wasn't a virtuoso but I was doing all right. I don't want to get into any of this cheating."

In their fourth year of therapy, Mr. Olympia had 154 sessions for a total of 602; and Mrs. Olympia had 172 hours for a total of 555. During the year it was necessary to have one conjoint session. The latter was due to Mr. Olympia's beginning to take pills again, a mood energizer so he could become more productive at work and a barbiturate to calm him down later. His taking pills disrupted both Mrs. Olympia and his office help. It was necessary because of Mrs. Olympia's great anger to shift the focus of therapy from analytic to primarily supportive and advisory. First I shall present her year's therapy.

Mrs. Olympia's first dream (fourth year) was an excellent example of resistance to change: "I had trouble making my appointment here. Many obstacles. Some force like a wind holding me from walking forward. I kept grabbing onto grass or sticks to propel myself forward. I am having a difficult time. Still thought I could make it yet everything was trying to prevent it."

At the end of the first month (fourth year) she reported: "Things at home increasingly better. Jack and I are communicating more. He is really interested in music now. I had a dream: I am painting a new picture. A conductor is watching me. There is a new format."

In her associations she commented that she has a new format of living, a new way of looking at things: "You are the orchestral conductor leading both Jack and me in new healthy ways of living and working."

In her sixth week (fourth year) Mrs. Olympia came in looking both angry and depressed. "I've decided to stop treatment for myself. I want to be free to make whatever decisions necessary on my own. Although things are fine now, I want to stop coming. I am sure Jack took pills or drank several times the past week."

I told her that I would use her appointments but hold them for a month should she reconsider her decision, but that I strongly suggest she continue.

Mrs. Olympia called two days later and asked to return. Upon her return the next day she related the following dream: "Very vivid dream. Lot of people. A revival meeting. All the people were emotionally stirred up.

"The dream was very vivid. I was in the midst of it. They seemed to have faith in God—his omniscience and omnipotence. People like that are in an uncontrollable happy state of emotion. Irrational, and that is what happened to me. I am glad to be back here." (This is a good example of the dyadic transference neurosis endowing the analyst with God-like qualities.)

In her third month (fourth year) she related a dream which revealed both her erotic and dyadic transference neurosis: "I was here on your couch. I had a very sharp pain in my side. You put your hand where the pain was and poked very hard as you leaned over me to do it. It was a comfortable feeling. I leaned my head against your chest.

"This is a pretty regressive dream. Childish dependency. In my childhood I always had a pain in my side and it was always poked at by the doctor I was so fond of and who was always encouraging me that I would grow up to be beautiful."

In her next hour she stated: "I've been thinking about our last session. Mother had the "baby blues" when I was born and was sick for a long time. Father didn't like you to touch him. He said that children's hands are dirty or sticky. My grandfather and uncle were leaders of the community, and I was expected to dress and act differently. Maybe that is why my father was always so neat and clean. Mother told me I was not wanted, and that my father was disgusted at my arrival."

Her fourth month of therapy (fourth year) dealt with concern about being like her mother, who was so rigid and moral, "especially when I disliked Mother so. On the other hand, she was very sociable, I am not like that. Perhaps when I was, before I knew it, I was involved and ended up getting hurt. I am getting along with people much better, but I don't know I like them any better." (Concern about her emotional involvement with me and fear of rejection. Further, an example of the encoding of some of Mother's moral values becoming "parental" voices in her "records.") The month ended with the following dream, which also illustrates how the couple in the triadic approaches discuss their therapy with each other:

"A bookkeeper of one of our accounts came to our office. An error had been made. I was trying to correct it. But nothing I could do would satisfy her. In another room I could see this oriental man. He said to me, come on in. He was chopping noodles. Then he would run his hands through them. They were supposed to rise, but didn't. I just stayed in there. He didn't seem concerned that the noodles didn't rise.

"I must be the bookkeeper too. I don't understand the part about the noodles. When Jack told me about his chop suey dream and your interpretation of it, I was surprised. I imagine you are the oriental man. Perhaps I am chopping people up. You would condone me for chopping them to bits."

I pointed out that she was correct, I was the "inscrutable oriental" who sits behind her, unreachable, and chops up "noodles" (brains). That she was wondering what she had to do to get a "rise" (reaction) out of me. In the dream she is wondering whether she has made an "error" in getting involved in therapy as it is so frustrating.

In her fifth month of therapy (fourth year) Mrs. Olympia was depression free; she related that the relationship between her husband and her had improved, particularly in the areas of communication and companionship. Her self-image showed continual improvement, and her month of therapy ended with the following comments: "Jack is doing well. I was busy all day. I did not feel tied up in knots. I am running the office very well. I've never seemed important to anyone before. It is true that Jack sees me differently now. There always had to be someone else in his life, and I always had to know about his affairs. I never could understand why he married me. There were always other women in his life, even during our courtship."

In the fifth month (fourth year) Mr. Olympia commented: "You know I've been married twenty-five years and didn't really understand my wife. This morning for the first time Ann said that she has another person now besides Dr. Greene that she can talk with."

Mrs. Olympia telephoned two days later that she was very upset. "Jack is either taking pills or liquor and I am leaving the office, shall I go home?"

I suggested that she stay and wait for him to return. Then go home together. If he should refuse, then she should leave by herself, and I would check with her later by telephone. When I phoned two hours later, they had returned home together. The next day she was depressed and angry.

"I was sure that he had taken something yesterday. I could tell from his eyes and behavior. I panicked yesterday. I didn't want to call you. We've been through another month of bulges. He throws everything into a turmoil at the office. My tolerance is low. I thought I would be a disturbing factor if I stayed in the office. I wanted the reassurance of your voice. It helped."

At the end of the month she brought in both a Dexedrine and a barbiturate capsule that he had secreted in a small container in his attaché case. "I had been questioning my sanity as to his recent reactions. I called you and did as you told me. He doesn't know I found these pills. He was real nice this morning. He kept asking me if I loved him. I managed to control myself. That night he asked me if I thought he was a weakling. I said I don't think so, but that you do. I don't want you to see me as a first sergeant. I want you to come and go from the office as a real person. I think he has been taking Dexedrine as a stimulant for the past two months. My apprehensions have been building up. I could tell from his general behavior he was taking something. As I look back over the last two months he has been able to keep going only by taking pills or liquor. In addition, he has been building up a head of steam toward our chief account executive, who brings in 50 percent of the new business and who keeps making more and more financial demands. I think since his hospitalization he has probably taken pills—but in a controlled way. Only occasionally too much. I don't know if Jack is capable of running a business now without a prolonged vacation. He can't run the whole world."

I suggested that she now sit up and that I did not think she could cope with both analysis and the business as well as her rage toward her husband. My role now would be both supportive as well as active. That when the situation permits, we would continue the analysis (example of flexibility on the part of the therapist.)

During the sixth month (fourth year) Mrs. Olympia came in very angry and depressed.

"After you talked to him he was all right for two weeks. Yesterday it became noticeable to me. He has admitted taking pills, but not as much as I thought. I told him I knew it. He swears that he absolutely had not taken any drinks, just pills. He said it started two months ago after a furious argument with Jim. I did not press him for facts. I thought it was better for him to talk to you, that I couldn't help him. He said he was going to tell you. If you discharged him he would have to accept it."

I suggest that I would raise the issue with him that afternoon. If he continued on the pills, we would have a conjoint session to decide how to handle his problem.

That afternoon, Jack stated: "I am a lousy liar. In April I began to take Dexedrine and an occasional phenobarbital. But I promise I will stop. I know Ann can spot it immediately. I am very frightened, the lie and deceit to both of you. But I will stop. Give me another chance."

He was told that if he started taking drugs again, we would have a conjoint session and decide on a course of action.

Three days later Mrs. Olympia called, extremely anxious and angry, an acute emergency had occurred that afternoon. She felt that Jack had taken, either pills or alcohol during a three-hour business absence from the office. Although he strongly denied this, his gait, speech and eyes revealed it. I suggested that I would stay in my office later for an emergency conjoint session. A two-hour conjoint session was held that evening. Mr. Olympia was angry, evasive and circumstantial. He denied taking anything, although his physical condition showed that he was under the influence of alcohol, drugs, or both. At one point he was quite angry at me, calling me a "prosecuting attorney," and at his wife for her reaction.

"I feel I have to report in and out every time I go to the washroom. I know I am to blame for this circumstance because of my past behavior. But now I resent this surveillance. I know in the past she has been right 80 percent of the time, but not now."

I specifically stated that he had taken something, but that I am still willing to treat him. He then admitted taking pills, but wanted another chance. I agreed and suggest they go straight home.

Mrs. Olympia replied that every time in the past when she did, he would take out his revenge on her by going off on an alcoholic binge for several days and would have to be rescued by her. A room clerk would call and she would go get him and bring him home.

I stated that she is not to do this again. I would be available day or night should either one have need to contact me. If Jack felt like he was on the verge of a binge, to phone me and I would hospitalize him again. Both agreed.

At Mrs. Olympia's next session she reported a nice weekend. "I think Jack would like to stop taking pills and alcohol. He is trying to the best of his ability. Pills are harder to stop than alcohol, and he has easy access to them. I don't know if he can. He was very glad he had an appointment with you today. I felt awful after I left here. Jack can get violently angry when he feels boxed in. I had him pinned to the cross in front of you. I didn't know what he would do, either to himself or to me."

She was given assurance that I would help her in this crisis. But, if he went on a bender, she was not to rescue him. She could run the business without him, and he would have to face the consequences of his behavior.

At the beginning of the eighth month of therapy (fourth year) she came for her session very angry and upset. She had gone through his clothes and discovered some pills. She confronted him, and a good conversation ensued without anger. "We are both involved in the business. I had to know what he planned to do. He said he would stay away from the business. I have become more assertive in my dealings with everyone. I am beginning to feel like a human being. I owe all this to you. He changed, and for the past twenty-four hours everything has been fine."

A month later Mrs. Olympia called acutely upset. She was given a double session. She described a typical hypomanic reaction in her husband at the office with everybody in a turmoil. She was furious at him. She was given considerable reassurance. I telephoned Mr. Olympia in front of her, and asked him to come right over.

Following the emergency meeting with Mr. Olympia, his wife stated he had stopped gyrating. Her dreams and associations revolved upon her rage at her husband for his lack of attention in the past. She complained that he had always indulged himself in the most expensive clothes while she dressed modestly.

It was pointed out to her that she felt very guilty about her murderous impulses toward him and punished herself by both self-depreciation and self-denial of her needs. Gradually her depression lifted.

In her last session of the year, she reported that Jack had a good week in all areas. "I've always been afraid of expressing my anger. I always knew I would not, but recently I was not so sure. What could the box of bakery goods represent in the dream? It was small. I didn't know what was in it. The things I miss. The things I feel I was deprived of? Jack certainly has been a luxury item. He has cost a lot of money to maintain his hobbies. I see myself differently now. I bought a new outfit the other day. The people in my office have noticed the change."

For the first six weeks (fourth year) of Mr. Olympia's therapy, there were no problems: "I am doing very well. Working efficiently. Our marital relationship is harmonious." (It was at this time that Mrs. Olympia wanted to stop treatment, since she wanted to be free to make her own decisions as she felt her husband was back on pills or alcohol.)

In the third month (fourth year) Mr. Olympia stated he was doing fine and related the following dream: "I was with you. We were in front of my garage. The car was a beauty except for two areas on the trunk lid. Dirty, maybe grease. I go in and get a cloth and worked like a son-of-a-bitch on these two areas until the car looked immaculate. The car was a beauty. An Ace-Bentley. It took hard work on my part to get it cleaned."

"I asked: "What are the two areas you are trying to clean up?""

"One area with Jim. Second to keep myself from getting too compulsive and getting into a high spin. Ann thinks I have been terribly angry at Jim. He is very greedy."

I asked if the two spots on his expensive car could be pills and alcohol.

No! Lots of times I get pissed off at Jim and Ann. I know she is justified at her suspicions, but I resent her surveillance.

In his fourth month (fourth year) Mr. Olympia commented he had been doing well at home and at work.

"I had a good dream last night: I was in a very comfortable home, furnished excellently but with simplicity. It was my home. President Kennedy and his son coming to spend the weekend with us. They arrive, and we chat like old friends.

His boy was ten years old and real sharp. All so easy and real. His boy puzzled me. The dream was so vivid and real. I have had three house dreams before this. The last one was not finished. Here is a visitor, President Kennedy, in our home: Not lavish, in good taste. This home. Simplicity, very livable, a place you like to be. Not ornate. In good taste. Beautiful blending of color. Air of dignity and quietness about this home."

My comment: "You have changed quite a bit."

"It's about time. I know I have changed. In the last two years home has meant something. Ann painting. Before this last bloodbath, I had to be on the go. External things were more important. In the dream I felt so much at peace."

(A week later his wife reports that he has been spiraling all week about his new marketing idea. Before it used to be his drinking. When he is spiraling he won't listen to anyone. Then when it's over he has that letdown feeling. But not an unpleasant weekend. He is much better. (An advantage of triadic sessions—another dimension of information about the partner.)

At the end of his fifth month (fourth year) therapy, he stated: "I'm tired but no longer depressed. Ann has been easier to live with. She is more relaxed. I've got to deal with my driving bulges. Things are much better. I know I was mad. That I was feeling sorry for myself. I knew I had to get this marketing idea off the ground. This was the point before when I took off.

"Jim was giving me a rough time. In the past I would say: 'piss on them—let them run the show' and I took off on a bender. But now I'm riding with it. You have me back on the bicycle and I'm pedaling pretty well! Before I was in such a damn turmoil and sweat for a month.

At the next session, he related a weekend of arguments with his wife and that he had told her he was going to go away alone for two weeks to think things through. I related his wife's fear that recently he has taken pills. He angrily denied her charge, the pills she found were from long ago. Three days later he confessed to his wife that he had been taking pills and stated: "I am a lousy liar. In April I began to take Dexedrine and an occasional barbiturate. I know that she spots it immediately. The fear. The lie and deceit. The real danger. I know I can stop now."

Emergency conjoint session three days later. At first he denies taking any pills but later admits it. He rationalized that he began again because of his wife's surveillance. I raise the issue of hospitalization, and he asks for another chance.

In his next session he commented: "I was pretty shaken up after I left here. For me to be put in a box makes me damn mad. I don't like to be put in a position where I am constantly defending myself. If you give up on me now I'll end up on skid row."

In his seventh month (fourth year) of therapy, Mr. Olympia commented: "I feel good today. We had a nice weekend. I want to get the record straight with you. Last September I began to take Dexedrine after that big argument with Jim. No alcohol. An occasional barbiturate. Sometimes when Ann thought I was driving myself, I had taken some Dexedrine. One reason I feel better is that I decided to tell you yesterday. I feel like a guy who has had a bath. I know I don't have to be a damn liar. I know I am to blame for the depression and anger Ann has had. It all depends on me."

In the beginning of the eighth month (fourth year) of his therapy, he related that the other night Ann had found some pills in his coat. He wondered why he had left them there?

I suggested perhaps it was an unconscious plea for help from Ann and me to help him stop taking pills. He had stopped drinking because alcohol meant death and that now if he did not stop taking pills, it would end in economic ruin, destroy his image in the business world, and, most important, destroy his marriage.

Two weeks later he reported that he had had a painful impacted molar tooth removed. "I did a silly thing later. I sneaked out and took two barbiturate pills. I did not notice anything unusual, but Ann could tell. I told her I didn't want to lie. I think she is very happy that I told her the truth."

I commented: "I will give you another chance. Please contact me if you feel you will need a pill. Otherwise you will have to be hospitalized, and if the three of us decide you need to restrict your pressures from your business, then that will be fully discussed. If this is not acceptable, then I suggest we terminate our relationship." (Mrs. Olympia was told the same thing at her next session.)

In the ensuing week, he reported having a rugged time: "I had to reach for a little patience and a little guts at times. I think Ann had a nice relaxing night. She slept like a baby. I know I've got to do it hour by hour. Yesterday I told you a great deal of this Dexedrine thing was that I felt I had to take it to keep this bounce. Go! Go! Go! To keep up a flamboyant appearance. I didn't realize until I was in the hospital two years ago how screwed up I had been. I never want to go back there again."

He continued to show improvement until a month later when Mrs. Olympia called completely upset: It took two hours to calm her down. She described a typical hypomanic reaction in her husband with flight of ideas and motor hyperactivity. At the end of her sessions with me, I telephoned Mr. Olympia and said that I did not think he had taken any drugs, but I did wish to discuss his behavior with him. He was seen that evening.

The next morning at his regular appointment he stated: "Coming over here last night gave me a lot of relief. Both of us were much nicer to each other that evening. I don't know what got into me. I did not take any drugs, but I felt all pepped up. My mind was racing with all sorts of ideas and I couldn't sit still."

When questioned as to any previous periods like that, he described a period of depression before his marriage.

"Nothing seemed to hold my interest. I was depressed for six months. Before, I was the top salesman then tapered off. Before that I was really on the go. I sold more merchandise than half the salesmen put together. Three years later I married Ann. You've never seen me like I was the other day. I felt like a rainbow."

He was told that some people swing higher and lower than others, and he could not help what was happening, that his motor was racing but he would be all right now. His wife had misinterpreted his behavior as due to Dexedrine. When she said, "You are really high, Buster," it really angered him.

That afternoon Mrs. Olympia commented: "Things are much better thanks to you. We had a nice evening. I think the fact that you saw him last night did a lot of good in helping him come down to earth."

She was reassured that her reaction was normal; but this time his behavior was psychological (hypomanic) and not pharmacological—artificially induced by drugs.

Mr. Olympia showed slow but progressive improvement as he began the tenth month of therapy (fourth year) by stating: "I did a very silly thing. Damn fool cowardly thing for me to do. I was afraid I wouldn't make the hill Friday. I got four Dexedrine tablets. But I didn't take any. Saturday, I had a severe headache, so I bought some tablets from the pharmacist for it. I didn't take anything. On Sunday I told her I was still susceptible. I have come 90 percent of the way. Six weeks ago I would have taken the pills. If I had taken one, I would have felt defeated."

Four weeks later he said: "The most wonderful thing happened in the way Ann and I can communicate together. We talked until two in the morning. If you think I am windy you should have heard her last night. I told her: 'You have just begun to find out about your fine mind and sensitivity.'"

In the twelfth month of therapy (fourth year) he began to take an occasional pill. At first he denied this but later admitted it. "I don't have to tell you I lied at our last session. A lousy combination of rebellion against anyone who tries to make me conform and my rage at Jim. But if I don't stop, I'll go into the hospital."

A week later he reported he was in good condition: "I had a good day. Ann even kissed me last night. I've been a selfish bastard and abused the hell out of her. But I am going to change." And so ended the fourth year of his therapy.

In their fifth year of therapy, Mr. Olympia had fifty-one sessions for a grand total of 653 and Mrs. Olympia had eighty-six sessions for a grand total of 641. Because of a therapeutic impasse, regular conjoint sessions were also started—fifty-three conjoint sessions during the year. Another important indication for the conjoint sessions is the need for the therapist to help the Olympias in discharging their key employee, Jim, who was taking advantage of Mr. Olympia's condition by making all sorts of demands and further acting as though the business would crumble unless he assumed complete charge of the operation. The severance of Jim was first discussed in July but not completed until the end of December.

The Olympias were seen in a three-hour emergency session after Ann had called stating that her husband had taken some pills that morning. During this long session he denied taking any pills, but her observations of his behavior contradicted his denial. He was given the option of four choices: (1) he could run the business entirely and Ann would stay at home; (2) Ann would operate the business and he could stay at home until we felt he should return; (3) hospitalization; and (4) liquidation of the business.

At her next individual session Mrs. Olympia was depressed and furious at her husband. Following the last conjoint session, he had gone on a one-day alcoholic and pill spree and was now at home. We decided that he have the option of staying at home for an indefinite period of time while she operated the business, or he would enter a hospital.

At her next session she stated: "He reacted to the two choices by threatening to commit suicide. He said he couldn't go back to the hospital. I told him I knew all about the pills, but that now he had two people to help him. The next day he said he did want our help, that he hoped you wouldn't desert him. He talked about the pills. He has never been off of them completely since he left the hospital, and that it was getting worse. He began to cry. I told him that I would give him another chance. He could stay at home, that there were plenty of bars and pharmacies around. I was going to work, and if he wanted to disappear he could. Also, I would immediately freeze the bank accounts to have money to take care of him if the police called or if he needed hospitalization. On the other hand, I pointed out his great creativity and ability. But I was never going to play "patsy" and rescue him again."

Mrs. Olympia was advised to have her husband telephone me.

Mrs. Olympia, when next seen, reported: "After he spoke to you he seemed very happy that you weren't angry at him. The next morning he was an entirely different person. You had suggested that we take walks, and we did. He said physically he was doing well but not emotionally as he wanted."

At the end of his first month of therapy (fifth year), Mr. Olympia returned for his first appointment since his stay at home. He looked bright and alert. I suggested that he continue to stay home but to come to my office for his regular appointments. Mrs. Olympia showed a complete grasp of the business, which ran smoothly. Her only problem was with Jim, who was, at times, demanding and condescending—expecting her to be unable to run the business. She was becoming increasingly furious with him.

At the beginning of his second month (fifth year) Mr. Olympia stated: "I don't know how to stop this act of proving myself. I do it when there is no reason to do it. I know what I am doing and hate my guts for doing it. It's a compulsion that I've got to keep proving myself."

Mrs. Olympia continued to run the business successfully and in her second month (fifth year) commented: "I wonder if I'm pretty aggressive, although I feel mousey and timid. I think I'm capable of a lot of aggression. I think I'm more aggressive than Jack is. In a dream last night I was on top of someone."

In the middle of his second month (fifth year) he noted: "I guess I've always been on the selfish side, thinking only of me. For a long time as a child I couldn't move three inches without asking someone's permission. And no explanations. I don't like to be put in pockets. I want a choice. The sad thing is that I'm following some of my father's domineering attitudes. I know I'm doing some of the things my father did." (Example of the "parental" voices in his "records.")

At the end of the second month (fifth year) Mr. Olympia was in excellent spirits. "I'm fighting the battle of the bulge—calories; the battle of the pack—cigarettes; the battle of the big bottle—alcohol; and the battle of the little bottle—pills, and I'm winning."

Two and one-half months after staying at home, Mr. Olympia returned to work.

During this time, Mrs. Olympia became more self-assured and a very competent executive in all aspects of the business. In the middle of her third month (fifth year) she stated: "Jack and I have had several good talks about a new philosophy in the operation of our business. He worked well all three days; quietly, efficiently, and on an even keel. He seems fine and feels he has a better chance now."

In the fourth month of therapy (fifth year) Mrs. Olympia phoned for an emergency conjoint session (second emergency call of this year).

"I caused trouble yesterday. My stomach got so upset. I was furious at Jack. I was determined to make Jack understand when he gets involved with the personal problems of the office help it undoes the things I have finally structured. I couldn't let it alone. Neither of us slept last night. I am so afraid he will rebel. He said we could work it out."

In the middle of the fifth month of therapy (fifth year), Mrs. Olympia was again very depressed and also very angry, stating that her husband had taken some pills yesterday. I told her I would discuss it with her husband that afternoon at his appointment.

During Mr. Olympia's session he stated: "I feel like a criminal again. No pills for four months and yesterday I took some. Ann confronted me, and I didn't lie like before. I have been going too fast. Too ambitious. Trying to prove myself. I still feel like a rookie in camp trying to make the team. But I know I can stop."

At the end of the month Mr. Olympia stated: "I feel very much better. The last two weeks I haven't had any pills. After that last jamboree with the pills, when I thought of moving out and when I thought I was driving Ann nuts, then I really got scared. I was also afraid I would start the booze again. In fact, as I look back, I was planning on it. That's when I stopped the pills. Until then I had been taking pills on and off. It was only when I got into the barbiturates that she found out. In spite of what she says, she didn't know I was taking Dexedrine. In this off and on thing, I was pretty sly."

In the seventh month of therapy (fifth year) things were going along well except for the increasing anger both felt toward their chief account executive, Jim. It was suggested that we try the combined approach, individual sessions plus two conjoint sessions weekly to discuss their current business problems. I stated that their extreme rage at Jim was unhealthy for them and they should consider discharging him.

Jack was angry at Jim's ingratitude after training him, and now he is asking for a large bonus when he knows they are short on capital. Ann was furious at Jim for his selfish and condescending manner toward her, as though he were waiting for both of them to collapse so he can take over the business.

At her next individual session she commented: "I think the conjoint sessions are most helpful because we need help for our pressing current problems."

In the middle of the tenth month of therapy (fifth year), Mrs. Olympia noted: "Jack has been performing wonderfully. He renegotiated our most important account for two years. He has been so complimentary and kind to me. It has been a very nice relationship. A relationship we've never experienced before. In all areas. There is a difference between seeing you alone and with Jack present. I don't feel unfamiliar with you alone. In the conjoint session it is different. You think about it differently. You react to it differently. I have to be more straightforward then. When we are alone it doesn't make any difference how it sounds. In the joint session there is a different kind of communication and relating. I think unless Jim goes, Jack will go back on pills."

At the next conjoint session, I congratulated Jack on his excellent performance of the past two weeks.

He replied: "I've done well. But Jim has to go. We had a three-hour conversation, and I told him he was fired and given three months severance pay. It came as a surprise to him."

Mr. Olympia had a rough time with Jim about his severance and at one period for two weeks took pills again. In their final conjoint session of the year (fifth year), The Olympias remarked they had a very nice weekend. They did not have to face the bullying pressures from Jim.

During the sixth year of therapy, Mr. Olympia had thirty-six individual sessions for a grand total of 689, whereas Mrs. Olympia had eighty-three sessions for a grand total of 724. When I felt I had gone as far as I could with Mr. Olympia, during the middle of the eleventh month, I terminated the sessions. He was still taking pills but not as often. Mrs. Olympia continued on a twice weekly basis, receiving both analytic and supportive therapy. In addition, both had twenty conjoint sessions for a grand total of seventy-five. It was during this time that Mr. Olympia had to be hospitalized for the second time for use of alcohol and pills.

Mrs. Olympia began her sixth year of therapy by stating she felt much better: "We had a very nice weekend. Jack talks very logically now. He said he was pleased with the return to the concurrent approach but that perhaps periodically hoped we could have a three-way session."

In the middle of her second month (sixth year) Mrs. Olympia reported the following dream: "The knight he has no mirth at all when the knave is fraught with laughter. I woke up with that thought. The two sides of the coin. The knight was dressed in armor while the knave was in rags. I have been very angry recently at the manner Jim treated us."

I suggest that perhaps while acting as the court's jester, she had been furious internally.

She replied: "You are right. I was playing the part of the placid 'stupe' and when I changed, I turned into nothing but a lawyer fighting everyone. I have not found the middle road yet. I'm either one way or the other. Jack is doing well."

Mr. Olympia began his third month of therapy (restarted after hospitalization) by noting that he is gradually improving. "I could see that Ann was getting upset, so I asked her what was wrong. She told me, and I realized I was spiraling, so I stopped. This pleased her tremendously. I realized I was calling people and taking phone calls that wasted two hours a day. Our communications are getting so much better."

He was advised to pace himself, both as to the demands others made on him and as to his own demands for performance—playing his father's "records."

In the middle of the fourth month of therapy (sixth year), conjoint sessions were again started when Mrs. Olympia became concerned about Jack taking pills again. At first he denied this but later admitted that she was right. She gave him an ultimatum of staying home or going into the hospital. Mr. Olympia remained at home for two weeks; Mrs. Olympia successfully operated the business. During this time she was given considerable reassurance and support in her sessions.

At the beginning of the fifth month of therapy (sixth year), The Olympias came in for a conjoint session. Jack looked very good. Mrs. Olympia commented: "We had a very good talk about changing our format at the agency. Pacing ourselves differently. Since then everything has been fine. I know I can run the business alone now. I've changed."

The first week in their fifth month of therapy (sixth year), I received an emergency call from Mrs. Olympia that her husband was on pills again. When they got home and she confronted him with this, he got furious and left in the middle of a thunderstorm stating that he didn't want to cause her any trouble, that he loved her, and that he needed several days alone to think things out. He promised he wouldn't take any pills or get drunk. I suggested she "sit tight." The next morning he called her from a hotel. He had been drinking all night and stated that he did not want to see me again. I offered to meet her at the hotel, as she was frightened at what he might do. Mrs. Olympia thanked me but felt she could convince him to go into the hospital. He was readmitted to the same hospital where he had been four years previously. After eight days he was discharged. While he was in the hospital I saw him every other day for psychotherapy. After several weeks at home he returned to work.

At their next conjoint session, the beginning of their sixth month of therapy (sixth year), I unequivocally stated that Mrs. Olympia was about to come apart emotionally and that I had her on tranquilizers. I had advised her to leave him if he took pills or drank again, but that I still felt he could make it.

At the first conjoint session in the seventh month (sixth year), Jack was again taking pills. I told her she will now have to make a decision.

"If he takes a pill once more, then I will have to leave. If Jack can't stop, it's only a matter of time until the business folds up. In a way I would not like to see that happen. His condition is now so obvious to other people. When I get to the office, I fear I won't make the day. I get so depressed and infuriated. But, the next time is it!"

At her next session she stated: "A very good week. I believe we have a real good chance. He is doing fine. Pacing himself and handling himself beautifully."

I called Jack at the office to congratulate him. At his next session he thanked me for the call and added: "Now that I've got my buttons back, I know I can do it. I'm so aware of the six years lost. I know I can't permit myself to get frustrated. I have to pace myself."

In the eighth month of therapy (sixth year), Mr. Olympia took some Dexedrine pills again. In a conjoint session he was told that if he went back on pills I would terminate our visits. This was his last opportunity with me, but he could see another psychiatrist if he wished. He was advised to stay at home all that week.

At Mrs. Olympia's next session she commented: "He was very frightened after leaving your office. I told him I didn't care if he left me. I could run the agency. I know I can. He was pretty frightened that you were going to discharge him. He doesn't want to lose you, above all things."

At the start of the eleventh month of therapy (sixth year), Mr. Olympia stated that tomorrow is his birthday, also related the following dream: "I am doing an excellent job for our chief client. I have a great new marketing idea. But I have to check it out with our CPA. You are the CPA. I am doing well and feel excellent."

Three weeks later, after he had taken some pills, Mr. Olympia was discharged from therapy.

At Mrs. Olympia's next session she reported that things were fine. "Sunday, in a choked up voice, he talked about you. Perhaps it was the best thing to terminate his treatment. This morning he wanted to return to the office and work. His anger and rebellion is gone. I said he could. For the first time I think he knows I will leave him if he drinks or takes pills."

I note that perhaps my discharging him and his feeling that you will leave, since you have me for support, may help him overcome his problem.

Two weeks later with continued improvement in Mrs. Olympia, her sessions were decreased to twice a week.

In the seventh year of therapy Mr. Olympia was not seen individually; Mrs. Olympia had 82 sessions for a grand total of 806 sessions. In December there were two conjoint sessions for a grand total of seventy-seven.

In the meantime a strategy was devised with Mrs. Olympia as to the procedure she would follow if her husband took pills or alcohol. Since Mrs. Olympia had the controlling shares in the corporation, she decided to either operate it or sell it. Mr. Olympia was advised of her decision and for four weeks he was fine but then went on an alcoholic bender and spent a large sum of money. Mrs. Olympia did not rescue him, and he came home on his own.

Mrs. Olympia began her second month of therapy (seventh year) as follows: "I accomplished the mission. He asked me if I meant right away, and I said, Yes. He called our lawyer at his home. The next morning he asked me if we should review what we planned to discuss. I told him there wasn't any story to be painted. He began to rebel. He was worried that his reputation would be ruined, fearful of being declared mentally incompetent. He didn't want any paper containing that in writing. It was very painful for me. I got so upset, I went to pieces, and this too shook him up, not with anger but I was just falling apart myself. This frightened him a great deal. He went to work with me the next morning and seemed a different person. A calm and collected and efficient man. That afternoon we went to our lawyer's office.

"Our lawyer couldn't believe it. I told him I didn't want Jack's stock but power to close the business orderly if indicated. We talked very plainly. He asked about you. I said, No, that you were no part of this. The matter was to be handled only as a legal problem. Jack was no longer your patient. I told him that when Jack took pills, he was a very angry, retaliatory person. All I wanted was the power to close the business if I wanted to. I told him we had almost used up our working capital. Jack said he too wanted the paper signed—to put pressure on him. It gave me power of attorney. It's locked up in the lawyer's safe with the stock certificates. Jack said he hoped the paper would turn yellow with age."

For four months Mr. Olympia was fine and then began to take some pills, although he denied this.

Mrs. Olympia in the sixth month of therapy (seventh year) related the following: "Friday night I told him he was gyrating. I could tell from his eyes and behavior he had taken some pills. He denied this and got furious. I told him he couldn't go to the office for a week. This made him angrier. But I was not afraid. I've come a long way since I started treatment. When he said he wanted to take a week off to think the thing through, I said, fine! I gave him eighty dollars in cash I had and four checks for one hundred dollars each. He said he was going to leave town and make a new start elsewhere."

"He was fed up with all my suspicions and restrictions. He left the next morning. I didn't call you. I had decided what I should do. Sunday morning he called and said he had been on a drunk. He had spent all his cash and only one check. He wanted to know if he could return home. I said, 'Yes.' He came home on his own. I was no longer going to play the 'rescue game.' He agreed to stay home until I thought it necesary, and also agreed to have unlisted phone numbers at home. He could be the power behind the throne, but I would run the agency."

From then on, Mr. Olympia stopped taking pills and alcohol. The business began to prosper again. In November Mr. Olympia suffered an acute moderate coronary occlusion. Six weeks later he was seen conjointly, twice for moderate anxiety.

In the eighth year of therapy Mr. Olympia was seen once for a grand total of 690 sessions. Mrs. Olympia was seen ninety times for a grand total of 896 sessions. Mrs. Olympia continued to show progressive improvement of her potential and self-image.

In the ninth year of therapy, Mr. Olympia was not seen individually at all. He continued to do well at his business, ceased taking pills and alcohol. Mrs. Olympia was seen individually fifty-seven times for a grand total of 953 sessions. The last three months of that year they had ten conjoint sessions for a grand total of eighty-seven. They sold their business and were financially independent. Treatment was discontinued.

This couple demonstrates the great need for flexibility on the part of the therapist. An important advantage of the combined approach is its flexibility; it lends itself to both the styles of various therapists and the marked variability of marital patterns. The triadic sessions are fairly standardized, but great variations are possible in the dyadic sessions. One partner may receive supportive psychotherapy while the other is analyzed, both may be analyzed synchronously, both may receive psychotherapy, one may receive psychotherapy while the other participates only in the triadic sessions, or one may be in analysis, while the other participates only in the triadic sessions.

In the triadic sessions the spouses sit upright facing the therapist, who usually sits equidistant between them at the apex of a triangle, a design which makes for easier observation. In the dyadic interviews, either the upright or the couch position is used, depending on the clinical material. I use dreams extensively in both the dyadic and triadic sessions. Dreams afford valuable insights, not only into each partner's personality and behavior, but also into the marital transactions.[12] Dreams reported in the triadic sessions provide verification and clarity of understanding of the marital transactions and also of the various levels of transference phenomena. In the triadic interviews I observe how the ideas of one spouse elicit reactions in the partner. Although one spouse may continue to discuss his partner's concepts, soon his own unconscious feelings and thoughts gain the upper hand and reveal his true attitudes and bring to light areas of conflict. This type of communication makes possible a new dimension in understanding the couple. At the end of the session, I usually summarize and add a more comprehensive interpretation. I view dreams as having both a biological function in promoting physiological recuperation, and a psychological function in the attempt to solve problems. In the triadic setting dreams offer a point of departure for communication.

Combined therapy is a useful therapeutic tool when both triadic and dyadic transactions are necessary, either for the successful treatment of the marital disharmony or of one of the partners. The form and character of the treatment processes using these different treatment settings are determined by the training and goals of the therapist.

CONJOINT FAMILY THERAPY IN MARITAL DISHARMONY

In conjoint family therapy, a child or the children of the couple are included in the therapeutic setting. In my experience, contrary to the observations of other family therapists, only occasionally is it necessary to include the children in the therapeutic setting when the presenting complaints of the couple are those of marital disharmony. Frequently when the marital situation improves, the behavior of the children changes in a positive direction. On the other hand, should the child cause a therapeutic impasse in his parents' therapy, then he is invited to participate in the therapy or, in some cases, is sent to another therapist for individual help.[13] Family therapy is now well into its second decade as a therapeutic innovation. There are at least ten different ways of treating families.[14] As yet no one knows the best way to treat families.

The following clinical extract illustrates conjoint family therapy:

The Marcellas were referred by their rabbi for marital counseling. Married twenty years, they had a son seventeen years old, who was completing his last year of high school. A handsome couple in their early forties, there had been increasing arguments because of Dr. Marcella's almost total involvement in his work.

Mrs. Marcella began her initial interview as follows: "Actually most of our other problems seem to derive from lack of communication. I feel our arguments are chiefly initiated by me, and I often wonder if it's because I would rather have *any* kind of communication than none. Bob has always acted unilaterally about everything without consulting me: the house, neighborhood, furniture, you name it. My husband is devoted to his practice and his son. I feel there is little energy and devotion left for me. We have had very little vacation time alone. He always insists on taking our son along. My husband does not really understand why I feel a need for this."

Dr. Marcella, when seen alone, stated: "I love my wife very much. If not for that, our marriage would have collapsed. Part of her unhappiness stems from the fact that my practice requires a considerable portion of my time. She has many insecurities. It has been a difficult problem for me to provide her with reassurance. I am a taciturn person who doesn't easily engage in light talk. At times she feels I am unattentive. I come from a typical old New England family who is quiet. A recurring theme is that she thinks I devote too much time to my work. This has been explosive. At times I have felt I was precluded from doing what I would like to do. I have normal obligations to patients that I feel I should do. What really upsets me is that she thinks I am too involved with our son. Disagreements have developed over the proper handling of discipline. For my part, I have been distressed at the harshness expressed by my wife to my son at times. I have feared the effect of the pressures so produced on the boy.

The Marcella's were started on conjoint marital therapy in an effort to open up avenues of communication between them. Dr. Marcella, beneath his cold and intellectualized facade, was very anxious and frightened. Mrs. Marcella fluctuated between periods of anger and moderate periods of depression. Early in the sessions, Mrs. Marcella complained about her husband being overly concerned about their son, his friends and dates.

Dr. Marcella replied: My son and I have been close. Closer than the relationship between my wife and son. This has been a source of tension. I was insensitive to this until after the situation developed. My wife has told me in recent years that she has felt excluded. It is true. My wife has, in various degrees of intensity, resented this, and it lead her to be very harsh to him. When I protest, she interprets this as a preference for my son. She has said that I've given him attention that I should have given her.

An attempt was made to structure the marriage so that the son was permitted to begin his individuation from his father. The boy reacted to this attempt to stop his parentification by his father by joining a group of hippies at his school. When his mother discovered some marihuana cigarettes secreted in his room, I suggested that they invite him to join therapy, and conjoint family therapy was started. The Marcella family was seen weekly in one and one-half hour sessions for about one year.

THE COMBINED-COLLABORATIVE APPROACH IN MARITAL DISHARMONY

The last type of the combined approach is that of combined-collaborative. In this clinical setting each spouse has individual sessions with his own therapist, and once a week the couple and their therapists get together for a conjoint session. In the past few years there has been an increasing literature[15] on the use of this technique. An important indication for this approach is a therapeutic impasse where one or both spouses will need a continuing relationship for his own maturation and/or help with the mourning process should the couple separate.

The following clinical extract is illustrative:

The Roxanas were treated for a period of nineteen months, for a total of 120 sessions: seven months of the combined approach—single and conjoint sessions, then eight months of weekly combined-collaborative sessions (CCS), and finally, the classic approach with Mr. Roxana for four months individually and terminated while Mrs. Roxana continued with her therapist.

Mrs. Roxana was an attractive, thin young woman, smartly dressed and neatly groomed. Initially tense and apprehensive, she stated that she was willing to seek marriage therapy so that she could be shown how to change her behavior to prevent destroying her marriage completely. Mrs. Roxana very readily was willing to assume a fair share of blame for her marital difficulties, berating herself for her immature ideas. She described herself as basically not an unhappy person, but as having a lot of troubles in her marriage. She talked of her mistake in being selfish, demanding and too interested in material things. She added that she and her husband had been separated for the past two months and had come for treatment at the advice of her lawyer, who had recommended marital counseling before proceeding with the divorce.

Mr. Roxana, a tall, well-built, extremely intelligent man, ten years older than his wife, was pessimistic about the value of marital counseling in their marriage. He described his marriage as having been a continual setting of tension with no surcease. Whenever he spoke of his wife, a vehement flavor crept into his voice. He took responsibility for walking out of the house, since he felt he was growing even more bitter and did not want to subject his two children to more conflict than has already been extant. Although he denied it when directly asked, it seemed that he was merely going through the motions of seeking marriage therapy and had already emotionally divorced his wife once and for all. He stated he was curious to become a better person with his wife or the next. At no time during the initial interview did he convey any feelings other than controlled anger and passive compliance with the demands of the situation.

At the CDD I suggested that we try the concurrent approach, that they remain separated, and recommended each to be seen twice weekly.

In Mrs. Roxana's next session she complained that she was very unhappy. "I didn't realize how much a demand marriage was. I am basically immature. I thought marriage had to do with love and sex. I found out that marriage is work. We are two different people. We have had no sex since our second child was born. No sex for two years. I am afraid of taking the pill, and he doesn't want anymore children. Sex has never been too important to my husband. Only on Sunday morning because he has to get up early during the week. I have never had an orgasm."

In his next session, Mr. Roxana stated: "I was always very critical of Joan. The way she walked and talked. I always felt she was immature and flightly but felt I could mold her into becoming a woman. My parents were glad that I was getting married because they were concerned that I was enjoying bachelorhood. I knew my wife was naive but I was always hoping that marriage and responsibility would straighten things out. But it only made things worse. Our two children were not planned. Each time she said she had her diaphragm in but later told me she forgot. So no sex for the last two years."

Mrs. Roxana began her second month of therapy by stating: "I've done a lot of thinking in the past month. A lot of self-analysis. He hasn't called nor invited me out. I was surprised when he was with us on Thanksgiving day. We were very congenial and friendly. I've been letter perfect as to money. I've been very lonely the past months. I miss the George I want. Not the one swearing at me. Not the constant bickering. Until I got married, my mother did everything for me."

At his next session Mr. Roxana commented: "I am unable to get along with Joan. This melodramatic nonsense on her part. I find my wife to be a harassment with the children when I visit. 'Why aren't you playing more with them. Why aren't you rolling on the floor with them.' If she wants a TV husband, she isn't going to get one. I don't have the patience to be with the children for a long time. I suppose I never really was a child, always on guard."

In the next three weeks Mrs. Roxana described her idyllic state when she was single, her doting parents, and how ill prepared she was for marriage. I suggested that she and her husband were ready for their first date and to begin courting again. Either they would start moving closer to each other or away. I felt her husband wanted to move back home, and I would suggest the courting process to him.

At her next session she stated: "About last night. I tried to make it like a first date. Like you told me to do. It was very pleasant! We had a very nice evening."

At his next session Mr. Roxana commented that their first date was very nice: "If only she could be that way most of the time, instead of her incessant demands. Ninety-nine percent (99%) of what she does infuriates me. From the beginning I sat down with her, after a month of marriage, and tried to explain there are certain duties to perform even though you don't like it. You have to carry your weight. She didn't see it that way. I would go into a blind rage when I paid the bills. She would ring her hands and say it wouldn't happen again. I was pulling my weight and she wasn't pulling hers. I would always be angry at her. There was never any adult response on her part. Her parents would talk to her, but she was complaining morning, noon and night. You have no idea. Still, I would like to move back home if you think it is the thing to do."

A week later at a conjoint session the question was raised about Mr. Roxana moving back home, and both agreed.

At his next session Mr. Roxana stated: "I've moved back home. It's been fine. I was happy to get home. I missed the children and the surroundings. I hope it works out, but I am afraid Joan can't change. She is too much of a child. She makes promises but can't keep them."

Everything went along fine for two weeks, and then Mrs. Roxana reported: "I feel a great deal of the arguing this weekend was my fault. I want to be a good patient. Why can't I grow up. I know better, yet I spend money foolishly and he gets furious." Two weeks after his moving home she stated: "We went out last night. It worked out fine. He was very witty. It was fun to be with him. Besides, I had been on my best behavior that week. Very enjoyable. We had sex. The first time in about two years."

Two weeks later Mr. Roxana came in furious at his wife. "She says, 'What do you want of me?' I said, 'I want harmony.' I don't want to be confronted with her problems—ten thousand bits of trivia. She is extremely immature. I went over the bills. I went completely mad. Hundreds and hundreds of dollars spent on unnecessary clothes. We had decided on one hundred dollars a week for food, yet I found four checks for fifty dollars made out to Jewel Food Store. She said, 'just figures.' I said, 'We are spending twice as much as I make.' Her answer was, 'So get a bank loan.' I hit the ceiling."

At her next appointment, I suggested to Mrs. Roxana that we try the combined-collaborative approach. Perhaps she felt I was prejudiced toward her and that her own therapist might be more helpful. She was very resistant and reluctant to the idea, and I suggested we have a conjoint session in three days to discuss my suggestion further. In my own mind this was a desperate last effort to save the marriage as Mr. Roxana was reaching the limit of his tolerance. Also, I felt Mrs. Roxana would need her own therapist to help her over a divorce should the combined-collaborative approach fail. At the next conjoint session, I recommended the new approach, a three-month target date and to terminate therapy if no improvement.

Mrs. Roxana began her first combined-collaborative session (CCS) by stating that she liked her new therapist. They had worked out a budget which was agreeable with her husband, and she was going to adhere to it. (I had previously suggested this in an effort to decrease the variables

in their marital discord so that we could get to the basis of their relationship.) "I had a frightening dream last night: My mother was there. She
said, 'I am unhappy with your marriage. You have to get along better
with your husband.' The scene changes. I am in our house. Very dark.
See someone else. See a rat. I start screaming with fear. Someone said it
is not a rat, only a mouse.

My mother was always very protective of me. Even when I was away
at college, she would write and tell me what to do. I was very frightened
in the dream." Mrs. Roxana commented that she liked her new therapist
even though she was young.

(Comment: Mrs. Roxana approaches the CCS with great fear and
attempts to reassure herself that it is not as threatening as it appears—not
a rat, only a mouse.) Ten days later in his individual session, Mr. Roxana
reported: "My wife has been much better. One incident last night. I blew
my cool over nothing." Three days later before the fifth CCS he stated:
"A good week. Joan is trying very hard. Last night a very slight disagreement. She started to regress a bit. The material things her friends had. I
did as you had suggested. I didn't escalate but left the room. Later in
bed I said, 'Joan this is the first time you caused me to leave the room
since our four-way sessions. Why do you do it?' She said she was sorry.
I'm much happier with what's going on. I think she likes her therapist
very much. I really would like the marriage to work, but I doubt it. She
will soon revert to her infantile behavior. I hope not."

In the sixth CCS, the main issue was her husband's complaint that
although he had told her they were overdrawn at the bank and had
suggested she only make necessary purchases, that evening she had purchased an expensive purse: "It was such a bargain she couldn't resist. It
had been marked down 50 percent." This had resulted in a furious argument. Mrs. Roxana's only retort was that all her friends had these things
and why couldn't she.

In the tenth CCS, Mrs. Roxana was unable to come in as her children
were ill. Mr. Roxana came in alone and with controlled anger stated:
"Tuesday, believe it or not, she talked about needing a new dishwasher
like her best friend just got. And here I'm trying to get caught up
financially. Sure, I can borrow more money, but I'm getting deeper in
debt. I make a very good salary and think we should live within our
means. I don't mind drawing on our reserves for this treatment. She is
just a vicious bitch. The tirade I got over the telephone at work because
the cleaning woman was ill and couldn't come. And here I am busy with
my salesmen. I don't think she has made any change. She is so immature,
a bitterness, an aggressiveness. I had a dream I don't understand: Joan
and I at her folks' house. A real battle ensued. They were attacking Joan
for her incessant demands upon me. I grabbed Joan and left. I was
furious at them. I resented them being unpleasant to Joan."

It was pointed out that he was furious at the two therapists for the
lack of change in his wife.

Dr. ——, the co-therapist, suggested that he be patient and take her out once a week as a regular date, since his wife complained they didn't do anything.

At the eleventh CCS, the issue of Joan wanting a new dishwasher was raised. Although she admitted it was not wise since the old one was functioning well but, it was the old-fashioned kind, not the pull out type; and she complained all her friends had everything they needed, although their husbands made less money than her husband. Mr. Roxana retorted that their parents bought these for them, and he felt they should live within their means. At this, Joan began to cry.

At his next session, Mr. Roxana said his wife wanted a divorce. After three days of noncommunicating he had told her that he was going to leave. "I don't love you. I don't think I can love you. After this everything was fine."

At their twelfth CCS, the Roxana's reported a good week and sex for the first time in many, many months.

At his next individual session, Mr. Roxana was very depressed and said that he and his wife had been quarreling for three days. I suggested that perhaps we try the classic approach, no communication between the therapists, with the goal being what was best for each individual and with the marriage secondary. That I would suggest a structured relationship at the next CCS that would attempt to avoid arguing (TSD). They would either move closer or further apart.

At the next CCS, Dr. —— opened the session by commenting that Joan, at her individual session, was quite upset and concerned about their financial situation, and that she was very sorry she was acting the way she had been.

Mrs. Roxana stated: We have both improved. Mr. Roxana commented: After I left your office the other day I was very upset about the whole thing. I decided it was unfair to have it sprung on her today at our four-way session. So for two hours last night we talked. The first time since our marriage.

I suggested the classic approach with a six-month target date. They should live together, but on a landlord-boarder arrangement. The financial aspect was to be structured realistically as if they were divorced.

At the next CCS, both reported a good week, and that both were trying very hard to meet each other's needs. Mr. Roxana observed: "I'm not as pessimistic as before. I feel either we will have a good marriage or separate."

A month later at the eighteenth CCS the discord had returned. Mr. Roxana began the session as follows: "It's been a miserable two weeks. Her behavior has been as though we never have been here. She blows like the wind. This morning she was screaming like a fishwife over nothing. All the grief is self-inflicted. She created an incident over nothing: I had forgotten to bring home some egg rolls with the chop suey. I see it as a pattern of behavior that can't change. Either she needs to be changed or needs a new husband who is equally as goofy."

With no improvement in the following month, the CCS were discontinued, eight months after the original CCS. All participants mutually agreed on the classic approach. Mrs. Roxana's closing comment was: "I am wholly in favor of the individual approach."

Five months later, Mr. Roxana decided to stop coming; he was going to see his lawyer about a divorce. "The marriage is no better. She is a very, very bitter girl. She has a good relationship with her therapist but is as immature as always."

This couple illustrates the failure of the combined-collaborative approach to reequilibrate this conflicted couple. However, the wife was anchored in therapy with her therapist and needed two more years of therapy, although stormy, to weather the divorce trauma without falling apart. To date the combined-collaborative approach has been successful with one-half the couples.

NOTES

1. M. Robert Gomberg, Family-oriented treatment of marital problems. In *Social Casework in the Fifties* (Cora Kasius, Ed.). New York, Family Service Association of America, 1962, pp. 198–212; Ernest N. Gullerud and Virginia Lee Harlan; Four-way joint interviewing in marital counseling, *Soc Casework*, 43:532, 1962; Eugenia Huneus; A dynamic approach to marital problems, *Soc Casework*, 44:142, 1963; Gisela Konopka: Group work techniques in joint interviewing, in *National Conference of Social Workers Social Welfare Forum*. New York, Columbia Univ. Press, 1957; Dwaine R. Lindberg and Anne W. Wosmek: The use of family sessions in foster home care, *Soc Casework*, 44:137, 1963; Otto Pollak and Donald Brieland; The midwest seminar on family diagnosis and treatment, *Soc Casework*, 42:319, 1961; Frances H. Scherz: Multiple-client interviewing; treatment implications, *Soc Casework*, 43:120, 1962; Pauline M. Shereshefsky. Family unit treatment in child guidance, *Social Work*, 8:4, 1963; Helen S. Sholtis: Management of marriage counseling cases, *Soc Casework*, 45:71, 1964; Rex A. Skidmore: The joint interview in marriage counseling, *Marriage Fam Living*, 17:4, 1955; Alexander Thomas; Simultaneous psychotherapy with marital partners, *Amer J Psychother*, 10:716, 1956; Sue Vesper: Casework aimed at supporting marital role reversal, *Soc Casework*, 43:303, 1962; Viola W. Weiss: Multiple-client interviewing: An aid in diagnosis, *Soc Casework*, 43:14, 1962; and Carl A. Whitaker: Psychotherapy with couples, *Amer J Psychother*, 12:18, 1958.

2. Oscar Guttman: The dynamic shift of transference in combined

individual and group analysis, *J Psychoanal Groups*, *1*:76, 1962; James Jackson and Martin Grotjahn: The treatment of oral defenses by combined individual and group psychotherapy, *Int J Group Psychother 8*:373, 1958; Asya L. Kadis and Max Markowitz: Group psychotherapy, in *Progress in Clinical Psychology*. New York, Grune & Stratton, 1958, Vol. 3, pp. 154–183; Helen Papenek: Combined group and individual therapy in private practice, *Amer J Psychotherapy*, *8*:679, 1954; Clifford J. Sager: Concurrent individual and group analytic psychotherapy, *Amer J Orthopsychiat*, *30*:225, 1960; and Emanuel K. Schwartz and Alexander Wolf: Psychoanalysis in groups: some comparisons with individual analysis, *J Gen Psychol*, *64*:153, 1961.

3. Nathan B. Epstein and John M. Cleghorn: The family transactional approach in general hospital psychiatry: experiences, problems, and principles, *Compr Psychiat*, *7*:389, 1966.

4. Fritz Reider: Perceiving the Other Person, in *Person Perception and Interpersonal Behavior*. (Renato Taguiri and Luigi Petrullo, Eds.). Stanford, Stanford Univ Press, 1958, p. 30.

5. Solomon E. Asch: *Social Psychology*. Englewood Cliffs, Prentice-Hall, 1952, p. 163.

6. Harry Stack Sullivan: *The Interpersonal Theory of Psychiatry*. New York, Norton, 1953.

7. The triangular setting is more demanding of the therapist's observational span. His personality exerts a strong impact on the couple. He must therefore be capable of warmth and sensitivity. He can set an example for identification. His attitude should be one that encourages self-esteem. There are so many things happening simultaneously in the triadic session that only by selective attention to some problems can the therapist avoid becoming confused. The triangular setting and the face-to-face confrontation of the partners necessitate greater activity on the part of the therapist and greater use of the freer aspects of his own personality. It is in this area that the triadic operational approach makes perhaps its greatest contribution. See also Clifford J. Sager: Transference in conjoint treatment of married couples, *Arch Gen Psychiat*, *16*:185, 1967.

8. James Jackson and Martin Grotjahn, *op. cit.*

9. A.H. Richmond and A. Lauga: Some observations concerning the role in children in the disruption of family homeostasis, *Amer J Orthopsychiat*, *33*:757, 1963; See also Emanuel K. Schwartz and Alexander Wolf (The interpreter in group therapy, *Arch Gen Psychiat*, 18:189, 1968), who give a clinical example of how a parent may take over and manipulate a child.

10. Shirley Gehrke and Martin Kirschenbaum (Survival patterns in family conjoint therapy, *Family Process*, *6*:67, 1967) describe the scapegoat

child in terms of the survival myth as a homeostatic function of the family. For a good discussion of scapegoating, see Nathan W. Ackerman: *Treating the Troubled Family*. New York, Basic Books, 1966, pp. 77–86.

11. A good bibliography and description of the "home visit" is found in an article by Constance C. Hansen: An extended home visit with conjoint family therapy, *Family Process*, 7:67, 1968.

12. Roy M. Whitman, Milton Kramer, Paul H. Ornstein, and Bill J. Baldridge: The physiology, psychology, and utilization of dreams, *Amer J Psychiat, 124:287*, 1967.

13. Nathan W. Ackerman, in a recent article written with Marjorie L. Behrens (The family approach and levels of intervention, *Amer J Psychother, 22:5*, 1968), writes: "Our experience leads us to take a stand against the implied bias of the assigned theme: family therapy therapy *versus* individual therapy. . . . The key note is flexibility in treatment. The required orientation is to the specific needs of family and family members at different stages of the life cycle, at different levels of relations of family and individual, and in connection with particular crisis in the life stuation. . . . The indicated level of intervention may be the family method, therapy of a pair or of an individual, or any combination of these."

14. The following books and articles on family therapy are of value: Irvin M. Cohen: *Family Structure, Dynamics and Therapy*. Washington, Psychiatric Research Reports, 1966; Harold T. Christensen (Ed.): *Handbook of Marriage and the Family*. Chicago, Rand McNally, 1964; Daniel J. Safer: Family therapy for children with behavior disorders, *Family Process*, 5:243, 1966; John E. Bell: Comment— Family group therapy—a new treatment method for children, *Family Process*, 6:254, 1967 (reproduces a paper read in 1953); John J. Sigal, Vivian Rakoff, and Nathan B. Epstein: Indicators of therapeutic outcome in conjoint family therapy, *Family Process*, 6:215, 1967; Murray H. Sherman, Nathan W. Ackerman, Sanford N. Sherman, and Celia Mitchell: Non-verbal cues in family therapy, *Family Process*, 4:133, 1965; Mordecai Kaffman: Family diagnosis and therapy in child emotional pathology, *Family Process* 4:241, 1965; Peter H. Schween and Alexander Gralnick: Factors affecting family therapy in the hospital setting, *Compr Psychiat*, 7:424, 1966; Gerald H. Zuk: Family therapy, *Arch Gen Psychiat*, 16:71, 1967; Frank S. Williams: Family therapy: a critical assessment, *Amer J Orthopsychiat*, 37:912, 1967; Martin Grotjahn: Clinical illustrations from psychoanalytic family therapy, in *The Psychotherapies of Marital Disharmony:* and *Psychoanalysis and Family Neurosis*. New York, Norton, 1960; Vivian Rakoff, John J. Sigal and Nathan B. Epstein: Working-through in conjoint family therapy, *Amer J Psychother*, 21:782, 1967; and C. Christian

Beels and Andrew Ferber: Family therapy: a view, *Family Process,*
8:280, 1969, a scholarly article with extensive bibliography.
15. See Israel W. Charny: Integrated individual and family psychotherapy,
Family Process, 5:179, 1966; Joachim Flescher: The dual method in
analytic psychotherapy in *New Frontiers in Child Guidance* (A. H.
Esman, Ed.). New York, Int. Univs. Press, 1958, p. 50, and *Dual
therapy and Genetic Psychoanalysis.* New York, D. T. R. B. Editions,
1966; Ian Alger and Peter Hogan: The use of videotape recordings in
conjoint marital therapy, *Amer J Psychiat, 123:*1425, 1967; J. C. Sonne
and G. Lincoln: Heterosexual cotherapy team experiences during
family therapy, *Family Process,* 4:177, 1965; Carl A. Whitaker: Family
treatment of a psychopathic personality, *Compr Psychiat,* 7:397, 1966;
Georges R. Reding, Lois A. Charles, and Michael B. Hoffman: Treatment of the couple by a couple. II. Conceptual framework, case presentation and follow-up study, *Brit J Med Psychol, 40:*243, 1967;
Georges R. Reding and B. Ennis: Treatment of the couple by a
couple, *Brit J Med Psychol,* 37:325, 1964; Ian Alger: Joint sessions:
psychoanalytic variations, applications, and indications, in *The Mar-
riage Relationship* (Salo Rosenbaum and Ian Alger, Eds.). New York,
Basic Books, 1968, pp. 259–262; David Rubinstein and Oscar R.
Weiner: Co-therapy teamwork relationships in family psychotherapy.
In *Family Therapy and Disturbed Families* (Gerald H. Zuk and I.
Boszormenyi-Nagy, Eds.). Palo Alto, Science and Behavior Books,
1967, pp. 206–220, give a good review of co-therapy and bibliography;
Gertrude Aull and Clifton E. Kew: Treatment by two therapists,
Pastoral Counselor, 4:23, 1966; Herbert M. Rabin: How does co-
therapy compare with regular group therapy, *Amer J Psychother,*
21:244, 1967; R. K. Greenbank: Psychotherapy using two therapists,
Amer J Psychotherapy, 18:488, 1964; Rudolph Dreikurs, B. H. Shul-
man, and H. Mozak: Patient-therapist relationship in multiple therapy,
*Psychiat Quart, 26:*219, 1952; Elizabeth E. Mintz: Male-female co-
therapists, *Amer J Psychother,* 19:293, 1965; Titus P. Bellville, Otto
N. Raths, and Carol J. Bellville: Conjoint marriage therapy with a
husband-and-wife team, *Amer J Orthopsychiat,* 39:473, 1969; Michael
Courtenay (*Sexual Discord in Marriage.* London: Tavistock Publications Limited, 1968, p 46) describes the gradual extension of their
techniques to include combined-collaborative: "An extension of the
technique of one couple-two doctors, whereby all four persons concerned were present at one interview, developed from the earlier
combinations described, and here the interaction between the doctors
led to further insight by both doctors and patients." Finally, Carl A.
Whitaker offers many interesting observations about co-therapy in his
chapter The Growing Edge in *Techniques of Family Therapy,* New
York, Basic Books, 1967, pp. 307–314, while Jay Haley and Lynn
Hoffman raise a number of issues about this technique.

XXVII

THE THERAPIST: ATTRIBUTES AND PITFALLS

The phenomena of transference was discussed for many years with apparent detachment until years of experience forced the awareness and admission of countertransference. In Chapter XIV I briefly presented the five foci of transference phenomena—the reaction and the feelings of the patient toward the therapist. Countertransference can be defined as the reaction and feelings of the therapist toward his patient. Countertransference, like transference, includes both conscious and unconscious (unawareness) levels of feelings, thoughts, fantasies and reaction. Freud from the outset was conditioned by his training as a physician. A patient was a patient and must therefore be viewed with cool, calm, collected objectivity. What was considered decisive and dangerous was the therapist's possible sexual involvement with his patient—an acting out in the literal sense of countertransference. In this chapter I shall present the attributes of a therapist, the transference and countertransference phenomena, and finally, the phenomena of acting out.

ATTRIBUTES OF A THERAPIST

The relationship between the therapist and patient is an affective one involving both positive and negative feelings. The therapist is concerned with the thinking, feeling and behavior of the spouses, whether the behavior be real or fantasied. On the other hand, therapy involves the therapist's own experiences and feelings. Thus the "records" in the jukebox of the therapist influences the manner in which he observes, organizes and categorizes information about the conflicted couple. All the activities of the therapist, psychological as well as others, in a therapeutic relationship with a spouse involve a personal situation. Hence, the values and attitudes of the therapist are crucial.

Cappon[1] has described the values that a physician brings into the therapeutic relationship that are equally applicable to the clergy as to all members of the helping professions. He comments:

Being tolerant, permissive and relatively free from prejudice and value bias does not imply being amoral or lacking values. In being a man who has to survive and a member of society, the psychiatrist is in human bondage to his own and his people's system of values. . . . However, morality and religion are equatable with health, and no good psychiatrist can deny this, provided one defines morality as a search for harmony, which is good for the individual and his society; and religion as man's deepest solicitude.

Browning[2] comments on the therapist are also helpful:

It seems to me that in "helping" and "treatment" situations the ultimate and most effective control on how the professional person accomplishes his work with his patient-client has to rest on *informed individual integrity*. We must do everything possible to keep the inner "test lamp" running, so that we are aware when we are *involved* [italics added] with a case or situation that we are *not competent* to deal with entirely unassisted.

Interestingly, the Reverend Mr. Bollinger[3] concludes his article on pastoral work by noting: "In all of this, it may not be too inaccurate to remark that the work of the ministry in our day requires greater skill, freer imagination, and *stronger personal integrity* [italics added] than have ever been demanded before." Thus integrity becomes an important attribute for the therapist.

Elkes[4] comments on the medical student are pertinent for any therapist:

. . . he must be made aware . . . that behavior and subjective experience are not only phenomena but also instruments of high inferential value; that skill in observation of behavior including his own behavior, though more native to some than to others, can be both taught and learned; that such learning requires conceptual tools of its own; that it can never be didactic and always has to be experiential; and that relative absence of hardware in clinical psychiatry and human psychology in no way reflect in its ability to measure, conceptualize and predict. In short, the student must learn to respect the use of himself as much as of his slide rule and statistical tables. In this self-acceptance and growing self-knowledge there can be a source of much power.

Educators have been tardy in awareness of the need for training therapists in the physiology and psychology of sexuality. Retrospective data obtained from many couples who had consulted their clergy or other therapists for help with their sexual difficulties revealed unhappiness with advice received. A sense of adequacy and comfort in the sexual area is contingent on the extent the therapist has worked through his own sexual conflicts and achieved an understanding of his own attitudes and beliefs which might affect his therapeutic methods. No discussion on sex can avoid the occasional patient's complaint of homosexuality and masturbation.

Important for the therapist is how to deal with the sexually provocative patient.[5] Also the therapist must have adequate knowledge of recent research on sexology.[6,7] Keeping abreast of current studies on sexology may help therapists to develop, as they mature, liberalization of their sexual attitudes and beliefs.[8] When therapists are queried explicitly about their attitudes toward masturbation beyond adolescence and homosexuality, many displayed considerable anxiety. Not infrequently I still hear from some spouses with college exposure that masturbation can produce weakening of the back, insanity, or even cause homosexuality.[9]

According to Klaus Thomas, clergymen have their own specific problems, prominent among which are "ecclesiogenic" neuroses.[10] He finds that "ecclesiogenic" neuroses are common and the result of upbringing and education by or on the behalf of the churches. The term *ecclesiogenic* neurosis has been used medically in Europe since 1955. Thomas states, the syndrome is "caused by the widespread 'tabooizing' education in which the sexual and erotic areas of life are banned from open discussion (and are) considered immoral, forbidden or even threatened with punishment." The main symptoms consist of perversions (e.g. homosexuality), compulsions, anxiety, scrupulosity, and may lead to ultimate despair and suicide.

In addition to groping with his own sexual feelings, the therapist must also control his hostile impulses toward his patients.[11,12] It is doubly difficult to be objective about hostility.

Usually it is repressed into the unconscious, in contrast to conscious suppression of anger. Unconscious hostility of the therapist may surface as boredom, forgetting an appointment, a struggle to remain awake while the patient is talking. Also a severe headache or a depressive complaint that the patient is very resistant to change or difficult to manage is indicative of hostility.

The subject of confidentiality[13] can be a most taxing one for the therapist. Our patients, despite their hesitations and anxieties, gradually trust us. This trust mobilizes moral forces within the therapist to be discreet. However, in a case of suspected suicide, the therapist should break the seal of privileged communications and warn whomever he deems wise of the possible dangers, thus sharing the responsibilities with someone else.

The characteristics[14] a therapist should attempt to develop require time and patience. Of prime importance is the ability to be empathetic. Accurate empathy is necessary to relate to another's emotional feelings, thoughts and behavior with judicious objectivity. Flexibility is essential in his relationship to his patient, yet within appropriate limits for both. Sensitivity to all nuances of communication evidenced by his patient, e.g. slips of tongue. Personal integrity and genuineness in all areas of his behavior. Serenity as to his own emotional and interpersonal processes. Capability to be inactive in an emotional relationship without tension, i.e. to maintain his "cool." Another important quality is to have a good memory.[15] Finally, to remember that where there is no hostility, there is no therapy—a meaningful relationship is ambivalent. Thus the therapist should have a thorough knowledge of psychodynamics, including the role of unconscious forces in everyday living. It is the integration of all these attributes, charged with a great deal of affect, that encompasses the therapeutic relationship.

On the Nature of Tranference Phenomena

When we view the constructs of transference and countertransference as reciprocal processes in the therapeutic relationship,[16] and introduce two persons into the therapeutic settings, we have conceptualized a new transactional model.[17] The complexities of transference-countertransference mount geometrically as we try to define its relation to reality, maturation and social learning.[18]

Excellent reviews of the semantic and conceptual problems in transference have been published.[19] When Freud speaks of transference neurosis, two meanings of the term *transference* are involved; first, the transfer of libido (positive feelings such as warmth, tenderness, love) contained in the ego (individual) to objects (significant others); and second, the transfer of affective relations exhibited toward objects in infancy onto contemporary objects. This second meaning of the term, the transference neurosis, is today the one most frequent referred to, to the exclusion of other meanings.[20,21] We agree with Loewald,[22] who considers transference in its "original richness of interrelated phenomena and mental mechanisms which the concept encompasses in contrast to trends in modern psychoanalytic thought to narrow the term transference down to a very specific limited meaning." Benedek,[23] Alexander[24] and others[25-31] have pointed out countertransference as an active, constructive element in the therapeutic relationship.

In marital therapy five foci of transference phenomena are differentiated: (1) the relationship to the therapist as a real person and a new object, (2) those situations where the therapist is experienced as a symbolic figure endowed with qualities of existing fantasies, for example, persecutory, and (3) the regressive phenomena (the hearing of old "records" by the patient as though the music was originating in the therapist's jukebox—projective identification) manifested in the dyadic (one-to-one) transference neurosis. These first three foci are basic in all transference relationships. In the triadic settings where the therapist sees both spouses, either concurrently or conjointly, the triangular transference transactions become manifest. These transactions occur because the transference reactions of both spouses are directed toward the same therapist as well as toward each other. Thus the fourth (4) focus is the triangular transference neurosis (old "records" of childhood of a different type than those played in the dyadic transference neurosis are heard coming from the therapist's jukebox, especially of the triangular type associated with the competitive situation in relation to father and/or siblings). In the fifth (5) focus, the triangular transference transactions concern the production of adaptive feedbacks, not only toward the therapist but also to the other spouse, who in turn feeds back to his spouse, to the therapist, or both.[32] One example is the displacement of the positive sexual transference from the therapist to the marital partner. A cyclical transactional process is thus set in motion.

In the combined approach of individual and conjoint sessions, the transference phenomena with the therapist undergoes important qualitative changes. In some patients tensions produced in individual interviews are markedly reduced in the conjoint session, thus hastening therapeutic change. Very often one can observe dynamic shifts in transference phenomena in the alternation of individual and conjoint sessions—the replaying of different "records." Fantasy reenactments toward one parent may alternate with those toward the other parent in such shifts. The triangular transference transactions may help to encode new "records" toward peers and authoritative figures. For example, the preoedipal character traits, such as hostile dependency and submissiveness towards a controlling, rejecting, and overprotective mother, are handled therapeutically in the warm and unaggressive atmosphere of the individual session. This is further aided by the corrective emotional experience in the nonjudgmental, objective, impartial but dedicated manner of the therapist, who offers a very different "parental" voice. Most patients have to be prepared for the joint sessions (triadic). The one-to-one (dyadic) relationship works through a little of the disturbance of the very early phase with mother (preoedipal) before the patient can cope with the higher socialization processes (oedipal phase and the relationships with siblings). This can be observed in the dramatic change of behavior of some patients between individual and joint sessions. There are patients who in individual sessions are submissive and unaggressive, accepting all the interpretations of the therapist. In the triadic setting the same patients may become very argumentative, even disputing the interpretations already accepted in the dyadic sessions. On the other hand, the therapist may react, differently towards such a patient in the conjoint session. Such alternating and contrasting behavior patterns in the therapeutic relationship may produce invaluable material.

The varying transference phenomena are demonstrated in the following vignette:

This vignette is a composite of the clinical material of a series of couples seen concurrently in psychoanalysis. Each couple had several years of analysis, with the women on the couch—frequently with marked annoyance at this position—and with the men, also, on the couch, offering no resistance to this position. The women were usually very attractive, aggressive, intelligent, buxom and seductive in dress and behavior, but usually frigid sexually. These women were typical of Katharina in Shakespeare's *Taming of the Shrew*, shrewish, bad-tempered with a notorious disposition. On the other hand, the men were passive, well-dressed and well-groomed, gracious gentlemen, whose disposition outside of the marriage was like that of Bianca's, Katharina's sister, sweet and lovable. Outwardly, these men suppressed and repressed their hostility, but psychosomatically occasionally revealed this by essential hypertension (elevated blood pressure on a functional basis) or anginal (heart), pains, with or without premature ejaculation (urinating on their wives instead of fornicating—used here in the nonlegal sense). The marriages were characterized by frequent games of "Uproar," à la *Whose Afraid of Virginia Woolf*, in which the content of the arguments varied from finances to in-laws. In my experience, psychoanalysis has been moderately successful in both taming the shrew and emotionally maturing the man.

Mr. and Mrs. Katharina came for counseling because of years of quarreling. Mr. Katharina felt that he had been unduly criticized by his wife for his interest in his mother. Mrs. Katharina felt that she could not stand her husband's close relationship to his mother because she rejected her as a daughter-in-law. Mr. Katharina, because he felt that his wife alone was the cause of their marital problems, was angry and reluctant about therapy. His individual diagnostic interviews revealed his premature ejaculation, which he had never disclosed to anyone before. He went into great length about his feelings of inadequacy as a man and his wish to be cured.

Mr. Katharina's "confession" of his premature ejaculation was his response to the therapist as a real object (focus one as described above under transference phenomena). Relating of his problem indicated that he saw me as a real person, that he accepted me as an individual and wanted help. On another transference level, the symbolic one, I represented the omnipotent, omniscient doctor who cures illnesses. His revealing his secret was both a plea for help and a fantasied wish for cure by the powerful physician.

In his next session, Mr. Katharina brought in his first dream (the following are excerpts): "My wife is on a horse. Horse skids and falls. I think that now they will have to destroy the horse. My wife gets up and tearfully says she had lost the buckles off her shoes. I tell her angrily to forget the buckles, as long as she is all right. She suddenly has only a slip on and is exposed. Her cousin comes up. He has a stupid facial expression. I tell him about the horse incident. He looks unconcerned and bored."

His associations revealed great anger toward his aggressive wife, who he characterized as a "shrew" and who was always putting pressure on him to be more successful. He is also angry at the therapist, who he feels may hurt him ("destroy the horse." This anger is not expressed openly, but revealed in the dream as the "stupid cousin.") Moreover, he is angry at both his wife and his therapist for making him reveal himself as an inadequate male—a woman who has "only a slip on and is exposed." These are unconscious negative transference feelings toward the therapist.

Mrs. Katharina, who was being seen separately but synchronously with her husband, continued to be cooperative in her therapy. In her behavior, dreams, and associations, the emerging libidinal dyadic transference (to the therapist as a real object) became apparent as seen in a dream reported in the fifteenth week of therapy: "I am at a hotel in Acapulco. I am in bed with a short man with curly hair. He asked me to marry him." (I am of short stature and have curly hair.)

Mr. Katharina's response to the interpretations of his anxiety about the nature of his repressed hostility led to excessive anxiety which required the use of tranquilizers.

In his third month of therapy he reported the following dream: "My mother and I are in the operating room. I am on the operating table. The doctor was putting on surgical gloves. He was going to perform a circumcision on me. I look down at my groin after the preparation and see that I have no testicles."

In his associations, the mother seemed to be the doctor's assistant. He related how his mother was both possessive and castrative. She was always belittling his father and him in front of the family. As a result he was an underachiever in school. Currently, he commented, his sexual performance at home was the poorest it had ever been, nocturnal emissions and even impotence now (sexless in the dream and castrated). This is a good example of the classical psychoanalytic transference neurosis (dyadic) in which feelings and fantasies from childhood in regard to the mother are transferred onto the therapist.

In his fifth month of therapy, Mr. Katharina complained of being very irritable and having feelings of "boiling inside with rage." A dream at that time revealed hostility at a regressive level heretofore not manifested: "My wife, me, and another man in a restaurant. Waiting for a table. Very crowded. Lots of tables available for two but not for three.[33] Go to the captain and get very angry at him. I shouted, and walked out. As I walked out my baby sister walked in."

This dream indicated anger at having to share the therapist with his wife—a frequent type of dream in triadic therapy (two is company but three is a crowd). Further, the dream revealed reactivation of feelings experienced when his younger sister was born. In his associations there was a wealth of memories about his hostile feelings toward both his mother and younger sister in his childhood. Mr. Katharina has not, as yet, been able to express overt hostility toward his therapist. Unconscious repression was due to hostile components in the sibling rivalry transactions toward his wife in the triangular transference neurosis (the fourth focus of transference phenomena). On a deeper level the triangular transference involves the oedipal constellation.

The fifth focus of transference, triangular transference transactions producing adaptive feedbacks, became more manifest beginning with the tenth month of therapy when Mr. Katharina reported a change in his wife, from a "shrill-sounding shrew to a soft-spoken and pleasant woman." Concomitant with Mrs. Katharina's improved self-image was her increasing libidinal feelings toward the therapist, which were being directed toward her husband. The next two months of therapy was stormy for the couple.

However, Mr. Katharina began to report progressively more aggressive attitudes at home and at his office. He was in excellent mood when he reported the following dream: "Listening to a naval officer giving a speech. He tells about beginning as an enlisted man and going up the ranks to become an admiral. I ask where he went to school. He said, Annapolis."

His first association was that "Annapolis is similar to analysis." It was followed by a number of early close and positive memories about his father (focus one—the therapist as a real object). We see in this dream identification with the therapist with the encoding of new "records." He is the enlisted man who has become commander of his ship.

At this time the Katharinas left for a vacation, and upon return, Mr. Katharina was in excellent spirits and proudly reported: "Don't ever remember having performed as well sexually in my life. We had a wonderful time. It was like a second honeymoon. It is one year since we first started coming to you." Mrs. Katharina expressed similar thoughts about their vacation.

Therapy was continued for another two years before the therapeutic changes were concretized.

The psychological relationship between patient and therapist is of an affective nature. The relationship usually involves positive affects of the patient toward the therapist. Occasionally the positive feelings on the part of the patient may become so strong that they may be openly stated. Not infrequently the therapist may respond to his patients overt declaration of love—a situation to be avoided at all costs. At all times it is important to remember that the relationship is professional and not social. Since ambivalence is the core of all relationships, at times the manifestation of negative feelings by the therapist can destroy the therapeutic relationship; on the other hand, some expressions of hostility, verbal only, can be expressed by the therapist when justified by the patient's behavior, e.g. being consistently late for appointments.

The following clinical material of Mrs. Eulalia illustrates the two sides of the coin of ambivalence—both the positive and negative feelings toward the therapist:

"In the beginning, we had a good rapport, but somewhere along the line, this has broken down, and now I feel stifled, inhibited, and I just cannot communicate. I am sure it involves many factors. For one thing, I am overcome with the feeling of 'What's the use?' Either way, I am wrong. You have managed, so far, to blame me for everything. Your advice is contrary. For instance, if Mel is childish, it is my fault because I mothered him. Ten lousy ugly married years is all my fault because 'I wanted it this way.' And then you turn around and advise me to baby him, mother him, excuse his childishness and give him sex, all the things that were so wrong before. Now you suggest they are right, and frankly, it doesn't make sense.

"I feel that you do not understand me, and really never did. I feel, you do not believe me, even though I have never made a statement in your office that I could not prove by examples. Yet, you very readily believed Mel's crazy, wild accusations, with no proof whatsoever. But, mostly, I feel I have failed from the beginning to impress upon you the seriousness of the whole situation (you keep referring to this whole thing like it is a game) and here I think is where the problem lies. This, or else I am seeing the wrong doctor.

"I do not wish to imply that I have any doubts as to your capabilities or your qualifications. On the contrary, I think you are the greatest. But your efforts and your service is directed toward trying to save this rotten, ugly marriage, which I feel is beyond repair. There have been many minor improvements in our daily living as a result of Mel's sessions with you. I know I have learned a great deal from my sessions with you, but if anything, it has left me more confused than ever. But I think the most important thing I have learned is that there is something wrong with me too, that it does not begin or end with Mel, and that something can be done about it. And it is this "something" that I am now looking for. And this is why I question whether you are the right doctor for me."

Mrs. Eulalia expressed considerable negative feelings toward me, insisted she wanted her own therapist, questioned my impartiality, and wanted a therapist whose orientation was not on the marriage. Since Mr. Eulalia had originally resisted any therapy and was showing progressive improvement, Mrs. Eulalia was referred to another therapist for the classical approach. Ten months later, after Mr. Eulalia had shown considerable improvement in the totality of his behavior, therapy was discontinued. Shortly thereafter, I received the following telephone call from Mrs. Eulalia revealing the opposite side of the coin of ambivalence—her positive feelings:

"I'm laughing with tears in my eyes. I just found out that Mel has not been seeing you for the past month. And now I feel like the biggest jackass on earth. All the months I was with Dr. ——, the hardest thing to bear was the overwhelming desire to flee his office and come back to you. But since you were Mel's doctor, I did not want to interrupt your work with him, and I absolutely could not, and would not, go back to the double visits we used to have.

"Two months ago I stopped treatment with Dr. ——. This was a mutual arrangement, as we both felt no further progress was being made. I intended to call and ask you for another referral. But since Mel is no longer your patient, I don't want another referral, I would like to return to you. I know you are a very busy man, but I also know you are a very good doctor, the best in the city as far as I am concerned, and if you do not have time right now, then I will wait until you do."

Mrs. Eulalia's session and telephone call illustrates the two sides of the coin of ambivalence—the positive and negative feelings each patient has toward their therapist. Although therapy moves forward in the climate of bilateral positive feelings, the therapist should control the level of these feelings. Thus the therapeutic setting should be structured, if possible, so that all sessions are in a professional setting (office and not at home). If the patient begins to display overt seductive behavior by act or dress, an excellent ploy is to shift the interviews from dyadic to triadic. Occasionally some private fantasies of a libidinal nature will occur in the therapist. These fantasies will cause no trouble provided they remain private. The therapist should guard against double entendres, which reveal his covert feelings. This leads us to the next topic to be discussed, acting out on the part of the patient or therapist or both.

The Phenomena of Acting Out

The usage of the term and the concept of acting out as a behavioral manifestation covers a wide spectrum of phenomena.[34] All three systems are involved but in varying degrees in acting out, and the behavioral manifestations vary in complexity. There is considerable variation in the degree acting out dominates the personality of any individual. Acting-out phenomena are best visualized as units of communication. Acting out as a circumscribed manifestation is best illustrated in the two following vignettes:

Mrs. Judith had been in intensive therapy for the treatment of obesity. Laboriously and painfully she lost twenty-five pounds in the past six months. At this point I took my annual winter vacation of two weeks. When I returned I found she had regained her weight loss. Exploring the determining forces behind this act revealed the following: (1) conscious anger at me for going away and leaving her, (2), unconscious anger of her "inner child" at being rejected, (3), feeling frustrated and unloved, she fed herself, using the equation food equals love, i.e., her symbolic communication stating: "I have to feed myself, since you no longer love me by going away."

Mrs. Julia, who was in treatment at the same time, reacted by becoming pregnant extramaritally. This created a "severe headache" for everyone concerned, especially her therapist. The unconscious motive was most dominant, that of revenge, which overlayed her strong rejection anger.

Acting out as a circumscribed manifestation also can occur as an hysterical conversion symptom. In the past two decades the incidence of hysteria is progressively decreasing. The following vignette is illustrative:

Mr. Jeanne was referred by his eye doctor because of "tubular or gun barrel" vision. He was unable to see anything except directly in front of his eyes and had no peripheral vision at all. The recent onset of his eye difficulty occurred while attending his first out-of-town convention. A deeply religious and moral man, he was shocked at the behavior of some of his fellow conventioneers. His eye difficulty followed shortly after a suggestive comment by a model. The unconscious communication was not to wander from the straight and narrow and to focus on reaching his own room and not glance to the "happenings" in some of the surrounding rooms.

Another type of neurotic acting out can occur in individuals who make episodic suicidal attempts. All suicidal thoughts or attempts should be considered seriously as the person may inadvertently commit suicide. For example, in a recent case the wife made several suicidal attempts, each structured so that the husband would rescue her at five o'clock when he returned from work. A flat tire on his automobile caused an hour's delay, and upon arrival home, his wife was dead. A suicidal threat may be an unconscious message for help.

In dealing with a psychotic spouse, the therapist should keep in mind the possibilities of that individual acting out, i.e. whether he will act upon his unrealistic perceptions and impulses, e.g. homocidal behavior. A physical attack may be the acting out of hallucinations or delusions. This assaultive behavior is unrealistic but consistent with the delusional ideation or hallucinatory distortions.

Another type of acting out is that exhibited by psychopathic personalities who react to their inner conflicts by behavior rather than by developing neurotic symptoms. An example is the behavior of Mr. Joan:

> Mrs. Joan had consulted me about her husband. After two years of sobriety, he recently went on an alcoholic spree and spent large sums of money on a prostitute. Mrs. Joan stopped divorce proceedings when he tearfuly promised to stop drinking and accept psychiatric help. She stated that two years ago, on his last alcoholic binge, he took off for New York, and she didn't hear from him for two weeks. During this two-week interval he managed to marry two women, one eighteen years old and the other thirty years old.

Not uncommonly, acting-out behavior can be observed in "normal" appearing individuals who tend to react in a stereotyped manner in certain situations. In these persons their stereotyped behavior is so ingrained in their style of living that they are clinically classified as having character disorders. Since their behavior patterns are part of their character, they are unaware of the inappropriateness of their reactions. Examples of this type of behavior are seen in seductive women who are being continually raped after leaving a tavern with a stranger who ostensibly is going to take them home; or by women who repeatedly permit themselves to be exploited by conniving men. It is as if these persons, when confronted with a set of stimuli, respond with inappropriate behavior as though

programmed by a computor. These individuals do not profit
from experience, since they do not connect their painful behavior with their unconscions motivations, but blame it on fate.
Berne's[35] conceptualizations of games people play are valuable
in understanding these individuals. In effect, these persons react to an unconscious script and do not realize the inappropriateness of their behavior.

The therapist must also be aware that his own countertransference may encourage acting out in his patients. Further, and
of greater danger to all concerned is when the therapist himself acts out particularly in the sexual area. The following vignette is illustrative:

Dr. Juliana called for a supervisory session for advice on how to cope
with a counselee who was sending him daily love letters. He had been
seeing the Juliettes weekly for the past six months for marital discord.
Initially Mrs. Juliette had "come on" in the conjoint sessions as a "hostile
bitch." After four months of therapy, the marital relationship had become
harmonious. At this point she had asked for an individual appointment,
declared her love for him, and began sending him daily love letters.

At the next conjoint session with the Juliettes, he announced that he
would be away on a vacation. That evening Mrs. Juliette called him,
extremely upset, and only calmed down when he agreed to permit her to
continue writing to him between their therapy sessions and that he would
send her a postcard while he was away. (This was a technical error on
his part, as Mrs. Juliette reacted to this card as a return of her love.) The
next morning he received the following letter:

I keep thinking of you and feel better when I put my thoughts down
on paper and send them to you. The talk you gave John (Mr. Juliette)
yesterday worked as he was trying to be very attentive and passionate
last night. I still had to have you in my thoughts to get satisfied sexually. (A good example of the triangular transference transaction.)
Honey, I got panicky that maybe you won't love me anymore if John
and I get along. I need you to love me honey as you do great things
for me. Stay with me, don't leave me. I called you last night because
I couldn't say what I wanted to say at your office with John there.
You handle John and me so beautifully. When I am sitting across from
you, it's so hard not to be able to touch you. I can't wait until you
return from your vacation. You mean so terribly much to me. Don't
ever stop loving me. I know you have important matters in your life.
Could you find a little place for me.

I LOVE YOU

This woman demonstrates the development of a strong sexual transference in a triadic conjoint session. It was suggested

that he no longer see her individually after explaining to her that her letters showed marked improvement in her self-image, that she now felt so much better about herself that she could have fantasies about him, but that he was her doctor and not her lover—and their relationship was a professional one, not a social one. Further, the letters must stop, or else he would have to transfer both her husband and her to another therapist. It was also suggested to Dr. Juliana that he point out to her that frequently an individual visualizes her doctor as omnipotent and omniscient. At the next session Dr. Juliana reported that Mrs. Juliette tearfully accepted his suggestions, stopped writing letters to him, and that three months later, with progressive improvement in the marriage, he discontinued therapy.

In the following clinical example, we see where transference and counter transference phenomena between a patient and her family physician almost resulted in disaster:

Mr. and Mrs. Katherine were referred by their minister for therapy because of marital disharmony. Mrs. Katherine became quite upset at her husband's interest in their neighbor's wife. Although this interest was purely platonic, she resented his doing little errands for her while her husband was out of town on business. His refusal to stop what he considered "being neighborly" had resulted in progressive arguments.

In her individual diagnostic sessions, Mrs. Katherine stated: "For the past six months I had gotten to know our family physician pretty well through our PTA meetings. When things began to get difficult for me, I had thought of talking to him about Jim (Mr. Katherine). I also knew I was attracted to him several months ago. I accepted my feelings toward him as nice and normal. I didn't plan to do anything about it. But I felt I had to talk to somebody about our problems. I felt the only person I could trust was this doctor and his wife. One night I got so upset that I went to this doctor's house. He wasn't home, but his wife was. I told her about our marital problem. I felt better. Later that evening Edward (the physician) came to our house, and I told him what was going on, and that Jim was accusing me of having a dirty mind. Edward was very helpful. I felt he was helping me. He suggested that I tell Jim how upset I was becoming by his behavior.

"The next night I told Jim. He got very angry but said he would chop off the relationship with the neighbor if that is what I wanted. Our marriage was most important. The next day he was lying on our bed. He seemed woe begone and said, I've lost a friend, and started to cry. I've never seen him cry before. And this, a reaction to losing a neighbor. Something happened inside of me and I called Edward again. He suggested I come in to his office. He has done a lot of counseling. When I arrived I told him I hadn't eaten for a week and perhaps if we could talk over lunch, I could get some food down. We went to a nearby restaurant and I had coffee and a sandwich.

"He said: 'Shall I analyze this?' At this, bells started ringing in my ears. Shall we talk in your house, he asked. As Jim was at work and the children at school, I said, yes, and wondered why. We did go to my house and he started talking about his feelings for me and mine for him. In a sort of clinical way. Then he asked me if I trusted him and I said, Yes. He asked me to sit on his lap. I threw caution to the winds and did. I felt I belonged there. No feelings of guilt. I felt rather turned on. He was very nice. Not demanding. He just held me. He didn't take advantage of me. He told me that he had been attracted to me for some time since our PTA meetings. One light kiss and he left. I thought all about it the next day. Here I was involved. He knew I cared about him and he about me.

"The next day I called his office. He suggested I come for another appointment. I knew his nurse was there and asked him if he would make a house call. He did. It took me a long time but I said: I love you. He held my hand for a moment trying to be the doctor. I could see he was struggling with himself. Suddenly he left.

"As he walked out I felt great. I had dumped my problems into his lap. The same lap I had sat on. I felt I could eat. I cleaned the house feeling great. The next morning the phone rang. It was Edward. It was the first time he said: 'I want to talk to you.' I felt it was important and said, 'Yes.' He came out. He told me he had been through a big struggle. He couldn't eat a thing yesterday. That yesterday he felt in control of the situation, but that today, no. He said: 'I feel so strongly about you. I want to express it physically. I feel stripped of all controls. I could go to bed with you right now. Would you?' I said, 'no.' So we talked. He said he loved me. After a time he thanked me for saying, No! We both had our puritanical backgrounds. We sat there and kissed. I felt very loving and comfortable with him. He left.

That evening he called again. Told me how grateful he was that I had said, no. That he loved his wife. That he couldn't see me again. In fact that he was going to stop being a psychiatrist and just be what he was trained to be—a general practitioner."

At this point Mrs. Katherine began to cry bitterly. A near tragedy had been averted.

SUMMARY

In this chapter I have presented some important attributes that every therapist should strive to attain. Being in a helping profession requires a continuous commitment to keep abreast of current therapeutic innovations and to strive continually for self-analysis and improvement. The importance of the recipro-

cal emotional character of the therapeutic relationship was presented in terms of psychoanalytic concepts of transference and
countertransference. The affective relationship between patient
and therapist consists of both conscious and unconscious feelings, phantasies and, unfortunately at times, acting-out behavior of a destructive nature. Finally, the phenomena of acting
out was described, illustrated, and suggestions offered to cope
with them on the part of the therapist.

NOTES

1. Daniel Cappon: Values and value judgement in psychiatry, *Psychiat
Quart*, July, pp. 1, 1966; Monroe S. Arlen (Conjoint therapy and the
corrective emotional experience, *Family Process*, 5:101, 1966) discusses
the role of the therapist and lists eight functions. See also Herbert
Silverman: The influence of values on psychotherapeutic tactics and
strategy, *Voices*, 2:71, 1966.

2. Thomas B. Browning: Psychiatry and the nonmedical psychotherapist,
Amer J Psychiat, 122:1065, 1966. See also C. Knight Aldrich (Brief
psychotherapy: a reappraisal of some theoretical assumptions, *Amer
J Psychiat*, 125:858, 1968), who comments on informed optimism as
an attribute of the therapist; and Lawrence S. Kubie's succinct comments in Pitfalls of community psychiatry, *Arch Gen Psychiat*, 18:257,
1968.

3. Richard A. Bollinger: Mental aspects of pastoral work: vignettes with
comment, *Pastoral Psychology*, 17:1, 1966.

4. Joel Elkes: On meeting psychiatry: a note on the student's first year,
Amer J Psychiat, 122:121, 1965; see also Berkley C. Hawthorne: Presidential address: continuing education—a must for pastoral counselors,
Pastoral Counselor, 5:21, 1967; Jules V. Coleman (Aims and conduct
of psychotherapy, *Arch Gen Psychiat*, 18:1, 1968) begins his article
as follows: "Many therapists are too *ambitious* [italics added]"; also
Richard B. Lower: Psychotherapy of neurotic dependency, *Amer J
Psychiat*, 124:514, 1967; Albert E. Scheflen: Quasi-courtship in psychotherapy, *Psychiatry*, 28:245, 1965. This illustrated article should
be read by all therapists. O. Spurgeon English: Contributions to the
development of a psychotherapist, *Amer J Psychother*, 22:431, 1968;
Richard D. Chessick: Greed and vanity in the life of the psychotherapist, *Psychiat Dig*, May, pp. 40–43, 1967; and Arthur A. Miller and
Alvin G. Burstein: Professional development in psychiatric residents,
Arch Gen Psychiat, 20:385, 1969.

5. Marc H. Hollender (The prostitutes two identities, *Med Aspects Hum*

Sexuality, 2:45, 1968) presents an interesting concept on how the same person can be both saint and sinner in terms of identity. In my conceptual frame this means playing different "records" containing different "parental" voices. These voices come from different "significant others" or from the same person who consciously expresses one value—be good—and unconsciously another value—be a sinner. These types of "records" may explain the seductive female patient.

6. The following are of value: Donald W. Hastings: *A Doctor Speaks of Sexual Expression in Marriage.* Boston, Little, Brown, 1966; Aaron L. Rutledge: *Pre-Marital Counseling.* Cambridge, Shenkman, 1966; Ruth and Edward Brecher: *An Analysis of Human Sexual Response.* New York, New American Library, 1966; Judd Marmor: *Sexual Inversion: The Multiple Roots of Homosexuality.* New York, Basic Books, 1965; and Isadore Rubin: Transition in sex values-implications for the education of adolescents, *J Marriage Family,* 27:185, 1965.

7. Lionel S. Lewis and Dennis Brissett: Sex as work: a study of avocational counseling, *Med Aspects Hum Sexuality,* 2:14, 1968.

8. An amazing recent report from Britain prepared by a committee of ministers and laymen (Reverend Kenneth Greet, Chairman, Chicago Daily News, Oct. 17, 1966, p. 30) after two years of research on sexual practices refused to condemn adultery and stated that casual sex could be "trivially pleasurable or mildly therapeutic," and further noted that the traditional "thou shalt not" approach of the church is outdated.

9. Serwyn M. Woods and Joseph Natterson (Sexual attitudes in medical students: some implications for medical education, *Amer J Psychiat,* 124:323, 1967) found that a large group of medical students felt that mental illness was frequently caused by masturbation. Many of the students were concerned with problems of potency, masturbatory anxiety and shame, and fears of latent homosexuality. Often their standards of normalcy were unreasonable and inaccurate and acquired from superstition or popular novels. Married students were anxious about the significance of occasional masturbation after marriage.

10. Klaus Thomas, MD., Ph.D., and D.D., of West Germany, in a paper delivered as a meeting held in United States before the Academy of Religion and Mental Health stated that prevention of "ecclesiogenic" neurosis cannot be fulfilled by any group other than by the churches themselves. Dr. Thomas during 1964–1965 was a staff psychiatrist at St. Elizabeths Hospital, Washington, D.C., and professor of Pastoral care at Wesley Theological Seminary and Gettysburg Lutheran Seminary. Among the first 1,000 neurotics reporting to his suicide prevention center, 389 (39%) were ecclesiogenically ill, verifying the "definite and extremely dangerous correlation between suicide and 'ecclesiogenic' neuroses." Pastors with this neurosis "less frequently consider suicide

as a solution, being generally preserved by their deep Christian faith." Although the ecclesiogenic neurosis is not found exclusively among clergymen, its correlation with the religious professions makes it "almost a vocation disease," among 186 neurotic pastors, 90 percent suffered from this condition.

Thomas described the childhood history of patients as similar: parents or grandparents were all very pious, upbringing was generally strict, all sexual questions were taboo. In addition, there was ignorance of sexuality and anxiety about their own sexual feelings, which were equated with sin. They had guilt feelings about their permanent failures to stop masturbation or other manifestations of their natural sex impulses.

The guilt feelings about their sexual feelings or behavior often cause marital problems, some of these may be caused by a frigid wife who usually, also exposed to a strict, religious upbringing, also suffers from "ecclesiogenic" neurosis: possible infidelity may result, deepening religious conflicts. "Where natural relations to the other sex are blocked by the so-called Christian judgement that "they are sinful," homosexuality and other perversions are the most frequent result and one of the most frequent symptoms of an "ecclesiogenic" neurosis. Compulsive reading of pornographic literature, and the uttering of strongly obscene words in the cadence of liturgical expressions are the most common and most uniform of these sexual compulsions.

Thomas suggests that religion must develop "a realistic theology of sexuality, but above all a theology of eroticism." In many instances, the meaning of the message of the Bible has been misunderstood or misinterpreted and therefore requires clarification. Certain words and sections "just do *not* have the sexual or erotic sense" attributed to them.

At the same meeting, Dr. Gelolo McHugh, professor of psychology, Duke University, noted that his studies revealed "that the most serious problem of the clergyman or church worker is in the sexual field. In this area the pastor's knowledge is below and absolutely inadequate for proper counseling of others and for helping himself."

See also Carl W. Christensen (The occurrence of mental illness in the ministry: family origins, *J Pastoral Care 14:*13, 1960), who found as Thomas did that the family groups were of a fundamentalistic faith.

11. D. W. Winnicott: Hate in the countertransference, originally published in 1947 and reprinted in Voices, 1:102, 1965. In this paper the author examines "one aspect of the whole subject of ambivalence, hate in the countertransference." His comments are valuable for every therapist.

12. Otto Kernberg in his paper, Notes on Countertransference, presented at the fall meeting of the American Psychoanalytic Association, New York, Dec. 7, 1963, describes the contrasting approaches in regard to the concept of countertransference, namely, the "classical" and the

"totalistic." In an erudite presentation, including an excellent bibliography, he describes the importance of "concern" as an important force in coping with aggression and self-aggression in the countertransference.

13. Ralph Slovenko: Sex counseling and the law, *Med Aspects Hum Sexuality*, 3:4, 1969.

14. R. Bruce Sloane: The converging paths of behavior therapy and psychotherapy, *Amer J Psychiat*, 125:879, 1969; C. B. Truax and D. Wargo: Human encounters that change behavior for better or worse, *Amer J Psychother*, 20:499, 1966; Margaret L. Ferard and Noel K. Hunnybun: *The Caseworker's Use of Relationships*. Springfield, Thomas, 1962, see Chapters 3 and 4, Meeting The Client and The Helping Process, pp. 27–84; George Robinson: A new theory of empathy and its relation to identification, *J Asthma Res*, 1:49, 1963; G. T. Barrett-Lennard: Significant aspects of a helping relationship, *Canad Mental Health*, Suppl 47, July, 1965; Carl R. Rogers: Characteristics of a Helping Relationship, *Canad Mental Health*, Suppl, 27, March, 1962; Joost A. M. Meerloo: Why do we sympathize with each other, *Arch Gen Psychiat*, 15:390, 1966; Robert E. Gould: Dr. Strangeclass: or how I stopped worrying about the theory and began treating the blue-collar workers, *Amer J Orthopsychiat*, 37:78, 1967. Finally, E. Fuller Torrey (The case for the indigenous therapist, *Arch Gen Psychiat*, 20:365, 1969) quotes the research of R. R. Carkhuff and C. B. Truax (Training in counseling and psychotherapy, *J Consult Psychol*, 29:333, 1965) advocating three qualities of the therapist—accurate empathy, nonpossessive warmth and genuiness.

15. Samuel Futterman: The memory of the psychotherapist, *Amer J Psychotherapy*, 20:284, 1966. He states that "in any search for the qualities necessary for good therapists, one never sees a good memory listed as an asset." He made a careful study of the literature and found little except for several pages in Freud. Yet "patients frequently remark with surprise at the psychotherapist's memory of the many things in their lives." He presents a psychology of memory which has to do with the process of incorporation and introjection of new material—what I refer to as cutting new "records."

16. B. Wolstein: *Transference. Its Meaning and Function in Psychoanalytic Therapy*. New York, Grune & Stratton, 1954; and *Countertransference*. New York, Grune & Stratton, 1959.

17. Bernard L. Greene and Alfred P. Solomon: Marital disharmony: concurrent psychoanalytic therapy of husband and wife—the triangular transference transaction, *Amer J Psychother*, 17:443, 1963. See John J. O'Shea (A six-year experience with nontraditional methods in a child clinic setting, *Amer J Orthopsychiat*, 37:56, 1967), who describes transference phenomena graphically: "This broadening and intensification of the data collection process promotes early clarifica-

tion of personal roles and of interpersonal interactions. To put it more figuratively, seeing the family in action in the home has the dramatic power for enlightenment that is symbolized by the saying, 'A picture is worth a thousand words'. It has something of the power to clarify that is inherent in the process of exemplification, so widely employed in almost all learning situations. It has the dramatic power of live theater, with the most authentic of stage settings."

18. Nathan W. Ackerman: Transference and countertransference, *Psychoanal Rev*, 46:17, 1959.

19. Douglas W. Orr: Transference and countertransference, a historical survey, *J Amer Psychoanal Assn*, 2:567, 1954.

20. R. Waelder: Introduction to the discussion on problems of transference, *Int J Psychoanal*, 37:367, 1957.

21. W. Hoffer: Transference and transference neurosis, *Int J Psychoanal*, 37:377, 1957.

22. Hans W. Loewald: On the therapeutic action of psychoanalysis, *Int J Psychoanal*, 41:26, 1960.

23. Theresa Benedek: Dynamics of the countertransference, *Bull Menninger Clinic*, 17:201, 1953.

24. Franz Alexander: Address before the annual meeting of the Academy of Psychoanalysis, May 7, 1961, Chicago, Illinois.

25. Franz Alexander: Current problems in dynamic psychotherapy in its relationship to psychoanalysis, *Amer J Psychiat*, 115:324, 1959.

26. Lucia Tower: Countertransference, *J Amer Psychoanal Assn*, 4:224, 1956.

27. Frieda Fromm-Reichmann: *Fundamentals of Intensive Psychotherapy.* Chicago, Univ. Chicago Press, 1950.

28. Harry Stack Sullivan: The theory of anxiety and the nature of psychotherapy, *Psychiatry*, 12:3, 1949.

29. Michael Balint: Changing therapeutic aims and techniques in psychoanalysis, *Int J Psychoanal*, 31:117, 1950.

30. Paula Heiman: On-countertransference, *Int J Psychoanal*, 31:81, 1950.

31. Mabel Blake Cohen: Countertransference and anxiety, *Psychiatry*, 15:231, 1952.

32. Greene and Solomon, *op. cit.*

33. John E. Bell (Contrasting approaches in marital counseling, *Family Process*, 6:23, 1967) writes: "Consequently there are certain problems and limitations imposed by this method of approach (Conjoint). The old saw that 'Two's company, three's a crowd' has more than surface validity."

34. James Naiman: The role of the superego in certain forms of acting out, *Int J Psychoanal*, 47:286, 1966; and, John M. MacDonald: Acting out, *Arch Gen Psychiat*, 13:439, 1965.

35. Eric Berne: *Games People Play.* New York, Grove Press, 1964. See also K. Michael Lipkin and Robert S. Daniels (The role of seduction in interpersonal relationships, *Med Aspects Hum Sexuality,* 3:79, 1969), who present seductive behavior as a developmental sequence which may be traced from infancy to maturity.

XXVIII

PREVENTION OF MARITAL PROBLEMS

It is sad to face the fact that so many marriages begin in heaven and end in hell.
———Rudolf Dreikurs[1]

In a recent address I stressed the importance of prevention in premarital and marital situations and in divorce.[2] I have been influenced by the pioneering studies of Gerald Caplan[3] and his co-workers on preventive psychiatry. Bolman[4] recently has attempted "to connect theory, general programmatic approaches, and specific programs related to family-oriented programs in a systematic and meaningful way." He distinguishes between three types of preventive intervention. He writes:

First, prevention is characterized as primary, secondary, or tertiary, depending upon the point in the course of disorder at which a given program is aimed. Primary prevention attempts to prevent a disorder from occurring, secondary prevention attempts to diagnose and treat at the earliest possible point so as to reduce the length or severity of the disorder, and tertiary prevention attempts to minimize the handicap or chronicity of the disorder.

This chapter shall be organized along the three types of prevention just defined.

GENERAL COMMENTS

The foundation of a meaningful existence for the individual and the prevention of disorders either intrapersonally or interpersonally is contingent upon an appropriate philosophy of living. A pragmatic philosophy is that of O. Spurgeon English's,[5] who succinctly states: ". . . an emotionally healthy person can entertain himself, entertain someone else, entertain a new idea, and work productively." In my therapeutic contacts with individuals, I draw four circles (see Fig. 10, Ch. XVII) to illustrate English's philosophy in promoting a healthy personality and thus preventing individual and intersocial problems.

In explaining this preventive philosophy, it is pointed out that each individual is unique in his own existence and with untapped potential. Developing one's potential is an ongoing process that should begin as early as possible. It is one's prerogative how he allocates energies into the four circles. Obviously priorities in the allocation of energy will be dependent on both the current phase of the marriage cycle and necessary life tasks. I describe each circle. For example, to entertain himself, the individual must consider four areas: creativity,[6] curiosity, play,[7] and sensuality (or, what Freud described as the libido). To entertain someone else includes meaningful relationships with members of one's nuclear family, with kinship networks, and with friends. To entertain a new idea involves the creativity and curosity of one's "inner child," e.g. art, literature and technological discoveries. To work productively involves adequate commitment to one's instrumental or nurturant-affectional role. However, working productively at the expense of the other circles can lead to many problems personally and interpersonally, for example, peptic ulcers or marital disharmony when the wife is competing with a "mistress" (her husband's work).

All therapists, particularly the clergymen[8] because of their multiple and longitudinal contacts with their congregants, are in a unique position to expound the value of prevention.

Primary Prevention of Marital Problems

Primary prevention attempts to eradicate marital disharmony. There are three main areas of primary prevention in marriage:
1. Premarital counseling.
2. Marital counseling—the "Well-marriage Unit."
3. Remarital counseling.[9]

In 1965[10] I stated: "Our focus in the Marital Department (Forest Hospital) is on *prevention* stressing (1) premarital counseling—an old established procedure; and, (2) the 'Well-Marriage Unit'—similar in philosophy to the well-baby clinics. . . ." Before discussing premarital counseling, I should like to describe the Well-Marriage Unit.

Since it was first established in 1964, the Well-Marriage Unit has undergone progressive change in goals. Its function now subserve both primary and secondary preventive interventions in marriage. Its original goal was that of offering couples an opportunity to come for periodic marital checkups.[11] At first no recommended time intervals were suggested. A couple could come in at any phase in their marriage. Currently, in my private practice, at the conclusion of successful premarital counseling, I suggest that the couple return yearly after marriage for three visits, then every three years for three visits, and then once every five years. The periodic marital checkup offers the couple and the therapist the opportunity to explore the current condition of their marriage. Since the family can be conceived as a social organization that goes through four phases of development in its life cycle with differences in life tasks, in the marital checkup we observe the manner in which the four dimensions of need complementarity are being dealt with by each spouse. We follow the suggestions of Otto Pollak[12] (see Ch. XI). The two other functions of the Well-Marriage Unit are in the field of secondary prevention: (1) where couples can come for therapy in the early phases of marital crises, and (2) where any competent therapist can bring a couple under treatment for consultation.[13]

Premarital counseling centers about primary marital prevention and involves two main groups of couples: (1) those who are engaged and to be married for the first time,[14] and (2) those in which one or both of the individuals have been previously married—remarital counseling (see under tertiary prevention). Since 50 percent of the presenting marital complaints in couples seeking help for their marital discord were found to have been present during the courtship, preventive premarital counseling is of crucial significance. Aaron Rutledge's book, *Pre-Marital Counseling*,[15] is a must reading for every therapist. A wide variety of individual, interpersonal, and environmental factors may warrant postponement of a marriage or a decision not to marry at all.[16]

The complexity of our society results in a great variation in marital patterns. At present we do not know what a "normal" marriage consists of, and any attempt to define the "contraindications" is complicated by the conscious and unconscious prejudices of the observer and the culture in which he moves. In premarital counseling each couple must be evaluated in the context of their individual personalities, their relationships with others, and the social field in which they live. A contraindication for one couple may not necessarily be so for another.

In Chapter XVII I described four main categories of personality configurations. Leon Salzman's[17] presentation of obsessive-compulsive defenses from an adaptive point of view along a spectrum of severity can be most helpful in evaluating a potential marriage. He delineates three levels: obsessive tendencies, obsessive personality and obsessive-compulsive neurosis (see Ch. XVII). Doubt is a characteristic trait of obsessives, and frequently severe anxiety results from paralyzing indecision about marriage. In these situations it is better to err in favor of advising against marriage. In the following couple, although marriage was advised against, the couple married with the ensuing poor result:

Mr. Rosalind and Miss Roxanna came for premarital counseling at the suggestion of her parents—former patients of mine. They were getting increasingly annoyed at Mr. Rosalind, who had, after all arrangements had been made, postponed the wedding three times. They wanted their daughter to stop seeing Mr. Rosalind, but she had been uncooperative.

Mr. Rosalind was a tall, thin, very polite, extremely intelligent, well-dressed man in his twenties. He carefully selected his words as he related the following: "We actually get along fine except for two or three things about her that I strongly object to. Most of the things I know about her I like very much. But at times I don't like her physical appearance. When I get strong doubts about this, I get very upset and that is why I have postponed our marriage. Ann is a very thin girl. It upsets me much just to talk about it. The bridge of her nose is a little convex. This embarrasses me to talk about it. It is displaced a little, due to falling off a bicycle as a child. With my encouragement she had an operation on her nose. Her parents were against the operation. I didn't exactly insist, but I made my feelings known in no uncertain terms. It is still not right, a little indentation at one point.

"Once in awhile she actually uses a phrase that is grossly wrong. That bothers me. The rest of the relationship could not be better. I like her and I don't like her. I have a feeling I will never find a person as good for me. I'm kind of a domineering person, and she tends to be submissive. Her greatest pleasure is to do things for me. She just subjugates herself to me. I don't want another girl. I want her. But on the other hand, I don't want to get married, yet I do. Yet I can't give her up. We've been engaged going on two and one-half years. Several times we've discussed separating. She says if this will make you happy, I'll give you up and she really means it. I'm always the one who goes back to her. I don't know what to do."

Miss Roxanna was a concerned, thin, pleasant, cooperative, simply dressed girl. She began the interview by stating that she had come at the request of her parents, Since finishing high school, she had worked in her father's office doing clerical work. "I'm at a loss to understand both my feelings and behavior. My common sense tells me to forget about Jim, but I can't. Basically I think he doesn't love me. I don't think he possibly could because he criticizes me so much. I am very sensitive to rejection.

"He is a perfectionist with the objects he owns. He goes through the same things with me that he does with his car and stereo set. I had plastic surgery done on my nose because of him. With his emotions he is selfish. Any time the subject of marriage is brought up, he gets very annoyed. I used to joke about it. Then he would get so upset about it, and so I stopped talking about it and then he would bring it up.

"When I started dating Jim, I was really surprised when he first asked me. It worked out so well. He reminds me of my father. But not so critical. They look alike physically. Neither one is very verbose in stating their emotions."

The diagnostic interviews and the CDD revealed Mr. Rosalind to have a severe obsessive-compulsive neurosis and a six-month period of premarital counseling was suggested. This suggestion was not accepted, and the couple eloped. Shortly after their marriage, her parents reported that the young couple were having repetitive quarrels.

People with other psychoneurotic reactions, such as anxiety states, hysterias,[18] and conversion states, do much better than the obsessives.

Individuals with the two main types of psychotic reaction, manic-depressive and schizophrenic, should marry only after very careful deliberation. Schizophrenics in remission make poor marriage material because an acute crisis, such as the birth of the first child,[19] could precipitate a recurrence of the psychotic symptoms.

Cyclothymic reactions present a difficult challenge to the

therapist in predicting the outcome of a marriage. The cyclothymics outgoing life-of-the-party, hail-fellow-well-met personality frequently attract inhibited individuals who want to participate more in life rather than observe. As previously described (see Ch. XVII), cyclothymic reactions form a continuum but may be divided into three main categories. In the cyclothymic personality if the individual's past life history reveals several depressive episodes of increasing frequency and duration, caution is indicated in advising marriage. Often the severe cyclothymic personality later develops manic-depressive psychosis and has a turbulent marital history. The following vignette is illustrative:

The Sabinas came for help following a severe suicidal attempt by Mrs. Sabina when she discovered her husband had a mistress. Married fifteen years, four children, Mrs. Sabina was moderately depressed at her first interview. An intelligent, attractive woman of forty, she described herself as always being outgoing and gregarious. In high school she was a cheer leader and active in all school activities. Her first serious suicidal attempt was at the age of sixteen when she became depressed following her parents refusal to permit her to get engaged. After being out of school for two months, she made a complete recovery and was well until twenty when she had another severe depression. For a month before this depression, she described a period of tremendous energy during which time she got involved with a lifeguard. Again she wanted to get engaged, and again her parents objected. She spontaneously recovered in two months and returned to school. At this time she met the man she later married. He was quiet, studious and shy. Their courtship was uneventful, and they were married just before college graduation. Her next severe depression occurred two years later following the birth of their first child. At that time she received electroconvulsive therapy.

Mr. Sabina, a quiet, reserved, intelligent man described a most difficult marriage. "Until the first baby was born, we got along fine. However, in the last ten years, we have had a difficult time. When she is good, she is terrific. But when she is depressed or racing her motor, she becomes most difficult to live with. Her alternating moods had upset the children, two are now seeing psychiatrists. I didn't want any more children after the first one, but she insisted. Following the birth of the last child, she has been chronically depressed and rejected everyone. She has been seeing a psychiatrist for the past three years. After awhile I turned to someone else to meet my emotional and sexual needs. I'm not sure anyone can help her or our marriage, but I'm willing to try."

This vignette illustrates how recurrent episodes of either hypomanic spiraling or severe depressive reactions with or without suicidal attempts can be devastating to the other spouse and frequently disturbing to the children. Not infrequently the partner does not understand that his spouse is ill, and may regard the depressive withdrawal as rejection. Occasionally hypomanic behavior with boundless energy may lead to extramarital affairs with resultant severe marital discord.

Manic-depressive psychosis is characterized by severe mood swings. I currently take an unequivocal position against marriage when there is a medical history of hospitalization, either in a psychiatric hospital or in the psychiatric service of a general hospital, for manic-depressive psychosis.

The projective defense reactions, described in Chapters X and XVII, are frequently contraindications to marriage.

The fourth configuration of personality disorders consisting of antisocial and dyssocial behavior are most difficult to change. These individuals make poor marriage partners.

In conclusion, there are no absolute contraindications to marriage, but if there seem to be too many real or potential areas of conflict, a marriage should be postponed until adequate exploration can be carried out.

SECONDARY PREVENTION

Secondary prevention in marriage attempts to recognize and treat a marital crisis at the earliest possible time so as to reduce the length or severity of the problem.[20] An example of this type of intervention is shown in the following clinical vignette:

Mr. and Mrs. Phoebe had been previous patients of mine about seven years ago and had received marital counseling with good results. Shortly after the completion of their therapy, Mr. Phoebe was transferred to the main plant of his corporation on the East Coast. They had been very happy until two years ago when he was sent back to Chicago to straighten out a research project. Both had been unhappy about this, especially Mrs. Phoebe. Because of personnel problems, Mr. Phoebe had run into a series of disappointments and sabotage from his superiors. At first he reacted with anger and later with depression. To add insult to injury, Mrs. Phoebe had impulsively made some very expensive purchases without consulting her husband, and this at a time when he was seriously considering changing his employment.

The Phoebes were seen conjointly for one and one-half hours. Mr. Phoebe was moderately depressed as he explained his situation at work. He was given considerable reassurance ("Greene" stamps) about his superior intelligence and creativity and was told he would have no problem at all in getting a better position if he did not get the cooperation from his superiors.

Mrs. Phoebe interrupted to state that perhaps she was at fault too and went into detail about her impulsive expenditures. She knew that, although her husband was silent about this, he was angry at her.

When asked if these purchases were impulsive, she replied in the affirmative, and I then strongly suggested her husband handle all the finances. That his suppressed rage was only deepening his depression and what he needed most of all at this time was TLC—tender, loving care. The interview ended with the suggestion they try to follow the many suggestions made and to call me again if they had not solved their problems.

A week later I received the following letter from Mrs. Phoebe:

Dear Doctor Greene:

I want to thank you for your positive suggestions. Last week I was so angry at you, hurt, frustrated, because I couldn't verbalize my feelings, and depressed. I could have cheerfully strangled you. This morning I could hug you.

The proof of the pudding is in the eating. Last night for the first time in nearly two years, Jim and I had intercourse successfully (this complaint had not been raised in the interview with them). For the very first time in my life I had absolutely no sense of guilt about it. He warmed up like an eighteen year old. Most surprising of all, for weeks I had been extremely depressed. This morning every trace of that depression has vanished. Apparently, I needed this love making as much as he. He was so happy and so was I. I wish you could see the difference.

Pursuant to your request, I immediately consigned all our money to Jim. I signed statements authorizing the banks to put our checking and savings' accounts in Jim's name only. We are each taking a weekly allowance for personal needs from our weekly budget.

One of my reasons for always acting unilaterally is my inability to verbalize my wants, even with Jim. Rather than ask, I have taken. It's hardly the way to conduct a marriage. My fear of rejection is one of the prime reasons for my inability to say no to a salesman.

I am now working (another suggestion I had made in the session was that she go back to work).

For my part I will do everything I can to help Jim by applying liberal doses of TLC. It worked last night and ought to again. Thanks for helping out.

This couple's reaction is an example of secondary marital prevention. Since they were former patients of mine, not only did they come in with positive transference feelings toward me, but more important perhaps, was that I knew their components in their three systems and could be very active in my management of their problems.

TERTIARY PREVENTION

Tertiary prevention in marital disharmony attempts to minimize either the repercussions to the request for a divorce or consists of divorce therapy per se.[21] In divorce or remarital therapy, I have combined divorce therapy (tertiary prevention) with remarital counseling (primary prevention) because frequently the same forces are present, any one or combinations of the following situations obtain:

1. Mourning process by a spouse.
2. Where a spouse is still a "phallic symbol" to the mate.
3. Rage reactions toward spouse due to rejection, to separation from the children, and, finally, to protracted legal maneuverings by lawyers or at the terms of the separation.

In addition to the above, an important phase of divorce counseling centers around requests for advise and guidance in the management of the reactions of the children during and after the divorce proceedings.[22] Currently the United States has approximately seven million children under eighteen whose parents have been divorced. At all times I offer to talk to the children during or even after the divorce. Invariably they are frightened youngsters, bravely trying to hold back their tears. I try to give them reassurance and support that they are not responsible for the separation of their parents.

It is important that the divorced spouses submerge their imaginary or real grievances against each other and work together for their children's best interests. In an excellent article Jack H. Pollack[23] points out a number of "sins committed by countless divorced parents:"

1. ". . . arguing bitterly in front of children before, during, and after a divorce."
2. ". . . denigrating the absent mate to the child."
3. ". . . encouraging children to choose sides. . . ."

4. ". . . suddenly overturning a child's way of life."
5. ". . . in having their children live half a year with one parent and the other half with the other."
6. ". . . fighting over visiting regulations."
7. Trying to wheedle gossip out of the child concerning the ex-mate's activities.
8. Breaking promises or dates with the child.
9. Trying to buy their children's affection.
10. "A child of divorce needs assurance that he isn't being abandoned or deserted."

If divorced parents keep the above ten "sins" in mind, they can make the emotional trauma to their children less painful. Divorce can be a maturing experience for all parties concerned, both adults and children, if the parents ". . . put their youngsters' best long-range interests above their own short-term bitterness. . . ."[24]

Individuals can react in various ways to divorce. Tertiary prevention is important at this time to minimize the handicap or chronicity of reactions to divorce. A not uncommon reaction to divorce is the unconscious mourning for the ex-mate. This mourning process varies from individual to individual, and can become chronic in some persons and interfere with other interpersonal relationships, e.g. by withdrawing from new or even old relationships. Usually this process is hastened when the individual is made aware that his depression is due to mourning. The following vignette is illustrative:

Mr. Marion consulted me at the suggestion of his family physician. An extremely handsome, intelligent, tall, impeccably dressed male in his early thirties, he appeared moderately depressed as he stated: "I am in the process of getting a divorce. Three months ago we separated when she announced she no longer loved me and wanted a divorce. I was very upset. It had come out of the blue. But I should have suspected something was wrong. Our sex life was once very wonderful but for the last year, virtually nil. She was not interested. I was a little overbearing about it. She didn't feel it and didn't want it. 'Go get a mistress if you want it that badly.' She said she felt dead in the relationship emotionally and wanted out. At first we decided to separate physically in the house, so I moved into another bedroom. That arrangement did not work out, so I moved out at her suggestion."

The courtship had been uneventful and smooth and two years in duration. After three years of marriage, Mrs. Marion accidentally became pregnant. Although the baby was not planned, she was a good mother. When the child was three years old, Mrs. Marion, according to her husband, complained of being tied down and wanted more excitement in their activities. It was at this time that he noticed a change in her attitude toward him.

His background was normal. The oldest of three children, he got along very well with his parents, siblings and peers, did well academically and socially. Upon college graduation he became associated with his father's business. Currently he felt depressed, disinterested in his work and had trouble concentrating. He blamed his feelings of depression and inability to concentrate on his marital situation.

In his sixth session he brought in to the discussion a dream in which he was in a funeral home but that this was all he could remember. His associations centered about his favorite grandmother, who had singled him out as her favorite grandchild. She had died while he was in high school, and he mourned her loss. Following my interpretation that perhaps his current emotional state could be due to a mourning process, a normal reaction to the loss of a loved object, he began to show small but progressive improvement.

Two months later, at his tenth session, he reported he was back to his old self again, in good spirits and productive and creative at his work. "You've given me a lot of help, not only in relation to the divorce but in myself. When I first moved away from my home, child and wife I was very traumatized. Your exposure to the mourning process was very valid and helped me a great deal. I've rediscovered who I am. I think I can now carry on alone. But I should like to feel I can call upon you if I need to."

He was told he could call upon me anytime, and therapy was discontinued.

Dealing with the mourning process can prevent serious emotional reactions.

Tertiary prevention in divorce therapy is indicated when a spouse reacts with panic or rage to his partner's request for divorce, either during the divorce proceedings, or after finalization of the divorce.[25] This type of reaction places a great responsibility upon the therapist, since the individual can become very violent and attempt to disfigure or even murder his former spouse. Occasionally the individual may even turn the rage upon himself and attempt suicide. The following clinical extract is illustrative:

The Nadias came together for their initial interview at the suggestion of their lawyers. Mr. Nadia, an intelligent and athletic man, spoke with a slight stammer. He was relatively calm and well poised throughout the entire session. His view of the marital strife which had led his wife to ask for a divorce was quite heavily loaded in the direction of demeaning his wife. He felt he had gone as far as he could in tolerating some of his wife's behavior and attitudes toward him and concluded he was fighting a brick wall. His major complaints about his wife suggested that he saw her as taking advantage of him, especially at times of financial adversity. He characterized himself as being an easygoing person, while admitting he had a volatile but short-lived temper. He admitted working almost seven nights a week at his business but was only doing this for his family's security. Although his wife had been complaining about their lack of social life and even occasionally threatening to divorce him, he was very surprised when she carried out her threat. This surprise soon gave way to furious resentment and rage. At first he thought there must be another man and even threatened to kill her.

Mrs. Nadia was short, attractive woman who was meticulously groomed and consistently spoke in a very soft voice. She commented that she and her husband had been ready to break up their marriage for some time but put it off for the sake of their daughter. Mrs. Nadia initially complained about her husband's neglect of her and their social life, feeling that he was concerned only with business success. Later, however, she admitted that the primary difficulties was his rejection of her as a woman. She characterized herself as a sensitive person and suggested that both her sensitivity and intolerance of her husband's behavior had increased with the onset of the climateric.

She was at a loss to understand her husband's behavior at her request for a divorce. Not only had he been violently angry but also accusing her of being in love with someone else. Recently she had observed him trailing her surreptitously while she was shopping. Worse yet, he had threatened to kill her if she did not stop divorce proceedings.

At this point in the session, I suggested that each be seen individually while I explored the marital problem.

In her individual sessions, Mrs. Nadia was adamant about the divorce but agreed to suspend divorce proceedings until her husband was anchored in therapy. Mrs. Nadia was referred to another therapist.

It took four months of therapy before Mr. Nadia was emotionally receptive to allow his wife to proceed with the divorce. Typical of his dreams during his second month of therapy was the following nightmare from which he awakened in a cold sweat: "I am on my way to the airport to board a plane. I am late. I glance down at my shoes and see that I am wearing women's high heel shoes. I am embarrassed and look around for a shoe store. All sorts of obstacles. Tremendous amount of anxiety in being able to buy some shoes and still make the plane."

This dream illustrates why he had reacted to his wife's request for a divorce with such anxiety and rage. Without his wife he did not feel masculine. No wonder the rage at her at what he felt unconsciously to be castration. He was threatened with becoming a woman, his wife being his alter phallus.

Tertiary prevention in divorce therapy frequently includes the rage of one spouse toward his ex-partner due to rejection, to separation from the children, and to protracted legal maneuverings at the terms of the separation. Occasionally the anger of the individual may be turned inward with depressive reactions such as inability to sleep, and/or severe mental and physical retardation.

Mr. Lena called for an emergency appointment. When seen that evening he appeared quite depressed and stated that he had been furious at his wife since their divorce two months ago. At first all he could think about was his fury at his wife for separating him from his children. Visitation rights had been set for the weekends only. He felt his wife had been most unreasonable in her settlement demands and further, he was furious at her lawyers for their prolonged legal maneuverings. For the past two weeks he had been unable to concentrate at his office, he slept fitfully and had lost ten pounds. Recently he had nightmares which had awakened him in a cold sweat. In some of his dreams he was strangling his wife, who would turn into a huge lizard. However, it was his last night's dream which prompted him to call: "I see a man behind me. Like Frankenstein. He put on a black mask and said, 'alms for the poor.'

"I woke up. I was scared out of my mind. I was terrified. I have no financial problems. But this divorce has turned me into a monster. I don't miss Helen, but I do miss the children. We had a very close relationship. Before I kept thinking of all sorts of ways to kill her, so I could get the children. I almost turned into a Frankenstein."

As Mr. Lena talked about his rage, his depression began to lift. Four months of therapy was necessary before he settled down emotionally and began to accept the repercussions of his divorce. At this point he began to date and worked out some realistic arrangements on his visitation rights.

In this chapter I have stressed the strategic position therapists are in to recognize and practice prevention in premarital, marital, and postmarital situations.[26] I have defined three types of preventive intervention. If possible, not only should therapists do premarital counseling of an intensive type, but also establish a Well-Marriage Unit.

NOTES

1. Rudolph Dreikurs: Determinants of Changing Attitudes of Marital Partners Toward Each Other, in *The Marriage Relationship* (Salo Rosenbaum and Ian Alger, Eds.), New York, Basic Books, 1968, p. 85.
2. Bernard L. Greene: Training clergymen in marriage counseling:

Pastoral Counselor, 5:42, 1967. Prevention is particularly important, since the divorce rate in the United States is 41 percent (William J. Lederer and Don D. Jackson: *The Mirages of Marriage.* New York, Norton, 1968, p. 53).

3. Gerald Caplan: *Principles of Preventive Psychiatry.* New York, Basic Books, 1964. See also Gerald Caplan and Henry Grunebaum: Perspectives on primary prevention, *Arch Gen Psychiat,* 17:331, 1967.

4. William M. Bolman: Preventive psychiatry for the family: theory, approaches, and programs, *Amer J Psychiat,* 125:458, 1968. This excellent paper contains an extensive bibliography. See also Stanley Lesse (The influence of socioeconomic and sociotechnologic systems on emotional illness, *Amer J Psychother,* 22:571, 1968), who states: "The optimum contribution that psychiatry and psychotherapy can make will be in the nature of prophylaxis. In the broadest sense of the term, these prophylactic techniques, to be most effective, should be part and parcel of the sociocultural matrix, an integral part of the sociopolitical structure. The basic design of any new sociopolitical institution should be formulated with its central focus being in the service of each man's psychophysical welfare."

5. O. Spurgeon English: Changing techniques of psychotherapy, *Voices,* 2:91, 1966. This article should be read concomitantly with the thought-provoking paper by Jacques Ellul (Reflections on Leisure, reprinted from *Interplay,* December 1967, in *Reflections,* 3:1, 1968), a professor of economics at the University of Bordeaux. He concludes: "First of all, it is a question of fighting against despair, and leisure must be used to this end. . . . We must accept the imperfection that is linked with any human creation. It is better to sit down at a piano and play a bit of music badly than to listen to a perfect recording. . . . Secondly, in order for leisure to mean something, it must be completely personal and must be filled with individual initiative. . . . Finally, the third approach consists in exercising criticism toward the society in which we live."

6. Emanuel F. Hammer: What is human creativity, and Curt Boenheim: The importance of creativity in contemporary psychotherapy, *Psychiat Opinion,* 4:17, 1967.

7. Lionel S. Lewis and Dennis Brissett (Sex as work: a study of avocational counseling, *Med Aspects Hum Sexuality,* 2:14, 1968) comment: "Concomitant with this increasing amount of leisure time, and the attendant problem of learning how to play, it has been observed that the *play of most Americans has become a laborious kind of play* [italics added]." Also see Edward Greenwood: The importance of play, *Menninger Quart,* 2:22, 1968.

8. Elizabeth D. Ossario: Parish clergy and community health, *Psychiat Opinion,* 3:9, 1966; Lester A. Kirkendall (Sex Education, *Med Aspects*

Hum Sexuality, 2:40, 1968) in an article that contains an excellent bibliography writes: "The church has an important and essential contributions to make to a comprehensive sex education program because it plays a vital role in the formulation of ideals and in the development of moral values. Instruction concerning ethical and moral standards must be approached positively and should include all aspects of life and all periods of the life cycle. The central problem is always the development of a *philosophy of life* [italics added], the creation of a set of socially meaningful and understandable values, and the enthronement of a wholesome personality for oneself and for others as a major goal of life"; see also Carroll A. Wise: The pastor as counselor, *Pastoral Counselor*, 5:4, 1967; and Elihu S. Howland: The challenge of mental health, to the christian community, *J Religion Health*, 5:314, 1966.

9. Monica D. Blumenthal: Mental health among the divorced, *Arch Gen Psychiat*, 16:603, 1967. Her findings indicate "significantly more mental disorder among persons who have been divorced at one time or another than among persons who have never been divorced."

10. Bernard L. Greene: The Family in Therapy, in *The American Family in Crisis*, Des Plaines, Forest Hospital Found., 1965, pp. 35–46. See also Celia S. Deschin: The future direction of social work: 1. from Concern with problems and emphasis on prevention, *Amer J Orthopsychiat*, 38:9, 1968.

11. Leslie Navran (Communication and adjustment in marriage, *Family Process*, 6:173, 1967) in a study used two test instruments, developed by Dr. Harvey J. Locke and his co-workers—Marital Relationship Inventory (MRI) and Primary Communication Inventory (PCI) that could be of potential value in the Well-Marriage Unit. The original publications of Locke and his co-workers are listed in this article. Navran's findings suggest that MRI "validly measures marital adjustment." Using both the MRI and the PCI tests, he found that the "results show marital adjustment to be positively correlated with capacity to communicate." Another statement made in this article pinpoints a concept later developed in this chapter: "Since there is a positive relationship between age and length of marriage, the low correlations between age and the MRI scores support the widely held conviction that *marital adjustment must be striven for constantly* [italics added] and cannot at any time be considered achieved and stored away as one would a prize possession." Another test has been developed by Tom Leland and John Warkentin: See-through D.A.P. test in couples therapy, *Voices*, 2:52, 1966. See also David R. Mace (The present status of marriage in the United States, *Med Aspects Hum Sexuality*, 2:14, 1968), who cogently says: "One of our problems in American Marriages today is that too many people are expecting

too much out of married life in return for *too little effort* [italics added]." This article should be read along with the paper of Natalie Shainess: Images of woman: past and present, over and obscured, *Amer J Psychother,* 23:77, 1969. See also Clark E. Vincent: Sex and the young married, *Med Aspects Hum Sexuality,* 3:13, 1969.

12. Otto Pollak: Sociological and Psychoanalytic Concepts in Family Diagnosis, in *The Psychotherapies of Marital Disharmony* (Bernard L. Greene, Ed.). New York, Free Press, 1965, pp. 15–26.

13. Reed Brockbank: Aspects of mental health consultation, *Arch Gen Psychiat,* 18:267, 1968; H. Neil Karp and James M. Karls: Combining crisis therapy and mental health consultation, *Arch Gen Psychiat,* 14:536, 1966.

14. Esther O. Fisher in her book (*Help For Today's Troubled Marriages.* New York, Hawthorn, 1968, pp. 194–202) describes three kinds of premarital counseling: "education for marriage, personal (clinical) therapy, and counseling that focuses on immediate preparation for a marriage that is already decided upon." Increasing clinical experience indicates the need for a courtship of at least one year. About 45 percent of the couples seen privately had a courtship of less than one year (see Table XIX) Wm. J. Lederer and Don D. Jackson arrive at the same conclusion (*The Mirages of Marriage.* New York, Norton, 1968, p. 182) when they write: "The occurrence of the quid pro quo action-reaction pattern is inevitable. In these exchanges the man and woman negotiate their total conjoint behavior, and at the same time become acquainted with the other's total personality. *This is why a long and intimate courtship is desirable* [italics added]."

15. Aaron Rutledge: *Pre-Marital Counseling.* Cambridge, Schenkman, 1966. Dr. Rutledge was head of the psychotherapy program of the Merrill-Palmer Institute in Detroit, Michigan, and former president of the American Association of Marriage Counselors. I agree with his viewpoint that premarital counseling offers the most opportune occasion in an adult's life for the resolution of personality differences and for a positive investment in individual and family health.

The book written in two parts covers every important aspect of preparing a couple for marriage. The first part is a general discussion of such premarital transactions as preparation for marriage, the nature of marriage, communication in marriage and in counseling, beginning a new family, and concepts of sexology. He presents concepts of sexology from a modern point of view, espousing neither a moral nor an ethical stand but taking into account new scientific data, especially that of Masters and Johnson, and the changes that have occurred in our cultural attitudes toward sex. His suggested plan of "package" services to engaged couples (pp. 84–88) is worthy of serious consideration by leaders in preventive medicine and theology.

Part two provides the background orientation requisite for the counselor in such fields as psychology, religion, genetics, medicine, psychiatry, economics and law. See also Charles E. Flowers, Jr., Changing concepts of the premarital examination, *Med Aspects Hum Sexuality, 1:*51, 1967; and Richard A. Bollinger: The dynamics of divorce, *Messenger, 115:*1, 1966.

16. Bernard L. Greene and Noel Lustig: Contraindications to marriage, *Med Aspects Hum Sexuality, 2:*4, 1968. See also Gail Jackson Putney: Marriage, American style, *The Single Parent, 9:*4, 1968.

17. Leon Salzman: The therapy of obsessional states, *Amer J Psychiat, 122:*1139, 1966.

18. L.L. Langness (Hysterical psychosis: the cross-cultural evidence, *Amer J Psychiat, 124:*143, 1967) finds this condition to be a "widely distributed type of abnormal behavior to which the term could be legitimately applied, and the term may therefore have greater utility than has hitherto been supposed." He was influenced to do his research by the previous study of Marc H. Hollender and S.J. Hirsch (Hysterical psychosis, *Amer J Psychiat, 113:*1046, 1957). Women most vulnerable to this disease according to Hollender and Hirsch have hysterical personalities—coquettish and seductive, histrionic, impulsive, suggestible and a tendency to live for the present. There is a diagnostic continuum of female psychiatric patients who fall within the diagnostic category of hysteria: hysterical personality, hysterical neurosis and finally, hysterical psychosis.

19. Z. Alexander Aarons (Therapeutic abortion and the psychiatrist, *Amer J Psychiat, 124:*745, 1967) writes: "We have said nothing about the psychotic prospective father for whom the birth of a child is a threat. . . ." See also William H. Wainwright: Fatherhood as a precipitant of mental illness, *Amer J Psychiat, 123:*40, 1966.

20. Another type of marital crisis has been described by Houston McIntosh: Separation problems in military wives, *Amer J Psychiat, 125:*260, 1968. See also Chester A. Pearlman, Jr.; Separation reactions of married women, *Amer J Psychiat, 126:*946, 1970.

21. John A. Ross: *How To Be Happily Divorced.* New York, Paperback Library, 1968. See also Morton M. Hunt: Strange courtship customs of the formerly married, *McCall's,* Sept., 94,156, 1966; and, Ivan B. Gendzell: End of a marriage—how do I find intimacy?, *The Single Parent, 12:*4, 1969.

22. John F. McDermott: Parental divorce in early childhood, *Amer J Psychiat, 124:*1424, 1968.

23. Jack H. Pollack: When Parents Separate, *Today's Health,* June 1967, pp. 17, 60, 66. A recent book by Robert V. Sherwin (*Compatible Divorce.* New York, Crown, 1969) is recommended for those contemplating divorce.

24. Pollack, *op. cit.*
25. Rubin Blanck and Gertrude Blanck: *Marriage & Personal Development.* New York, Columbia Univ. Press, 1968, p. 50.
26. Clark E. Vincent: The physician as counselor in post-marital and extramarital pregnancies, *Med Aspects Hum Sexuality,* 1:34, 1967.

Appendix

BIOGRAPHICAL MARITAL QUESTIONNAIRE

Date_____

Name_____Spouse_____

Address_____
             street   city   zip code

Phone: Residence_____ Business_____

1. Age_____ Of spouse_____
2. Marital status: First marriage? Yes__ No__ Duration of present marriage_____
3. Religion_____ Of spouse_____
4. Occupation_____ Of spouse_____
5. Education_____ Of spouse_____
6. Children? Yes   No   How many and give ages_____

---

7. Name of person or agency who referred you:
        Name_____
        Address_____

(Disposition: To be filled in at completion of evaluation or treatment.)

8. What are your specific complaints about your marriage?
First circle and then describe:
    a. Lack of communication
    b. Constant arguments
    c. Unfilled emotional needs
    d. Sexual dissatisfaction
    e. Financial disagreements
    f. In-law trouble   k. others_____ _____
    g. Infidelity   l.
    h. Conflicts about children   m.
    i. Domineering spouse   n.
    j. Suspicious spouse   o.

---

9. Why are you *now* seeking help? _____

10. If you have received any help with respect to your marriage, circle the following: psychiatrist, psychologist, physician, clergy, social worker, counselor, agency, other. Name of person and date. Give your opinion of the results:_____

11. Have *you* or *your* spouse ever attempted suicide? If so, give details:

12. The getting married phase:
    a. How did you meet your spouse?_____

    b. Describe your courtship, giving duration and whether smooth, stormy, etc. _____

    c. Did you have a honeymoon? Yes   No
       Describe your reactions, partner's behavior, etc. _____

13. Any previous marriages? Yes   No   If yes, did the marriages end by divorce, death, or desertion? Give details:__

14. Original family:
    a. Father: name_____ occupation_____
        age if living_____ age at death_____
    b. Mother: name_____ occupation_____
        age if living_____ age at death_____
    c. Brothers and sisters: First name only   age   sex

    d. Describe your parents, what they were like as people, and how they got along in their marriage. How did you get along with them? Describe your family's circumstances as you were growing up. Include anything else that would give a clearer picture of your family experiences and relationships:_____

15. Relationship with your children: Describe your children and your relationship with them. What are the problems and conflicts that arise, and how do you deal with them? How do you feel about being a parent?_____

16. Describe the kind of person you are: feelings of inferiority, sensitivity, anxiety, etc._____

17. School adjustment: How well did you do as far as grades were concerned? What extracurricular activities did you

participate in? What problems did you have in school?_____

_____

_____

18. Medical History:
    a. Family physician, name and address:_____

    b. What is your present state of health?_____

    c. When did you have your last medical checkup?_____

    d. What serious medical illnesses have you had and when?

    _____

    _____

    e. What surgical operations have you had and when?_____

    _____

    f. Habits:
       1. What drugs are you presently taking?_____

       _____

       2. How much do you smoke?_____

       3. How much do you drink and how often?_____

       _____

       4. Do you think you drink too much?_____
19. Describe your participation in social and civic activities. What
    are your personal hobbies and interests? How much satis-
    faction do you get from these activities? What problems do
    you have in this area?_____

    _____

    _____

20. Describe your job or occupation. Describe your feelings
    about your work. How do you get along with your co-

workers and employer? Have you changed jobs frequently, and if so, give details?_____

_____

_____

_____

21. Religion: What is your religious preference? What religious and other church-sponsored activities do you participate in? How often is your participation? How have the teachings and values of your church and your faith influenced your marriage?_____

_____

_____

_____

22. Any additional comments you wish to make about your marriage? _____

_____

_____

_____

_____

_____

NAME INDEX

SUBJECT INDEX

A

Acting out phenomena, 393–397
  therapist and, 395
  cases illustrating, 395, 396–397
  types of, 393–395
Alcoholism, 124, 129–131, 146, 224
  "Alcoholic" game in, 129
  case extract in, 131
  definition of, 131
  statistics on, 124, 224

B

Biographical marital questionnaire, 11,
  20–21, 24–235, See Appendix
  additional comments in, 233–234
  age of spouse in, 24–26, *Also see*
    Marital disharmony
  childhood environment in, 178–191,
    Also see Childhood environment
  children and the, 124–126, *Also see*
    Children and marriage
  education of spouse in, 29–30, *Also*
    see Education of spouse
  evaluative use of, 11, 24–235
  financial disagreements in, 83–93,
    Also see Financial disagreements
  getting married phase in, 153–170,
    Also see Getting married phase
  infidelity in, 105–123, *Also see* Infidelity
  in-law information in, 94–104, *Also*
    see In-law problem
  marital complaints in, 32–44, *Also*
    see Specific marital complaints
  medical history in, 216–226, *Also see*
    Medical history
  miscellaneous marital complaints,
    124–133, *Also see* Alcoholism, *Also*
    see Conflicts about children, *Also*
    see Physical abuse by a partner,
    Also see Pygmalion syndrome, *Also*
    see Suspicious spouse
  occupation of spouse in, 28, 31, *Also*
    see Occupation in marriage

pathological communication explored
  in, 35–42, *Also see* Communication
personality in, 146–148, 204–209,
  Also see Personality configuration
previous help received in, 144–145,
  Also see Previous help received
previous marriages in, 171–177, *Also*
  see Previous marriages
reactions of spouses to, 20–21
relationship with children in, 124–
  126, 193–203, *Also see* Children
  and marriage
religion of spouse in, 26–28, 231–
  232, *Also see* Religion and marriage
request for help in, 134–143, *Also*
  see Sexual dissatisfaction
school adjustment in, 210–213, *Also*
  see School adjustment
sexual dissatisfaction in, 55–82, *Also*
  see Sexual dissatisfaction
social activities in, 227–228
source of referral in, 30–31, *Also see*
  Referral
suicide issue in, 145–151, *Also see*
  Suicide
unfulfilled needs in, 45–53, *Also see*
  Unfulfilled emotional needs

C

Childhood environment, 178–191
  encoding of values in, 179, 193–194,
    Also see "Parental" voice
  model of marriage in, 180
  ordinal position in, 180–187
  pathogenic parental traits in, 195–202
    over controlling, 195–197
      case illustrating, 195–196
    overindulgent, 201
      case illustrating, 201–202
    perfectionistic, 197–199
      case illustrating, 197–198
    submissive, 199
      case illustrating, 200
  role of father in, 193–194

Sexology, 56–62, 80–82ff
  cultural factors in, 57–58
  physiological studies in, 61–62
  sexual myths in, 59–62
    clinical vignette illustrating female
      nonaggressiveness, 59–60
    infant, 57, 62
    male embryological equality, 60–61
    masturbation, 62
    vaginal orgasm, 61
  statistics on sexual activity in, 80–
    81ff, 82ff
Sexual dissatisfaction, 58–82
  categories in men with, 55–56
    case illustrating frigity, see Frig-
      idity
  categories in women with, 55
    cases illustrating displeasure, 62–64
    cases illustrating frequency, 64
    cases illustrating poor partners per-
      formance, 64–65
    see Premature ejaculation
  frequency of, 55–56
Specific marital complaints, 32–44
  alcoholism as a, 129–131
  case illustrating multiple, 32–35
  conflicts about children as a, 124–
    126
  constant arguments as a, 42–43
  domineering spouse as a, see "Pyg-
    malion" syndrome
  financial disagreements as a, 83–92
  frequency of, 32
  infidelity as a, 105–121
  in-law interference as a, 94–102
  lack of communication as a, 35–40
  physical abuse as a, 131–132
  sexual dissatisfaction as a, 55–78
  statistics on, 32
  suspicious spouse as a, 128–129
  unfulfilled emotional needs as a, 41–
    53
Suicide, 144–150, 150–151ff
  case extract illustrating, 146
  depression and, 146–150
    case illustration of, 147
    case illustrating reactive, 149–150
  prevention of, 146, 150–151ff
  statistics on, 145, 146

Suspicious spouse, 17, 124, 208–209,
    247, 286
  "district attorney" syndrome form of,
    see "District attorney" syndrome

T

Therapist, vii, 12ff, 15, 18–29, 266–
    267, 274–275ff, 379–381, 385–397
  acting out and, 393–397, *Also see*
    Acting out
  ambivalence and, 391–392
    case illustrating, 391–392
  attributes of, 266–267, 274–275ff,
    382–398, 401ff
  confidentiality and, 385
  communication between blue collar
    worker and, 28–29
  counter-transference and the, see
    Counter-transference
  definition of, 3, 12ff
  "ecclesiogenic" neurosis and, see
    "Ecclesiogenic" neurosis
  initial interview between patient and,
    15
  memory and, 401ff
  transference phenomena and, see also
    Transference phenomena
    case illustrating, 395
Therapy, vii, 15, 29, 249–250, 257–
    267, 269–381, 336ff
  bibliography on marital, 269–274,
    276–277, 378–379, 380–381
  classic technique in, see Classic
    technique
  classification of, 257–258, 267–268
  collaborative technique in, see Col-
    laborative technique in marital
    disharmony
  combined techniques in, see Com-
    bined approach in marital dis-
    harmony
  concurrent technique in, see Con-
    current approach in marital dis-
    harmony
  confidentiality in, see Confidentiality
  conjoint technique, see Conjoint ap-
    proach in marital disharmony
  counseling, see Counseling in marital
    disharmony